Cloud Computing Demystified for Aspiring Professionals

Hone your skills in AWS, Azure, and Google cloud computing and boost your career as a cloud engineer

David Santana

BIRMINGHAM—MUMBAI

Cloud Computing Demystified for Aspiring Professionals

Group Product Manager: Mohd Riyan Khan
Publishing Product Manager: Surbhi Suman
Senior Editor: Athikho Sapuni Rishana
Technical Editor: Arjun Varma
Copy Editor: Safis Editing
Project Coordinator: Ashwin Kharwa
Proofreader: Safis Editing
Indexer: Pratik Shirodkar
Production Designer: Alishon Mendonca
Marketing Coordinator: Gaurav Christian
Senior Marketing Coordinator: Nimisha Dua

First published: March 2023

Production reference: 1060323
Published by Packt Publishing Ltd.

Livery Place
35 Livery Street
Birmingham
B3 2PB, UK.

ISBN 978-1-80324-331-3

www.packtpub.com

To my mother, Lucy, and to the memory of my father, Luis, for their sacrifices and for exemplifying perseverance in the face of all obstacles. And to my family and children, thank you for motivating me to dream and grind to make this and many more ambitions a reality. This work has been the culmination of decades of service to aspiring professionals and gratitude in educating and working alongside soldiers and veterans of the United States armed forces and helping veteran services such as JVS SOCAL and DAV. Finally, to my mentors Richard Luckett, who inspired me to do great things and to continue moving forward toward the noble pursuit of helping humanity achieve greatness through education!

Thank you, God, for this blessing.

– David Santana

Foreword

As someone rightly said, "Teachers are born and not made." I absolutely agree with that when I think of David. His breadth and depth of knowledge just always leaves me delighted. I have had the pleasure of knowing David through our collaboration on workshops for nearly five years now, and from the start I have admired his passion for technology and teaching, sharing a plethora of expertise and insights with the world.

If you're reading this, you're likely interested in learning more about cloud computing, a technology that has revolutionized the way we store, process, and access data. As an aspiring professional, you will understand the importance of staying up to date with the latest developments in your field, and mastering the fundamentals of cloud computing is a crucial step in that journey.

In this book, you will learn the fundamentals of cloud computing and how it differs from traditional computing models. You will explore the different types of cloud computing services and understand how they can be used to support various business needs. The book also covers key technologies and concepts, such as virtualization, containers, and cloud security.

Whether you're a complete beginner or have some experience with cloud computing, this book has something for you. It starts with an introduction to the core concepts and principles of cloud computing, explaining what it is, how it works, and why it's so important. From there, it dives into the different types of cloud computing, including public, private, and hybrid clouds, and explains the pros and cons of each.

As an entertaining presenter, active community contributor, passionate advocate, and ex-military, David imparts the knowledge, experience, and discipline gained through this period of progressive innovation. With easy-to-understand yet comprehensive descriptions, step-by-step instructions, screenshots, snippets, real-world examples, and links to additional sources of information, *Cloud Computing Demystified for Aspiring Professionals* facilitates the enhancement of skills that will enable successful careers in cloud engineering and beyond.

In today's fast-paced and competitive business environment, having a strong understanding of cloud computing is crucial for success. With *Cloud Computing Demystified for Aspiring Professionals*, you can gain the knowledge and skills you need to thrive in this exciting field. Having read it myself, I hope this book reaches as many learners as possible and lets the world know about David and his expertise.

Amit Malik

Chief Operating Officer, Spektra Systems

Contributors

About the author

David Santana is a multi-cloud engineer, certified trainer for Amazon, Microsoft, and Google, course developer, and cloud computing evangelist. His vast experience in cloud software engineering, data science, and managing training events have made him the Fast Lane US cloud director and lead subject matter expert. With over 20+ years managing training events, and developing, and implementing application workloads, with B2B consulting including leadership experience. He has been supporting Microsoft, Amazon, and Google cloud business partners such as, Deloitte, Accenture, Humana, ABB, and public government agencies such as CJIS, Dept of State, DoD, DIA, and Naval veteran services. He has authored other published works, such as *Azure Resources for AWS Architects*, showing IT professionals how to adopt a Microsoft and Amazon service including using AWS and Azure infrastructure as code tools.

About the reviewer

Amogh Raghunath is a software engineer with 5+ years of experience, building data platforms and implementing data pipelines on AWS and Azure. He is currently working at Amazon (Audible group) as a part of the data capture scrum team to help build data solutions for data science, marketing and BI teams. He has a master's degree in data science, with focus on data engineering, from Worcester Polytechnic Institute in Massachusetts.

Table of Contents

Part 2: Implementing Cloud Deployment Models

4

Developing Infrastructure Services Using Public Cloud Providers (IaaS)   79

Part 3: Cloud Infrastructure Services in Action

7

8

Launching Compute Service Resources for Scalability   181

9

Configuring Storage Resources for Resiliency   223

Part 4: Administrating Database and Security on the Cloud

10

11

12

13

Managing API Tools for Agility   351

Part 5: Roadmap for a Successful Journey in Cloud Engineering

14

15

Preface

If you want to upskill yourself in cloud computing domains to thrive in the IT industry, then you've come to the right place. *Cloud Computing Demystified for Aspiring Professionals* helps you to master the cloud computing essentials and the important technologies offered by cloud service providers that are needed to succeed in a cloud-centric job role.

This book begins with an overview of the transformation from traditional to modern-day cloud computing infrastructure, and various types and models of cloud computing. You'll learn how to implement secure virtual networks, virtual machines, and data warehouse resources including data lake services used in big data analytics — as well as when to use SQL and NoSQL databases and how to build microservices using multi-cloud Kubernetes services across AWS, Microsoft Azure, and Google Cloud. You'll also get step-by-step demonstrations of infrastructure, platform, and software cloud services and optimization recommendations derived from certified industry experts using hands-on tutorials, self-assessment questions, and real-world case studies.

By the end of this book, you'll be ready to successfully implement standardized cloud computing concepts, services, and best practices in your workplace.

Who this book is for

The book is mainly intended for those aspiring to become cloud engineers. Novice cloud practitioners, fresh college graduates, IT enthusiasts, and anyone looking to get into cloud computing or transform their career with a cloud engineering role in any industry will also benefit from this book. A basic understanding of networking concepts such as IP addressing, client and server devices, and communication protocols and experience in any programming language will be helpful for reading this book.

What this book covers

Chapter 1, *Introduction to Cloud Computing*, leads you through a journey from traditional infrastructure to the rise of cloud computing, and also describes in great detail what cloud computing is and its various advantages over traditional technology infrastructures.

Chapter 2, *Unveiling the Cloud*, demystifies the cloud by describing in detail the underlying technology that comprises cloud computing services. Here, you will learn how these technologies support core services such as compute, storage, and containers.

Chapter 3, Understanding the Benefits of Public Clouds (AWS, Azure, and GCP), helps you understand the benefits of the Azure, AWS, and GCP cloud infrastructure. Here, you will learn about their worldwide infrastructure presence, service availability, cloud scaling capability, built-in resilience, and how adhering to well-architected frameworks optimizes overall operational costs.

Chapter 4, Developing Infrastructure Services Using Public Cloud Providers (IaaS), takes you through how **infrastructure as a service** (**IaaS**) solutions are implemented. You will learn how to architect, deploy, and manage networking components, compute services, and storage resources, and you will gain the knowledge required to maintain IaaS workloads throughout their life cycle by understanding the responsibility you share with the cloud provider.

Chapter 5, Developing Platform Services Using Public Cloud Providers (PaaS), takes you through how **platform as a service** (**PaaS**) solutions are implemented. You will learn how to architect, configure, and manage core application services, serverless resources, object-level storage services, and database resource types, and you will gain the knowledge required to maintain PaaS workloads throughout their life cycle by understanding the responsibility you share with the cloud provider.

Chapter 6, Utilizing Turnkey Software Solutions (SaaS), takes you through how **software as a service** (**SaaS**) solutions are implemented. You will learn how to configure and utilize at a high level core Microsoft Office 365, Amazon WorkDocs, and Google Docs services. You will also learn about the role of the SaaS marketplace, and you will gain the knowledge required to maintain SaaS workloads throughout their life cycle by understanding the responsibility you share with the cloud provider.

Chapter 7, Implementing Virtual Network Resources for Security, takes you through implementing various fundamental networking services. You will also learn how to set up a public load balancer and a site-to-site (hybrid) virtual private network, and you will reinforce concepts and configuration procedures by completing review questions.

Chapter 8, Launching Compute Service Resources for Scalability, takes you through implementing various fundamental compute services. You will also learn how to set up a virtual machine, web application services, container services, and serverless function services. You will reinforce concepts and configuration procedures by completing review questions.

Chapter 9, Configuring Storage Resources for Resiliency, takes you through implementing various fundamental storage services. You will also learn how to set up object-level storage services, file-sharing services, key-value storage services, and message-queueing services. You will reinforce concepts and configuration procedures by completing review questions.

Chapter 10, Developing Database Services for APIs, takes you through utilizing key database services, including how to create relational databases and non-relational database resources. You will reinforce your learning by completing review questions.

Chapter 11, Building Data Warehouse Services for Scalability, takes you through building instrumental data warehouse databases, and Data Lake storage resources. You will reinforce concepts and configuration procedures by completing review questions.

Chapter 12, Implementing Native Cyber Security Controls for Protection, takes you through implementing native-cloud cyber security features. You will also learn how to configure built-in database, storage, compute, and network security features, and you'll learn about the concepts of defense-in-depth while exploring these capabilities.

Chapter 13, Managing API Tools for Agility, takes you through configuring native fundamental cloud management API tools. You will learn how to manage resources utilizing web-based portals and interfaces and web-based CLIs, and you will learn how to use cloud-native infrastructure as code tools to efficiently develop IaaS and PaaS resources.

Chapter 14, Accelerating the Continuous Learning Journey, takes you through utilizing supplemental learning resources to successfully master cloud computing. You will learn about online learning communities and self-paced, live instructor-led, and mentorship resources.

Chapter 15, Driving Growth, and the Future of the Cloud, the final chapter of the book, explores the significance of certifications, role requirements, examination preparation resources, and best practice testing strategies, which inevitably will lead you to a milestone in your successful journey in cloud computing.

To get the most out of this book

You should have a basic understanding of networking and computer concepts, including networking topologies, IP addressing, routing, and DNS, and basic experience with command-line and programming languages such as Python and C#.

Software/hardware covered in the book	Operating system requirements
AWS, Microsoft Azure and Google Cloud Platform.	Windows, macOS, or Linux

If you are using the digital version of this book, we advise you to type the code yourself or access the code from the book's GitHub repository (a link is available in the next section). Doing so will help you avoid any potential errors related to the copying and pasting of code.

Download the example code files

You can download the example code files for this book from GitHub at `https://github.com/PacktPublishing/Cloud-Computing-Demystified-for-Aspiring-Professionals`. If there's an update to the code, it will be updated in the GitHub repository.

We also have other code bundles from our rich catalog of books and videos available at `https://github.com/PacktPublishing/`. Check them out!

Download the color images

We also provide a PDF file that has color images of the screenshots and diagrams used in this book. You can download it here: `https://packt.link/rmL2p`.

Conventions used

There are a number of text conventions used throughout this book.

`Code in text`: Indicates code words in text, database table names, folder names, filenames, file extensions, pathnames, dummy URLs, user input, and Twitter handles. Here is an example: "Mount the downloaded `WebStorm-10*.dmg` disk image file as another disk in your system."

Bold: Indicates a new term, an important word, or words that you see onscreen. For instance, words in menus or dialog boxes appear in **bold**. Here is an example: "Select **System info** from the **Administration** panel."

> **Tips or important notes**
> Appear like this.

Get in touch

Feedback from our readers is always welcome.

General feedback: If you have questions about any aspect of this book, email us at `customercare@packtpub.com` and mention the book title in the subject of your message.

Errata: Although we have taken every care to ensure the accuracy of our content, mistakes do happen. If you have found a mistake in this book, we would be grateful if you would report this to us. Please visit `www.packtpub.com/support/errata` and fill in the form.

Piracy: If you come across any illegal copies of our works in any form on the internet, we would be grateful if you would provide us with the location address or website name. Please contact us at `copyright@packt.com` with a link to the material.

If you are interested in becoming an author: If there is a topic that you have expertise in and you are interested in either writing or contributing to a book, please visit `authors.packtpub.com`.

Share your thoughts

Once you've read *Cloud Computing Demystified for Aspiring Professionals*, we'd love to hear your thoughts! Scan the following QR code to go straight to the Amazon review page for this book and share your feedback.

https://packt.link/r/1803243317

Your review is important to us and the tech community and will help us make sure we're delivering excellent quality content.

Download a free PDF copy of this book

Thanks for purchasing this book!

Do you like to read on the go but are unable to carry your print books everywhere?

Is your eBook purchase not compatible with the device of your choice?

Don't worry! Now with every Packt book you get a DRM-free PDF version of that book at no cost.

Read anywhere, any place, on any device. Search, copy, and paste code from your favorite technical books directly into your application.

The perks don't stop there. You can get exclusive access to discounts, newsletters, and great free content in your inbox daily.

Follow these simple steps to get the benefits:

1. Scan the QR code or visit the link:

https://packt.link/free-ebook/9781803243313

2. Submit your proof of purchase.
3. That's it! We'll send your free PDF and other benefits to your email directly.

Part 1:
The Journey to
Cloud Computing

This part provides an introduction to cloud computing, its foundation, and architecture.

This part comprises the following chapters:

- *Chapter 1, Introduction to Cloud Computing*
- *Chapter 2, Unveiling the Cloud*
- *Chapter 3, Understanding the Benefits of Public Clouds (AWS, Azure, and GCP)*

1

Introduction to Cloud Computing

As organizations today continue to move their customer interfacing services and internal **line-of-business (LOB)** applications to the cloud, it becomes imperative that IT professionals, developers, and enthusiasts understand the essentials and tenets that formed cloud computing. Practitioners should understand and explore the core advantages ingrained in cloud computing that empower users of any skill level to deploy, configure, and manage with confidence cloud-hosted applications, modern services, and core infrastructure resources optimally.

This chapter will lead you through a historic journey from traditional infrastructures to the rise of cloud computing as we know it and then describe in detail cloud computing and its various advantages over traditional technology infrastructures.

In this chapter, we're going to cover the following topics:

- Genesis
- Monolithic on-premises technology
- The advent of cloud computing
- Cloud computing explored
- Advantages of cloud computing

The fact that you're reading this implies you know that cloud computing is not some fad on its way out to be discarded to the annals of time. It's also an excellent modern technology to master, however improbable, due to its ambiguity and cosmic scale. I may be embellishing, but this is not a far cry from the undoubtable truth, which is there are no cloud gurus to speak of in the literal sense. It's also an exciting cutting-edge service-oriented technology that will expand your existing capabilities, and successfully mastering cloud computing through attaining industry-standard certifications subsequently leads to sustainable careers with the promise of future growth in some of the most prestigious organizations in the private and public sectors. I speak from experience, and when I tell you it's feasible, it is, because like you, I too was seeking but not finding, and my hopes are that you find your niche in modern technology by embracing the cloud.

Genesis

In this section, you'll learn about the history of key technology being used in cloud computing, and you will also learn how these technologies are derived from the traditional mainframes used in data centers. Lastly, you will come to understand a technology architecture pattern known as distributed systems.

I will describe **Advanced Research Projects Agency Network (ARPANET)**, Multics, and mainframes, and introduce virtualization.

> *"Ever since the dawn of civilization, people have not been content to see events as unconnected and inexplicable. They have craved an understanding of the underlying order in the world. Today we still yearn to know why we are here and where we came from. Humanity's deepest desire for knowledge is justification enough for our continuing quest. And our goal is nothing less than a complete description of the universe we live in." (Stephen Hawking)*

The future of tomorrow's technological wonders arose from the turbulent '60s, arguably an era of counter-cultural beginnings. Through this chaos, humanity rose to accomplish impossible feats, such as the US and Soviet Union's **Space Race**, but there are more developments that may have not been as significant to the public, such as the discovery of a rapidly spinning neutron star, the automotive industry's contribution to acceleration in the literal sense with vehicles such as the Ford Mustang, and nuances in size classes, which included compact, mid-sized and full-sized, coming into being.

The very first computers were connected in 1969, and this was only possible due to the beginnings of the **Advanced Research Projects Agency Network (ARPANET)** in 1966, a project that would implement the TCP/IP protocol suite. Out of the project rose many nuances such as remote login, file transfer, and email. The project over the years continued to evolve; internetworking research in the '70s cultivated transmission control programs' later versions. These later TCP/IP versions were then used in 1983 by the Department of Defense.

Scientific communities in the early 1980s invested in supercomputing mainframes and supported network access and interconnectivity. In later years, interconnectivity flourished to develop what is known today as the internet.

Practical application concepts on remote job entry became realized due to market demands in the 1960s for time-sharing solutions, led by vendors such as IBM and others. GE was another major computer company—along with Honeywell, RCA, and IBM—that had a line of general-purpose computers originally designed for batch processing. Later, this extended into full-time-sharing solutions developed by GE, Bell Laboratories, and MIT, wherein the finished product was known as the Multics operating system, which ran on a mainframe computer. These mainframes became known as **data centers**, where users submitted jobs for operators to manage, which became prevalent in the years that followed.

The mainframes were mammoth physical infrastructures installed in what later was coined a server room. It became practical for multiple users to access the same data and utilize the CPUs' power from a terminal (computer). This allowed enterprise organizations the ability to get a better return on their investment.

Following the early achievements of mainframes, corporations such as IBM developed **virtual machines** (**VMs**). VMs supported multiple virtual systems on a single physical node—in layman's terms, multiple computer environments coexisting in the same physical environment. VM operating systems such as CP-40 and CP-67 potentially pathed the way for future virtualization technologies. Consequently, mainframes could run multiple applications and processes in parallel, making the hardware even more efficient and cost-effective.

IBM wasn't the only corporation that developed and leveraged virtualization technologies. Compaq introduced Intel's 80386 microprocessor, the Deskpro 386, in 1986. The Deskpro 386 included platform virtualization in the virtual 8086 mode for Windows 386, which supported Microsoft Windows running on top of the MS-DOS operating system. The virtual 8086 mode supported multiple virtual processors, optimizing performance.

In the years to come, virtualization functionality could be traced back to the earliest implementations. Virtual infrastructures can support guest operating systems, including VM memory, CPU cores, disk drives, input devices, output devices, and shared networking resources.

Telecommunication pioneers in the 1990s such as AT&T and Verizon, who previously marketed point-to-point data circuits, began offering virtual networking resources with a similar quality of service, but at a lower cost. Various telecommunication providers began utilizing cloud symbols to denote demarcation points between the provider and the users' network infrastructure responsibilities.

As distributed computing became more mainstream throughout the years of 2000-2013, organizations examined ways to make scaled computing accessible to more users through time-sharing, underpinned by virtual internetworking. Corporations such as Amazon, Microsoft, and Google offered on-demand self-service, broad network access, resource pooling, and efficient elasticity, whereby compute, storage, apps, and networking resources can be provisioned and released rapidly utilizing virtualization technology.

The advantages of virtualization go far beyond what I have written here, but most notably include reducing electronic equipment costs, resource pooling (sharing), multi-user VM administration, and site-to-site internetworking implementation acceleration—moreover, decreasing exorbitant operational maintenance costs. Virtualization is one of the most pivotal protagonists that catalyzed organizations such as Microsoft, Amazon, and Google to introduce cloud resources in a fully managed **service-oriented architecture** (**SOA**) that presently spans the globe.

These virtualization ecosystems, now known as cloud computing services, are delivering turnkey innovations such as Amazon's e-commerce **software as a service** (**SaaS**), known as Amazon Prime, specializing in distributing goods and services. The business benefits are staggering: agility, flexible costs, and rapid elasticity to support highly available access. General statistics shows that millions of consumers rely on Amazon services to facilitate daily shopping needs, especially during the holidays.

Amazon has even surpassed retail organization giants such as Walmart as the world's largest online public retailer. These facts conclusively support the benefits of services delivered using virtualization infrastructure resources. As the age-old adage proclaims, *less is more*!

Monolithic on-premises technology

In this section, you will learn about the core traditional data center resources. Moreover, I will describe data centers by type, maintenance, compliance, implementation, **business continuity (BC)**, cost, energy, environmental controls, and administration.

To understand the advent of the cloud, we need to address the elephant in the room—while this is figurative in nature, this closely resembles the enormity of the current subject matter: the traditional on-premises data center. I'll elaborate on the term *on-premises* in the current context in a later section of this chapter. For now, let's focus on the traditional data center architecture.

In an unembellished but detailed description, data centers are physical facilities that host networking infrastructure services that manage data resources. The data center is known to house thousands of servers, formerly known as mainframes, and data centers are comprised of various resources, such as computers and networking devices, including utilities and environmental control systems supporting the physical infrastructure.

All data centers, regardless of type, include networking infrastructure resources such as media (cable), repeaters, hubs, bridges, switches, and routers to connect computer clients to servers. Networking devices support internetworking connectivity with internal and external networks. Even the traditional data center supported remote connectivity and had the capability to implement networking topologies such as site-to-site connectivity using an array of networking technologies that supported customers and remote workers who had to connect to the enterprise organization from outside of the company's private local area network securely.

Storage system resources were prevalent and consisted of infrastructure resources such as **storage area network (SAN)**, **networked attached storage (NAS)**, and **direct-attached storage (DAS)** devices. Regardless of the data structure, volume, velocity, and accessibility pattern, data was stored in one of these primitives. Later, I'll elaborate on the variances to help you not only differentiate but to better understand the advantages and disadvantages, which may ultimately drive organizations of all sizes to adopt modern cloud computing data services.

It's important to note the essential legacy data center infrastructure hosted services on physical servers, which served as the compute infrastructure, typically mounted on physical racks and occasionally installed into cabinets. Here are some important facts: statistically, data centers are in office buildings or similar physical edifices, and data centers have either raised or overhead floored architecture that contains additional equipment, such as electrical wiring, cabling, and environmental controls required to sustain the data center services.

Overall maintenance is another important factor to consider for traditional data centers. This includes administering and maintaining industry-standard regulatory and non-regulatory business best practices, which is a perennial expense. Planning, preparing, and deploying new applications, as well as existing LOB applications or services, using monolithic infrastructures typically incurs substantial costs that directly impact capital and operational expenditures. And innovation, experimentation, and deployment iteration while plausible are not cost-effective in monolithic environments, which delays—if not prevents—new services from general availability. Decommissioning these hardware infrastructure resources is a process within itself, and nigh impossible for some organizations who do not have either the internal talent or budget to successfully complete the project. This more often than not leads companies to try other solutions based on different data center implementations.

The content herein only scratches the surface of traditional on-premises infrastructures' compliance considerations, such as business requirements and system maintenance concerns. But make no mistake—whether your company is small or large, regulatory compliance policies are very important. I highly recommend reviewing governance and compliance documentation for any technology. Similarly, later sections will elaborate on various compliance controls that organizations such as Amazon, Microsoft, and Google must adhere to. Organizations that implement and manage data centers, traditional or cloud, must adhere to compliance controls set forth by various governmental or non-governmental agencies. My apologies—I have digressed a little from my previous paragraph's subject. So, let us continue our journey regarding different data center implementations.

Did you know that on-premises data centers come in various implementations? Enterprise data centers are the most common. They are owned and operated by the company for their internal users and clientele. Managed data centers are operated by third parties on behalf of the organization. Companies typically lease the equipment instead of owning it. Some organizations rent space within a data center, where the data center is owned and operated by third-party **service providers** (**SPs**) that offer off-premises implementations known as colocation data center models. Each implementation includes redundant data center operational infrastructure resources, such as physical or virtual servers, storage systems, uninterruptable power systems, on-site direct current systems, networking equipment, cooling systems, data center infrastructure management resources, and—commonly—a secondary data center for redundancy.

High availability (**HA**) and **disaster recovery** (**DR**) are other important factors to weigh up. Data center infrastructures are categorized into tiers, which is an efficient way to describe the HA (or lack of HA) infrastructure components being utilized at each data center. Believe it or not, some organizations do not require the HA that a tier 4 data center proposes. Organizations run a risk if they do not plan carefully. For example, organizations that invest in only a tier 1 infrastructure might make a business vulnerable. However, organizations that decide on a tier 4 infrastructure might over-invest, depending on their budget constraints.

Let's have a look at the various HA data center tiers:

- Tier 1 data centers have a single power and cooling system with little, if any, redundancy. They have an expected uptime of 99.671% (28.8 hours of downtime annually).

- Tier 2 data centers have a single power and cooling system with some redundancy. They have an expected uptime of 99.741% (22 hours of downtime annually).

- Tier 3 data centers have multiple power and cooling systems with redundancy in place to update and maintain them without taking them offline. They have an expected uptime of 99.982% (1.6 hours of downtime annually).

- Tier 4 data centers are built fault-tolerant and have redundant components. They have an expected uptime of 99.995% (26.3 minutes of downtime annually).

The **total cost of ownership** (**TCO**) may be too costly for some start-ups. Most enterprise organizations are looking to offload these costs using third-party vendors but learn eventually the upfront capital expenses are too much to bear, so they continue investing in their own on-premises data center. The public cloud provides advantages regarding capital expenditures and HA. We will discuss these topics in more detail in the section titled *The advantages of cloud computing*.

What about utility costs? Data centers use various IT devices to provide services, and the electricity used by these IT devices consequently converts to heat, which must be removed from the data center by **heating, ventilation, and air conditioning** (**HVAC**) systems, which also use electricity.

Did you know that utilities and environmental control systems are other important items to consider when reviewing on-premises data center costs? On average, on-premises data center infrastructure systems containing typically tens of thousands of network devices require an abundant amount of energy. Several case studies illustrate that traditional data centers use enough electricity to power an estimated 80,000 homes in the US.

These traditional on-premises data centers' HVAC infrastructure systems are also sometimes not efficient and require the capability to deliver central and distributed cooling, which is costly due to some buildings' older architectural designs. Moreover, to be more cost- and energy-efficient, newer modular data center models are required for optimal cooling paths, but that's not always feasible in older structures. Achieving optimal performance from your computing infrastructure requires a different modern modular design that can support the ongoing business demands of today.

Managing a traditional data center requires employing large teams, and supervisors of varying skill sets. Operations team members are responsible for the maintenance and upkeep of the infrastructure within a data center. Governing data center standards for networking, compute, and storage throughout an organization's application life cycle may not be efficient due to the monolithic architectural design of most traditional data centers. If a company required scaling, it would have to invest in expanding its data center resources by procuring more hardware, which is inevitable. Upgrading the on-premises hardware technology also requires multi-vendor support and sometimes even granting those third parties access to the data center, which poses numerous risks. These concerns would be far fewer if the overall quantity of physical servers in a traditional data center were proportional to the services rendered. But that idea becomes a reality when virtualization becomes prevalent.

Let's summarize—traditional data centers are listed as a type, such as enterprise data centers, implemented and managed by the company. Data center locations are physical buildings and can include offices and closets. Data centers incur a myriad of costs, some functional and others non-functional. Data center governance includes conforming to policies, laws, regulations, and standards. A data center's architectural design may impact energy and efficiency. More importantly, data center designs based on type have an impact on our environment. A data center's power and cooling system design require consistent monitoring and optimization, which consequently will decrease emissions and energy consumption and decrease TCO. Finally, the quintessential traditional data center has a 1:1 ratio between physical servers and services published by an organization. This method of implementation is to be expected because of monolithic architecture. Consequently, this method incurs substantial capital and operational expenditures that have a direct negative impact on an organization's **return on investment (ROI)**.

The advent of cloud computing

In this section, I will introduce, describe, and define virtualization types and vendors, and I will describe how virtualization is different from physical servers. Then, I will explore the distributed computing API architecture. I will also describe how demand has driven technology. Finally, I will define cloud computing models.

This section's objectives are the following:

- From physical to virtual
- Virtualization contributions by vendor
- Distributed computing APIs
- Exponential growth

From physical to virtual

Cloud computing technology emerged from a multitude of innovations and computing requirements. This emergence included computer science technology advancements that leveraged the underpinnings of mainframe computing, which changed the way we do business. Let us not forget the fickle customer service-level expectations related to IT BC.

The mainframe system features and architecture topology would be one of the important legacy technologies that, through several joint ventures from various stakeholders and evolution, contributed to the advent of cloud computing.

As described in the *Genesis* section, CP-40 provided a VM environment. Mainframes such as IBM's 360-hosted CP-40, which supported multiple cloud computing engineer VM operating system instances—arguably, are the very first hardware virtualization prototype.

Let us define virtualization first before we explain how Amazon, Microsoft, and Google use this underpinning to drive their ubiquitous services.

In the *Genesis* section, we saw how achievements in virtualization technology played an important role in the emergence of cloud computing. Understanding the intricacies of VMs—arguably referred to as "server virtualization"—is critical in the grand scheme of things.

Virtualization abstracts physical infrastructure resources, which support running one or more VMs guest operating systems that resemble a similar or different computer operating system on one physical computer host. This approach was pioneered in the 1960s by IBM. IBM developed several products, such as CP-40 and CP-67, arguably the very first virtualization technologies. While virtualization is one of the key technologies in the advent of cloud computing, this book will not delve into virtualization implementations, such as hardware-assisted virtualization, paravirtualization, and operating system-level virtualization.

Over the years, many technology-driven companies have developed different virtualization offerings of varying types.

Virtualization contributions by vendor

VMware is a technology company known for virtualization. VMware launched VMware Workstation in the '90s, heralding virtualization software that allowed users to run one or more instances of x86 or x86-64 operating systems on a single personal device.

Xen is another technology company known for developing hypervisors that support multiple computer operating systems running on the same hardware concurrently.

Citrix is a virtualization technology company that offers several virtualization products, such as XenApp (app virtualization), which supports XenDesktop (desktop virtualization). There is even a product for Apple devices that hosts Microsoft Windows desktops virtually. Citrix also offers XenServer, which delivers server virtualization. Additionally, Citrix offers the NetScaler product suite: in particular, **software-defined wide area networking** (**SD-WAN**), NetScaler SDX, and VPX networking appliances that support virtual networking.

Microsoft, known for its personal and business computer software, has contributed as well to virtualization. Microsoft started offering application virtualization products and services. Microsoft's App-V delivered application virtualization, and soon thereafter, Microsoft developed Hyper-V, which supported server virtualization.

There are many more organizations that, through acquisition or development, have contributed to modern advancements in various virtualization nuances that are the foundation of cloud computing wonders today. But I would be remiss if I didn't elaborate on the ubiquitous cloud's distributed nature—or, more accurately denoted, distributed computing architecture.

Distributed computing APIs

Distributed computing, also known as **distributed systems**, rose out of the '60s, and its earliest successful implementation was the ARPANET email infrastructure. Distributed computing architectures categorically are labeled as loosely coupled or tightly coupled architectures. Architectures such as client-server are the most known and were prevalent during the traditional mainframe era. N-tier or three-tier architectures provide many of today's modern cloud computing service architecture characteristics: in particular, sending message requests to middle-tier services that queue requests for other consuming services—for example, in a three-tier web, application, and database server architecture. The application server or application queue-like service would be the middle-tier service, and then queue input messages for other distributed programs on the same server to consume (input) and if required send (output). Another aspect of distributed computing architectures is that of **peer-to-peer** (**P2P**), where all clients are peers that can provide either client or server functionality. Each peer or service communicates asynchronously, contains local memory, and can act autonomously. Distributed system architectures deliver cost efficiency and increased reliability. Cloud computing SPs offer distributed services that are loosely coupled, delivering cost-efficient infrastructure resources as a service. This is also due to distributed systems utilizing low-end hardware systems. The top three cloud computing providers are decreasing, if not eliminating **single points of failure** (**SPOFs**), consequently providing highly available resources in an SOA. These characteristics are derived from distributed computing.

Exponential growth

The rise of cloud computing is also arguably due to the exponential growth of the IT industry. This has a direct correlation with HA, scalability, and BC in the event of planned or unplanned failures. This growth also resulted in mass increases in energy consumption.

Traditional IT computing infrastructures must procure their own hardware as capital expenses. Additionally, they must encounter operating expenses, which include maintaining the computer operating systems and the operational costs incurred by human services. Here is something to ponder— variable operational costs and fixed capital investments are to be expected. Fixed or capital costs are upfront, which could be lowered by increasing the number of users. However, the operational costs may increase quickly with a larger number of users. Consequently, the total cost increases rapidly with the number of users. Modern IT computing infrastructures such as the cloud offer a pay-per-use model, which provides cloud computing engineers and architects greater control over operational expenditures not feasible in a traditional data center.

Meeting the demands of HA and the capability to scale becomes more and more important due to the growth of the IT industry. Enterprise data centers, which are operated and managed by the corporation's IT department, are known to procure expensive brand-name hardware and networking devices due to their traditional implementation and familiarity. However, cloud architectures are built with commodity hardware and network devices. Amazon, Microsoft, and Google platforms choose low-cost disks and

Ethernet to build their modular data centers. Cloud designs emphasize the performance/price ratio rather than the performance alone.

As the number of global internet users continues to rise, so too has the demand for data center services, giving rise to concerns regarding growing data center energy utilization. The quantity of data traversing the internet has increased exponentially, while global data center storage capacity has increased by several factors.

These growth trends are expected to continue as the world consumes more and more data. In fact, energy consumption is one of the main contributors to on-premises capital and operational expenses.

Inevitably this leads to rising concern in electricity utilization, consequently voicing concerns over environmental issues, such as **carbon dioxide** (**CO2**) emissions. Knowing the electricity use of data centers provides a useful benchmark for testing theories about the CO2 implications of data center services.

The cost of energy produced by IT devices impacts environmental and economic standards. Industrialized countries such as the US consume more energy than non-industrialized ones. The IT industry is essential to the global economy and plays a role in every sector and industry. Due to the frequency of IT usage, this will no doubt continue to increase demand, which makes it important that we consider designing an eco-friendly infrastructure architecture.

On-premises data centers, which are also referred to as enterprise data center types, require IT to handle and manage everything, including purchasing and installing the hardware, virtualization, operating system, and applications, and setting up the network, network firewall devices, and secure data storage. Furthermore, IT is responsible for maintaining the infrastructure hardware throughout an LOB app's life cycle. This imposes both significant upfront costs for the hardware and ongoing data center operating costs due to patching. Don't forget—you should also factor in paying for resources regardless of utilization.

Cloud computing provides an alternative to the on-premises data center. Amazon, Microsoft, and Google cloud providers are responsible for hardware procurement and overall maintenance costs and provide a variety of services you can use. Lease whatever hardware capacity and services you need for your LOB application, only when required, thus converting what had been a capital expense or fixed into an operational expense. This allows the cloud computing engineer to lease hardware capacity and deliver modern software services that would be too expensive to purchase traditionally.

Cloud computing explored

In this section, you will learn about the cloud computing concepts derived from the **National Institute of Standards and Technology** (**NIST**). Then I will describe the cloud computing models used by cloud computing providers today. Additionally, I will describe cloud computing deployment models.

Cloud computing plays an increasingly important role in IT. Therefore, as an IT professional, you must be cognizant of the fundamental cloud principles and methods. There are three main cloud computing deployment models: public, private, and hybrid. Each provides a range of services but implements the resources differently. Equally important to consider are the cloud computing service models: **infrastructure as a service (IaaS)**, **platform as a service (PaaS)**, and SaaS. They are the core tenets from which cloud computing is defined.

By now, you should understand the historic journey that led us to cloud computing. However, if you are still unsure, I highly recommend you revisit the section titled *Genesis* and then correlate the researched data with the section titled *The advent of cloud computing*. Nevertheless, the cloud is the culmination of evolutionary technological advancements in human history.

To understand cloud services, we first refer to standards.

There are undoubtedly many organizations that develop standards built to ensure we measure, innovate, and lead following industry best practices to reach an overarching goal, and that is to improve our quality of life.

These standard entities may be deemed regulatory or non-regulatory. For simplicity's sake, regulatory organizations such as the **International Energy Agency (IEA)** are appointed by international legislation to devise energy requirement standards, and entities such as NIST are non-regulatory because they define supplemental standards that are not official rules enforced by some regulation delegated through legislation. However, in cloud computing, NIST is the gold standard.

NIST proclaims the following regarding cloud computing services:

"Cloud computing is a model for enabling ubiquitous, convenient, on-demand network access to a shared pool of configurable computing resources (e.g., networks, servers, storage, applications, and services) that can be rapidly provisioned and released with minimal management effort or service provider interaction."

The cloud computing model(s), which we will define in grandiose detail in later sections, are derived from NIST standards, which you can review at your leisure, by navigating to their online website. You can use the URL located at `http://csrc.nist.gov/publications/nistpubs/800-145/SP800-145.pdf`.

Cloud computing provides a modern alternative to the traditional on-premises data center. Public cloud providers such as Amazon, Microsoft, and Google are responsible for hardware procurement and continual maintenance, and the public cloud provides on-demand resources. Rent hardware to support your software whenever you need it; organizations can convert what had been an upfront capital expenditure for hardware to an operating expense. This allows you to rent resources that would be traditionally too costly for some companies, and you pay if the resources are being utilized.

Cloud computing typically provides an online website experience, making it user-friendly to administrators who are responsible for managing compute, storage, networking, and other resources. For example, administrators can quickly define VMs by compute size, which includes VM capacity settings, such as virtual CPU core quantity, amount of RAM, disk size, disk performance, an operating system image such as Linux, preconfigured software, and the virtual network configuration, and then has the capability to deploy the VM using the described configuration anywhere in the world, and within several minutes securely access the deployed compute instance where the IT pro or developer can perform role-based tasks. This illustrates the rapid deployment capability of cloud computing defined by NIST.

Cloud computing supports various deployment options as well, such as public, private, and hybrid cloud. These options are known as cloud computing deployment models, not to be confused with IaaS, PaaS, and SaaS cloud computing models.

You will have a general understanding of the public cloud deployment model once you have completed reading this book. So, let me take a moment to elaborate on private and hybrid. In a private cloud, your organization creates a cloud environment in your on-premises data center and provides engineers in your organization with access to private resources. This deployment model offers services similar to the public cloud but exclusively for your users, but your organization remains responsible for procuring the hardware infrastructure and ongoing maintenance of the software services and hardware. In a hybrid-cloud deployment model, enterprise organizations integrate the public and private cloud, permitting you to host workloads in whichever cloud computing deployment model meets your current business requirements. For example, your organization can host highly available website services in the public cloud and then connect it to a non-relational database managed in your private cloud.

Planning, preparing, and implementing a cloud service model is as imperative as deciding whether to remain utilizing traditional systems built using monolithic architecture topology or choose an all-in cloud approach. From a consumer's point of view, the myriad resources that cloud computing providers such as Amazon, Microsoft, and Google provide are daunting to the untrained eye. Thankfully, Amazon, Microsoft, and Google organize their distributed services into three major categories, referred to as cloud computing models.

One of the first cloud computing models is known as IaaS. In this model, the customer pays the **cloud SP (CSP)** to host VMs in the public cloud. Customers are responsible for managing the VM guest operating system, including hosted services or applications. This cloud computing model offers the customer complete control and flexibility.

The second cloud computing model is known as PaaS. In this cloud computing model, customers are responsible for the deployment, configuration, and management of applications in an agile manner using the cloud platform. The CSP manages the application runtime environment and is responsible for managing and maintaining the platform's underlying VM guest operating system.

Another widely utilized cloud computing model is known as SaaS. In this model, clients utilize turnkey online software services such as storage, or email software managed by the cloud computing provider. Customers access cross-platform installable and online apps. These products are typically pay-as-you-go.

Cloud computing providers Amazon, Microsoft, and Google offer all three cloud computing models: IaaS, PaaS, and SaaS. These services are made available as consumption-based offerings. The cloud computing service models form three pillars on top of which cloud computing resources are administered.

All three service models allow the cloud computing engineer to access the services over the internet. The service models are supported by the global infrastructure of the CSP. Every service includes a **service-level agreement** (**SLA**) between the provider and the user. The SLA is addressed in terms of the services' availability, performance, and general security controls.

To help you better understand these service models, I'll describe in detail IaaS and PaaS enterprise implementation by sharing real-world examples in later chapters from Amazon, Microsoft, and Google.

All three major cloud providers' solutions are built on virtualization technology, which abstracts physical hardware as a layer of virtualized resources for networking, storage, and processing. Amazon, Microsoft, and Google add further abstraction layers to define specific services that you can provision and manage. Regardless of the unique technology that one of these organizations uses to implement cloud computing solutions, the characteristics commonly observed remain on-demand, broad network access, shared resource pools, and rapid elasticity, and include metering capabilities, which allows enterprise organizations to track resource utilization at a cloud scale.

Cloud computing resources are built-in data centers that are commonly owned and operated by the cloud provider. The cloud core platform includes SANs, database systems, firewalls, and security devices. APIs enable programmatic access to underlying resources. Monitoring and metering are used to track the utilization and performance of resources dynamically provisioned.

The cloud platforms handle resource management and maintenance automatically. Internal services detect the status of each node and server joining and leaving and do the tasks accordingly. Cloud computing providers such as Amazon, Microsoft, and Google have built many economically efficient, eco-friendly data centers all over the world. Each data center theoretically houses tens of thousands of servers.

Here is a layered example of the cloud computing architecture: infrastructure, platform, and application. These layers are implemented with virtualization and provisioned in adherence to each cloud provider's well-architected framework, which will be explored in a later section for each cloud provider. The infrastructure layer is implemented first to support IaaS resources. This infrastructure layer serves as the foundation to build PaaS resources. In turn, the platform layer is a foundation to implement the application layer for the SaaS.

This begs the question: *What are the benefits of said services?*

Advantages of cloud computing

In this section, you will learn to describe the advantages of cloud computing architecture. I will describe the benefits of trading capital expense for variable expenses, cloud economics, capacity planning, optimized agility, improved focus, and leveraging global resources in comparison to the traditional architecture, and will review and define HA and BC.

Cloud computing offers many advantages in comparison to traditional on-premises data centers. Let us review some of the key advantages.

Trade capital expense for variable expense

Organizations generally consider moving their workloads to the cloud because of the expense advantages. Instead of having to invest in data centers and servers before organizations know how they are going to use them, only pay when you consume cloud computing resources, and only pay for how much the organization consumes. This expense advantage allows any industry to rapidly get up and running while only paying for what is being utilized.

Benefit from massive economies of scale

Using cloud computing, organizations can achieve a lower variable cost than they can get on their own. Because usage from tens of thousands of customers is collected and combined in the cloud, cloud computing providers such as Amazon, Microsoft, and Google can achieve higher economies of scale, which translates into lower subscription prices.

And cloud computing providers such as Amazon, Microsoft, and Google invest in low-end commodity devices optimized for large-scale clouds instead of purchasing high-end devices. The volume of subscription purchases coupled with lower-cost commodity hardware grants cloud computing providers the ability to lower prices for new customers.

Stop guessing about capacity

As aforementioned, enterprise organizations only pay when utilizing cloud computing resources. Organizations access as much or as little as needed, and scale up and down, in and out as required on-demand.

Capacity planning is not only arduous but tedious and error-prone, particularly if you do not know what the customer's response will be. Customers' demands fluctuate dynamically, and the capability to scale becomes critical. Cloud computing engineers can demand more capacity during real-time shifts and spikes in customer demand, reduce costs using commodity compute, storage, and networking resources pooled by the cloud computing provider, and can be provisioned at a moment's notice. For general concerns such as whether your LOB application needs more compute resources to meet increasing customer demands, hosting your workload in the cloud can help keep your customers satisfied. Does a decline in business mean that you don't need all that capacity your cloud computing service is providing for your LOB applications? Cloud computing engineers can scale down compute capacity to control costs, offering a huge advantage over static on-premises data center solutions.

Increase speed and agility

On-premises data centers can take generally several weeks to months to provision a server. With cloud computing ecosystems, organizations can provision tens of thousands of resources in minutes, and the ability to rapidly scale your workloads both horizontally and vertically allows you to address SLAs that are in constant flux. Developing new applications in the cloud can significantly decrease

time to market (**TTM**), which is an improvement over traditional monolithic development for several reasons. You do not have to deploy, configure, and maintain the underlying hardware for the compute, storage, and networking on which your applications will run. Instead, use the infrastructure resources accessible to you by your cloud computing provider.

Another reason why cloud computing-developed applications are faster to deploy has to do with how modern applications are developed. In an enterprise setting, developers create and test their applications in a test environment that simulates the final production environment. For example, an application might be developed and tested on a single-instance VM, also known as the dev environment, for eventual deployment onto two VM instances clustered across different **Availability Zones** (**AZs**) for HA and fault tolerance, which is common for production environments. Inconsistencies between your development and production environments can impact the development sprint cycle for business applications because problems might be missed in testing and only become apparent when the applications are deployed to production, which consequently necessitates further testing and development until the applications are behaving as intended. But with cloud computing, organizations can perform development and testing in the same kind of environment that their applications will be deployed upon. This allows you to quickly create resources and experiment iteratively. For start-ups, cloud computing grants them to start at a very low cost and scale rapidly as they gain customers. Start-ups would not encounter large upfront capital investment to create a new VM. This empowers any enterprise with the flexibility to rapidly set up development and test configurations. These can be programmed dynamically, giving you the ability to instantiate a development or test environment, do the testing, and tear it back down. This methodology keeps the cost very low, and maintenance is almost nonexistent.

Focus on what matters

Cloud computing lets organizations focus on their customers, rather than on expanding their data centers' resources, which includes investing in infrastructure, racking, stacking, and powering servers.

Cloud computing providers have already done the heavy lifting for you. For most enterprises, their most inadequate resource is their software engineers, now referred to as developers. Development teams have various priorities and tasks that need to be successfully completed. It is an advantage to focus those resources on projects that move the organization's campaign forward, rather than planning, procuring, preparing, and implementing an underlying infrastructure.

This makes economic sense for organizations when it comes to hardware acquisition costs because the cloud computing provider provides the core hardware resources. Traditionally, enterprises have often purchased and deployed large, scaled SANs from third-party vendors to meet business requirements. By utilizing storage resources from a cloud computing provider instead, enterprise organizations can significantly decrease overall storage procurement and long-term maintenance costs.

Cloud computing providers manage the data center, which means you do not have to manage your own IT infrastructure. Cloud computing enables you to access computing services, regardless of your location and the equipment that you use to access those services.

Go global in minutes

Cloud computing providers such as Amazon, Microsoft, and Google are constantly expanding their global presence to help all customers of varying sizes achieve lower latency and greater throughput and to ensure that an enterprise's most important asset—that is, data—resides only in the region they specify. As organizations and customers continue to grow their businesses, cloud computing providers such as Amazon, Microsoft, and Google will continue to provide the infrastructure that meets any organization's global business requirements.

Only the largest global enterprises can deploy data centers around the world. So, using Amazon, Microsoft, and Google entitles enterprises of any size to the capability to host an application or workload from any region to reduce latency to end users while avoiding the capital expenses, long-term commitments, and scaling challenges associated with maintaining and operating a global infrastructure.

In a later section, I will divulge each cloud provider's mammoth global infrastructure regions and zones in detail. But before I do, here's a brief insight into HA and DR, which are addressed by utilizing cloud computing global infrastructure.

An overview of HA

IT systems are considered critical business tools in most organizations. Outages of even a few hours reflect poorly upon the IT department and can result in lost sales or loss of business reputation. HA ensures that IT systems can survive the failure of a single server or even multiple servers.

Availability refers to the level of service that applications, services, or systems provide, and is expressed as the percentage of time that a service or system is available. Highly available architectures have minimal downtime, whether planned or unplanned, and are available more than 99% of the time, depending on the needs and the budget of the organization.

Here are some common target availability considerations:

- Cloud data center infrastructure
- Server hardware
- Storage
- Network infrastructure
- Internet
- Application services

> **Note**
> This is not an exhaustive list.

Cloud computing providers support the capability of any organization to design a highly available architecture. Cloud computing data centers are organized into AZs. Each AZ comprises one or more data centers, with some AZs having three to six data centers.

Each AZ is designed as an independent failure zone. This means that AZs are physically separated within a region and are in a specific flood zone by region. In addition to having separate uninterruptable power supplies and onsite backup generators, they are each connected to different electrical grids from independent utilities to further reduce SPOFs. AZs are all redundantly connected to multiple transit providers.

Enterprise organizations are responsible for selecting AZs where their systems reside. Some services can span multiple AZs. Every organization should design its systems to survive temporary or prolonged failure of an AZ if some disaster occurs. Utilizing distributed computing methods, organizations can distribute applications across multiple AZs, allowing them to remain resilient in most failure scenarios, including natural disasters or typical system failures.

An overview of DR

DR planning is an essential requirement for fulfilling SLAs. These agreements define when a service needs to be available, and how quickly it must be recovered if it fails. To ensure that organizations meet SLA requirements, site resiliency becomes a business requirement. Site resiliency is the ability of one or more systems and services to survive a site failure and to continue functioning using an alternate data center.

One of the advantages of cloud computing is the capability to implement multi-region with multiple AZs for DR and HA. The alternate data center is a site that can be in another region within a separate AZ dedicated only to DR. For example, the alternate data center could be another location in the same geographical region, such as the Johnson & Johnson primary data center, which is located in Virginia but has its secondary data center in Ohio; it's in use but has sufficient capacity to handle the Ohio facility's services in the event of an unplanned failure.

In summary, AZs are equivalent to a cluster of data centers. Amazon, Microsoft, and Google isolate their data centers using AZs so that they are not easily affected by natural disasters at the same time. AZs are a distinct group of data centers, whereas a region is made of multiple AZs to support the capability of spreading compute resources across multiple power providers.

> **Tip**
>
> Cloud computing providers recommend provisioning your resources across multiple AZs. If you implement multiple VM instances, you can spread them across more than one AZ and get added redundancy. If a single AZ has a problem, all assets in your second AZ will be unaffected. All recommendations are derived from online artifacts and can be corroborated by reviewing each cloud computing provider's well-architected framework document. The well-architected frameworks define real-world best practices that support cloud adoption and ongoing governance and management for any workload.

Summary

In this chapter, you learned about the genesis of key technologies used in cloud computing and reviewed core traditional data center service concerns. You also learned how data center technologies transitioned into virtual offerings, reviewed key patterns to distribute workloads efficiently, and learned how the demand for data requires a cloud-scaled infrastructure. We also explored cloud computing underpinnings and key advantages over traditional on-premises data centers.

In the next chapter, you will learn the underlying technology that comprises cloud computing services.

Further reference

For more information about topics covered in this book, you are referred to the following resources:

- NIST: `https://www.nist.gov/`
- Amazon Well-Architected Framework: `https://aws.amazon.com/architecture/well-architected/`
- Microsoft Well-Architected Framework: `https://docs.microsoft.com/en-us/azure/architecture/framework/`
- Google Cloud Architecture Framework: `https://cloud.google.com/architecture/framework`

Questions

1. Who is ARPANET?

    A. Defense Advanced Research Projects Agency

    B. Department of Defense

    C. Bell Laboratories

    D. Advanced Research Projects Agency Network

2. You are a cloud engineer tasked with deploying a Linux VM instance for Pharmakinematics, an enterprise organization. The IT department needs you to make use of the appropriate cloud computing service model. Which model do you make use of?

    A. FaaS

    B. PaaS

    C. Public

    D. IaaS

3. Which design strategy should you consider when planning cloud computing architectural recommendations for distributed computing services across AZs that provide a highly available architecture?

    A. Design for agility

    B. Design for scalability

    C. Design for failure

    D. Design microservices

4. Which data center tier supports an annual downtime of 26.3 minutes?

    A. Tier 4

    B. Tier 3

    C. Tier 2

    D. Tier 1

5. Which of the following refers to company-owned and operated enterprise data centers?

    A. Off-premises

    B. Cloud

    C. Co-located

    D. On-premises

6. What is virtualization?

    A. Docker resources

    B. Apple iOS

    C. The abstraction of physical resources

    D. Linux kernel

7. What is the Microsoft application virtualization service?

    A. Citrix

    B. Container

    C. App-V

    D. Hyper-V

8. What are some attributes that distributed computing systems display? (Choose all that apply.)

    A. SOA

    B. Monolithic

    C. DevOps

    D. Queue

9. NIST declares the following regarding cloud computing (Choose all that apply):

    A. On-demand self-service

    B. Resource pooling

    C. Rapid elasticity

    D. Poly Cloud

10. In terms of HA, what does an AZ provide?

    A. Fault tolerance

    B. Regional redundancy

    C. Energy reduction

    D. Identity and Access Management (IAM)

2
Unveiling the Cloud

This chapter will demystify the cloud by describing the underlying technologies, patterns, and concerns that comprise cloud computing services in comparison to traditional on-premises services. Here, you will learn how these technologies support core services.

The following topics will be covered in this chapter:

- Cloud computing unveiled
- Cloud-managed data centers
- Virtualization
- Microservices

Cloud computing unveiled

In this section, you will learn about what the cloud is like compared to on-premises infrastructure.

While the cloud has a myriad of unique advantages over traditional on-premises data centers' architecture services, it would be remiss of me if I did not demystify it to further enlighten you, the reader, about its similarities. Through this lesson, you will learn to understand its amorphous fabric and perhaps even learn to trust cloud computing.

With on-premises infrastructure, hardware systems such as IT cabinets (racks) of physical blade servers and disks, including networking devices and networking media, are owned and operated by the enterprise corporation. The hardware and software are often owned or sometimes leased for long periods of time by the corporation. A traditional on-premises service requires organizations to either spend a significant amount of money initially to purchase IT equipment or agree to lengthy terms.

Traditionally, this has led to hardware procurement decisions focused on scaling up, which is purchasing a blade server with more cores to satisfy a performance need. With cloud computing, you launch a **virtual machine** (**VM**) instance hosted on hardware provided by the cloud computing provider. Cloud computing providers utilize commodity hardware, which is significantly more cost-effective than scaling up through expensive commercialized hardware.

The major cloud computing providers such as Amazon, Microsoft, and Google build their hardware infrastructure from commodity components. Commodity, in this context, refers to using equipment from uncommon/unknown manufacturers who are less costly than their common brand-name competitors.

Cloud computing providers design their cloud data centers with extensive compute, storage, and network resources. Providers optimize their investment by efficiently renting these resources to customers.

Vast resources and the capability to quickly change resources between customers facilitate cloud computing providers to preposition resource allocation more efficiently than traditional on-premises data centers. Before providing a description of cloud computing data centers, we must unveil the ubiquitous foundation that supports cloud computing services as we know them.

Cloud computing's physical and logical architectural foundation has evolved from several concepts, such as cluster, grid, and distributed computing. For example, cluster and grid computing use parallel computing to unravel rather difficult scenarios. Similarly, cloud computing uses a multitude of infrastructure resources to deliver unparalleled services to consumers and supports sharing access to these unique resources from anywhere at any time across any platform. Thus, cloud computing providers' web services are developed and accessible over the internet. These resources can communicate with each other around the globe, thereby delivering services in a scalable and efficient manner to end users, which aligns with distributed computing.

The essential core of cloud computing is the cluster—to be more accurate, a VM cluster. We will elaborate shortly on this topic of virtualization and, moreover, on how virtualization is used as one of the underlying components or layers of cloud computing. Virtualization has already been explained in layman's terms in the previous chapter.

The VM cluster nodes are used as compute resources. A few are control nodes used to manage and monitor the cloud. The scheduling of jobs requires work delegation to various VM clusters. There are even external access points, referred to here as gateway nodes, that lead to the public internet.

The infrastructure layer is the first foundation that supports **infrastructure as a service** (**IaaS**). This layer supports the platform layer, which supports native cloud platform services, and **software-as-a-service** (**SaaS**) solutions, such as Slack (Google), Chime (Amazon), or Teams (Microsoft). The platform layer is a foundation to implement the software layer, known as SaaS. You will be able to understand and describe the IaaS, **platform-as-a-service** (**PaaS**), and SaaS solutions through detailed examples delivered in later chapters—specifically, *Chapters 4, 5*, and *6*. However, I recommend completing this chapter first to better understand the underpinnings, which will help you truly comprehend cloud providers' responsibilities. In turn, this will assist you in cloud adoption decisions when assessing the **total cost of ownership** (**TCO**). Let's say you decide on a private cloud implementation mirroring the in-house public cloud SaaS offering. Understanding a modicum of these foundational layers truly breathes foresight into the overall capital and operating costs and why leasing public cloud-native services is beneficial to organizations of any size in comparison to owning and operating the infrastructure required to meet current and new customers' expectations.

Operating and managing the cloud data center to address your customers' needs is by no means a simple feat, especially when you must consider not only the logical architecture but that of the physical architecture and everything it encompasses. In the next section, we continue to pull back the curtain unveiling cloud computing data centers' physical infrastructure.

Join us while we ask the question that is on everyone's mind these days, and that is: *What is the cloud?*

Cloud-managed data centers

In this section, you will learn about Microsoft, Amazon, and Google data centers.

What is the cloud?

It is a fair question, but the answers remain somewhat complex. If what you have read so far has enlightened you, then you can surmise from earlier lessons that it is more than just a buzzword. The cloud has grown from what *was* to what *is*, and in its incubation period, various technologies, disciplines, and architectural patterns have birthed ubiquitous architecture. However, we have only peeked into the logical architecture, not the physical aspects, but the physical aspects are required to truly demystify today's modern technological wonders.

Consider today's technology—remote workers collaborating from across the globe in online meetings using services such as Google's Slack or Microsoft's Teams, cross-platform gamers from Microsoft's Xbox to Google's Stadia, and where industries such as healthcare unite to do battle with pandemics such as COVID-19. It is the cloud computing-managed data centers that breathe life in and support all we do as humans in today's fast-paced society. Mobile platform applications store and retrieve data in nanoseconds; if you lose your device, simply download the data from the cloud! To be more precise, download it from a cloud-managed data center. While the app is installed on your mobile phone, there is an almost unlimited amount of data generated and consumed by your mobile iOS or Droid device. These devices would never be able to contain all that data. Someone or some organization must manage the cloud-managed data center that houses the world's data in an efficient manner and provide the reliability that we have come to depend on in our personal and business lives. It is more than just Verizon's vast network that distributes data—it is the **cloud service provider's** (**CSP's**) data center that is home to our unique personal and business data. Services such as YouTube, which provide business and personal services to any consumer, generate terabytes of data stored in a cloud-managed data center. It is not stored on your computer's browser or Apple device; the underlying service and—more importantly—the data are stored in what you will come to learn is the cloud-managed data center.

Figure 2.1 shows a cloud-managed data center:

Figure 2.1 – Cloud-managed data center

Cloud infrastructure

Infrastructure is not as ambiguous as the concept of the cloud, but one would agree that it is ubiquitous. Cloud-managed data centers are a globally interconnected network of millions of servers in modular and non-modular designs, where cloud computing providers are frequently experimenting with new architectural designs, such as submerging data centers to improve cooling costs. If you can fathom this, these cloud-managed data centers are supporting an infinite number of internet-accessible services, referred to commonly as online services. The scale of these infrastructures is sometimes daunting, and to learn that the cloud-scaled data center is taking traditional technologies to limits unheard of before and thus allowing developers to create the future of tomorrow today is incredible!

Figure 2.2 illustrates the cloud computing global infrastructure regions:

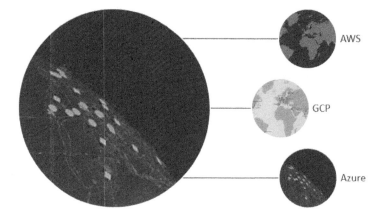

Figure 2.2 – Cloud computing global infrastructure regions

Cloud-managed data centers, like traditional on-premises data centers, are buildings with electrical and mechanical equipment. Presently, any one of the cloud computing providers' data centers operates in numerous countries around the globe and they're interconnected using powerful optical fiber networks, and each provider is frequently expanding its digital footprint.

Figure 2.3 shows interconnected data center equipment:

Figure 2.3 – Interconnected data center equipment

As aforementioned, the cloud is a culmination of scientific and technological innovations due to the need or desire to improve life. Obviously, traditional data center architecture limits us but motivated us to innovate, and throughout the years, data centers have transformed into more efficient infrastructure and optimized compute systems. Modern data center designs are motivated by those various factors' limits and the ongoing challenges to decrease power consumption in hopes of it one day becoming carbon neutral.

Cloud-managed data centers are using best practices and optimized systems and infrastructure that are increasing server and rack density and improving portability, wherein CSPs can relocate cloud compute systems to auspicious locations on-demand and with lower costs in environmental controls, which supports reducing overall operating costs, including ongoing infrastructure maintenance tasks that incur additional operational costs.

The previous paragraphs denoted key characteristics of a modular data center. Each cloud computing provider mentioned in this compendious volume has invested in this efficient data center design in contrast to the traditional on-premises design we described in an earlier chapter. Here is a glimpse into the modular data center design.

Modular

A modular data center looks like a container, and inside there are blade servers that are contained in racks. Additionally, there is a multitude of powerful fans that force heated air generated by the blade servers to go through equipment designed to exchange heat for cool air, which consequently cools the blade servers. Modular data centers were motivated by the demand of lowering energy and cooling costs, which are also managed using environmental controls. Furthermore, the modular data center compute system utilizes custom commodity hardware, which is a business practice with cloud computing providers' equipment replacement methods to control costs.

Figure 2.4 shows a modular data center:

Figure 2.4 – Modular data center

Before I get too far afield, let me remind you that managing a data center involves more than racking and stacking server blades into cabinets. While it is true that cabinet design—and thus data center infrastructure design—impacts operating costs, a less efficient data center design negatively impacts operations. As mentioned in the previous chapter, traditional data center infrastructure included designing cooling systems with efficient pathways and deploying and managing electrical equipment. Cloud-managed data centers' modern modular and non-modular designs are by far more energy efficient in comparison to traditional on-premises data centers that are owned and operated by corporations. Cloud computing providers are responsible for implementing and managing the cloud data center's environmental control systems and planning, preparing, and configuring the physical server resources. For on-premises data centers that are owned and operated by corporations, whether the business is a start-up or enterprise-level, ultimately the business is responsible for decreasing energy consumption in today's data-driven era.

Data and energy growth

The continuous influx of digital information, dubbed data, today is staggering. The massive volumes of data include structured, semi-structured, and unstructured data from different data origins, and in different sizes that range from gigabytes to petabytes of our country's digital information. Considering collecting and analyzing this ever-growing data with traditional infrastructure and resources is almost impossible. The large volume of digital information can also be historical or in real time and ranges from digital streams of social media-generated messages to batches of historical transactions, and from thousands of server logs to sensor data from manufacturing plants. This reminds us that innovation is not just for the sake of innovation but because of real-world scenarios that force us to adapt, and thus innovate. Statistically, the world consumes more and more data each year, and new forms of services, such as the **Internet of Things** (**IoT**) and **machine learning** (**ML**), are compute-intensive; consequently, data center usage or—more precisely—data center energy consumption increases dramatically as we continue to develop as a civilization. Various studies offer many insights into the drivers of energy utilization. However, generating a report to support our observations is time intensive; therefore, reports don't appear frequently, and creating a report to prove the obvious is counterproductive. Let me state the obvious: statistical data models estimate total energy use by data center market growth indicators, such as global internet traffic or data center investments, and tend to estimate large increases in data center energy usage. Some studies indicate that global data center energy consumption has doubled in the last decade and is constantly incrementing. No matter the study, all data reinforces the common belief that rapidly growing demands for data directly impact data center energy generation and consumption.

Ecosystem

In a cautionary tale, the substantial energy utilization of traditional data centers gives rise to concerns over CO_2 emissions. A handful of organizations, including Amazon, Microsoft, and Google, publicly report their observations. These findings help other businesses understand the importance of transparency and indicate how these technology giants who own and manage some of the world's largest cloud-managed data centers operate efficiently toward renewable and sustainable clean energy usage. Google, Microsoft, and Amazon monitor their CO_2 emissions periodically and have set attainable goals with actionable plans to continue the global effort in improving our ecosystem for future generations. Not many on-premises data center owners and operators can drive technology into the future while ensuring that we are here to enjoy the fruits of our labor.

The path forward lies in investing in next-generation data center design such as cloud-managed data centers with technologies that can improve cooling systems using products that leverage renewable energy with sustainability in mind. These nuances will be required to avoid potentially steep energy utilization increases soon and minimize the climate implications of data center energy usage.

Amazon, Microsoft, and Google's energy-efficient cloud-managed data center resources—such as compute, storage, and networking infrastructure—have improved substantially due to the technological progress by IT manufacturers and each cloud computing provider's unique customizations, which have been trialed and tested by their massive consumer base. Secondly, greater use of virtualization technologies, which support multiple applications running on a single server, has dramatically reduced energy consumption and is one of the fundamental physical layers in a cloud-managed data center that is supporting IaaS. For example, **Amazon Web Services (AWS)**, **Elastic Compute Cloud (EC2)**, Microsoft Azure's **Virtual Machines**, and **Google Cloud Platform's (GCP's)** Compute Engine are all examples of compute services that are supported by each cloud computing provider's virtualization technology. And lastly, organizations from every industry, whether enterprise or start-up, have started to migrate their workloads to the cloud, which utilizes various environmental controls to decrease energy consumption not feasible to many on-premises data centers.

Virtualization

In this section, you will learn to describe virtualization, and we will explore virtualization technologies, or—more importantly—how virtualization software such as hypervisors are the building blocks for cloud computing. Moreover, we'll look at how Amazon, Microsoft, and Google use this technology in combination with distributed computing architecture methods such as a grid as the underlying vehicle for creating and releasing resources, which is an attribute of elasticity, for cloud computing services today.

The virtualization program or software, which develops what is known as a guest machine (VM) on a physical machine, is referred to as the **host**. The program or software is referred to as a **hypervisor**, in modern technology nomenclature. Here is where we begin educating you, the reader, on various hypervisors, particularly those utilized by Amazon, Microsoft, and Google cloud platform providers.

Figure 2.5 illustrates a VM architecture:

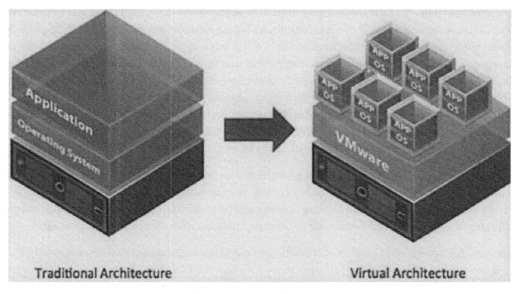

Figure 2.5 – VM architecture

Amazon (AWS), Microsoft (Azure), and Google (GCP) cloud computing hypervisors enable sharing cloud compute, memory, storage, and networking resources across multiple VMs. As aforementioned, this is the same technology that originated from the mainframe era in the 1960s. Virtualizations and hypervisors became more and more pervasive throughout the early 1990s, which I explored at a modest level in a section labeled *Genesis*, located in *Chapter 1*. Something to note before we venture too far: while there are many different types of hypervisors, they all fulfill similar pursuits, allowing one or more physical server resources' CPU, memory, and storage to be shared to multiple VM guest operating system instances, whether Windows or Linux.

Hypervisor

The virtualization **hypervisor** is the bedrock of all cloud computing service models, such as IaaS, PaaS, and SaaS, whether those services are procured as resources to a single customer or to multiple customers from any cloud computing provider. Consequently, virtualization has helped birth new terms such as **multitenancy**, coined in our cloud computing era. This is one of the many capabilities that drive the economics of most cloud computing offerings.

Figure 2.6 illustrates a virtualization hypervisor:

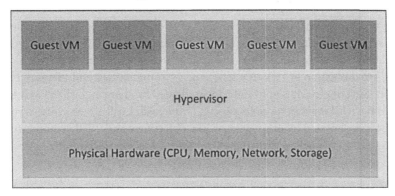

Figure 2.6 – Virtualization hypervisor

Microsoft, Amazon, and Google hypervisor services implement the portability that enables assets and workloads to easily be migrated from on-premises to public cloud computing and even between different cloud computing providers. This essentially drives organizations of any size, whether start-ups or enterprise corporations, to rapidly scale and thus extend from on-premises servers to cloud computing server instances at a cloud scale when frequent increases in utilization occur due to various use cases such as market growth; this can include unplanned failure events that require on-demand resources. All this is possible due to the innovations of virtualization.

These hypervisors also help cloud computing providers reduce the amount of physical hardware space while reducing the amount of energy needed to power and cool the vastness of the modern cloud computing global infrastructure.

You may still feel reluctant to trust these hypervisors within the context of multitenancy, so allow me to decrease your anxiety by describing one of the many security attributes and exploring later each cloud provider's choice of infrastructure virtualization software. Recall, if you will, that hypervisors abstract the underlying servers from VM guests. The VM guest operating system requests server resources; requests are then reviewed by the hypervisor host, which manages and allocates resources upon request. VM guest operating systems typically run in a least privileged or unprivileged mode compared to the hypervisor host, so they cannot negatively impact the operation of the hypervisor host or the other VM guest operating systems. VM software (hypervisor) such as Xen, **Kernel-based Virtual Machine** (**KVM**), and Hyper-V provide various security features based on their *type* that have subtle differences but similar overarching objectives—that is, to secure the hypervisor host and ensure unique enhancements in security-shield VM hard drives using various attestation and encryption methods that are controlled by a hypervisor host or a **Trusted Platform Module** (**TPM**) service.

While my goal is to educate you regarding virtualization and its role in cloud computing, I need to enlighten you on virtualization types and how these types correspond to the hypervisors utilized by our major cloud computing providers. Let us begin with an introduction to virtualization types and then describe Amazon, Microsoft, and Google virtualization software. There are several hypervisor types, which we will refer to herein as **type 1** and **type 2**. A type 1 hypervisor is considered by many IT pros and enthusiasts as a lightweight operating system and runs directly on the physical server's hardware. A type 2 hypervisor runs on or with the Linux or Windows operating system as a software program. Again, let me repeat: if the hypervisor runs directly on top of the hardware, it's type 1. If the hypervisor operates on a separate layer because there is an operating system present, it is type 2. This concept is open to discussion in various science and IT communities, and that is due to no present standardization. Nevertheless, it is used and widely adopted by many, and while I may utilize my vast experience and the wisdom of other great experts in the field, I will always educate you, the reader, on what can be corroborated by other great works objectively and, furthermore, what is deemed empirically a fact. I do not believe in using buzzwords unless I am debunking or demystifying the nuanced concept.

Virtualization types

Type 1, known as hardware virtualization, is used widely in IT environments, supporting the subdivision of a single physical computer's hardware capacity, and sharing that capacity with multiple VM guest operating systems. Type 2, paravirtualization, is considered lightweight virtualization. For example, paravirtualization does not require additional virtualization extensions configured from the CPU architecture. To further elaborate, Amazon's (AWS) Xen hypervisor supports paravirtualization and full virtualization types of virtualizations. Hardware-assisted virtualization or **hardware VM** (**HVM**) provides similar support to full virtualization. As such, HVM provides the capability to run an operating system directly on top of a VM host without any modifications and includes complete hardware isolation. I will expound on Xen in a bit. Let's return to our current topic.

Figure 2.7 illustrates type 1 and type 2 virtualization architecture:

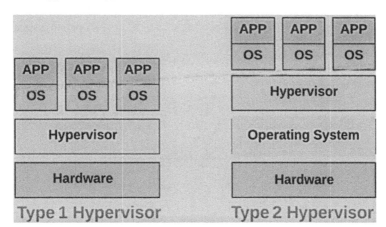

Figure 2.7 – Type 1 and type 2 virtualization architecture

Hardware virtualization has many benefits that are utilized by cloud computing providers behind the scenes. Cloud computing's use of virtualization centralizes administration, which provides visibility into overall data center hardware utilization. Additionally, VM guest operating systems can run in parallel on a single CPU, and an organization of any size can better manage dynamic updates to the operating system and guest applications without incurring downtime, which subsequently impacts VM guest operating system end users and can consequently impact customer loyalty.

Another benefit of virtualization is the capability to take a snapshot of the VM's state at any time and use that snapshot to restore services, very similar to incremental backups. You can have a stack of snapshots with different **point-in-time** (**PIT**) states as a single hard disk drive, supplementing your **business continuity** (**BC**) measures. Furthermore, the snapshots can be rehosted—thus moved to another virtual host—and then resume service, like a migration of sorts. Because we can migrate the VM disk to any host, then we can use this method in a failover strategy for any planned or unplanned event, such as a VM host failure. Many of the capabilities described in this lesson will correlate with Amazon, Microsoft, and Google's cloud computing IaaS model advantages.

Now that we've covered various types and the history of virtualization, let's review AWS, Azure, and GCP hypervisor technologies.

The art of Xen

As mentioned before, the Xen hypervisor is a type 1 hardware or bare-metal virtualization program, utilized by many organizations around the world, including AWS. However, current reports suggest that Amazon is also utilizing KVM and perhaps may be migrating away from Xen. No matter—both technologies have been utilized by Amazon as the infrastructure layer, so they are both relevant. First, let us describe the Xen architecture. Xen is situated between the computer operating system and the hardware; as such, it provides a virtual environment wherein a kernel can run. The major elements of any system applying Xen are the following: hypervisor, kernel, and VM guest operating system applications.

Figure 2.8 illustrates the Xen architecture:

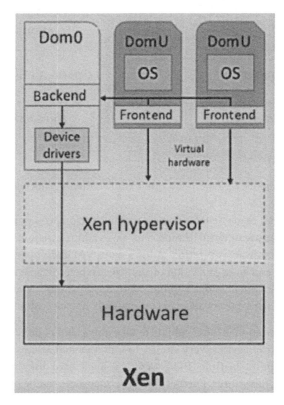

Figure 2.8 – Xen architecture

Xen supports multiple VMs; each VM can run its own operating system on one or more physical servers. While this book introduces you to Xen and—more importantly—Xen's role in cloud computing, I strongly recommend further research and experimentation to truly grasp Xen's logical architecture.

Xen's hypervisor creates a VM guest operating system known as **Domain 0**. Domain 0's unique privileges grant the guest operating system access to the hardware. Domain 0 utilizes the Xen management tools to govern the Xen hypervisor and additional VM unprivileged guest operating systems. The default Xen tooling includes the command line; however, Xen also supports various web-based management tools, even from third parties.

The Red Hat way

Google's (GCP's) IaaS foundation utilizes a security-hardened KVM hypervisor. KVM is an open source developed project that later merged into the Linux kernel. KVM supports hardware-assisted virtualization and transforms Linux kernels into hypervisors. Many CPU architectures, particularly from manufacturers such as AMD and Intel, offer known AMD-V and Intel VT CPUs that meet the virtualization requirements to support KVM.

Figure 2.9 illustrates the KVM architecture:

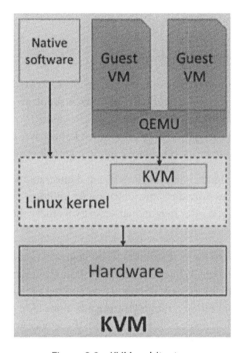

Figure 2.9 – KVM architecture

The Hyper-V call to arms

Microsoft (Azure) uses a customized version of Hyper-V. Microsoft's Hyper-V is a type 1 virtualization that is included with Microsoft's **line-of-business** (**LOB**) applications, better known as enterprise applications. Hyper-V lets you configure and run multiple VM guest operating systems on one or more physical servers. Microsoft has also developed other virtualization products such as Virtual PC and Virtual Server; however, Microsoft's Hyper-V has replaced the other legacy products and remains prevalent today.

As mentioned before, Microsoft's Hyper-V is included in Microsoft's enterprise applications, such as Windows Server and Windows (non-server), as a feature configurable via Windows Server role options. It is also important to note that Microsoft's Hyper-V can be downloaded, installed, and deployed as a standalone service.

Several core components underpin Hyper-V: the Windows hypervisor VM management service, **Windows Management Instrumentation** (**WMI**), essentially an operating system interface for communication, a VM bus, a **virtualization service provider** (**VSP**), and lastly, the virtual infrastructure driver. These core components are implemented when you either configure Hyper-V via Windows Server or Windows or elect to install the standalone product.

The management tools are separate from the core components; however, the tools are recommended but optional. Here is a list of the current operational or administrative Hyper-V tools:

- Windows PowerShell

- Hyper-V Manager

- **Virtual Machine Connection** (**VMConnect**)

Microsoft's virtualization technology provides several benefits such as virtual storage and networking features and, as with many other virtualization hypervisors, it supplements BC patterns. For example, eventually, everything fails, as the truism goes, so if you need to restore services, Hyper-V creates copies of VMs for backup and restore scenarios. There is even a feature known as live migration, which streamlines moving VMs to virtual hypervisor hosts, whether the infrastructure is on-premises or in the public cloud.

Security is paramount to each cloud computing provider and integrated with its version of IaaS—hence, native to each cloud computing provider's virtualization technology. Trialed and tested hypervisors such as Xen, Hyper-V, and KVM offer heightened security features that safeguard against malware and exfiltration tactics from anomalous actors.

Xen, KVM, and Hyper-V hypervisor virtualization technologies have made cloud computing possible for Amazon, Microsoft, and Google. While each brings its unique but subtle key feature differentiators, objectively, virtualization makes the ideals of distributed computing a reality—particularly, breaking free of the monolithic, server-to-application 1:1 ratio. Any organization's LOB application or service can then become loosely decoupled utilizing virtualization, wherein the service-to-service (application) is a 1:N (one-to-many) ratio. This method starts us down the journey where we transition from a monolithic or server architecture to a **service-oriented architecture** (**SOA**), which is the underpinning of microservices.

Organizations are increasingly realizing cost efficiency, problem-solving, and optimized operations using microservices architecture in conjunction with containers. There are many product vendors with various services and tools that deliver container solutions to help companies build and deploy applications at a cloud scale.

Docker containers

Most IT pros arguably equate microservices to containerization, yet containers are another type of virtualization. Containerization, or—more accurately put—operating system virtualization, refers to an operating system feature wherein the kernel host supports the existence of multiple isolated instances. These instances are referred to as containers and are sometimes known as **virtual environments**, which appear as computer operating systems to users and applications. Services running inside a container can only view the container's contents and not the other operating system resources or containerized applications. This is one of the many advantages introduced by operating system virtualization.

Figure 2.10 illustrates a container architecture:

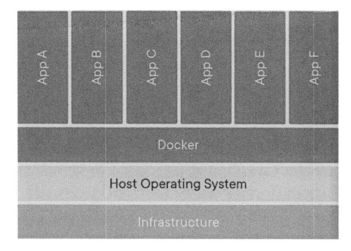

Figure 2.10 – Container architecture

The product or service is also a technique known as **containerization**, which software developers formally refer to as follows: **software engineers develop an application or service**, and its dependencies and configuration information are packaged as one unit or container image. One or more containers can run on the same computer and share the operating system kernel with other containers. Each container is individually running isolated processes in user space. These instances can take up less space than a VM, so they can manage multiple applications and require fewer VM guest operating system instances and hardware system resources. VMs provide resource isolation and allocation benefits but function differently. Docker containers virtualize the operating system, not the hardware.

Containers are also known for their architecture, which makes it feasible to package an application and its dependencies in a unit referred to as a container that can run in any environment, such as IoT devices, which include smart **heating, ventilation, and air conditioning** (**HVAC**) thermostats and more. Containers are portable, in contrast to traditional application development, wherein the application software could not be migrated to a different environment without numerous exceptions and inconsistencies due to environmental variables built into the other system.

Containers or—more accurately put—containerization methods streamline operations and development teams' ability to manage and automate software development and distribution. Containerization also facilitates another method known as **infrastructure as code** (**IaC**). In IaC implementations, the software engineer specifies infrastructure prerequisites via a configuration or manifest file used during repetitive idempotent deployments. Similarly, configuration or manifest files are utilized in containerization.

I'd love to just get down to brass tacks and explore container orchestrators such as Kubernetes and OpenShift and how they tie into cloud computing; however, I would be remiss if I did not describe the overall architecture or core components of a container or Docker. Similar to virtualization hypervisor technologies, containers' components are integrated into many cloud-computing services.

Goods to be transported by a container

There are several building blocks for containerized applications, which are listed as follows:

- Container runtime (also known as container engine)
- **Container Runtime Interface (CRI)**
- Container image
- Image repository

A runtime is also known as a **container engine**, which is operating system-level virtualization. It is software that can run containers on a host operating system, and it's responsible for loading container images from a repository, monitoring resources, isolating processes, and governing the container life cycle.

Container runtimes work with container orchestrators such as Kubernetes. The orchestrator is responsible for configuring and managing the cluster of containers, while the container runtime is responsible for managing the containers running on each compute node in the cluster.

Here is a non-exhaustive list of container engines:

- Windows containers
- Docker
- containerd

I will spend my energies thus focusing on only two engines from this bulleted list—that is, Docker and Windows containers—because of their relevance to Amazon, Microsoft, and Google cloud computing.

Docker is the leading PaaS, offering a holistic feature set that includes utilizing and modernizing operating system-level virtualization, and it is the default Kubernetes container engine, aggregating image details, supporting native CLI tools, and providing an image-building service. I will spend more time on Docker later, but let's not lose this momentum and continue to the next runtime summarization.

Microsoft has several options: Windows containers offer an abstraction, such as Docker or Hyper-V virtualization. Hyper-V containers provide efficient portability because they have their own kernel, so you can run isolated disparate applications on the host system.

Due to the rise of containerization methods, there were various container engine innovations, which increased complexity when incorporating two or more runtimes into orchestrators such as Kubernetes. That's because it would be far too difficult to maintain an extensive integration between each new container runtime and the orchestrator's source code.

The Docker container communities created an interface with functions that a container engine would need to put in place on behalf of their orchestrator, known as the CRI. The CRI is a plugin interface that supports the kubelet agent running on each node in a cluster and is supported by several different container engines. Its objective is to streamline administrators' and developers' capability to make use of multiple container runtimes and enable efficient integration with orchestrator ecosystems.

While container engines and interfaces are critical, I would argue that the majority of IT pros and developers correlate containers or Docker containers with container images. Container images are static files that include executable code that can create a container on any computer operating system. The container image is immutable, which means it cannot be altered, and it can be deployed in any environment consistently.

Container images include all dependencies, such as the container runtime, system libraries, configuration settings, and application or service that will run on the container. A container image also shares the operating system kernel of the host.

These images are composed of one or more layers, aggregated to a parent or base image. The layers make it feasible to reuse components and configurations across various images. Creating layers can help reduce the container image size and even optimize performance.

As aforementioned, a container image or a Docker container image is a group of files, libraries, source code, and other resource dependencies required to deploy a container environment. Here are two methods for creating Docker images:

- Create a Dockerfile, which is a configuration file where the developer details what a Docker image should contain

- Secondly, you can run a container image, modify the container, and then save the updated image as a new image version

The following code block is a Dockerfile:

```
FROM mcr.microsoft.com/dotnet/aspnet:5.0 AS base
WORKDIR /app
EXPOSE 80
EXPOSE 443

FROM mcr.microsoft.com/dotnet/sdk:5.0 AS build
WORKDIR /src
COPY ["dockerFileExample.csproj", "."]
RUN dotnet restore "./dockerFileExample.csproj"
COPY . .
WORKDIR "/src/."
```

```
RUN dotnet build "dockerFileExample.csproj" -c Release -o /app/
build

FROM build AS publish
RUN dotnet publish "dockerFileExample.csproj" -c Release -o /
app/publish

FROM base AS final
WORKDIR /app
COPY --from=publish /app/publish .
ENTRYPOINT ["dotnet", "dockerFileExample.dll"]
```

There are many misconceptions about container images and containers. Allow me to clarify the distinction: Docker container images describe the container environment. The container is an instance of that environment, hosted on a Docker engine—or container runtime, to be more accurate. Cloud computing engineers and developers can create multiple container instances from the same image, and each container instance will contain a similar configuration because of the container image. I will not delve into how to use Docker layers in this book, but it's worth researching. So, I highly recommend you research Docker images and layers to understand how to use base and parent images. We must continue focusing on core components and their relation to cloud computing.

Figure 2.11 shows a Docker container and image:

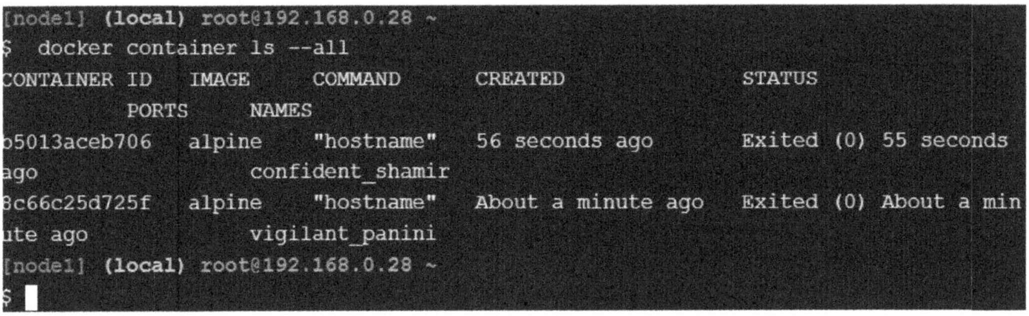

Figure 2.11 – Docker container and image

> **Note**
>
> The $ docker container ls --all command was utilized to list all containers.

Moving forward I will refer to containers as Docker containers since they are setting the standard when it comes to containers. Where were we? Oh, yes—Docker container images include a file called **manifest**. A manifest file is a **JavaScript Object Notation** (**JSON**) file type that defines the image, layers, size, metadata, digital signature, and additional documentation. I find it curious that JSON file types are used widely in cloud computing; particularly, IaC plays a large role in configuring various IaaS and PaaS resources declaratively. Think back to a previous section in this chapter, where we started describing containers. Here is an excerpt to help jog your memory:

In IaC implementations, the software engineer specifies infrastructure prerequisites via a configuration or manifest file used during repetitive idempotent deployments. Similarly, configuration or manifest files are utilized in containerization.

In a later chapter, you will learn which cloud computing service utilizes JSON files to configure and create IaC. Similarly, a Dockerfile is as important as a manifest file. It contains instructions for building a Docker image and commonly contains scripts with text lines that define the image, installation instructions, applications, and files. I highly recommend you review the Dockerfile illustrated in the preceding code block if you have not done so already. It's important to note that containerization and Docker container commands and resources are used in cloud computing across Amazon, Microsoft, and Google cloud platforms, and therefore it is essential to understand this technology. Docker containers are a proponent for distributed computing, which has been modernized and thus transformed into microservices that are at the heart of various cloud computing logical and physical architectures.

A very important question when it comes to planning and preparing container implementations is this: *Where do we store our images?* The answer to that question is a container repository. A container repository provides storage for images. As previously described, container images are utilized to create new container instances based on the configuration defined in the image. Subsequently, images are stored in a container image repository. Container images stored in a repository can then be used to create new container instances.

Cloud computing providers are well known for their cloud-scaled storage, which benefits containerized workloads because containers use container repositories. Here are some of the benefits:

- **High availability (HA)**—Consider retrieving images over the public internet from a repository. This resource becomes core to an organization's application architecture. If the repository is unavailable, the images will not be accessible during the downtime event. Private container repositories deliver flexibility, control, and optimized availability due to the cloud computing provider's scalability.

- **Improved performance**—Not all images are small; some are very large and can cause performance issues when accessed over the internet. Alternatively, images can be accessed from a private repository and implemented from a hybrid cloud computing deployment model.

- **Multi-cloud integration**—Orchestrating containers utilizing cross-cloud services such as Kubernetes is powerful. Developers can retrieve Docker container images from remote private repositories and deploy them using DevOps techniques to any platform.

There are also public and private repositories to choose from when deciding on a container repository. Public repositories facilitate storing and sharing container images with the public. Conversely, private repositories are used to store and share images with your organization's internal development teams. Private repositories offer greater security benefits over public shared storage services.

Cloud computing providers have several built-in offerings to meet private and public access business requirements.

> **Information**
>
> AWS offers an **Elastic Container Registry** (**ECR**) service, which is managed by Amazon and supports scalability, including public and private container repositories, to meet various compliance controls. I will elaborate on and explore this AWS resource in *Chapter 5*.
>
> Azure provides an Azure Container Registry service that is fully managed by Microsoft and is renowned for its scalability, and Azure includes public and private container repositories for additional business needs. I will elaborate on and explore this Azure resource in *Chapter 5*.
>
> GCP includes an Artifact Registry service that is operated by Google and delivers the promise of cloud scalability. Furthermore, Google includes public and private repositories. I will elaborate on and explore this GCP resource in *Chapter 5*.

As you can imagine, containerization, which is technologically operating system virtualization, and the pattern or strategy referred to as containerization and Docker container resources are at the root of various Amazon, Microsoft, and Google cloud computing services. The advantages delivered by these cloud providers are well known. Allow me to summarize here—in later chapters, I will describe in detail how these cloud computing providers' services deliver overall advantages over traditional on-premises architectures.

Docker container registries can either negatively or positively impact the availability of your applications or services. When planning your architecture to meet HA requirements as documented in your customer's **service-level agreement** (**SLA**), multiple alternatives will optimize resiliency.

Security is the foremost important deciding factor other than cost when implementing containers. Factoring in organizational requirements and regulatory compliance controls is very important and sometimes becomes the decision breaker ultimately. Cloud providers have various tools and native security resources that should improve administrative efforts and security analysis when deciding on container orchestrators and even image repositories.

All in all, Docker containers and containerization are part of the core compute services offered by the major cloud computing providers, and for good reason, considering cloud computing providers offer more PaaS resources that perform optimally when organizations embrace the microservices architecture. This surprisingly accelerates **time to market** (**TTM**) while in parallel decreasing operating costs due to its convenient offerings that are derived from further abstraction, wherein IT professionals and developers alike are no longer responsible for the VM guest operating system.

As an instructor and **subject-matter expert** (**SME**), I've noticed more and more that when practitioners research operating system virtualization they tend to find containers. Moreover, you will come across Docker containers or just Docker. I believe it's my duty to clarify misconceptions about Docker to enlighten you, the reader, on Docker's role in microservices. Docker is a suite of services that utilize operating system-level virtualization to distribute packaged containers. Docker is presently the standard in the container industry, supported by the Linux and Windows environments. There are numerous articles and tutorials online available to educate you on how to use Docker on your local Linux, Mac, or Windows operating system. This compendious volume is enlightening you on the logical and physical concepts including architecture on containers but not Docker's vast command-line arguments. However, in a later chapter, you will have the opportunity to use a Docker container and the cloud computing **service provider's** (**SP's**) orchestrator to reinforce commands and their efficiency at a cloud scale.

To conclude, Docker containers can be hosted anywhere—on-premises, in private clouds, and in the public cloud. And Docker containers are very useful for implementing microservices application architectures, which consist of a multitude of distributed disparate isolated applications or services—some of the key characteristics of containers.

The next section should come as no surprise since I have been mentioning microservices throughout the last section on virtualization due to their importance in containerization patterns.

Microservices

In this section, you will learn to describe the microservices architecture.

In the early 1960s, virtualization was in its infancy, but so too were distributed computing architectural patterns or strategies, if you will, and practitioners of these patterns' initial seed bore many fruits. IT pros, in conjunction with development teams, later devised various alternatives to the monolithic application architecture patterns to optimize testability, decoupling, dependencies, and singularity, and improve development sprint cycles with small but proficient teams. As you would expect, cloud computing SPs—Amazon, Microsoft, and Google architectures—provide the building blocks for modern alternatives to the monolithic application development pattern utilized traditionally on-premises.

This new architecture, known as microservices, was derived from distributed computing patterns' service-oriented nature. Due to the architecture's position on singular capabilities, one would assume small or micro over large in terms of application features or capability. Microservices is a befitting name based on key attributes of the architectural strategy. So, as you would imagine, microservices require an architecture that consists of smaller services. If optimization is one of the goals, then we would require autonomous services that are self-contained, which further leads to efficient developer testing. For example, it's easier to manage bugs or hotfixes when the code base is smaller. Developers can update a service without having to redeploy the entire application solution composed of multiple projects and separate code files, and even roll back an update if something goes awry, as eventually, something always does go wrong.

A microservices architecture would recommend smaller teams for a singular capability, wherein developers can plan, prepare, build, test, and deploy efficiently over a larger team with multifaceted capabilities.

Because microservices lack built-in dependencies, thus leading to greater autonomy and isolation, this consequently ensures each service will not disrupt another, hence negatively impacting an entire solution. If the microservice becomes unreachable and the other components are designed with fault tolerance, then our microservices architecture can deliver fault isolation and subsequently greater reliability.

Microservices' independent architecture can support each service to scale independently, allowing any service to scale due to its unique demands. Cloud computing providers offer a multitude of cloud-scaled orchestrators such as Kubernetes for more efficient utilization of computing resources.

Additionally, microservices' architectural resources should implement persisting state data utilizing decoupled services. Here is some insight: in contrast to a monolithic architecture, microservices' data layers are loosely coupled from the microservice, whereas monolithic data layers are disconnected but tightly coupled and centralized.

Cloud computing providers' ecosystems are accessed and managed using well-defined APIs, and it so happens that microservices architectures communicate with each other using the same method. Also, the communication details of each microservice are obfuscated from other services augmenting security protocols.

Containers—or as you learned within this chapter's sections, Docker containers—are widely used in microservices architectures. Arguably, IT pros and developers may refer to Docker containers as microservices, but I strongly suggest you recall that microservices are an architecture, not a type of virtualization.

Here is a concern your organization will encounter with microservices architecture.

A microservices strategy for creating decentralized applications or services may lead to problems, such as maintaining a multitude of various programming languages. My recommendation to your organization is to standardize supported protocols for each project to help control multi-language complexity.

Real-world example

As a certified instructor and consultant with over 15 years of experience, I've worked with numerous cloud providers' business partners. In one of the many project deliveries, I was tasked by *Global Knowledge*, a cloud computing training and consulting partner for Amazon, to provide consulting services after educating one of the many AWS business partners on cloud computing services based on their unique business requirements. The AWS cloud business partner was Johnson & Johnson. I am not at liberty to discuss what was mentioned internally or provide any company proprietary data, but what I can share is the following: Johnson & Johnson experimented successfully with microservices and learned to define project-wide API standards to prevent future obstacles, leveraging AWS IaC and microservices orchestrators to govern the decentralized services efficiently. The key takeaway here is that an enterprise organization followed best practices, which resulted in a successful microservices architecture by defining and enforcing governance.

> **Tip**
>
> I highly recommend you create a Docker Hub account and review the Docker docs online. The *Docker docs* is a great resource to start your journey with Docker containers. It includes resources such as guides, manuals, references, and free videos. I recommend mastering Dockerfiles and Docker Compose files. This will prepare you before learning how to utilize Kubernetes across all three major cloud computing providers.

Summary

In this chapter, you learned about the foundational infrastructure, systems, and services used to support the physical and logical architecture of cloud computing. Those resources included similarities to on-premises, cloud-managed data center designs, the virtualization layer (including containerization), and microservices architecture. We delved into what makes the cloud, including cloud-managed data centers, and in the next chapter, we describe the benefits of cloud-managed data centers' global infrastructure.

In the next chapter, you will learn about the benefits of the AWS, Azure, and GCP cloud computing providers. You will also learn about the cloud's infrastructure layer's virtualization, which is working behind the scenes to support various HA, elasticity, and fault-tolerant functional and non-functional features.

Questions

1. Which technology supports IaaS?

    A. iOS

    B. Java

    C. Virtualization

    D. Cisco CSR 1000

2. Who is responsible for maintaining the infrastructure in an on-premises data center?

    A. Google

    B. Microsoft

    C. Amazon

    D. Enterprise corporation

3. AWS uses best-in-class commercial hardware for its data centers from which vendors?

   A. Dell

   B. Apple

   C. HP

   D. None of these—cloud-managed data centers use custom commodity hardware

4. Azure uses best-in-class commercial hardware for its data centers from which vendors?

   A. Dell

   B. Apple

   C. HP

   D. None of these—cloud-managed data centers use custom commodity hardware

5. GCP uses best-in-class commercial hardware for its data centers from which vendors?

   A. Dell

   B. Apple

   C. HP

   D. None of these—cloud-managed data centers use custom commodity hardware

6. What is virtualization?

   A. Peer-to-peer (P2P)

   B. Apple iOS

   C. Abstraction of physical resources

   D. Linux kernel

7. Which of the following connect cloud-managed data centers? (Choose all that apply)

   A. Media

   B. Routers

   C. Digital subscriber line (DSL)

   D. Wi-Fi

8. Where can cloud-managed data center equipment be located? (Choose all that apply)

    A. On the cloud

    B. In a building

    C. Underwater

    D. In modular containers

9. Which of the following characteristics do modular data centers have? (Choose all that apply)

    A. Portable

    B. Static

    C. Decrease server density

    D. Optimize cooling

10. Who is responsible for the rack and cabinet design in a cloud-managed data center?

    A. Customer

    B. Provider

    C. A third party

    D. AI

11. Cooling systems are part of:

    A. Data

    B. Infrastructure

    C. Availability Zones (AZs)

    D. Networking equipment

12. CO_2 emissions correspond with which of the following?

    A. Data center fires

    B. Data center energy utilization

    C. Statistical data models

    D. Data warehouse

13. Which of the following virtualization software is used to host VM guest operating systems?

    A. Docker

    B. Hypervisor

    C. Kernel

    D. macOS

14. Which of the following do hypervisors enable sharing? (Choose all that apply)

    A. Memory

    B. Firmware

    C. BIOS

    D. Storage

15. Which VM guest operating system do Xen and Hyper-V support?

    A. Android

    B. Mac

    C. iOS

    D. Linux

16. Which VM guest operating system does KVM support natively? (Choose all that apply)

    A. Windows

    B. Debian Linux

    C. Red Hat Linux

    D. macOS

17. AWS, Azure, and GCP use traditional architecture to support IaaS resources.

    A. True

    B. False

18. Which of the following options is considered type 1 virtualization?

    A. Docker container

    B. Hardware virtualization

    C. Operating system virtualization

    D. VirtualBox

19. Which virtualization BC capability is like incremental backups?

    A. Live migration

    B. Software-defined networking (SDN)

    C. Virtual private network (VPN)

    D. Snapshot

20. Which of the following options defines microservices?

    A. Docker

    B. Microchip

    C. Small web services

    D. Architecture

3

Understanding the Benefits of Public Clouds (AWS, Azure, and GCP)

More and more industries require secure, yet efficient infrastructure to support growing customer demand. Additionally, they require a highly-performant global, fast, and resilient network architecture that powers line of business and non-business services, all while ensuring data stays on a secured private backbone, thus ensuring they provide the best overall experience to their end users.

This chapter will describe the benefits of the AWS, Azure, and GCP cloud architectures. You will learn about each architecture's global software-defined network, **high availability** (**HA**) infrastructure, scalability infrastructure services, fault-tolerant infrastructure, and how to optimize your organization's workloads by conforming to cloud architectural best practices using documented frameworks.

In this chapter, we're going to cover the following topics:

- Global infrastructure
- Fault-tolerant infrastructure
- HA infrastructure
- Cloud -scaled infrastructure
- Optimizing architecture using cloud frameworks

Global infrastructure

In this lesson, you will gain the knowledge to describe the cloud computing global infrastructure and its many advantages. Additionally, you will learn helpful tips and about potential pitfalls that encumber beginners.

As we explore the cloud computing global infrastructure, I will describe the benefits of regions, edge zones, wide area networks, and cloud computing architecture sustainability. Furthermore, I will define patterns and anti-patterns when considering designing regions and edge locations.

Whether you need to deploy your organization's application or service across the globe efficiently, or whether you want to develop services in proximity to your consumers, cloud computing architecture is always available where you need it and when you need it, on-demand!

Before we explore the global infrastructure, it is important that I introduce each of the cloud computing providers. Furthermore, I'll explain my selection of cloud computing providers. In brief, why Amazon, Microsoft, and Google?

As you might imagine, my experience plays a role in the selection process, and based on my experience, I prefer to use qualitative analysis methods that rely on market trends. Additionally, the data must be sourced from some governing body – whether it is regulatory or non-regulatory is arbitrary – but it should also be beyond reproach and corroborated using empirical data.

Cloud computing rating reports

For us to select a report, we should establish a well-defined criterion that has been tried and tested. As mentioned earlier, NIST solicits cloud characteristics that are deemed the gold standard for cloud computing vendors, also known as providers. Utilizing those standards, the governing body analyzes a cloud computing provider's ability to achieve its vision; therefore, the cloud computing provider should measure a service's financial viability, and development, and ensure market responsiveness. So, let's review this: the criteria in the analysis should include the ability of the cloud computing provider to achieve its vision and ensure it is financially viable. It just so happens that there exists a report generated by Gartner that meets our requirements.

> **Note**
> Gartner is a technology research organization that was founded in 1979. For further information, I recommend navigating to their online site.

Gartner's Magic Quadrant research regarding cloud computing leaders published in 2021 scores a cloud computing provider and then positions the provider in one of four quadrants:

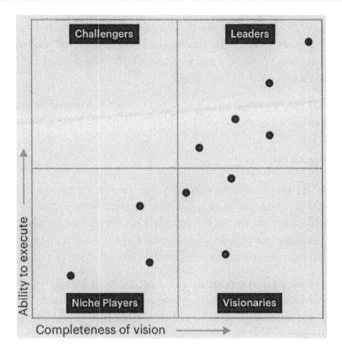

Figure 3.1 – Gartner's Magic Quadrant

Providers positioned in the niche players quadrant are focused on single markets. Typically, they adapt their services to emerging markets and are not ready to execute their vision.

Providers positioned in the visionaries quadrant offer new services that are of importance but have not displayed the ability to get ahead in the market. Start-ups and privately held smaller organizations fit into this category.

Providers deemed challengers participate in competitive markets with leaders but usually lack the size or influence of a leader provider.

AWS, Azure, and GCP are positioned in the leaders quadrant, where leaders can execute and achieve visions. A provider in the leaders quadrant has a sizable market share, credibility, and profitability, and delivers innovations that change the face of technology.

Cloud computing providers such as Amazon, Microsoft, and Google understand the cloud landscape and develop a point of view that can be shared in IT communities and with business leaders from start-ups to enterprise corporations. These cloud computing leaders can assess strengths and provide insights for upcoming providers. Additionally, they assist organizations of any size in planning for the future by soliciting actionable recommendations and intelligent considerations for cloud adoption, development, governance, and management.

Based on the criteria we defined earlier, along with proven research from Gartner, I have selected Amazon's **Amazon Web Services** (**AWS**), Microsoft's Azure, and Google's **Google Cloud Platform** (**GCP**) as the cloud computing providers that I will explore throughout this compendious volume to educate you about the cloud and all its intricacies.

For brevity's sake, I will refer to Amazon's cloud service as AWS, Microsoft's as Azure, and Google's as GCP moving forward.

Geographic regions

Cloud computing services are available from specific regions that are managed by the cloud provider. The regional locations are in geographies such as North America, South America, Europe, Asia Pacific, South Africa, the Middle East, and more. Geographies are divided into regions and zones. We will explore zones in the *Fault-tolerant infrastructure* section. Organizations can choose a region to deploy their solutions in to meet business requirements, such as latency, cost, and compliance.

Cloud computing providers' datacenters are designed as clusters in geographic regions globally. These datacenters are always online and are ready for the eventuality of a planned or unplanned event that will incur downtime, and automated services redirect traffic from any non-healthy datacenter to a targeted healthy datacenter.

Each datacenter within a region has a discrete uninterruptable power supply and onsite backup generators connected to isolated electrical grids and more. We will describe this further in the *Fault-tolerant infrastructure* section.

Cloud regions are connected to multiple internet service providers and a private global network that provides consistent cross-region high-speed network latency.

Each cloud provider is frequently expanding its global presence to support customers with business requirements, such as data residency, or to achieve higher throughput.

There is even a securely isolated GovCloud region designed to support the workloads of the United States armed forces, public government, and federal and state agencies that are deemed sensitive or classified by addressing their regulatory compliance control requirements.

> Tip
>
> If your organization has data compliance requirements, you have many cloud computing region options that are in proximity to your data residency. This should make it simpler to meet regional data compliance requirements. Cloud computing leaders, such as AWS, Azure, and GCP, adhere to **General Data Protection Regulation** (**GDPR**) standards and support a myriad of tools to help you construct a GDPR-compliant architecture in the public cloud. Organizations of any size or industry, including the public sector, have the capability to meet their compliance goals.

Edge zones

To understand the benefits of edge zones or locations, also referred to as **points-of-presence (PoP)**, we must introduce a process called caching. Caching stores data locally so that subsequent end user requests for data can be accessed rapidly. There are various caching types or methods, such as browser caching. Browsers such as Chrome, Edge, and Safari store copies of data on your local computer and use the cached data instead of traversing the public internet to the origin server, which decreases the time it takes to locate and render the data, thus reducing latency.

Cloud computing providers use edge servers, commonly referred to as PoPs for caching to improve the end user's experience. Cloud computing leaders provide a content delivery network service that allows developers to manage a shared cache. In a shared cache managed by a content delivery network, data is requested by an end user and, subsequently, can be accessed by other end users. This process decreases the number of end user requests to the origin cloud service or virtual machine.

Based on what you have read so far, caching is important to how a content delivery network speeds up delivery and decreases the origin service request load. Additionally, the content delivery network tactically stores data on servers that are closer in proximity to end users. Consider that most online traffic is web-based; therefore, the content is either HTML documents, images, or videos, so the cloud computing provider's content delivery network can handle much of your request by reducing network latency and ensuring the cached data is close to hand by reducing the distance. Furthermore, content delivery network caching decreases cost and additional resource dependencies for any cloud computing origin service.

Currently, AWS has 313 PoPs (300+ Edge locations and 13 regional mid-tier caches) in over 47 countries:

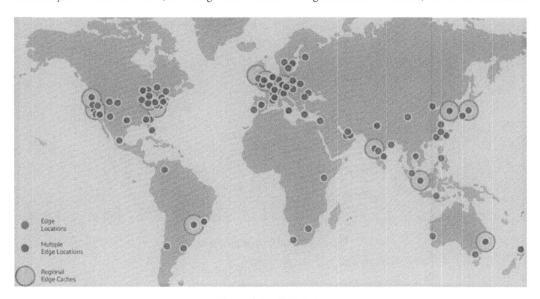

Figure 3.2 – AWS PoPs

Azure currently has many edge locations. For an exhaustive list by region, you can go to `https://docs.microsoft.com/en-us/azure/cdn/cdn-pop-locations`:

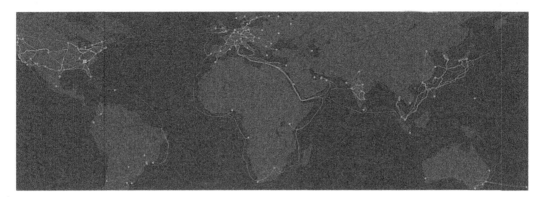

Figure 3.3 – Azure edge locations

GCP currently has edge locations all around the globe. For further insight into the locations, go to `https://cloud.google.com/vpc/docs/edge-locations`. The following screenshot has been sourced from the URL:

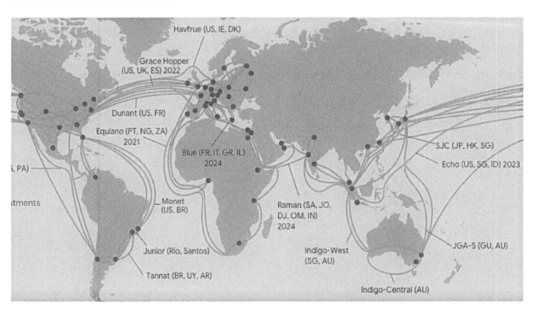

Figure 3.4 – GCP Edge locations

Wide area networks

A cloud computing provider's infrastructure is interconnected using a vast private global network. This software-defined network spans the globe, connecting cloud services and customers around the world.

The wide area network is a critical part of the cloud delivery system, connecting resilient datacenter services across an expansive cloud architecture, which includes geographic regions and edge locations globally, is implicitly HA, and is purpose-built with sustainability in mind.

Whether you are completing an online transaction, making a checking account deposit, or withdrawing from your checking account, you are utilizing the cloud. Every business or customer request is ingress, or inbound, internet-sourced traffic, which enters a global network through a PoP, also known as an edge location. Whether they are connecting from Washington to California or Africa, the traffic data travels through cloud-optimized routes, going over a wide area network to its final destination based on the customer's request. And subsequent requests are cached in proximity to the customer, optimizing response times and, thus, improving your customer's experience. Moreover, most client traffic for cloud-hosted services located across numerous regions globally is routed within the cloud computing provider's global network and does not traverse the public internet. This strategy provides the best performance and security.

Each cloud computing leader, as mentioned earlier, has extensive cloud computing experience, coupled with unfathomable investments for continuously expanding their footprint, ensuring best-in-class network performance, and offering agile virtual networking resources and cutting-edge services – pun intended!

Sustainability

Ask any data steward of information technology, or review current studies from captains of industry – research will show that cloud computing infrastructure is several times more energy efficient than a traditional on-premises datacenter. Cloud computing is more energy efficient than enterprise datacenters because cloud computing leaders have comprehensive efficiency programs that reach every facet of their facilities. From renewable energy and water conservation to hardware recycling, cloud computing leaders AWS, Azure, and GCP are committed to constantly improving datacenter sustainability:

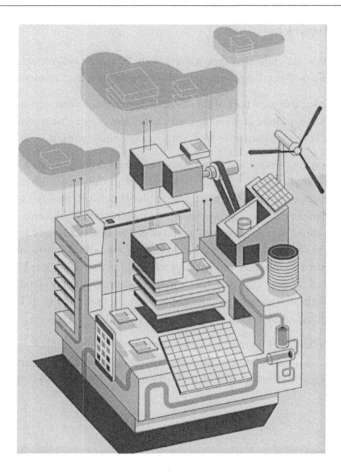

Figure 3.5 – Energy-efficient cloud computing infrastructure

Each cloud computing provider has made commitments to shift to renewable energy, and to be carbon negative in the foreseeable future. Cloud computing datacenters are repurposed, and datacenter hardware and servers are recycled. Every cloud computing leader shares environmental data and technology to help other organizations make informed decisions. Modern cloud computing datacenters use eco-friendly solutions to cool infrastructure resources, which, in turn, consumes less electricity and less water than traditional on-premises datacenter cooling systems. Here is a brief overview of how these innovative systems cool millions of pieces of hardware and server infrastructure: cooling system designs, while unique for each cloud computing provider, all have a similar objective. Cooled air is blown down a cold aisle to cool the server racks, while heated exhaust air is then guided back to an air handler by way of a hot aisle, to be cooled again, and again, and reused to continue the cycle. Cloud computing leaders such as AWS, Azure, and GCP have numerous initiatives to use local water much more efficiently and use less human drinking water to cool their global infrastructure. Cloud computing leverages water-use patterns by reviewing climate patterns for each cloud computing geographic region, local community water management, and any opportunities to conserve water.

By taking a holistic measure, cloud computing companies assess both water and energy consumption for cooling solutions to use an efficient strategy.

Because each cloud computing leader uses large economies of scale, this means that cloud computing commonly operates with greater operational efficiency than traditional on-premises datacenters. For further insight into the benefits of massive economies of scale, review the *Advantages of cloud computing* section of *Chapter 1, Introduction to Cloud Computing*.

Not to mention server utilization – or, more accurately put, virtualization – where higher server utilization rates equate to the same amount of work being done with fewer physical rack servers. Consequently, this leads to less energy consumed per useful output.

Advancements in cloud computing infrastructure across all three cloud computing leaders' datacenters have reduced electricity requirements for lighting, cooling, and power. The power usage effectiveness ratio of overall electricity usage at the datacenter to the electricity delivered to information technology hardware is a form of measuring datacenter electricity efficiency. It's no surprise that cloud computing datacenters can achieve better power usage effectiveness (PUE) than traditional on-premises datacenters. AWS, Azure, and GCP are committed to innovating continuously to further improve their power usage effectiveness as this has a direct correlation with carbon emissions.

With higher demands for cloud computing, cloud computing leaders can procure green power, which brings renewable energy products. Over the years, cloud computing has been relying largely on wind, solar, and hydropower electricity. This will shift all services and operations to 100 percent renewable energy, which will create agreements for green energy for carbon-emitting electricity resources.

In one of Amazon's analyses, there was an observation that found shopping online generated less carbon than a consumer driving to a store, because a single Amazon distribution can take an estimated 100 round-trip vehicle journeys off the road on average. The study was able to find that, averaged across various basket sizes, online deliveries generate lower carbon emissions per item compared to shopping in a physical location. Our continuous use of online services is indirectly and without our knowledge helping our ecosystem.

> **Tip**
> When considering distributed systems and the apps that reside on said systems, be aware of the location (region) privacy and compliance requirements, such as EU Data Privacy Directive. Your organization is responsible for selecting the region that will store data based on your regulatory or company compliance controls.

Fault-tolerant infrastructure

In this section, you will gain the knowledge to describe the native fault-tolerant infrastructure and its advantages. Additionally, you will learn helpful tips and aboutpotential pitfalls that encumber beginners.

Regions and zones

Cloud computing's global infrastructure is built inside geographic regions and availability zones. A region is a physical location where the cloud has multiple availability zones. And the availability zone's infrastructure contains datacenters, redundant power, and networking, in separate physically distanced locations to provide fault isolation.

Availability zones

Each cloud computing provider's region offers greater fault tolerance and stability with availability zones, which are unique physical locations that span the datacenters within a region. Every availability zone can access one or more datacenters that have independent power and cooling, and each availability zone in a region is connected through low-latency links. Additionally, it's common for each cloud computing region to have an average of three separate availability zones. For example, the physical separation of availability zones within a geographic region increases an IaaS virtual machine's resiliency against datacenter failure. Cloud computing providers such as GCP support the capability to place virtual machine instances and store data within multiple regions as well as across different availability zones within a cloud region. The availability zone is designed as an independent failure zone, wherein the availability zones are separated within a city and are in specific flood zones adhering to best practices. They have independent power substations and availability zones that are all redundantly connected to internet service providers such as Verizon.

Your organization is responsible for selecting the availability zones where your service resides. Services can span multiple availability zones. You should design your services to survive temporary or sustained failures of an availability zone if a disruption occurs. Any disruption across multiple availability zones allows them to remain resilient in most failure scenarios:

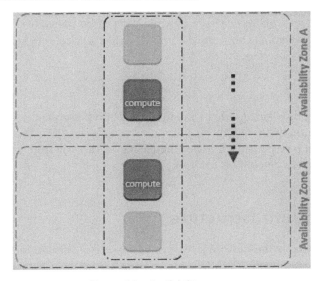

Figure 3.6 – Availability zones

IaaS built-in HA

If your organization's workload is not deemed business- critical, then its average time available for use should be below 99.9% availability, meaning that you do not have to configure it for HA, and can deploy a single virtual machine. You can still use cloud computing scalability features to automatically scale out the single virtual machine to help with load. But deploying a single virtual machine without configuring, at the very minimum, multiple different availability zones inside a geographic region offers only 99.9% availability or, in other words, considers the single virtual machine as a zonal resource, wherein a zonal outage could impact the resources in that zone. And if an availability zone is logically a deployment area for one or more resources within a region, it's considered a single point of failure within a region. So, to develop a fault-tolerant virtual machine with HA in mind, implement a minimum of two virtual machines across multiple availability zones in a region.

While many argue that the cloud includes, by default, HA within every resource, it's common architectural knowledge that one of anything is considered a point of failure. I also mentioned scalability features in the previous paragraph; however, if you're concerned that we have not defined scalability and its objectives, do not fret, as I will explore that marvelous concept in a later section of this chapter. Furthermore, I also used the term availability and an average denoted as a percentage of availability. We will explore what availability is in the section that follows.

I need to make it abundantly clear that 99.9% availability is not considered by many industry experts as being HA or resilient against the loss of an entire region due to planned downtime or unpredictable catastrophic events that we have no control over. It still provides some semblance of resilience, especially if compared to traditional on-premises datacenters including the majority of modern enterprises' datacenters. Now that might seem a bit presumptuous of me, but there are numerous articles and studies that would corroborate my point. However, I digress, so let's resume. Each cloud computing provider supports a cloud-managed disk for their compute resources, such as a virtual machine, built into the cloud service. These disks are replicated within a datacenter zone, on different server cabinets, to provide high durability. For example, if one or more replicas experience hardware component failures, the remaining help ensure your data is tolerant against failures.

Nevertheless, it is important to note that IaaS compute resources, such as a single virtual machine, by default are not considered as HA due to the architectural significance of a single point of failure in terms of numerous factors, including AWS, Azure, and GCP well-architected framework best practices.

This leads us on to our educational journey to explore HA infrastructure.

HA infrastructure

In this section, you will gain the knowledge to describe HA infrastructure and its advantages. Additionally, you will learn helpful tips and about potential pitfalls that encumber beginners.

Resilient architecture

Every app or service design requires building resiliency and availability. Regardless of the deployment model, such as all in the cloud or hybrid, planning and preparing for HA should be incorporated at every stage of development.

Availability

There are many reasons that organizations elect to migrate a workload or an entire line of business service or resource to the public cloud. Nevertheless, one factor is key in any endeavor – while we understand security is paramount, resiliency is one of the priorities.

Resiliency is a key capability for any service to recover from disruptions, attain resources to meet business needs, isolate faults, and remedy disruptions to service. Of course, other factors impact resiliency and could lead to suboptimal performance. Each cloud computing provider has several guiding principles that help achieve reliability, which we will explore later in the chapter when I elaborate on well-architected frameworks and their correlation to resiliency.

First, let us grasp service availability, commonly referred to as availability, which is used as a metric to measure resiliency. In other words, availability is the percentage of time that a service is available. This is calculated over a period, typically one year. And a service's availability is reduced anytime it is not available, which may include scheduled and unscheduled disruptions to availability. There are other commonly used terms that refer to the percentage of uptime or availability period, known as the number of nines; for example, "four nines" translates to 99.99% availability.

Here is a table that contains examples of each availability tier:

Availability	Annual maximum unavailability
99%	3 days and 15 hours
99.9%	8 hours and 45 minutes
99.95%	4 hours and 22 minutes
99.99%	52 minutes
99.999%	5 minutes

Table 3.1 – Table showing each availability tier

> **Tip**
> Numerous services have tightly coupled dependencies on other services and resources. If a disruption in a dependency consequently disrupts the invoking service, then the invoking service's availability is the product of the dependent service's availabilities. Nuances in architectural patterns have emerged to mitigate dependency failures, such as microservices, which advocate a loosely coupled architecture.

Generally, cloud computing offers various infrastructural resources and services that use independent, redundant architecture, such as redundant IaaS virtual machines spread across multiple availability zones. For example, if a line of business application uses two independent virtual machines, each with an availability of 99.9%, the theoretical effectual availability of the application is 99.9999%, in other words, *six nines* availability. Additionally, some cloud computing resource types are implicitly HA without any post-implementation configuration required. That is because the cloud computing provider is offering a fully managed resource type. There is more on this topic of managed services in the section that follows.

AWS, Azure, and GCP offer various infrastructure resources to expand availability, such as availability zones, wherein a physically separate zone provides fault tolerance from other datacenter zonal failures. Alternatively, it can configure and manage a group of load-balanced virtual machines that can automatically scale out or in when needed. Each cloud computing provider supports storing copies or backups of your data so that it is protected from unplanned outages, transient failures, infrastructure power outages, and even natural disasters. And let us not forget, to ensure business continuity, cloud computing offers various recovery services that can leverage multi-region or even hybrid architectures because, eventually, everything fails, so we plan with that propensity in mind.

Did you know? Designing services and their resources for higher levels of availability incurs substantial cost increases, so mature information technology-centric organizations classify and categorize specific line of business applications as business- critical or something similar before embarking on architecting an application for high availability. While many subject matter experts argue that all services and those services' independent components should be HA, this might not be justified based on the unique business requirements, which vary from business to business. And these must be taken into careful consideration before making a costly decision that could impact the organization's return on investment. We must also factor in the requirements for testing failover and failback scenarios. This requires automation over manual processes for recovery and restore procedures.

Yet another concern is that additional costs in systems that need higher availability impact other workloads. At these higher service levels, the services that may not be required are labeled emerging technologies. And as the infrastructure supporting higher availability expands, it's common to find more purpose-built services and fewer newer technologies. Cloud -managed HA inherent services are cost -effective and help organizations support business critical applications and those services that are still in their infancy.

Managed versus unmanaged services

In cloud computing, there are services that are mostly managed by the provider. Therefore, responsibilities such as explicitly configuring redundancy and scaling are not the responsibility of the developer. To explore the logical concept of managed and unmanaged, I'll have you recall the cloud computing models. The AWS, Azure, and GCP cloud computing models adhere to the *National Institute of Standards and Technologies* declaration of IaaS, PaaS, and SaaS.

IaaS is unmanaged by AWS, Azure, and GCP and requires the user to respond to an increase in client traffic and restore services in the eventuality of a resource-planned or unplanned disruption. Resources such as virtual machines are classified as unmanaged and, by default, do not inherit high availability. If the organization requires high availability, it will have to configure infrastructure resources to provide fault tolerance.

PaaS offers an application hosting ecosystem that enables you to adopt a modern microservices strategy. The developer provides the code base artifacts, and the cloud provider includes the runtime environment and managed services that handle the heavy lifting and access to files and SDK packages. Additionally, Platform-as-a-Service (PaaS) resources are inherently fault tolerant and include a HA infrastructure.

SaaS is a managed online solution with many innate attributes such as being multitenant, fully managed, and reliable. In the following list, you will find some examples of modern SaaS that exude the attributes defined here:

- Office 365

- Amazon WorkDocs

- Slack

- Microsoft Teams

It's common knowledge that managed services require less configuration, so offer greater agility, and are cost-efficient in comparison to an unmanaged service that requires heavy lifting on your part but provides flexibility in terms of control. Unmanaged resources such as virtual machines permit developers to manage the underlying filesystem, enabling developers to support legacy applications and adhere to traditional compliance policies.

> Tip
>
> Managed and unmanaged are concepts, not services. However, at the time of writing, each cloud computing provider provides an offering or product known as **managed services** with unique features and benefits. But this is not the same as the concepts explored here.

Managed service constraints

All cloud computing services can be categorized as either IaaS, PaaS, or SaaS, so we can tag them as managed or unmanaged to better understand their native attributes such as built-in redundancy or scalability. You could also argue that some services have more constraints than others, and some have adjustable limits. For example, some limits are managed at a zonal or regional level. While both the preceding statements are true, they vary from service to service, even if either service has been categorized as PaaS, which is deemed a managed service and is inherently resilient due to its default redundant configuration. The question remains, does the service's implicit resiliency meet your business needs if it is local (a single datacenter), zonal, or regional, or is there a business justification for multi-regional? Let us explore further, shall we?

Datacenter/zonal

Cloud computing resources can be classified as zonal, regional, or multi-regionally managed by the cloud computing provider. And as mentioned earlier, each is unique and bears considerable examination to understand its constraints or limits in terms of features, and more importantly resiliency, which includes fault tolerance and elasticity.

Any cloud service that is managed by the provider at the zonal level has redundancy at the server rack scope, but if there is a planned or unplanned disruption at the datacenter, this will cause an outage because the service resides within a datacenter inside of one availability zone. For example, IaaS resources such as virtual machines are deemed zonal.

Regional

In contrast, geographic regional services are redundantly configured across multiple availability zones within a single region. This increases the availability of a resource classified as zonal. For example, PaaS object-level storage services are typically replicated redundantly across several datacenters in different availability zones inside a geographic region.

> **Tip**
> When planning which resiliency option is best for your scenario, factor in the trade-offs between lower costs and increased availability.

Multi-region/global

Organizations can replicate their line of business applications and their dependencies across cloud computing geographic regions. They can accomplish this by utilizing private high-speed networks or public internet connections to increase redundancy and provide low-latency accessibility to multi-region services across the world.

Furthermore, if your organization has its own data replication technology, you can use it to implement a secondary in-region zone or a multi-region disaster recovery site. And multi-region high availability is plausible; however, it requires a load balancer that can distribute inbound traffic globally. It so happens that each cloud computing leader has one or more services that offer global **Domain Name System** (**DNS**) traffic distribution.

Disaster recovery

First, let's summarize availability, which refers to the level of service that an application, service, or system provides, and is expressed as the percentage of time that a service or system is available. If a service is declared HA, the service has minimal downtime, whether planned or unplanned, and is typically available more than 99% of the time. Additionally, it's dependent on the requirements and the budget of the organization. Availability must be expressed so that there is no misunderstanding regarding the implications.

> **Tip**
>
> Any miscommunication concerning service-level expectations between the customer and the cloud service provider can result in inappropriate business decisions, such as unsuitable investment levels, and could impact customer loyalty.

Disaster recovery planning is essential for meeting **service-level agreements (SLAs)**. These agreements define when a service must be available and how quickly it must be recovered because, eventually, it will fail!

Even in the cloud, resiliency planning should include disaster recovery objectives based on recovery protocols your organization is responsible for developing in the case of a disaster event. Disaster recovery planning focuses on recovery objectives in response to natural disasters, region-wide failures, and more, which could vary based on the organization's industry or unique infrastructure and workload. Here is some insight: this is different than availability, which gauges average resiliency over a period in response to disruptions.

Recovery time objective

The recovery time objective is defined by an organization. This is the maximum acceptable time between the disruption and restoration of a service or system. This helps organizations to understand what an acceptable time frame for a service is to be unavailable.

Recovery point objective

The recovery point objective is also defined by the organization. This is the maximum acceptable time since the last data recovery point or backup. This helps organizations to understand what an acceptable loss of data from the last backup to the disruption of service is.

A cloud computing service's infrastructure resources fail over time, including VM instance operating system memory getting corrupted, and transient errors disrupt services, no matter the quality of hardware or software or whether on-premises or in the cloud. However, in cloud computing, you should be protected from most low-level hardware failures due to the built-in HA infrastructure, which isn't your responsibility when you transition from on-premises to cloud computing. For example, compute service disks are zonal where they are automatically replicated to protect you from a single point of component failure. And regional services such as cloud object-level storage services' data is replicated across several availability zones, providing increased resiliency. But your organization must choose a managed or unmanaged service wisely, based on factors such as resiliency, and consider costs before investing to meet certain SLA expectations. For example, certain public sector regulatory compliance policies require IaaS and exclude PaaS resources. This poses considerable operating costs to configure the service to meet increased resiliency requirements such as "four nines," which most certainly will require load-balanced IaaS virtual machines spread across, at the very minimum, two different availability zones within one region to ensure regional availability.

Here is some food for thought: backup data and data backups are not mutually exclusive for on-premises. You should identify and back up all data that will require increased resiliency to meet SLA expectations. Cloud computing offers many services and tools, such as object-level storage resource types and unique backup and restore replication services that have the capability to target one or more cloud or hybrid storage services as a backup destination for numerous disparate data sources. Even open source third-party backup systems can be procured, implemented, and utilized from a cloud marketplace. I really want to expound on the marketplace in this book, but I would lose myself in its bazaar-like variety and never return to the topic at hand. My apologies, I digress. Where was I? Oh, yeah… Alternatively, if data can be replicated from other sources to meet recovery point objectives, there may not be a need for a backup, but until you have assurances, back up everything.

Cloud computing also supports several methods of data encryption, using server-side encryption, even if your data was sourced unencrypted. Cloud computing then encrypts it before storing it persistently. Optionally, organizations can use client-side encryption, but they would be responsible for encrypting the data before it's backed up to one of the cloud computing storage services. Furthermore, either the client side or the server side can use the cloud computing key management services to create and store the key, or bring your own, and utilize the advanced identity and access management features that AWS, Azure, and GCP have to offer.

Cloud computing models support automatic data backup features based on a periodic schedule, even if there is a change in state. Most cloud computing resources include a backup feature, which may be enabled by default or disabled. This varies from unmanaged to managed service and should be researched by reviewing the online documents for AWS, Azure, and GCP, to understand each cloud service's backup feature constraints, which are defined in AWS, Azure, and GCP service quotas or limits online article.

Here is an example: `https://docs.aws.amazon.com/general/latest/gr/aws_service_limits.html`

Another important tidbit is validating that your backup strategy meets your recovery time objective and recovery point objective by performing a failover and a failback or recovery test successfully. Utilizing cloud computing, organizations can stand up a testing environment and restore services using backups to assess recovery time objective and recovery point objective capabilities and further ensure data integrity. Alternatively, some cloud computing services offer a point-in-time recovery feature that uses continuous backup, thus allowing you to restore services to the state they were in at a specific time and date.

As you have learned so far, disaster recovery considerations include the availability of the service or system to keep running in a healthy state, and disaster recovery works in the preservation of data if a disaster occurs.

> **Tip**
>
> High- availability failover in production should be quick, with no data loss, and have a limited effect on the service or system. In contrast, a traditional disaster recovery failover might have a longer period, which impacts the recovery time objective and recovery point objective with potentially minimal data loss, but it is inevitable.
>
> Organizations can take advantage of availability zones for both high availability and disaster recovery by utilizing different availability zones for their disaster recovery strategy.

Cloud- scaled infrastructure

In this section, you will gain the knowledge to describe cloud-scaled infrastructure and its advantages. Additionally, you will learn helpful tips and about potential pitfalls that encumber beginners.

Performance

Performance is key to many organizations, whether large or small, so cloud computing leaders have made substantial infrastructure investments to meet today's demands in a high-volume world, where the ability of your workload to scale to meet the fluctuating requirements of consumers is critical. Traditionally, on-premises datacenter owners purposefully over-provisioned infrastructure to support workload unpredictability. While this was a logical approach in enterprise datacenters because it guaranteed capacity availability during increases in service utilization, in later years, this was considered by most pundits to be costly due to significant decreases in utilization for long periods of time.

Planning for the eventuality of service utilization fluctuations in load is important not only on-premises but in cloud computing, too. However, one key differentiator is that, with cloud computing, you possibly no longer need to make upfront long-term assumptions or estimations of whether you will have enough capacity in the foreseeable future.

Additionally, to improve performance and redundancy, an organization's application workloads are commonly dispersed across, at the very minimum, two or more cloud computing virtual machines. And the virtual machine's inbound, or ingress, customer traffic is distributed through a load balancer to the target or destination virtual machine network's interface. Please note that I will delve into networking components or services in *Chapter 7, Implementing Virtual Network Resources for Security*.

Autoscaling

Cloud computing leaders support two or more virtual machines in a logical grouping, referred to by many as an autoscaled group. Each cloud computing provider's nomenclature has subtle variations of the name; however, the objective for this elastic group is similar, and that is to scale quickly, efficiently, and automatically, and to ensure exceptional performance at a reasonable cost only if utilized, thus paying only for what you need:

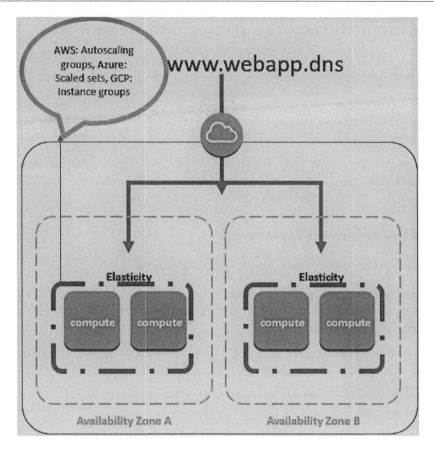

Figure 3.7 – Autoscaling group

AWS, Azure, and GCP provide a streamlined intuitive experience when configuring scaling. Organizations can view service and system utilization fluctuations using a simple but robust interface that provides a central pane of glass. Additionally, you can develop how your logical group responds to changes in state to support unique scaling requirements that are deemed complex. Autoscaling continuously monitors your services and systems to ensure they are operating within your SLAs. In a world where being flexible is crucial, elasticity becomes paramount, and autoscaling terminates any excess capacity in an effort to decrease operating costs. And best of all, this feature is *free* and included by all three cloud computing leaders.

> **Tip**
>
> While there is no additional cost for autoscaling, there is a cost for additional computes or services running. So, assess your service or system, find what you can and should scale, consider the business outcomes, such as cost or performance, track trends in near real time, and adjust your autoscaled configuration to meet your current demands. Then, rinse and repeat.

Optimizing architectures using cloud frameworks

In this section, you will gain the knowledge to describe architectural frameworks that help optimize cloud computing services. Additionally, you will learn helpful tips and about potential pitfalls that encumber beginners.

Well-architected frameworks are the cloud computing best practices, core principles, and standards required to provide a level of quality when building architectures to support applications and vice versa.

Cloud computing leaders such as AWS, Azure, and GCP provide in-depth guidance on how to optimize your organization's solutions, and the Well-Architected Framework encompasses IaaS, PaaS, and SaaS resource types.

AWS Well-Architected Framework

The AWS Well-Architected Framework consists of the following:

- **Operational excellence pillar**: To respond efficiently to meet fluctuating demands, Amazon has developed a core principle known as operational excellence, which delivers guidance on continuous improvement.

- **Performance efficiency pillar**: Here, Amazon's core principle objective is to guide organizations on how to efficiently allocate the appropriate capacity.

- **Security pillar**: Here, Amazon's core principle objective is to provide guidance on how to protect services.

- **Reliability pillar**: Here, Amazon's core principle objective is to help organizations improve availability and recovery processes.

- **Sustainability pillar**: Here, Amazon's core principle objective focuses on environmental impacts and details our shared responsibility.

- **Cost optimization pillar**: Here, Amazon's core principle objective focuses on controlling costs to prevent unsuitable investments.

Azure Well-Architected Framework

The Azure Well-Architected Framework consists of the following:

- **Operational excellence pillar**: Microsoft has crafted a principle known as operational excellence, which yields guidance on improving operational processes.

- **Performance efficiency pillar**: The objective of this crafted Microsoft principle is to guide you on efficiently adapting to changes in utilization.

- **Security pillar**: The objective of this crafted Microsoft principle is to provide guidance on how to protect your data and services against modern threats.

- **Reliability pillar**: The objective of this crafted Microsoft principle is to educate you on how to improve your service's availability and recovery processes.

- **Cost optimization pillar**: The objective of this crafted Microsoft principle concentrates on managing costs to ensure value.

Google Cloud Architecture Framework

The Google Cloud Architecture Framework consists of the following:

- **Operational excellence**: Google has curated a design recommendation known as operational excellence, which delivers insights into efficiently developing and managing cloud services.

- **Performance optimization**: The objective of this Google-curated design recommendation is tuning cloud resources.

- **Security, privacy, and compliance**: The objective of this Google-curated design recommendation is to provide guidance on maximizing security, privacy, and compliance standards.

- **Reliability**: The objective of this Google-curated design recommendation is operating resilient workloads.

- **System design**: The objective of this Google-curated design recommendation defining the architectural service requirements to support a workload.

- **Cost optimization**: The objective of this Google-curated design recommendation is to help you maximize your cloud investment.

As detailed at the beginning of *Chapter 1*, cloud computing leaders such as AWS, Azure, and GCP have a comprehensive perspective of the cloud computing ecosystem and curate design recommendations that can be disseminated by leaders, scientists, IT communities, and enthusiasts. As leaders in cloud computing, it is their duty to communicate how best to utilize cloud resources for the benefit of all.

If you reviewed the previous bulleted lists of well-architected framework principles, you should have noticed subtle similarities across the cloud computing leaders. This is profound, in that all three cloud computing providers understand the importance of these pillars and agree that these are core pillars that any organization, small or large, no matter the industry, must abide by to be successful and achieve the end goal, which is value.

Every business leader understands that people, processes, and services must have exceptional resiliency to ensure cloud computing customers can access what matters most to them anywhere, anytime.

Customers cannot value a service if they do not trust in its end-to-end privacy and the security of their data. Security is the cornerstone of customer trust, which establishes loyalty and breathes value into life.

People, processes, and services must operate at higher levels to ensure we organically change to the shifting tides of life, thus building customer confidence that we are here, and the cloud will adapt to life. This is essential; this will support our labors to always raise the bar in the hope of providing exciting levels of performance in each innovation and adaptation of cloud computing services.

Cloud computing leaders understand the importance of fiscal responsibilities and all their facets. Cloud providers know customers can be financially cognizant and thrive in the cloud by following the guidance of captains of industry, who through trial and tribulation have successfully digitally transformed their own organizations, to the financial gain of all stakeholders.

Moreover, using guidance derived from the well-architected frameworks, which are living and breathing documents of wisdom, should help customers drive adoption, loyalty, and perhaps even value the cloud.

Tip

Cost optimization is one of the well-known architected frameworks; however, most organizations fall short of its ideals. Balancing business goals with budget justifications is by no means simple. But assessing workloads holistically to reduce unnecessary expenses is feasible. Start small and scale out. Rather than investing in larger infrastructure, use cloud tools such as total cost of ownership calculators initially, establish budget baselines, and use pricing calculators and cost forecasting services frequently to build awareness. Lastly, establish transparent policies, budgets, and controls that prohibit unsuitable investments.

Organizations that shift resources to the cloud must plan and prepare a cost model. And procurement strategies in the cloud should encourage using tools to evaluate costs for IaaS, PaaS, and SaaS resources. You should generate actionable reports that support awareness and enforce budgets using intelligent notification services that can detect divergences that could create a future cost concern. You should continuously review services and systems that are underutilized and experiment using different cloud computing payment options to lower costs. Finally, weigh the cost versus each principal and include all stakeholders to ensure an agreed-upon action before investing further.

For example, if you consider using multi-region for increased resiliency, cost increases with the number of regions. Using services in cost-efficient regions does not nullify the additional costs of network ingress (inbound) and egress (outbound).

By now, you should have fundamental knowledge of how the cloud emerged, an insight into its core, and its value in everyday life. If you need to, go back and read earlier lessons. I highly recommend you do this because it's essential to understand the concepts that will be covered in the next chapter, as we will explore how to develop IaaS, PaaS, and SaaS cloud computing solutions.

Summary

In this chapter, you learned about the global infrastructure's resilient architecture, and how some cloud computing models may or may not be inherently HA. We described how some services are zonal, regional, and globally resilient. Finally, we reviewed the well-architected framework.

In the next chapter, you will learn about some of the core cloud computing resources, such as networking, compute, and storage resources, and architecting recommendations.

Questions

1. What criteria were measured and plotted in the Magic Quadrant research regarding cloud computing? (Choose all that apply.)

   A. Resiliency

   B. CPU

   C. The ability to execute

   D. The completeness of vision

2. What cloud location options are available to host your services?

   A. Datacenter

   B. On-premises

   C. Wi-Fi

   D. Region (for example, East US)

3. What are edge zones or locations?

   A. PoPs

   B. PPTP

   C. Perimeter

   D. Router

4. How are modern cloud computing datacenters more eco-friendly than on-premises?

   A. Comprehensive efficiency programs

   B. Apple hardware

   C. Dell hardware

   D. Tesla

5. What is a geographical region?

    A. Container

    B. Ephemeral

    C. Physical location

    D. Mainframe

6. What are the benefits of availability zones?

    A. Scale

    B. Performance

    C. Cost optimization

    D. Fault tolerance

7. Are cloud-managed disk types replicated to increase resiliency by default?

    A. Yes

    B. No

8. What is availability?

    A. RPO

    B. No failures

    C. The percentage of time that a service is available

    D. Scheduled availability

9. What are cloud computing virtual machines?

    A. Managed

    B. IaaS

    C. Kernel virtual machine hosts

    D. Docker cloud

10. Which of the following characteristics apply to virtual machines?

    A. Regional

    B. Global

    C. Zonal

    D. Rack

11. What are AWS S3, Azure Blob, and GCP's cloud storage (object-level storage types)?

    A. Archive

    B. Regional

    C. IaaS

    D. Databases

12. Do resilient cloud workloads require disaster recovery strategies?

    A. Yes

    B. No

13. What does RTO define?

    A. Acceptable loss of data

    B. Resiliency time options

    C. Fault tolerance

    D. Acceptable time frame

14. What does RPO define?

    A. Fault tolerance

    B. Kernel isolation

    C. Acceptable loss of data

    D. Acceptable time frame

15. Scaling optimizes which of the following?

    A. Unpredictable workloads

    B. Predictable workloads

    C. Availability

    D. Network bandwidth

16. Which of the following is autoscaling's minimum recommended architecture?

    A. One Availability Zone

    B. Two Availability Zone

    C. Multi-Region

    D. None

17. Amazon and Google, excluding Microsoft, created the operational excellence well-architected framework pillars.

    A. True

    B. False

18. Reliability is built into cloud computing and does not require design recommendations.

    A. True

    B. False

19. What are the costs, if any, of using two or more region locations?

    A. Pay for the site

    B. Manage the physical infrastructure

    C. Ingress and egress network traffic

    D. Free

Part 2: Implementing Cloud Deployment Models

This part of the book will help you comprehend utilizing underlying cloud computing models.

This part comprises the following chapters:

- *Chapter 4, Developing Infrastructure Services Using Public Cloud Providers (IaaS)*
- *Chapter 5, Developing Platform Services Using Public Cloud Providers (PaaS)*
- *Chapter 6, Utilizing Turnkey Software Solutions (SaaS)*

4

Developing Infrastructure Services Using Public Cloud Providers (IaaS)

In this chapter, you will learn how **infrastructure-as-a-service** (**IaaS**) solutions are implemented, as well as how to architect, deploy, and manage networking components, compute services, and storage resources. You will also gain the knowledge required to maintain IaaS resources throughout their workload's life cycle by understanding the responsibility you share with the cloud provider.

In this chapter, we will cover the following topics:

- Cloud computing models
- Common scenarios by industry
- Networking
- Compute
- Storage
- Sharing responsibility

Cloud computing models

Once an organization understands its responsibilities and how they apply to operating in the cloud, it must determine how they apply to its unique scenario. Responsibilities vary and are based on numerous factors such as regional laws and the cloud computing models or services they elect to meet their business requirements. For example, infrastructure maintenance tasks are the cloud providers' responsibility. This is similar across the cloud computing leaders – Amazon, Microsoft, and Google.

Infrastructure as a service

Organizations that elect to use IaaS decrease the complexity of procuring and managing the physical infrastructure on-premises. Each service is separate and scalable, and you only pay for what you use. Cloud computing providers such as Amazon, Microsoft, and Google manage the physical infrastructure.

> Note
>
> For more information on the physical infrastructure, review the previous chapters.

Common scenarios by industry

Every industry uses cloud computing, and each organization has unique service requirements for optimizing data, agility, sustainability, or fiscal outcomes.

Health and sciences

Over the last several years, we have seen epidemics that have spread out of control to grow into pandemics such as COVID-19. Our world's systems and processes were challenged and numerous limits in our traditional systems and processes were discovered. Organizations such as Amazon, Microsoft, Google, and Moderna were pivotal in helping the world find solutions. Breakthroughs are not feasible using traditional systems and processes.

Moderna was founded to deliver medicines for unmet patient needs. Their expertise included cardiometabolic diseases, infectious diseases, and more.

Like so many organizations in the health and science industry, it takes decades to bring new medicines to market. Moderna acknowledged the limitations of traditional drug development and distribution. So, to optimize the potential of mRNA, Moderna used cloud computing resources, which are inherent, highly available, elastic, built with agility, and deliver global data accessibility.

Moderna partnered with **Amazon** and leveraged its cloud computing service models such as IaaS to advance drug research, development, and overall organizational processes. For example, Moderna utilizes **Elastic Compute Cloud** (**EC2**) coupled with powerful autoscaling features to meet high-performance computing demands while controlling costs, without negatively impacting performance to champion their cause.

> Tip
>
> In the *Networking*, *Compute*, and *Storage* sections in this chapter, we will explore administrating essential AWS architectural resource types and their key resource factors recommended to efficiently implement an IaaS solution similar to the one used by PayPal.

Financial services

As more and more businesses understand the importance of putting customers first, even financial sector services need to distinguish themselves from other entities by delivering personalized experiences.

Take, for instance, **PayPal**, a global leader in digital transactions, a technology-driven company whose main objective is to serve as an online financial transaction service for personal and commercial use. PayPal has grown over the years through achievements in technology-driven systems and processes. But like most flourishing organizations, some scenarios cause entities such as this to pivot due to growing demands and to not only meet but exceed customer expectations. So, PayPal, like many other organizations, partnered with Google to adopt cloud computing infrastructure services and minimize its physical infrastructure footprint, migrating its various workloads from on-premises to the public cloud. Google has numerous business partners who help organizations such as PayPal accelerate adoption using best practices as frameworks to ascend to the cloud.

With Google's cloud computing platform, PayPal is leveraging IaaS resources and tools to adapt instantly to real-time fluctuations in financial transactional traffic demands.

Moreover, PayPal can quickly handle bursts in transactional traffic without incurring upfront capital expenditures that are encountered when using traditional on-premises data centers. This is because PayPal would have to extend its physical infrastructure to meet increasing demands.

> **Tip**
> In the *Networking*, *Compute*, and *Storage* sections later in this chapter, we will explore administrating essential GCP architectural resource types and their key resource factors recommended to efficiently implement an IaaS solution similar to the one used by PayPal.

Retail

Retailers offering goods and services such as Publix, Costco, Walmart, and Albertsons are undergoing major digital transformations to compete in their market space. As an example, **Albertsons** partnered with **Microsoft** to accelerate digital transformation. As the COVID-19 pandemic impacted retailers around the globe, online orders increased exponentially, accelerating Albertsons' plans of modernization. To quell concerns and deliver innovative services such as *DriveUp & Go*, Albertsons utilized the service advantages of Azure to adapt to market demands.

Like many retailers, Albertsons elected to go all in with the cloud and migrate to Microsoft Azure. The first of many steps was to establish a foundation using IaaS to pave the way for digital transformation.

> **Tip**
> In the *Networking*, *Compute*, and *Storage* sections in this chapter, we will explore administrating essential Azure architectural resource types needed to implement an IaaS used by Albertsons.

Networking

In this section, you will learn about the advantages of IaaS networking, illustrated by leading industry examples. You will also learn helpful tips and potential pitfalls that encumber beginners.

As mentioned previously, IaaS is the foundation on which many organizations from various industries such as health and sciences, financial services, and retail have established initial successes in cloud adoption. While cloud adoption strategies are unique to each company, there are subtle similarities in cloud computing services utilized by all three organizations. Let's focus on the facts – each cloud computing provider solicits IaaS. The core IaaS resource types include networking, compute, and storage.

Did you know that Moderna, PayPal, and Albertsons, while in different industries, required similar IaaS resources?

Cloud computing providers such as Amazon, Microsoft, and Google offer resilient yet scalable resource types such as networking, compute, and storage IaaS. In all three industry scenario examples, organizations implement fault-tolerant compute services configured to automatically scale based on implementing unique configurable conditions, which vary by industry and organization.

Did you know that IaaS VM network services are a core building block for either public or private compute network access? Each cloud computing provider network supports IaaS, PaaS, and SaaS resources securely communicating with each other, the internet, and in a bi-directional connection with on-premises networks, commonly referred to as a hybrid network, and supports multi-cloud connectivity between Amazon's, Microsoft's, and Google's cloud network.

Architectural considerations

When selecting network infrastructure resources, it's very important to assess your solution's needs for connectivity, communication, and reliability.

Architecting network services requires organizations to plan network topology and internet protocol addressing by factoring in standardized nomenclature, geographical locations, high-availability networks, cloud computing provider account restrictions, subnetting, internal and external internetworking, and network security.

On the following pages, you will find several network architectural examples for each cloud computing leader. These examples were created while utilizing each cloud computing leader's architecture icons, which are generally available to the public:

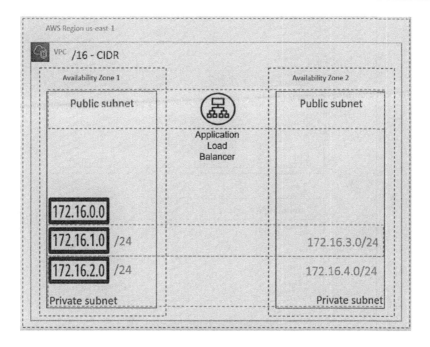

Figure 4.1 – AWS Virtual Private Cloud

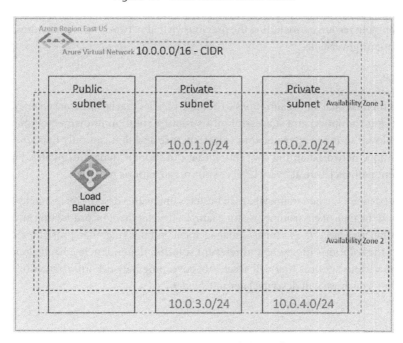

Figure 4.2 – Azure Virtual Network

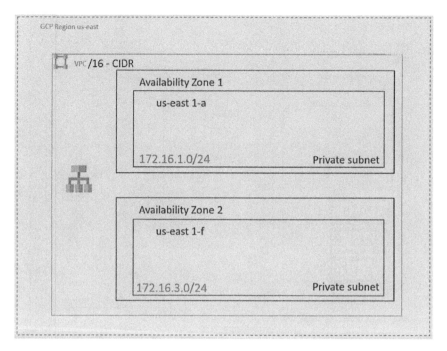

Figure 4.3 – GCP Virtual Private Cloud

All cloud computing resources, including the previous virtual networking architectures, must adhere to an organization's governance.

Governance

Governance is foundational for organizations to develop policies that ensure transparency and security, and facilitate cloud adoption and successful infrastructure solution implementation. All solutions should be deployed in the proper network infrastructure and that can only happen if we create a flexible and unique network naming convention that can support dynamic updates. First, you must apply consistent nomenclature at every level of your organization's hierarchy.

Then, you must define a method to manage each business unit with a descriptive hierarchy that describes the location and the type of environment – for example, development or production environments. If your organization uses projects as a form of management and tracking, then project logical containers should reflect the solution's life cycle and relevant solution dependencies. Each cloud computing provider offers various services that will accelerate governing network infrastructure planning and implementation, which we will describe later in *Chapter 7*.

Geographical locations

Cloud computing providers offer geographical regions, as explored in an earlier chapter. Cloud infrastructure services such as networking resources exist in regions. However, you can connect networks that exist in different geographic regions. Amazon, Microsoft, and Google provide a global footprint that can support solutions for worldwide business requirements. Organizations should factor in where many of their customers reside to ensure the lowest network latency. Another consideration is data residency and data sovereignty, and how to adhere to those corresponding regulatory or company compliance policies. Here, data residency requires organizations to utilize infrastructure and enforce data management within a specific geography. With data sovereignty, the data is subject to legal or regulatory enforcement from that country due to its laws. Next, we factor in reliability, where every organization, whether it's large or small, needs to consider resiliency.

High-availability networks

A business-critical requirement during the planning phase is deciding the level of resiliency. Let's consider a simple network for small, single applications, managed by a small group, mainly utilized for development, or in some instances for high-performance computing batch or stream processing before multiple networks can be implemented. A network in cloud computing provides inherent but not implicitly configured architecture resilience by utilizing fault-tolerant zones within the same geographical region for IaaS resource implementation. Organizations can elect to deploy resources such as compute to different zones within the same network, which provides a modicum of high availability known as fault tolerance through availability zones. Through reviews, you will find that the example solutions developed for this chapter to reinforce the common scenarios described herein utilize one network with multiple availability zones. This is because each example is a development demonstration, not a production workload.

For production workloads, consider a multi-zone network architecture or multiple networks and design cloud computing network resources such as compute for the eventuality of failure by incorporating failover resources into your cloud computing architecture. Cloud computing providers include highly available **domain name systems (DNSs)**, points-of-presence edge services, known as **content delivery networks (CDNs)**, and layer 4 and 7 load balancer services that support a multi-zone network. If you need more insight into these zones, review *Chapter 3*. Additionally, configure redundant connectivity between private networks and public networks in the cloud and on-premises. Google, Microsoft, and Amazon offer numerous direct physical connection options between your on-premises network and the cloud computing provider's network. Direct Connect and ExpressRoute, as they are referred to in cloud computing, provide a cost-effective model for procuring dedicated, reliable, persistent network connection and bandwidth without traversing the public internet.

Optionally, you can also consider creating multiple networks within the same region or in different regions! A disaster recovery strategy needs to be defined to meet recovery time objectives and recovery point objectives, and this is still very important, even in cloud computing. Amazon, Microsoft, and Google optimize your organization's disaster recovery processes by leveraging their geographic regions wherein a disaster recovery region is a cloud computing region other than the primary being utilized for your solution.

Subnetting

Organizations should ensure that cloud computing network IP address ranges are large enough to accommodate the solution's requirements, including factoring future network expansion of IP addresses across multiple availability zones. This includes and is not limited to compute resources and load balancers.

When you devise your cloud computing network, initially, you must define the IP address space, and always refer to the RFC article 1918. Here are some things to consider:

- Can your IP address space support more than one network per geographic region?

- Can your IP address space within the network support multiple subnets across multiple availability zones?

- In the event of traffic spikes, is there IP address space to meet the dynamic needs of your solution?

- Does your organization have policies in place to enforce non-overlapping private IP addresses?

Figure 4.4 shows several subnets:

Figure 4.4 – Subnets

Later in this chapter, you will learn that none of the cloud computing leaders support overlapping network IP addresses when peered or connected via a VPN, which includes IP address conflicts between the cloud computing network and traditional on-premises networks in hybrid or multi-cloud architectures.

Chapter 7, AWS, Azure, and Google Cloud Platform Networking Details

I'll elaborate on cloud computing networking concepts and configurations in *Chapter 7* in more detail. The sections covered in this chapter should help you understand planning and preparing before implementing a cloud network and reinforce the common scenarios by industry examples. Every organization, no matter the industry, must factor in cloud networking when adopting cloud computing.

Security

As you have learned in previous chapters, there are many responsibilities on-premises, including securing your infrastructure both physically and digitally. However, as your organization shifts to the cloud, your security responsibilities change. Organizations undergoing a digital transformation as it relates to cloud adoption should be cognizant of the additional potential vulnerabilities when extending their existing network to include public and private cloud services. Your on-premises defense-in-depth, known as a multi-layered defense model, likely involves a perimeter between the public internet and your internal network zones, where demarcation points are typically clearly defined. Regardless, when organizations move to the cloud, you introduce additional threat vectors beyond your on-premises demilitarized zones.

While we have yet to explore the Shared Responsibility Model, which is clearly defined by each cloud computing leader, it is indicative in those principles that you are responsible for how you set up and secure your cloud computing network.

One clear strategy adopted by cloud computing leaders is that your network trust model must change. The modern model is named zero trust, which means that no one person or system is trusted implicitly, whether they are inside or outside your organization's network zones. The zero-trust model recommends you verify each user or system and the condition of the request. This model is an additional control plane to your network controls that is recommended across all three cloud computing leaders.

The careful planning and management of your network architecture forms the core of how you provide secure resources for your solutions. IaaS solutions operate in a network classified as a **virtual private cloud** (**VPC**) and/or virtual network. This is interchangeable in the grand scheme of things. Amazon names its network **VPC**, Microsoft names its network a virtual network, and Google classifies theirs as a VPC (more on these resources later in this chapter). Nevertheless, these networks provide isolation and boundaries by default.

Configuring defense-in-depth network layers by subnetting resource types with dissimilar connectivity requirements in cloud computing virtual networks improves security. This layered strategy isolates incidents to subnets and protects any subsequent subnet layers. Those layers can have additional network security controls in place to further protect and isolate critical data in a multi-layered subnet defense, which can prevent unauthorized access.

Organizations can use advanced technologies in cloud computing to optimize controlling network traffic. They can filter network traffic to and from resources and subnets in cloud computing networks using various controls. Additionally, cloud computing providers create default routes for local traffic that can be overridden by the organization based on their unique business requirements. They can do this by developing and associating a route table that defines routing rules for managing the network traffic's path inside the subnet.

Cloud computing leaders solicit numerous services that implement analysis and proactive protection by inspecting and filtering traffic at each layer for any potential hacker attempt. They do this by providing automated self-defending network services that include the capability to use AI to optimize threat intelligence and detection.

In summary, trust no user or system, even if it's already trusted in your internal network controls. Secure all connections, including hybrid and multi-cloud, and secure your perimeter. Inspect in a proactive method and improve monitoring by leveraging cloud computing capabilities to streamline automating infrastructure protection.

In the next section, we will describe cloud computing's compute architecture and storage dependencies.

> **Common cloud configuration recommendations**
>
> Segment and secure your network resources by subnetting.
>
> Plan to control ingress and egress network traffic by identifying source-to-destination connectivity requirements.
>
> Cloud computing supports publicly routable endpoints that must be hardened and secured using various monitoring intrusion detection and prevention services that assess the flexibility, agility, and costs for each project before you make a decision.
>
> Utilize defense-in-depth strategies with cloud computing controls at each layer or subnet, including hybrid and multi-cloud networks.

I've included several cloud computing example solutions that reinforce one or more concepts and technologies derived from the previous health and sciences, financial services, and retail industry examples, which are located within this chapter, that correlate with IaaS. The example solutions are defined using **infrastructure as code** (**IaC**) methods and then implemented utilizing each cloud computing leader's API and tooling to streamline creation. The instructions defined in GitHub are high-level and assume working experience. This humble author recommends reviewing the examples at this time but returning later to attempt to develop the solutions after you have read and completed the example labs described in *Chapter 7*.

> **Tip**
>
> IaC facilitates your organization's development teams to automate the implementation of cloud computing resources such as applications, services, and infrastructure consistently and reliably. We will explore IaC in *Chapter 12, Utilizing Management API Tools*.

Please review the files located on GitHub if you wish to review example solutions associated with the common scenarios by industry:

- `https://github.com/PacktPublishing/Cloud-Computing-Demystified-for-Aspiring-Professionals/tree/main/Allfiles/Chapter4/iaasAWSexample`

- `https://github.com/PacktPublishing/Cloud-Computing-Demystified-for-Aspiring-Professionals/tree/main/Allfiles/Chapter4/iaasAZUREexample`

- `https://github.com/PacktPublishing/Cloud-Computing-Demystified-for-Aspiring-Professionals/tree/main/Allfiles/Chapter4/iaasGCPexample`

Compute

In this section, you will learn about the advantages of IaaS compute, as illustrated by leading industry examples. You will also learn helpful tips and potential pitfalls that encumber beginners.

Architectural considerations

Cloud compute planning includes design, and we must consider several key factors.

Compute options

Cloud computing VMs are the cornerstone for IaaS but are not the only resource categorized as compute; others include containers and functions. Compute resources share attributes such as being on-demand and scalable. Additionally, as denoted in the Shared Responsibility Model, customers are not responsible for procuring and maintaining the physical hardware infrastructure. Nevertheless, VMs are IaaS, along with networking and storage disks. As an IaaS resource, VMs provide customers with the greatest flexibility and control. For example, you can deploy whatever software and applications your organization wants, even if the application software is deemed legacy and unsupported in certain modern platforms that require developers to refactor the legacy application before hosting the workload. VMs in the public cloud have many similarities to the traditional on-premises architecture resources concerning administration but with the additional benefits derived from IaaS that promote elasticity, thereby controlling operating costs over on-premises physical and virtual servers.

> **Tip**
> Containers and functions will be explored in *Chapter 5*.

Cloud computing leaders allow you to accelerate creating VM instances using cloud computing APIs and tooling, allowing you to quickly update VM instance features in support of your unique business requirements. This empowers experimentation, which drives innovation. Cloud computing providers Amazon, Microsoft, and Google offer various VM images of Windows and Linux OS, including different performance options categorized into families or a series of varying sizes, and different storage options for VM disks. We will discuss storage disks later in this chapter.

Chapter 8, AWS, Azure, and Google Cloud Platform Compute Details

In *Chapter 8*, I'll elaborate on the cloud compute concepts and configurations in more detail. This chapter should help you understand planning and preparing before implementing compute, and reinforce the common scenarios with industry examples. Every organization, no matter what, must consider compute options, capacity, and scalability before adopting cloud computing.

Scaling compute

As mentioned previously, organizations commonly shift to cloud computing for several business outcomes that serve as the foundation for any transformation. These outcomes include such things as sustainability, global reach, eliminating capital expenditures due to upfront investment in hardware equipment, and some that correspond with core cloud computing principles such as reliability and performance, especially in today's technology-driven landscape, where customers assume services will always be available and always perform well. Scalability is one of the main reasons health and science organizations such as Moderna chose AWS, financial services companies such as PayPal selected GCP, and retailers such as Albertsons chose Microsoft's Azure to meet current growth demands.

Cloud computing providers such as Amazon, Microsoft, and Google provide the flexibility to expand or reduce your IaaS VM dynamically through a variety of features to meet unpredictable changes to customer traffic requests. AWS, Azure, and GCP offer performance metrics and logs, whereby any resource, such as compute, can automatically scale to changes in state and use its elastic features to meet even the most unprecedented demands. Furthermore, this elasticity meets dynamic demands, which can deliver cost savings when demand lessens.

Scaling can be done manually, but it is available by way of autoscaling, which is a service offered by each of the cloud computing platforms. Its main objective is to allocate resources to match performance requirements. Here is a good description of the scaling process: if utilization by traffic load increases, a solution needs more resources to maintain performance levels and adhere to SLAs, so you should scale by increasing capacity or adding more instances. And if utilization decreases, additional instances and resource capacity are terminated to control costs.

Autoscaling takes advantage of the scalability inherent in cloud computing architecture while reducing management operations. It does so by reducing the need for an administrator to continually monitor and configure performance features for services and assist with adding and/or removing infrastructure resources efficiently.

Compute capacity

Monitoring capacity utilization is a best practice on-premises and in cloud computing. Why? Because understanding how your organization's systems and services such as IaaS VMs perform by tracking and recording accurate resource utilization may lead to operational excellence and can optimize costs. Additionally, this logged data can be used to make informed decisions regarding near-real-time and future resource allocation.

All cloud computing technologies generate volumes of logged data, which is typically converted into numeric representations of performance data, also known as metrics and system event logs. Cloud computing providers offer monitoring services that can be used to observe, capture, analyze, and correlate data. For example, you can extrapolate VM metrics or logs in either a centralized or decentralized strategy, and provide methods for batch or stream analysis to gain visibility and insights into optimizing system operations.

After collecting and analyzing the logged data, system administrators can experiment with different compute types, also known as compute sizes, to select a VM instance of the right size to adhere to unique business requirements. These compute types or sizes include CPU core quantities and type, memory sizes, and network performance regarding throughput. Cloud computing leaders have even provided categories based on solutions or workload types to help any industry, no matter how small or large, make an informed decision when allocating compute capacity. For example, a compute-intensive workload, such as a retail industry web application, could be best served by using a specific cloud computing family of VM instances available under one of the many cloud computing categories, such as compute-optimized.

Managing

Organizations that use the public cloud benefit from a wide range of services and tools to efficiently create and manage IaaS, such as VMs. There are many native administrative and developer-friendly resources, including open source tooling, which we expound on in a later chapter. Nevertheless, these tools help organizations implement and maintain services and resources consistently at cloud scale. These tools allow you to automate managing your workload throughout its life cycle.

Furthermore, cloud computing providers such as Amazon, Microsoft, and Google offer a variety of tools for efficiently managing updates and supporting features that can be used in your autoscaled group of VM instances automatically without additional administrative intervention. These APIs and tools improve administration for patching security vulnerabilities, health performance, and updates, which can be orchestrated during slow traffic periods to prevent them from negatively impacting your customers' experience. All things considered, deployment management tools and strategies are essential in cloud computing.

Deploying

As mentioned previously, cloud computing provides a modern alternative to traditional on-premises. Typically, cloud computing providers offer a web-based management portal that streamlines deploying and managing network, compute, and storage disk resources. For example, your organization may use a web-based management portal to provision a VM configuration, commonly specifying the compute capacity (size, also known as type), root volume disk, and network configuration. In the next section, we will elaborate on VM disks in cloud computing.

I have chosen to mention deployment or provisioning because it is part of the IaaS solution's life cycle. However, it's important to note that I will expound on how to deploy cloud computing services by exploring different cloud computing APIs and tools in *Chapter 7*.

The example solutions I have created and deployed to reinforce the concepts covered in this chapter, including the common scenarios by industry, were achieved using cloud computing APIs and tools. In the cloud, you have considerable resources to help deploy solutions efficiently. In this chapter's example solutions, I have elected to create resources using IaC. Each cloud computing provider explored within this tome offers numerous services used in IaC. I will use one or more of the core native tools from AWS and CloudFormation, Azure and ARM templates, and GCP and Cloud Deployment Manager.

By employing AWS CloudFormation templates, I was able to easily create an elastic yet resilient service to support Moderna Therapeutic's growing demands by improving research and distribution with services such as autoscaling and Availability Zones.

Utilizing ARM templates, I was able to streamline deployment to support Albertsons' business requirements by improving scalability and resilience with services such as autoscaling and availability zones.

Lastly, by using Google Cloud Deployment Manager, I was able to accelerate development to support PayPal's customer demands by defining cloud-scaled and highly available services in a repeatable manner.

Monitoring

It's common knowledge that cloud computing reduces the amount of overhead required by customers. Tasks such as managing physical hardware and network media are things of the past. And cloud service models such as PaaS provide hosting services, where customers are not even responsible for managing the guest operating system. However, this does not mean that a customer shouldn't know the health of its services.

Like on-premises, there are a host of issues that can occur, such as host software issues, failed system checks, misconfigurations, exhausted CPU or memory, deviations from instance state, and more. That is why it's important to monitor services and their resources for their availability, performance, and operation even in the cloud.

The cloud includes monitoring capabilities that provide a holistic view of your organization's cloud-scaled digital estate, including extending its analysis abilities to provide visibility in network, hybrid, and multi-cloud architectures using agents, agentless, and SIEM services.

These services collect both system metrics and log files from your IaaS resources. It supports different VM images and enables you to select the specific metric, including its metric dependency, at a fine-grained level.

Events or activities that occur in the cloud are recorded along with any service event. And organizations can view, search, and even download historic or real-time events.

Data science analytics has become the new norm in IT, including in organizations that shift to the cloud. Cloud computing providers offer modern monitoring services that streamline analyzing metrics and logs using powerful charts and graphs. Built-in and add-on **artificial intelligence** (**AI**) services are also leveraged as features in cloud computing monitoring, introducing actionable insights derived from either historic or near-real-time metric values to give small to enterprise businesses the ability to predict how to optimize their cloud services in all facets, including performance, operations, security, reliability, and even optimizing costs by being more cognizant about their resource utilization across the entire enterprise's digital estate.

Common cloud configuration recommendations

Automate vulnerability assessment tools.

Automate operating system patches.

Automate inventory management.

Maintain security configurations.

Centralize management of anti-malware agents or software for all VMs.

Utilize defense-in-depth strategies with cloud computing controls at each layer, including hybrid and multi-cloud compute systems.

Please review the files located on GitHub if you wish to review the example solutions associated with the common scenarios by industry:

- ```
  https://github.com/PacktPublishing/Cloud-Computing-Demystified-
  for-Aspiring-Professionals/tree/main/Allfiles/Chapter4/
  iaasAWSexample
  ```

- ```
  https://github.com/PacktPublishing/Cloud-Computing-Demystified-
  for-Aspiring-Professionals/tree/main/Allfiles/Chapter4/
  iaasAZUREexample
  ```

- ```
  https://github.com/PacktPublishing/Cloud-Computing-Demystified-
  for-Aspiring-Professionals/tree/main/Allfiles/Chapter4/
  iaasGCPexample
  ```
  ```

Storage

In this section, you will learn about the advantages of IaaS storage illustrated by leading industry examples. You will also learn helpful tips and potential pitfalls that encumber beginners.

Architectural considerations

Cloud storage planning includes design, and we must consider several key factors.

Storage disks

In the public cloud, organizations can use durable, detachable, block-level storage, such as your computer's hard drive. But cloud storage disks are for your organization's IaaS VMs. Furthermore, cloud computing leaders offer options such as network or direct-attached storage services, and they can offer low latency between where the data is stored and where it is utilized. All cloud computing disks provide a level of persistence and are resilient, so the cloud-managed disks inherit the benefits of high availability and durability and include geo-redundant options inherent in cloud computing because of the massive, worldwide digital footprint of AWS, Azure, and GCP.

Scaling disk capacity

Public cloud-managed disks are scalable but include cloud provider restrictions by account, region, and type. But the minimal restrictions in the cloud do not prevent you from creating many VM disks in a single account. I may be embellishing a bit, so always review the cloud computing service quota articles that are maintained by the cloud service provider.

Cloud computing providers offer different disk types, such as **HPC** capacity types, wherein types are synonymous with size and performance. Cloud disks support standard hard disks and include **solid-state drives (SSDs)** for optimal performance and varying levels of persistence. Google, Microsoft, and Amazon all offer varying disk types, such as disk types that are best used for medium-sized and development environments, as well as disk types to meet the needs of **input/output (I/O)** intensive solutions that require persistent performance in terms of **input/output operations per second (IOPS)** ratios. This includes disk types for large data processing and long-term storage use. Cloud computing leaders understand the importance of optimizing costs, so they also offer a wide range of affordable disk types.

> Tip
> You should conduct performance tests to ensure the disk performance is sufficient. If it is not, consider aggregating more managed disks to the VM.

Managing disks

Configuring a cloud VM is only the beginning – there are several other factors that you should consider when managing the VM. Factors such as disk scalability, disk resiliency, and disk maintenance are but a few; however, these tasks are some of the most critical administratively. And these administrative management tasks are largely the customer's responsibility, as denoted in the Shared Responsibility Model.

Creating or capturing disk images is the customer's responsibility, so you must plan for this management task. For example, you might want to create several more VMs using the one you created as a template of sorts. This is known as capturing or imaging the VM, or creating a VM image. When you capture a VM image, you capture not only the disk but any additional disks too. Each cloud computing provider has developed platform services that centralize and accelerate this process at cloud scale to optimize the overall imaging process.

Organizations can elect to configure their disks as encrypted, to adhere to different data-at-rest encryption compliance policies. In cloud computing, you can create an encrypted disk and attach it to the VM instance; any data stored on the disk and even image snapshots created from the disk are encrypted. This encryption is handled on the cloud server that hosts the guest VM instance, supporting encryption of data in transit to and from the disk.

Configuring resilient disks

The public cloud offers disk backup and disaster recovery and improves overall business continuity because each cloud computing leader mentioned herein can replicate data through disks to redundant locations using their global infrastructure. Resilient architecture is yet another great reason organizations from industries such as health and science, finance, and retail have elected to migrate some of their most critical workloads to the public cloud.

Whether your organization elects to invest on-premises, in the private cloud, or in the public cloud, ensuring the risk of data loss is minimal to none, and that services and resources are highly available considering real-world situations such as server failures, power outages, and let's not forget unpredictable natural disasters, including pandemics, is a shared responsibility. Cloud computing can help keep your data safe and recoverable by utilizing modern backup services and leveraging best practices derived from the Well-Architected Framework provided by Amazon, Microsoft, and Google.

The cloud computing backup-centric services, including snapshots, provide disk persistence by creating many replicas in different zones or regions, with disk replicas distributed between different locations. Cloud computing disks are highly available resources and can be used in disaster recovery protocols. They not only support a server failure, but if one of the primary clustered data centers fails, the additional disk replicas in a secondary availability zone can be accessed quickly. Ultimately, this improves **service-level agreements (SLAs)**.

> **Common cloud configuration recommendations**
>
> Review disk optimization options.
>
> Measure the performance of your disks.
>
> Factor in your solution's disk performance, I/O, and latency.
>
> Track disk performance using cloud computing monitoring tools and services.

Please review the files located on GitHub if you wish to review the example solutions associated with the common scenarios by industry:

- https://github.com/PacktPublishing/Cloud-Computing-for-Beginners/tree/main/Allfiles/Chapter4/iaasAWSexample

- https://github.com/PacktPublishing/Cloud-Computing-for-Beginners/tree/main/Allfiles/Chapter4/iaasAZUREexample

- https://github.com/PacktPublishing/Cloud-Computing-for-Beginners/tree/main/Allfiles/Chapter4/iaasGCPexample

Sharing responsibility

In this section, you will learn how to describe and understand the cloud computing Shared Responsibility Model.

Shared Responsibility Model

It is very important that each organization, no matter its size, review and come to understand the Shared Responsibility Model in cloud computing. Moreover, you must understand which tasks are managed by the cloud provider and which tasks are managed by the customer. Responsibilities vary, depending on the cloud computing service model, such as IaaS, PaaS, and SaaS, and even then, some services and resources that fall under these categories may include or exclude some administrative tasks, which required any organization to review each cloud computing provider's services and resources in depth to grasp any unique differences in responsibilities. For example, compute resources such as VMs and container services may have subtle similarities in administrative responsibilities to the customer but vary if the container in this context is hosted on either a VM or PaaS resource type.

Whether you choose IaaS or PaaS, the cloud computing leaders are responsible for architecting, procuring, installing, maintaining, and securing the infrastructure that hosts all the services offered in the public cloud. This infrastructure is comprised of the hardware, virtualization software, networking media and devices, and the infrastructure facility utilities and environmental controls.

As mentioned previously, the customer's responsibility will be determined by the cloud computing service they select. This choice determines the amount of work the customer must perform as part of their responsibilities:

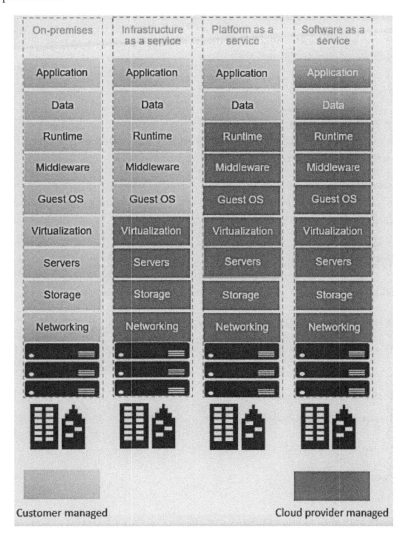

Figure 4.5 – Shared Responsibility Model

IaaS has no upfront costs, and customers only pay for what they consume. The customer is responsible for purchasing, installing, configuring, and managing their application software, systems, middleware, application service, and guest operating system. The cloud computing provider is responsible for ensuring that the underlying cloud infrastructure, such as the hardware infrastructure, including the facility, host VM, and storage and network infrastructure resources, is healthy, secured, and available for the customer.

Please note that the customer is responsible for ensuring the service they are using is configured correctly, up to date, and available to their end users. In brevity, IaaS requires the most user management of all cloud computing service models. The customer is responsible for managing the entire solution, application, data, and operating systems.

In the next chapter, you will learn about the PaaS model and how it has similar benefits and considerations to IaaS, but there are additional advantages.

Summary

In this chapter, you learned about the core IaaS resource type and services, namely the VM instance and its dependencies. You also learned factors to consider when architecting and recommending administration tasks while following well-architected frameworks.

In the next chapter, you will learn how PaaS solutions are implemented. In this chapter, we explored IaaS, but in the next chapter, you will learn how to architect, configure, and manage core platform resource types. You will also learn how to maintain platform services by understanding the Shared Responsibility Model.

Questions

Answer the following questions to test your knowledge of this chapter:

1. What is IaaS?

    A. Infrastructure as a software

    B. Infrastructure anywhere and systems

    C. Infrastructure as a service

    D. Infrastructure API as code

2. Where is IaaS implemented?

    A. Private cloud

    B. Public cloud

    C. Local Linux and Windows hosts

    D. On-premises

3. Which factors should you consider when architecting cloud network services?

    A. Installing network hardware

    B. Internet protocol addressing

    C. Configuring a VLAN

    D. None of the above

4. What governance factor should you consider when storing data?

   A. Tech manufacturer

   B. Internet service provider

   C. Data sovereignty

   D. NoSQL

5. Which statement is true regarding cloud computing IP addressing?

   A. Supports overlapping IP addressing

   B. Does not support overlapping IP addressing

   C. Supports classful IP addressing

   D. None of these options

6. Cloud computing providers manage and do not share responsibility for security in the cloud with customers.

   A. True

   B. False

7. What scaling options are available for cloud computing?

   A. Scale out

   B. Scale in

   C. Scale up

   D. Scale down

8. What do cloud computing monitoring services analyze?

   A. Firmware

   B. Metrics

   C. Voltage

   D. None of the above

9. Which of the following storage hard drives supports cloud devices?

   A. Floppy disk

   B. USB

   C. Solid-state drives

   D. Ephemeral

10. What does the customer manage in IaaS from the Shared Responsibility Model?

    A. Networking hardware

    B. Storage hardware

    C. Virtualization

    D. Guest operating system

Developing Platform Services Using Public Cloud Providers (PaaS)

In this chapter, you will learn how **platform-as-a-service** (**PaaS**) solutions are implemented and how to architect, deploy, and manage services and resources. You will also gain the knowledge required to maintain PaaS resources throughout your workloads' life cycle by understanding the responsibility you share with the cloud provider.

We're going to cover the following main topics in this chapter:

- Cloud computing models
- Common scenarios by industry
- API endpoints
- Platform application services
- Serverless
- Data services
- Sharing responsibility

Cloud computing models

In this section, you will understand the concepts and architectural benefits of platform services.

Responsibilities are shared in the cloud, and learning how this applies to developing and administrating platform services in the cloud is important. These responsibilities or tasks vary and are based on numerous factors, such as regulatory or non-regulatory policies that apply based on industry and geography, and include the cloud computing service you choose to meet your business requirements.

For example, as your organization adopts the cloud, some responsibilities transfer to the cloud computing provider. I'll expound on what the shared responsibility model is in a later section of this chapter—it is very similar for each of the cloud computing leaders, **Amazon**, **Microsoft**, and **Google**.

PaaS

Organizations that choose to use a PaaS typically develop and deploy applications to application architecture. The cloud computing provider supplies the application runtime, storage, and middleware— also known as integration—required to run the customer's application and is responsible for keeping the underlying infrastructure implicitly highly available, patched, scalable, and secure. This disencumbers an organization's developers and administrators from maintaining and managing the cloud infrastructure service resource types, consequently empowering them to accelerate and innovate development.

For example, organizations deploying a simple static website (HTML pages), or even dynamic web applications, utilizing PaaS do not have to download, install, and configure an operating system (OS image, or distro), web server (IIS or Apache), or even manage system updates. So, PaaS is defined as a holistic development and deployment environment, with resources that enable small-to-enterprise organizations with the capability to conveniently implement simple to robust cloud-scaled applications.

Common scenarios by industry

Every industry uses cloud computing, and each organization has unique functional and non-functional requirements and services needed to optimize data, agility, sustainability, or fiscal outcomes.

Business and multimedia

In the last several decades, people from around the world and businesses of all industry types have communicated and collaborated using online channels of communication at an unprecedented rate that emboldens us to create and share information with communities near and far. These communities access and share information using social media services; services are typically online via a website or a desktop or mobile application. Social media has become a cornerstone for communication—not only personal but business communication.

Here are some but not all of the current most popular social media services: **Facebook**, **TikTok**, **Twitter**, **YouTube**, and **Snapchat**.

Snapchat, the multimedia service (or **Snap Inc.**), was developed with the goal of delivering a new, more in-the-moment way of communicating and collaborating using pictures and messages with mobile devices. Snapchat's innovative features have grown the organization's user base exponentially rapidly.

As with many organizations in social media, Snap Inc. must continuously differentiate itself in this competitive market and manage its incredible growth in terms of its user base and nuanced service features.

The initial solution was clear—adopt cloud computing. Snap Inc. unraveled problems that impact any social media service in today's market—that is, managing a large set of services and features efficiently.

Snap Inc. partnered with Amazon and utilized its PaaS, **Elastic Kubernetes Service** (**EKS**), to help them manage more than 2 million transactions per second. Snap Inc. was able to reduce development costs associated with delivering new services and features.

Travel and transportation

Transportation services are critical to any industry, especially freight services. Freight services, also referred to as shipping, involve transporting freight by truck, train, ship, and plane. Supply chain services and logistics are required in the travel and transportation industry, and organizations such as **Maersk** have been delivering transportation and logistics services to meet customers' needs from every spectrum of the supply chain through global **end-to-end** (**E2E**) solutions.

Companies such as Maersk have adopted cloud computing to continue their digital transformation journey. Emerging technologies have played a key role in cloud integration. Maersk has embraced technologies that are capable of accelerating engineering innovation and that are also able to decrease administrative management tasks.

Considering the organization's cloud adoption objectives, Maersk elected to utilize PaaS cloud services such as Microsoft's **Azure Kubernetes Service** (**AKS**) to optimize managing its applications.

In a later section within this chapter, titled *Kubernetes*, we will explore the Kubernetes PaaS and provide a Microsoft AKS workload example used by Maersk.

Travel and hospitality

Emerging technologies and services such as cloud computing are also playing an increasing role in the hospitality service and, by extension, meal services, and goods and services such as pizza delivery are as commonplace globally as the air one breathes. When one considers practical applications where cloud computing has delivered "pun intended" solutions that touch not only businesses but our personal lives, many would agree that pizza stands out.

There have been many changes over the years that have defined how a consumer wants a good or service, such as pizza, and because of these changes, organizations such as **Pizza Hut** must stay competitive and agile by offering cutting-edge features across multiple platforms and devices.

Pizza Hut partnered with **Google Cloud Platform** (**GCP**) and chose a PaaS that improved their developer's capability to innovate quickly by using managed orchestration container services such as **Google Kubernetes Engine** (**GKE**).

In the *Kubernetes* section within this chapter, we will explore the Kubernetes PaaS and provide a GKE workload example used by Pizza Hut.

API endpoints

In this section, you will learn about **APIs** and **endpoints**. You will also learn helpful tips and potential pitfalls that encumber beginners.

Almost every individual and business on this planet has used or interacted with an API, but many don't know what it is or how it's part of our daily lives. For example, most mobile applications call APIs, and the API in turn calls a service, and then the service sends the calling mobile application whichever data the end user requested.

In a previous chapter, we discussed cloud computing's distributed nature and how its API architecture is based on design principles established in **service-oriented architecture** (**SOA**) strategies. Simply put, SOA is a way to design a distributed system or service where the services autonomously labor by sending data using specified contracts, also known in this context as API interfaces.

Allow me to preface this with the subtle similarities of APIs and middleware, but APIs will be our focus. If you reviewed the **shared responsibility model** in *Chapter 4*, you may have noticed a row across all columns that listed middleware. Well, both middleware and APIs are used to integrate systems and services. Middleware uses APIs and supports the extended capability and flexibility of isolated and non-isolated systems, thereby supporting complex service integration, while APIs are far simpler but more powerful.

Let's start by explaining what an API is first. **API** stands for **application programming interface**. An API is software that enables systems and services to communicate with each other. To elaborate, APIs are made up of different parts that act as a client and server, also referred to as the client and services. APIs interface with software libraries, which is why you may have researched C# or Python APIs when trying to use software on your computer or mobile device to interact with online services from cloud computing providers such as Amazon, Microsoft, and Google. So, the term *API* is used loosely because it correlates with different components.

To clarify any ambiguity, we are not referring to end user graphical interfaces that are mistakenly called APIs—that is a misconception. However, when end users interact with websites, a web API is an interface between a web server and the end user's client also known as a web browser, such as **Google Chrome** or **Microsoft Edge**.

The client and server in this API architecture require an interface; think of it as a contract between two systems or services. Remember—APIs are software, so the services are applications and so too is the client: yes, your browser. Back to the contract, the interface also known as a contract is a description of each method exposed from the service. This contract defines how the client and service communicate. For example, let's consider the travel industry—say, *Delta Air Lines*. My Delta Air Lines mobile application is the client, and the Delta Air Lines database is the API server or service in this client and service example. If I use my mobile app/client, then my client application makes API calls to the service methods exposed by Delta Air Lines defined in the interface contract.

In detail, services such as cloud computing and their clients communicate with each other by agreeing through an interface known as a contract. Understanding the notion of an interface is key to APIs. API will begin with defining a set of interface types that are used to represent a set of member methods for a given exposed service. APIs include an address, bindings, and contracts, wherein *address* describes the location of the service, commonly denoted as a URI or endpoint (we'll come back to this shortly), *bindings* specify network protocols, and *contracts define* the method exposed from the service.

The API must specify a binding used by callers to gain access to the service and its functionality. Various attributes can be adorned on public member methods of interfaces, such as by using **representational state transfer** (**REST**), which defines a set of methods, also known as functions—such as GET, PUT, and POST—that a client can use to access the exposed service or server.

Once you establish the contracts and bindings, the last component is to specify an address for the service. The client application or caller must be able to communicate with the remote service, and while it's common for a service to be singular, it is possible for a collection of unique addresses with similar or different bindings to exist. The term *endpoint* represents the address, binding, and contract together. Endpoints are expressed using URLs or URIs, services, and other online locations from where information is sent and received between systems and services.

> **APIs are everywhere!**
>
> An API is sometimes used to refer to software programming languages, libraries, packages, and even operating systems because it is software.

Cloud computing acts as a collection of services and resources designed to support the simple but agile use of cloud resources on-demand from anywhere, and above this collection is the Amazon, Microsoft, and Google APIs. Cloud computing APIs are a way for users to interact or interface with services and, by extension, deploy and manage resources. For example, if you use the GCP or Microsoft Azure portal or the **Amazon Web Services** (**AWS**) management portal, including their **command-line interfaces** (**CLIs**) or **software development kits** (**SDKs**), you are using clients (tools) that make API calls to the cloud computing API endpoints.

> **REST API**
>
> Remote APIs such as REST let software engineers, better known as developers, manage remote resources using communication protocols that permit different services, programming languages (**Python and C#**), and platforms to work together. REST and web APIs are useful in managing the abstraction in programming a service by invoking or calling a function or method (action) on the remote service and/or resource, such as creating an Azure **Virtual Machine** (**VM**) instance, or creating a GCP Private Service Connect endpoint. REST defines functions or methods using GET, PUT, POST, and so on.

Here's an example:

```
POST https://compute.googleapis.com/compute/v1/projects/
PROJECT_ID/global/addresses

{
"name": ADDRESS_NAME,
"address": ENDPOINT_IP,
"addressType": "INTERNAL",
"purpose": PRIVATE_SERVICE_CONNECT,
"network": NETWORK_URL
}
```

We will now look at some architectural considerations.

Architectural considerations

PaaS design is as important as IaaS architectural design—granted, there are fewer responsibilities, but it is crucial to plan and prepare availability, accessibility, and overall security.

Architecting services requires organizations to consider important factors, such as how cloud computing services can integrate with cloud network (**virtual private cloud** (**VPC**) or **virtual network** (**VNet**))-dependent resources securely and without impacting interoperability and performance. And because almost every cloud service offers a public endpoint, organizations share responsibility with the cloud provider to harden or secure accessibility. Cloud computing providers have answered the call by offering private access to these public service endpoints bidirectionally from cloud networks, whether all in the cloud or in a hybrid cloud architecture.

All of this is possible because of cloud computing's distributed API architecture!

The following is an AWS service endpoint architectural example for a cloud computing API:

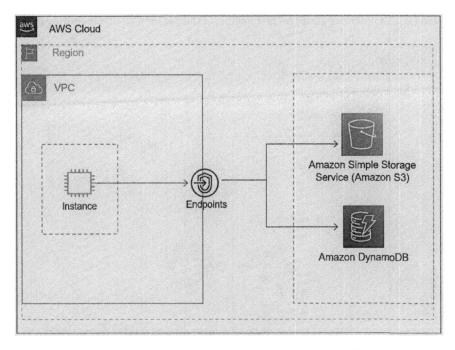

Figure 5.1 – AWS interface VPC endpoints (PrivateLink)

The following is an Azure service endpoint architectural example for a cloud computing API:

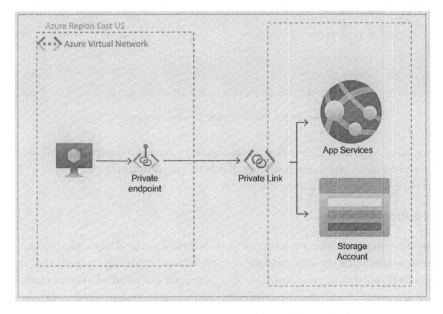

Figure 5.2 – Azure VNet private endpoint (PrivateLink)

The following is a GCP service endpoint architectural example for a cloud computing API:

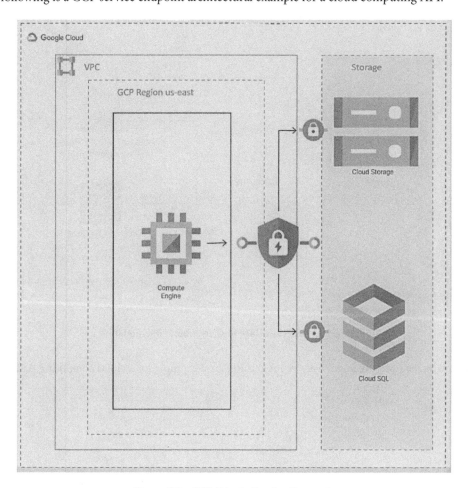

Figure 5.3 – GCP Private Service Connect

Cloud computing API endpoints are key in transitioning to cloud computing and the inevitable evolution toward a microservices architecture. But before we discuss this, let us review the security advantages of private endpoint access.

Private endpoint access

Cloud computing providers offer service access options that allow cloud-networked resources such as VM instances to communicate with endpoint services without requiring an external domain name, URI address, or IP address. In other words, your organization can create and utilize platform service endpoints using private IP addresses that you define and that are internal to your organization's cloud ecosystem of services and networks (VPC and VNet).

Cloud computing leaders offer the following services with some similarities but subtle differences in terms of service conditions:

- AWS offers a VPC endpoint service, with a variety of features that support connections between VPC and cloud services. At the core of this resource is the **PrivateLink** service, which enables organizations to configure private connection access to partner networks and also hybrid networks. PrivateLink is a fully managed, scalable, and implicitly highly available AWS service.

- Microsoft Azure provides a private endpoint service or interface that connects you privately to platform services—for example, connecting one or more VM instances hosting your organization's client applications to a destination such as Azure Storage services, such as **Blob Storage**. And Microsoft Azure Private Link extends the benefits and features of private endpoints by supporting private access to on-premises, peered networks, and even to cloud services hosted in different regions.

- GCP offers **Private Service Connect**, a service that allows private access to Google services from VPCs, whether the service is managed in a different project or even hosted in another business partner's organization. Private Service Connect supports global private IP addresses, configurable domain names, and network hybrid architectures, which include interconnecting on-premises enterprise networks.

Domain names

It is very important that your organization plans and configures domain names to private endpoint services to ensure the address resembles your unique application's endpoint. All cloud providers generate domain names that you can use to communicate with a service. However, for some cloud computing services, the provider allows you to configure a private **Domain Name System** (**DNS**) name to access the service using a preexisting domain name that your organization owns and operates. This way, you do not have to change the application's configuration.

Security

On-premises IT responsibilities such as securing your hardware and virtual infrastructure have changed after migrating to the cloud. However, organizations undergoing a digital transformation as it relates to cloud adoption should be aware of the additional potential vulnerabilities when adopting public and private cloud services.

One of the many strategies adopted by cloud computing leaders is the zero-trust model, which recommends you verify each user or system and the condition of the request. This model is an additional control plane to your network controls.

Careful planning, configuration, and management of your cloud services form the core of how you provide secure access to services efficiently. PaaS does not depend on a customer-developed network such as a VPC or VNet. However, these networks provide, by default, privacy and boundaries, which help secure E2E service connections.

Cloud system administrators can filter network traffic to and from platform services connected privately to cloud computing networks using various cloud computing network controls, such as AWS security groups, Azure network security groups, and GCP network endpoint groups. Furthermore, organizations should use best practices from strategies such as **defense-in-depth** (**DiD**), which advocates applying a layered security approach for both ingress and egress traffic.

Amazon, Microsoft, and Google offer numerous services that proactively analyze and protect by inspecting and either recommending or automatically mitigating the anti-pattern or configuration error of the platform service. For example, you mistakenly configured an Amazon **Simple Storage Service** (**S3**) service as publicly available! AWS immediately warns you by notification and describes the potential risks.

> **Common cloud configuration recommendations**
>
> Segment and secure your network resources by subnetting.
>
> Plan to control ingress and egress network traffic by identifying source-to-destination connectivity requirements.

Now that we have explored endpoint services and their security benefits, we can describe and learn about the platform application services accessible via the endpoints.

Platform application services

In this section, you will learn the advantages of PaaS application services and resources, illustrated by leading industry examples. You will also learn helpful tips and potential pitfalls that encumber beginners.

Architectural considerations

Cloud platform application management service planning includes design, and we must consider several key factors.

Platform services

Cloud computing platform services are resources designed to help users focus on application development, while infrastructure service administration is handled by the cloud computing provider. For example, platform services improve agility more than **infrastructure as a service** (**IaaS**) because your organization does not need to configure and manage the underlying VM compute service resources, such as hardening or securing the operating system image throughout the application's life cycle.

Cloud computing providers Amazon, Microsoft, and Google offer various platform services, and they are categorized to simplify research, with categories such as *compute*, *containers*, *storage*, and *database*. They include other categories such as *analytics*, *integration*, and *IoT*, and that's only scratching the surface. It's incredible to behold. For example, researching compute services not only leads consumers to view VM services and their resource dependencies, but also displays platform services such as **AWS Elastic Beanstalk**, **Microsot's Azure App Service**, or **Google App Engine**, and these services help organizations efficiently deploy developed applications and their environment with less operational overhead than using IaaS VMs.

> **Tip**
>
> Detailed information on implementing web applications utilizing Elastic Beanstalk, App Service, and App Engine is provided in *Chapter 8*.

Here are some but not all of the most popular platform services. You'll notice similarities across these products, even if the service is hosted by a different cloud computing provider. *How?* you wonder. Because they are platform services.

Elastic Beanstalk

In an era defined by accelerated innovation, organizations of varying industries are required to excite and improve customer experiences through iterative feedback that permits small-to-large businesses to deliver value! Cloud computing has not only supported these principles but also set the standard by helping organizations such as Snapchat, Maersk, and Pizza Hut with services they can use to quickly deploy and manage applications in the cloud, without concerns regarding the infrastructure services that host the application.

Organizations today need to repeat the same configuration steps to create application environments in production; however, manual configuration can potentially be error-prone, and frequently administrators and developers will need to apply the same configuration that they labored on in development and quality environments to production. There also may be numerous environments created and then destroyed during stress testing and functional testing application environments—this is before creating and then staging a production-ready environment. So, to recreate the same solution, you will need a way to define, automate, and duplicate efficiently the application environment.

Earlier in this book, I mentioned **infrastructure as code (IaC)**, and in the cloud, this is an appropriate approach. Some services are uniquely capable of delivering IaC methods. These services include—but are not limited to—**AWS CloudFormation templates**, Microsoft **Azure Resource Manager (ARM) templates**, and **GCP Deployment Manager**. Combined with platform services, not only are you able to optimize the environment configuration and application deployment process, but platform services also inherently utilize and improve IaC tools and methods to bolster reproducibility, and provide a developer-friendly user interface for those who are not yet comfortable with JSON or YAML configuration files. And while some developers can do it themselves using cloud computing-native SDKs that provide cloud APIs to help newcomers build constructs (software) that interact programmatically with existing cloud API endpoints in an efficient way, it is the simplicity of using platform services such as AWS Elastic Beanstalk, Microsoft Azure App Service, or GCP App Engine that decreases administration complexity without limiting the controls required by any organization to adhere to their unique application environment goals.

Platform services such as Elastic Beanstalk drive customers to adopt cloud computing. Elastic Beanstalk is all the buzz in social media. Why? Because enthusiasts read about or listen to news of application development agility, elasticity, driving costs down, and so on. It is platform services such as Elastic Beanstalk that are easy to use and build web applications with popular source code or container images of **Python**, **.NET**, **Node.js**, **PHP**, **Java**, **Docker**, and more. For example, if you want to upload your code and don't need to further customize the runtime environment or operating system files, Elastic Beanstalk will not just meet but exceed your expectations.

> **Note**
>
> Detailed information on implementing web applications utilizing Elastic Beanstalk, App Service, and App Engine is provided in *Chapter 8*.

Platform services such as Elastic Beanstalk can be used in different facets of application deployment management, such as infrastructure deployment, code management, application deployment, and container or runtime implementation.

The best practices documented in Amazon's Well-Architected Framework make it clear that Elastic Beanstalk has strong requirements for the way an application is designed. For example, Elastic Beanstalk is best utilized when designing an *n*-tier application architecture.

> **Tip**
>
> The *n* in *n*-tier refers to many—for example, two- or three-tier can be denoted as *n*-tier. Two-tier architectures are referring to two parts, where part one is the presentation, and part two is the business logic coupled with data access—for brevity, in layman's terms, a website and application program such as Python, and data in a database in separate tiers, where the tier represents a system or service in this context.

Additionally, Elastic Beanstalk deploys only to Amazon **Elastic Compute Cloud** (**EC2**) instances, which are VMs that are restricted from deploying to external service resources such as multi-cloud or hybrid architectures, which include on-premises servers.

As with most platform services, Elastic Beanstalk inherits cloud computing benefits associated with platform services, where services automatically handle all the details such as compute implementation, load distribution by load balancing, scaling, and built-in monitoring features designed to be developer friendly. Essentially, Elastic Beanstalk configures the infrastructure environment required to host your organization's application and resources based on your development stack.

> **Common cloud configuration recommendations**
>
> Review your application's key performance metrics—for example, throughput, latency, and so on.
>
> Stress-test your application by scaling incrementally to see how it performs under increased load.

As with AWS, Microsoft Azure provides an application platform service.

App Service

Microsoft Azure App Service helps organizations build, host, and manage web applications, mobile application backends, and custom APIs, and supports resource integration without having to manage the underpinning infrastructure services. Developers can build in their favorite programming languages, such as .NET, .NET Core, Python, Node.js, Ruby, and Java. You'll notice many similarities between App Service and Elastic Beanstalk because of their primary purpose, which is to simplify creating application-hosting environments.

As a platform service, Azure's App Service inherits built-in security and load distribution by load balancing and scaling, and Microsoft manages the underlying infrastructure. Additionally, Azure's App Service gets the added benefit of its DevOps features, such as **continuous deployment (CD)** from external services, and Docker Hub, Azure's DevOps service, including GitHub.

IInsight

Insight: Docker Hub is a developer resource where you can easily create, manage, and deploy container applications. Find out more at `https://hub.docker.com`.

Insight: GitHub is another developer open source resource where you create and manage repositories of code and share them with a vast developer community. Go to `https://github.com` to find out more.

Insight: Azure DevOps is a Microsoft online service where you can plan, collaborate, and leverage agile tools, **continuous integration (CI)** and **continuous delivery** services, and numerous more features to improve software delivery. For more information, go to `https://dev.azure.com`.

As with most platform services, App Service manages the built-in runtime environments of its underlying infrastructure. Platform services use the latest and greatest modern technologies, including application runtimes. Because of this, outdated runtimes are deprecated, but for good reason, if you understand that older runtimes have a greater potential for exhibiting vulnerabilities. Nevertheless, older runtimes are not supported in many cases. Remember—using the latest runtime is a security best practice; eventually, your organization will have to absorb the costs incurred to upgrade to the latest runtime version. Considering this, some organizations that support legacy application runtimes elect to use IaaS, where they can configure the underlying operating system to continue supporting the older application.

Tip

If the application runtime is not supported in App Service, you can deploy it with a container.

Additionally, platform services such as App Service support running scripts and executables, such as Microsoft PowerShell or Linux shell, also known as Bash shell. These scripts or executables can be configured during or post-deployment to further customize the application environment.

> **Tip**
>
> Detailed information on implementing web applications utilizing Elastic Beanstalk, App Service, and App Engine is provided in *Chapter 8*.

As with Azure, Google Cloud provides an application platform service.

App Engine

Google Cloud's App Engine is yet another platform service that is fully managed by Google and, as with Amazon's Elastic Beanstalk and Microsoft's App Service, it greatly simplifies developing and deploying applications and their environments.

As with the other cloud providers, GCP's App Engine provides standard and flexible options that allow your services to benefit from either offering. App Engine is also best used with application architectures that embrace the microservices approach instead of the *n*-tier architecture that is recommended for Microsoft Azure's App Service or AWS's Elastic Beanstalk, although both Microsoft and Amazon support containers. However, Google's App Engine provides a flexible environment that runs Docker containers on its IaaS Compute Engine VMs that you can still manage by remote access, but it is not the default.

> **Caveats**
>
> While Google offers a more flexible environment, it currently has many factors an organization must consider in terms of scale and availability if one decides to use the flexible option, but it includes supporting legacy runtimes by way of containers.

One more thing—these platform services are secure. Amazon, Microsoft, and Google's application environment deployment services adhere to numerous security and compliance controls such as **International Organization for Standardization** (**ISO**), **System and Organization Controls** (**SOC**), **Payment Card Industry** (**PCI**) security standards, and more. And let's not forget, Google, Microsoft, and Amazon provide best-in-class security features such as **identity and access management** (**IAM**) resources (for example, Microsoft's Active Directory) and support **multi-factor authentication** (**MFA**) with **single sign-on** (**SSO**) support from **identity providers** (**IdPs**) such as Facebook, Apple, and Google, whether your organization elects to use Microsoft Azure's App Service, AWS Elastic Beanstalk, or GCP's App Engine.

All these mentions of extending platform services to either support a microservices architecture or ensure legacy applications can run anywhere using containers leads us to a well-known resource: Kubernetes.

Kubernetes

Infrastructure deployment and configuration have evolved from the traditional on-premises hardware installation to automating the implementation on-premises using virtualization services, to accelerating infrastructure configuration and automation using cloud computing services. There is a trend here: to simplify by abstracting repetitive manual administrative tasks that have a greater potential for human error.

Automation and virtualization are included in different facets of deploying and managing our evolving environments, and new approaches are being discovered. Enterprise-level workloads require agility, so we learn to quickly start a new instance with Docker containers. And embracing open source resources that support the CI and CD of environments, which have transformed them from VMs to containers, frees us to focus on what matters most. Many would agree that Kubernetes is one of the services driving open source adoption.

Kubernetes is an open source orchestrator for distributing Docker containerized applications, and Kubernetes provides the services through which you interact with your cluster. Utilizing Kubernetes commands and services empowers your organization with the capability to automate the deployment and configuration management of your containerized applications, referred to as workloads.

Kubernetes is one of the most widely used open source resources in cloud computing today. It's a mature and reliable infrastructure orchestrator, especially for microservice workloads, which is the evolution of distributed systems, and it's practical for all-in-cloud and hybrid-cloud development. Furthermore, Kubernetes improves the speed or velocity at which you can deploy new services because of tenets such as immutability, declarative configuration, self-healing, and decoupling by defined APIs and service load balancers, and consequently, when you need to scale your service, Kubernetes' immutable and decoupled characteristics streamline scaling. Consider that Docker containers are immutable, and the number of containers is simply a declarative configuration value, denoted as a number. So, scaling your solution is done by changing that number value in the file—that's if you don't want to use autoscaling!

However, when considering scaling, one assumes that there is enough capacity in the cluster to support your request. While Kubernetes makes this administrative task simple, as aforementioned we are always striving to evolve and, by extension, further abstract underlying components and tasks.

Cloud computing provides that alternative—a way to optimize deploying and managing Kubernetes clusters by shifting the operational overhead to Amazon, Microsoft, and Google. As a cloud-scaled platform service, cloud computing leaders handle critical tasks, such as overall cluster health and maintenance.

Cloud computing providers offer numerous deployment options for Kubernetes; however, I will elaborate on the fully managed service that you can use to run Kubernetes on the public cloud without manually having to install, operate, and maintain your own Kubernetes cluster of nodes.

AWS's EKS is a managed service that organizations can utilize to deploy and maintain Kubernetes nodes. Amazon runs and scales the Kubernetes cluster across multiple fault-tolerant zones to improve reliability.

Amazon's EKS can detect and replace unhealthy nodes, and the managed service includes load balancers to handle distribution. Additionally, EKS integrates with Amazon's **Elastic Container Registry (ECR)**, a Docker container image repository, leverages Amazon's authentication services that optimize IAM for better security, and supports DiD by providing isolation using Amazon's VPC services.

As with Amazon EKS, Microsoft's AKS is a managed service that customers can use to deploy and maintain Kubernetes clusters at a cloud scale. Microsoft runs and scales the Kubernetes cluster, improving site reliability and performance.

GKE is a fully managed service that empowers developers to use simple interfaces and APIs to orchestrate container management at a global scale. Google Cloud manages and maintains the Kubernetes cluster across the globe, improving reliability by providing geo-redundant and zone-redundant availability options, which may not be feasible for some small start-up organizations.

This book includes cloud computing examples that reinforce the common scenarios by industry. The instructions are located and defined in GitHub but are high-level and assume working experience.

The recommendation is to return after you have read and successfully completed the example labs described in *Chapters 7 to 11*:

- `https://github.com/PacktPublishing/ Cloud-Computing-Demystified-for-Aspiring-Professionals /tree/main/Allfiles/Chapter5/ paasAWSexample`

- `https://github.com/PacktPublishing/ Cloud-Computing-Demystified-for-Aspiring-Professionals /tree/main/Allfiles/Chapter5/ paasAZUREexample`

- `https://github.com/PacktPublishing/Cloud-Computing-Demystified-for-Aspiring-Professionals/tree/main/Allfiles/Chapter5/ paasGCPexample`

Platform services are inherently highly available, but what can we expect from our provider? Let's review **service-level agreements (SLAs)**.

Built-in high availability and elasticity

Organizations typically shift to cloud computing for several business outcomes that serve as a justification for transformation. This includes such things as sustainability, agility, and fiscal and data democratization, and corresponds with cloud computing tenets such as reliability and performance, especially in today's technology-driven landscape, where customers assume services are highly available by default.

SLA

Cloud computing providers such as Amazon, Microsoft, and Google provide **high availability** (**HA**) implicitly for cloud services. Availability refers to the level of service that the PaaS type provides to customers and their end users, and it's expressed as the percentage of time that a service is available. Platform services are highly available and have minimal downtime, whether planned or unplanned, and each service has a unique SLA documented and shared by the cloud computing provider.

Every customer should understand availability expectations due to their impact on the overall operations of any workload. For example, if a start-up organization wants to gain a workload SLA of 99.99%, the level of operational configuration required by the workload is far greater than if the SLA desired was 99.9%.

It's key for any business, no matter the motivation to adopt the cloud, to define its unique target SLA for the holistic solution so that it can then decide whether the service and its default SLA are based on data center rack level, zonal, regional, and global redundancy, and service scalability features and limits.

The cloud computing leaders provide online articles that address all our concerns regarding service and accounts limits and quotas:

- `https://docs.aws.amazon.com/servicequotas/index.html`
- `https://docs.microsoft.com/en-us/azure/azure-resource-manager/management/azure-subscription-service-limits`
- `https://cloud.google.com/service-usage/docs/overview`

PaaS is inherently redundant, but what is redundancy? Let us explore this further.

Redundancy

Assessing capacity and SLA requirements is a best practice on-premises and in cloud computing. Why? Because understanding how your organization's services such as PaaS perform by tracking and recording accurate resource utilization improves performance and controls cost.

Additionally, organizations should consider what transpires when combining SLAs because multiple services are supporting your solution, and remember—each service has a different level of availability, and the potential of each service failing is independent of the combined SLA. But the combined SLA is lower than the individual SLA. Why? Because it has more potential failure points. So, redundancy is key; duplication of services can improve the combined SLA by creating a contingency.

Therefore, cloud computing leaders list not only the SLA for each service but also whether the service is highly available globally, regionally, or intra-zone. As aforementioned in *Chapter 3*, the public cloud global infrastructure hosts its services and resources in multiple locations around the world, and these locations—which are better known as regions and zones—not only provide isolation from infrastructure failures, but placing resources in different zones or regions provides an even higher availability by designing redundant distributed services across either multiple zones or regions.

As an example, multi-region implementations allow organizations to deploy workloads in more than one region and use various global traffic distribution services such as DNS or global load balancers to fail over if the workload fails in one region.

Vertical scaling

Platform services such as Amazon's Elastic Beanstalk or GKE automatically adjust the capacity (CPU) for a service to a larger or smaller size befitting the service's needs based on **key performance indicator** (**KPI**) metric utilization values. This is known as vertical scaling, and some cloud computing services support manual and automatic vertical scaling.

Horizontal scaling

Additionally, some platform services automatically scale the number of workloads or resources by creating copies of the resource, also referred to as creating instances, such as autoscaling VMs, thereby creating VM instances. Platform services can also either manually scale or automate scaling based on KPIs that you define. This method can help not only meet increased utilization demands, but if the service scales its workload or resources across different **availability zones** (**AZs**) or regions, it can potentially improve the availability of that service, thus increasing the service's SLA. For example, if you scale the service horizontally across at minimum two zones, behind a built-in load balancer, if one zone inside a region fails, you still have the other instance of the service hosted in the other zone. Another example: if the single zone or zonal service SLA is 99.95%, then the combined SLA for two zones equals 99.9999%.

Managing

Organizations that use the public cloud benefit from a wide range of services and tools to efficiently manage PaaS, such as Microsoft Azure App Service. There are many native administrative and developer-friendly resources, and these tools help organizations implement and maintain services at a cloud scale and allow them to automate managing their workload throughout the application's life cycle.

> Tip
>
> IaC helps your organization's development teams to automate the implementation of cloud computing resources such as applications, services, and infrastructure consistently and reliably. We will explore IaC in *Chapter 12*.

Diagnostics

Administrative tasks such as managing infrastructure storage, network devices, cabling, and racking and stacking physical server blades are a thing of the past for organizations that have adopted the public cloud, and based on the type of service one procures, such as a PaaS, customers are not even responsible for managing the VM guest operating system. However, this does not mean that a customer does not need to view the health of its services.

As with on-premises, many problems can potentially occur: misconfigurations, exhausting selected capacity, and more. That is why it's important to monitor services and their resources, even in the cloud.

Cloud computing providers Microsoft, Amazon, and Google offer monitoring services that centralize analyzing your digital estate, including extending its varying analysis capabilities to provide visibility into private, hybrid, and multi-cloud services.

These powerful monitoring services ingest metrics and logs from your platform resources and support selecting custom, more granular metrics, including any dependencies. All activities or interactions with your digital estate are recorded, and organizations can view, search, and even elect to share this data with third-party auditors to meet compliance requirements.

Artificial intelligence (**AI**) services are also leveraged as features in cloud computing monitoring, introducing actionable insights derived from either historic or near-real-time metric values and giving small-to-enterprise businesses the capability to predict how to optimize their cloud services in all facets, such as performance, operations, security, reliability, and even optimizing costs by being more cognizant about one's resource utilization across the entire enterprise's digital estate.

> **Common cloud configuration recommendations**
>
> Disable anonymous access requests to any API unless it's a business requirement.
>
> Enforce authentication by either manual application configuration or streamlining authentication using built-in IAM services.
>
> Secure backend services with IAM services and authenticate applications to a backend service, such as Amazon's DynamoDB, Microsoft Cosmos DB, Google Cloud Spanner, and so on.

Innovation leads platform services driven by SOAs to the inevitable microservices architecture where serverless is prevalent.

Serverless

In this section, you will learn the advantages of serverless function platform services. You will also learn helpful tips and potential pitfalls that encumber beginners.

Architectural considerations

Cloud serverless planning includes design, and we must consider several key factors.

Serverless services

In cloud computing, serverless is a type of resource that removes all infrastructure service operations, thus facilitating the software engineering experience. Cloud computing leaders provide many services for running code, managing data, integrating APIs, and more, without the need for manual administration of infrastructure services such as the underlying VM instance or underlying container host. While many new buzzwords such as **functions as a service (FaaS)** are here today but gone tomorrow, serverless technologies belong under the PaaS category. Serverless services inherit cloud computing's reliability features such as automatic scaling and native HA while removing infrastructure operations so that organizations can focus on developing better solutions to delight customers.

Functions

What if you could write code and simply upload the code, and then invoke the code to do anything? That's right: anything. I have your attention now—no, I am not embellishing. If I were using Python or .NET—well, almost any programming language—it is an agnostic environment, and I could easily copy and paste code into an online editor and then simply test the code, and finally publish the code and allow the magic of programming to do anything. Yes—it is that simple: for example, build a backend to process mobile API requests for iOS and Android devices. Imagine a touchless soda fountain dispenser—upon sensing your presence, an event is invoked that ignites your organization's code (also known as software) and its actions (also known as functions or methods in this context) to dispense delicious *Coca-Cola*. This is one of the many practical applications for serverless resource types known as functions. As COVID-19 shook the world to its core, organizations such as Coca-Cola continued innovating to help humanity in one of its worst moments to dispense beverages more safely by providing a touchless beverage experience.

The following is a serverless function example—a timer function:

```
def main(mytimer: func.TimerRequest) -> None:
    utc_timestamp = datetime.datetime.utcnow().replace(
        tzinfo=datetime.timezone.utc).isoformat()

    if mytimer.past_due:
        logging.info('The timer is past due!')

    logging.info('Python timer trigger function ran at %s',
utc_timestamp)
```

GCP, Microsoft Azure, and AWS offer serverless because they understand and even utilize APIs like functions to automatically validate policies and perform scripted automation tasks using functions that can be invoked by any event. Functions listen for events in private, public, hybrid, and multi-cloud architectures, and if coupled with other serverless resources, they can distribute events, addressing some of the most complex business requirements no matter the industry. And if the cloud computing leaders see a value in this and offer services that are the next step in the evolution from containers, then pivot, I say: drive evolution forward by using serverless technologies.

One of the most typical challenges is transitioning from a monolithic on-premises service to the cloud, especially to serverless. So, many organizations adopt an IaaS VM because of its familiarity. However, some organizations take advantage of this transitional period and modernize their application.

However, there will always be obstacles, as with all architectural decisions; implementing serverless should be done with careful consideration and planning.

Many serverless technologies do not support state data, but it makes serverless more resilient when it comes to scaling and there is no central point of failure. But if you do need state, then consider embracing a model that isn't serverless, such as Elastic Beanstalk, App Engine, or App Service.

Architecturally, you can design temporary platform data services to store state data, and cloud providers include additional serverless resources that provide support for state data but at a premium, with some constraints to performance in contrast to the typical functions.

Other factors to consider include the following:

- Functions are limited in terms of time allotted for running code
- Potential delays to startup due to the service being idle awaiting the event

Cloud computing providers' serverless platforms include more than functions. These serverless services have the capability to work together and integrate with other platform services from object-level storage types to **Structured Query Language** (**SQL**) or even NoSQL databases. And serverless is used in an array of big data solutions, from analyzing to feature engineering large volumes of ingested data for both batch and stream processing.

Whether it is a customer-developed cloud-hosted API, an application hosting resource, or a serverless resource type, data is either derived as is or is transformed before or after using **extract, transform, and load** (**ETL**) or **extract, load, and transform** (**ELT**) methods. So, it begs the question: *Which data type and service can be optimized in cloud computing?* But first, the data structure.

Data services

In this section, you will learn how to describe and differentiate object-level, relational, and non-relational data types by data structure and the advantages of cloud data PaaS. You will also learn helpful tips and potential pitfalls that encumber beginners.

Architectural considerations

Cloud data planning includes design, and we must consider several key factors.

Data structure

When it comes to managing data, you might agree the best method to employ is a suite of services that are optimized for their objective. Traditionally, most organizations made mistakes when setting up data storage by using only one solution—typically a SQL Server platform to handle most data storage scenarios. Although SQL Server and its distributors provide a superior product, this may not be the right tool for the job in question. A better solution may be a combination of data management services.

Many organizations going through data transformation will still use traditional tools and roles, but this is a mistake. Why? Because data structures or types are constantly changing, so we must classify the data to best serve or handle it in a performant and cost-effective way. Numerous formats of data are used in practical applications every day, including text, streaming data, video, audio, metadata, structured data, semi-structured data, and unstructured data.

Additionally, a quick and easy "lift and shift" to the cloud in the foreseeable future may not be enough to continue innovation in a cost-effective way. Customers from every industry are constantly trying to experiment to promote value with each service offered. For many, this means embracing platform services over infrastructure services. Consequently, organizations from around the world are using products that abstract more and more infrastructure responsibilities, such as platform service databases, better known as managed databases.

Cloud computing provides a comprehensive suite of data services to help organizations harness the ability to ingest, process, and analyze different data formats or structures optimally.

Types

There are several database management services based on data type or structure, as mentioned in the previous section. There are types such as semi-structured text, unstructured video, and audio files, also referred to as media (JPEG, PNG, and so on), and these support structured data found in worksheets that use tables or tabular datasets with a defined schema of column names and rows upon rows of column values. Boring, I know, but it's important to understand that the data structure is different, and therein lies the problem or obstacle. To overcome this and thrive in the cloud is to understand which services correlate to the data structure in question.

Once classified, then we move to improve database management by assessing the various services provided by each cloud computing leader. Any organizational resource can add value by assisting in designing by classifying datasets and optimizing performance and security. Streamlining an efficient **business continuity** (**BC**) plan that includes all data is obviously essential, but what drives businesses to excel is providing optimization throughout the entire solution, including its database management workloads.

Cloud computing-managed data services support a wide range of data structures or types such as object-level, relational, non-relational, and block-level (disk). Microsoft Azure, AWS, and GCP offer reliable services and API tools for all aspects of database management. The cloud computing leaders address core infrastructure operations such as maintenance without incurring downtime and backups and—optionally—include automating the failover process and built-in availability unique to each service, and support manual scaling or automating the scaling process to support high-volume workloads utilizing their global infrastructure.

Object-level storage

Whether you need to store media files such as photo images (unstructured), volumes of logged data generated from compute disks (semi-structured), or any type of data structure in its original format, it's preferable the data is unstructured. Object-level storage services in the cloud are designed to streamline object-level scale computing. Furthermore, cloud object-level storage services, which are also known as **blob** or binary-level object services, are an inexpensive option for storing unstructured data in the public cloud.

Cloud-scaled object-level storage is made for the internet, and each cloud computing provider delivers easy-to-use APIs that can be utilized to put and get any volume of data. These services give developers access to inherent platform service benefits such as reliability, performance, and security at a global scale.

Here are some but not all object-level storage services offered by Amazon, Microsoft, and Google:

- **Amazon S3** is a platform service that supports object-level data structures with all the accouterments of cloud computing's global infrastructure to improve HA, archiving, **disaster recovery (DR)**, and scalability.

- **Microsoft Azure Blob Storage** is also a platform service that optimizes managing massive object-level data structures with all the benefits of cloud computing's global infrastructure to deliver greater HA, archiving, DR, and scalability than traditional on-premises solutions.

- GCP's Cloud Storage is a platform service that helps manage object-level data structures with all the resources of cloud computing, delivering reliability at levels unattainable feasibly on-premises.

Moreover, cloud computing leaders offer different storage classes to save you money without sacrificing performance and ensuring once again better utility through awareness that you not only classify data by structure but also by the data's access patterns, such as how the data is being accessed and how frequently. Understanding these additional attributes that correspond to your datasets helps further optimize performance and perhaps over time will deliver a return on your investment in cloud computing.

Relational

SQL is used in programming specific to managing data.

The relational data structures are normalized or transformed into tables of data, which consist of columns and rows. Relational or normalized data is defined by its schema, and schemas in relational data management services are encompassing, enforcing table names, columns, and rows. They're known for supporting complex or advanced table-to-table relationships.

For example, the format or structure of the Microsoft Office 365 Excel worksheet shown next and utilized for technology problem analysis is modeled and thus configured as a relational dataset by default, and any data you add to the worksheet must adhere to the currently defined schema of columns and rows.

I'm sure you are thinking: But I can edit, right? The answer is yes, but your edit must comply with the current worksheet's schema. Ah! Or, create your own new worksheet by defining your own schema—tedious, right? I'll remind you about this little detail later in the *Non-relational* section to help you understand why sometimes we need to embrace change and leverage something more dynamic regarding editing or, as I like to call the editing action or process, as a write operation.

The following table depicts a Microsoft Office 365 Excel worksheet, which shows you the format supported by SQL:

PROBLEM AREA	OCCURRENCES	% OF TOTAL	CUMULATIVE %
Databases	35	23.18%	23.18%
License	25	16.56%	39.74%
Environment	21	13.91%	53.64%
Operating system	18	11.92%	65.56%
Operating system license	13	8.61%	74.17%
Servers	12	7.95%	82.12%
CPU per server	10	6.62%	88.74%
Core per CPU	7	4.64%	93.38%
RAM	5	3.31%	96.69%
Optimized by	3	1.99%	98.68%
Relational database management system (RDMS) version and edition	2	1.32%	100.00%

Table 5.1 – Microsoft Office 365 Excel worksheet

Cloud computing provides database services that are fully managed by the cloud computing provider, and cloud computing leaders support several different relational database services, including popular offerings such as Microsoft SQL Server and PostgreSQL. And because these services are powered by the public cloud, organizations can manually or automatically vertically scale by increasing the size or scale horizontally by adding database replicas based on the underlying database engine's unique availability features but at a cloud scale.

Here are some but not all relational database management services offered by Amazon, Microsoft, and Google:

- Amazon Aurora is another platform service that provides a managed relational database with similar features and compatibility to MySQL and PostgreSQL. Aurora includes native HA, DR, and scalability and has the capability to deliver exponentially more throughput than MySQL and PostgreSQL, thus optimizing its performance.

- Microsoft Azure SQL Database is a fully managed version of Microsoft's SQL Server, offered as a platform service. Powered by the Microsoft Azure cloud, this version of SQL Server includes preconfigured features such as an always-on availability group for HA, DR, and scalability without the operating overhead of the traditional on-premises Microsoft SQL Server.

- Google Cloud offers Cloud Spanner, a globally managed relational database that delivers cloud-scaled performance with no limits, helping start-ups to enterprise businesses focus on what matters most, driving value to their customers.

Non-relational

NoSQL (this is referring to non-relational) services are sometimes referred to as **not only SQL** to highlight that they may support SQL query languages.

Non-relational database tables commonly do not enforce schemas. Similar to relational database tables, there are key names used to help identify parts of the dataset in the table, to get or set (`edit` (`write`)) dataset values, entire column sets of data, and include getting semi-structured datasets such as text, JSON, XML, or other documents in the database management service, which may denote its datasets in a document-like format that is different from relational tables, which appear tabular—or, in other words, like an Excel worksheet.

JSON is a file format and is used widely in technology services to store and transmit data defined as value pairs. Here is an example of a JSON file:

```
{
    "Item":{
        "Authors":{
            "SS":[
                "Author1",
                "Author2"
            ]
        },
        "Dimensions":{
            "S":"8.5 x 11.0 x 1.5"
        },
```

```
          "ISBN":{
              "S":"333-3333333333"
          },
          "Id":{
              "N":"103"
          },
          "InPublication":{
              "BOOL":false
          },
          "PageCount":{
              "N":"600"
          },
          "Price":{
              "N":"2000"
          },
          "ProductCategory":{
              "S":"Book"
          },
          "Title":{
              "S":"Book 103 Title"
          }
      }
  }
```

Cloud computing also provides non-relational database services that are managed by the cloud computing provider. Cloud computing leaders offer different NoSQL database services in support of columnar database, document database, and graph database requirements, and they include in-memory database cache services to continue improving performance. While all these NoSQL types are used widely in various practical applications, I will focus on the document data storage type, as it is essential in cloud computing due to its popularity and utility.

Cloud computing leaders have invested significantly in non-relational database services due to utilization in combination with the majority of many microservices and other emerging technologies, and more semi-structured data is becoming prominent in data sources. Cloud-scaled NoSQL services are not only simple to use and cost-effective but also support retrieving any amount of data from almost any API client or service, and support online transactional processing speeds somewhere around single-digit millisecond latency—that's unheard of on-premises. Coupled with no strict schema, each item in the database can have a different number of attributes and, as such, deliver flexibility and support for almost any data type. Therefore this non-relational database service can support innovation, which would be more constrained in its relational counterpart.

Here are some but not all non-relational database management services offered by Amazon, Microsoft, and Google:

- **Amazon DynamoDB** is a fully managed and fast but predictable non-relational database management service. It's known for its streamlined scaling features and simple-to-use API tools.

- **Microsoft Azure Cosmos DB** is a managed database service that's known for not only its unparalleled performance and implicit HA and DR capabilities at a global scale but also includes support for several open source APIs such as the popular MongoDB platform.

- **GCP's Cloud Bigtable** is a scalable NoSQL fully managed database service for both transactional and analytical processing workloads backed by Google Cloud's global infrastructure.

Mastering relational and non-relational database engines

This book only includes the essentials; for you to truly master relational and non-relational data and database management services, you will have to dig deeper into durability, performance, and scale. I recommend attending an instructor-led course or class; however, that insight will be shared at the end of this compendious volume in a chapter that will cover mastering continuous training programs.

Sharing responsibility

In this section, you will learn how to describe and understand the cloud computing shared responsibility model.

Shared responsibility model

It is very important that each organization, no matter the size, reviews and comes to understand the shared responsibility model in cloud computing—that is, understanding which tasks are managed by the cloud provider and which tasks are managed by the customer. Responsibilities vary depending on the cloud computing service model, such as IaaS, PaaS, and SaaS, and even then, some services and resources that fall under these categories may include or exclude some additional administrative tasks, which requires any organization to review each cloud computing provider's services and resources in depth to grasp any unique differences in responsibilities. For example, compute resources such as VMs and container services may have subtle similarities in administrative responsibilities to the customer but may vary if the container in this context is hosted on either a VM or PaaS resource type, such as Microsoft AKS.

As mentioned, the customer's responsibility will be determined by the cloud computing service they select. This choice determines the amount of work the customer must perform as part of their responsibilities, which is shown in detail in the following figure:

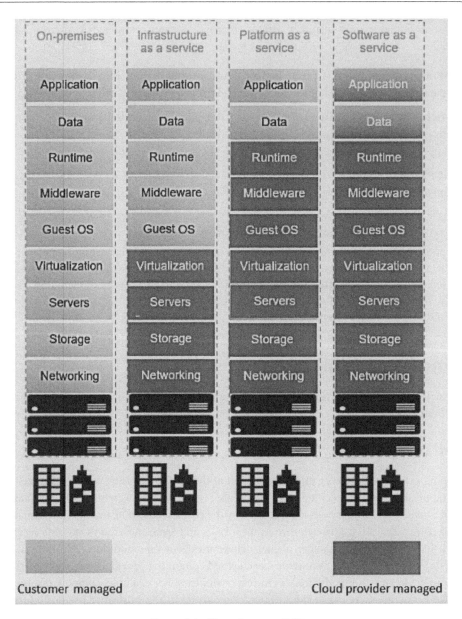

Figure 5.4 – Shared responsibility

PaaS provides greater convenience over control. The customer using this model is responsible for managing application service configuration, data, and the custom application code published, as well as securing connectivity and governing IAM.

Summary

In this chapter, the new skills you learned were how to describe and manage the essential PaaS type and its managed services—namely, the application, serverless, and database management services. You also learned factors to consider when architecting and recommending these platform services following public cloud leaders' Well-Architected Framework of best practices.

In the next chapter, you will learn about the **software-as-a-service** (**SaaS**) model and how it has similar benefits and considerations to PaaS; however, there are some pros and cons.

Questions

1. What does PaaS stand for?

    A.   Public access anywhere services

    B.   Private access anywhere services

    C.   Platform as a service

    D.   None of these

2. What does an API provide?

    A.   Software and protocols for systems and services to integrate or communicate

    B.   The iPhone user interface

    C.   An Amazon platform interface network

    D.   JavaScript

3. What is DNS?

    A.   IP address

    B.   Domain Name System

    C.   Wide-area network

    D.   None of these

4. Kubernetes falls under which category?

    A.   SaaS

    B.   Serverless

    C.   IaaS

    D.   PaaS

5. Elasticity includes which of the following options?

    A. I/O

    B. AI

    C. Horizontal scaling

    D. None of these

6. With serverless resources, you are responsible for which of the following?

    A. Application code

    B. Hardware

    C. Guest operating system

    D. Infrastructure

7. Which of the following are non-relational databases?

    A. RDMS

    B. Google Docs

    C. S3

    D. NoSQL

8. PaaS provides which of the following benefits?

    A. Greater control than IaaS

    B. Greater convenience than IaaS

    C. Completely customer managed

    D. None of these

6
Utilizing Turnkey Software Solutions (SaaS)

This chapter will take you through how **software as a service (SaaS)** is implemented. First, you will learn how to administer core Microsoft Office 365, Amazon WorkDocs, and Google Docs services at a high level. You will also learn about the role of the SaaS marketplace, and you will gain the knowledge required to maintain SaaS workloads throughout their life cycle by understanding the responsibility you share with the cloud provider.

The following topics will be covered in this chapter:

- Cloud computing models
- Marketplace
- Fully managed software
- Sharing responsibility

Cloud computing models

In this chapter, you will understand the concepts and benefits of SaaS. In the cloud, responsibilities are shared, and learning how it applies to administrating SaaS is critical. These responsibilities or tasks vary based on numerous factors, such as procurement and governance. For example, as your organization adopts the cloud service, also referred to as an online service, some responsibilities transfer to the cloud computing provider. I'll expound on what the Shared Responsibility Model is later in this chapter; it is very similar for each of the cloud computing leaders: Amazon, Microsoft, and Google.

Software as a service

Organizations that elect SaaS typically use and manage applications that are either accessible online or can be installed on different platforms and devices. The cloud computing provider is responsible for provisioning, managing, and maintaining the application's underlying infrastructure. This disencumbers an organization's engineers from managing and maintaining the on-premises or cloud infrastructure core services, which consequently facilitates a highly available, up-to-date, and secure online software service. For example, regarding an application, also referred to as a service in this context, that I use (end user), such as an app on my phone or computer, I am not responsible for managing its underlying infrastructure – Amazon, Microsoft, or Google would be responsible. That pretty much sums up most apps that you or I use daily, whether for business or personal needs.

> Note
>
> For more information on the on-premises physical infrastructure, and the cloud infrastructure as a service's responsibility, review the previous chapters, particularly, *Chapter 1*, *Chapter 2*, and *Chapter 4*.

Common scenarios by industry

The government uses cloud computing.

Did you know that local, state, and national government agencies utilize cloud computing? Amazon, Microsoft, and Google offer niche services that adhere to stringent local, state, and national compliance controls that focus on delivering unprecedented security at all levels.

Education

In the last couple of years, we have seen pandemics impact our society's way of life in all sectors, particularly the education sector. You may agree that remote working and remote learning were already on the rise. But COVID-19 ignited unprecedented changes in how we learn, thus accelerating the need for remote learning.

The benefits are uncontroversial; higher education institutions can use the advantages derived from cloud computing to address accessibility for students anywhere in the world from any device or platform, such as a smartphone.

Academic institutions such as **Arizona State University** (**ASU**), which has been a cornerstone of education since it was founded in 1885, known then as **Territorial Normal School**, adopted cloud computing with the support of Amazon.

ASU leverages the massive AWS global infrastructure and uses Amazon WorkDocs to benefit from securely sharing files and collaborating with internal and external (remote) users around the globe while ensuring the right people have the right access efficiently. This includes turnkey advantages, which provide a secure and auditable real-time content-sharing capability.

> **Information**
>
> In the *Fully managed software* section in this chapter, we will explore the SaaS offerings and provide a SaaS example used by ASU.
>
> Review *Chapter 3, Understanding the Benefits of Public Clouds (AWS, Azure, and GCP)*, to understand the inherent benefits of cloud computing when using any cloud computing service model such as SaaS.

Automotive

The automotive industry has been undergoing a digital transformation for several years that has reshaped its ecosystem. Cloud computing service models have been utilized to deliver improved analytics that optimize the quality provided by suppliers.

The public cloud has introduced many solutions that deliver better, smarter products incorporated into all aspects of automaking, which includes other facets, such as aftermarket, marketing, and sales and services. Furthermore, these various modern cloud turnkey solutions help automotive dealers optimize the engagement experience.

These advantages enrich the customer experience from end to end, delivering value that could not be achieved without the cloud.

Automotive business leaders such as **Volvo** adopted the Microsoft cloud to improve the way it does business across all business facets, including how they design and build. Part of its business strategy is to utilize the Microsoft 365 suite of services to help improve company culture and collaboration.

Volvo utilizes Microsoft 365 services such as OneDrive to bolster a culture of transparency by encouraging sharing at a company-wide level, which, in turn, drives efficiencies to its various initiatives.

> **Information**
>
> In the *Fully managed software* section in this chapter, we will explore the SaaS offerings and provide a SaaS example used by Volvo.

Manufacturing

In today's fast-paced market, manufacturers face many challenges, such as the need to innovate quickly and still provide great quality. Manufacturers require modern infrastructure and services to meet the needs of tomorrow today, for their customers. Successfully doing that is measured by a business's ability to create better relationships, share, and collaborate in real time, thus improving the way customer information is changed into delivering value.

Google helped **Whirlpool** meet its needs by migrating to Google's Workspace to optimize business processes. These services or tools helped Whirlpool streamline how the areas of the organization connected and accelerated productivity by simplifying how the business designs and collaborates.

> **Google Docs, Microsoft 365 Outlook, and Amazon WorkDocs**
>
> I am using Google Docs to collaborate with Packt Publishing regarding the details of this very book, as well as transmitting articles of compliance concerning licensing and invoicing using Microsoft Outlook, all while storing backups of any edited content in Amazon WorkDocs.

Whirlpool can leverage a wide array of resources, from email, calendaring, and online meetings, to storing resiliently in the cloud, to sharing in real time, using Google Workspaces.

> **Tip**
>
> In the *Fully managed software* section in this chapter, we will explore the SaaS offerings and provide a SaaS example used by Whirlpool.

Marketplace

In this section, you will learn about the cloud marketplace. First, we'll explain **buying** and **selling** software services in the marketplace. You will also learn helpful tips and potential pitfalls that encumber beginners.

The cloud computing leaders, Amazon, Microsoft, and Google, host a marketplace to help connect end users with partners, independent software vendors, and start-ups, offering niche services and solutions.

The marketplace allows customers of all levels, enthusiasts, IT professionals, and developers to locate, try, purchase, and provision applications from many top-leading service providers. Most software services can run on-premises or in the public cloud.

The marketplace is a curated catalog where you can filter by industry, service, publisher, product type, and more, and includes open source applications and services, pre-configured computer operating system images, data management services, developer resources, security tools, and even modern services such as blockchain, AI, or IoT. And that's not even scratching the surface – it's a modern-day science and technology bazaar for your organization to procure or sell native cloud and third-party software or services.

> **SaaS is everywhere!**
>
> Any application, also referred to as an app, regardless of platform or manufacturer, is constructed of software and its components or microservices, such as API components, or data access logic components, to provide a solution as a service to the end user or organization's customer. The majority of apps are downloaded to a destination device and/or device platform, such as Android (Google) or iOS 15 (Apple), or desktop and laptop computers running a Linux, Windows (Microsoft), or macOS (Apple) operating system. Alternatively, apps are accessed directly from the device and/or device platform's browser (Edge, Chrome, and so on) over the public internet by accessing its endpoint URL or URI. And lastly, you subscribe to the software service, which may offer different payment options.

SaaS considerations

A SaaS product purchased from the marketplace still requires proper planning and governance. Cost management is also very important – just as important as managing the IaaS cost. Granted, there are fewer responsibilities, but it is important to plan and prepare before implementing the SaaS product.

Architecting SaaS requires the end user or organization offering the SaaS as a managed service provider or reseller to consider important factors, such as how SaaS can integrate with their current framework and native line-of-business applications without impacting performance and productivity.

The following are some other factors to consider:

- SaaS distribution

- SaaS activations

- SaaS licensing depends on the cost model

- SaaS volume pricing

- SaaS consulting partner

> Tip
>
> Marketplace products are defined in detail and include intuitive cost model information to eliminate inaccurate pricing estimates.

Buying SaaS

The marketplace offers free trials and flexible pricing plans that vary from service to service. And there are different types of subscription options, such as monthly or annually.

> Tip
>
> Some SaaS product manufacturers will charge a usage fee instead of a monthly subscription. Make sure you read the details section for any product.

Some product manufacturers may use a combination of monthly subscription and usage rates.

> **Free is always limited**
>
> The majority of free (better known as a trial) subscriptions or plans are for a limited trial period. This trial period is managed by the product manufacturer. And typically, you either reach a usage credit limit or a trial period expiration date.

Selling SaaS

You must understand that SaaS is a **lucrative** market and that it's growing exponentially every year. There are current insights from Gartner illustrating that the SaaS market generates billions of dollars annually.

Why, you ask? Let's use an example. Most organizations that market products online, during periods of growth, face many challenges, and every business has some semblance of IT and requires IT infrastructure. If not, then it's outsourced or contracted.

Nevertheless, scalability becomes a challenge. Most SaaS start-ups, before the rise of cloud computing, elected to host their solution on-premises and therefore had to plan hardware procurement and expansion. If the organization did not install enough hardware, they may have missed an opportunity to sign up a new customer. However, if the organization installed too much hardware, it would impact profits and may have prevented future expansion needs.

Additionally, businesses must find a way to scale operationally. So, more customers means an organization needs to increase the number of IT resources, which includes employees and infrastructure resources to scale the SaaS product. So, automating processes to optimize operations also becomes critical.

Furthermore, challenges such as building customer loyalty mean delivering new service features rapidly. Customers are also becoming more knowledgeable about SaaS and know what to request from their manufacturer.

There are also concerns regarding data sovereignty and data locations, supplier agreements, high availability, little to no maintenance demands from customers, and more.

Any business, no matter the size, will face one or more of the challenges described herein. Building, marketing, and supporting SaaS is no easy feat, but if an organization can accomplish meeting the needs described here, it can continue to thrive in its niche market.

Alternatively, organizations can elect to build SaaS solutions while utilizing cloud computing, and then deploy the solution as SaaS and make it available for customers around the world. Additionally, customers can elect to sell their SaaS product to be resold or utilized by consumers. And the marketplace delivers great resources to help consumers and sellers, such as in-depth guidance on how to sell your SaaS product using each cloud computing leader's unique marketplace. Although each provider has its minor differences, the main objectives are similar; they help sellers focus on building while the provider manages billing, collections, and payments.

The cloud computing marketplace includes various methods to increase product visibility and help the seller engage more with potential buyers. And cloud computing providers allow various managed service consultants to assist with reselling the solution. This may include additional proprietary support services to add yet another great benefit for selling a SaaS solution.

> **Did you know?**
> Sellers have a wide range of payment options they can offer to buyers to accommodate almost any form of payment.

Fully managed software

In this section, you will learn about the advantages of SaaS offerings, as illustrated by leading industry examples. You will also learn helpful tips and potential pitfalls that encumber beginners.

Architectural considerations

We'll look at the various architectural considerations in the following sections.

Software services

Cloud computing SaaS products should be designed to help the end user by delivering one or more of these focus values:

- Replacing tedious tasks
- Adding value by doing the following:
  - Saving the end user money
  - Generating money
- Being simple to incorporate and simple to use
- Improving transparency for the business or end user
- Enriching the business or end user's life

These are some of the focus areas, but this is not an exhaustive list for any SaaS offering. Let's look at an example of a SaaS offering: Microsoft 365 Outlook email services. Microsoft is responsible for provisioning, managing, and maintaining the application's underlying infrastructure throughout the application's life cycle.

Cloud computing providers such as Amazon, Microsoft, and Google offer various SaaS products, such as Amazon WorkDocs, Microsoft 365 OneDrive, and Google Workspace Docs. These services help organizations and their end users by providing one of the many SaaS focus values listed previously, and without the operational or capital expenses incurred if the end user decided to implement their own SaaS architecture using one of the deployment models, such as on-premises, private cloud, or public cloud service models such as **IaaS** or **platform as a service (PaaS)**.

> **Information**
> Let's look at some but not all of the most popular SaaS offerings. You may notice minor similarities across these products, even if the service is hosted by a different cloud computing provider.

Amazon WorkDocs

Amazon WorkDocs is a SaaS product; it delivers secure content creation and storage and includes features to improve collaboration. Organizations can streamline creating, editing, and sharing files, and it's hosted on AWS' global infrastructure, so you can access it from anywhere. It facilitates features that allow sharing content while receiving feedback in real time.

Organizations that choose to use Amazon WorkDocs are typically deprecating a legacy file-sharing system and are migrating these files to the cloud. Amazon includes an API so that you can interoperate with existing systems.

SaaS products such as Amazon WorkDocs can be used in enterprise content management strategies. Due to Amazon's massive infrastructure, which adheres to various compliance controls, Amazon WorkDocs can be used across different industries to optimize operations:

Figure 6.1 – Amazon WorkDocs

> **Tip**
> There are no upfront fees with Amazon WorkDocs.

The following are common cloud configuration recommendations:

- Administrators can integrate Amazon WorkDocs with Microsoft Active Directory, which can greatly improve identity and access management processes

- Developers and operations teams can work together to integrate any activity data with either customer-owned or AWS analytics tools and services to optimize how they monitor Amazon WorkDocs

Please review the files located on GitHub if you want guidance on how to trial SaaS services utilized by industry leaders in education, automotive, and manufacturing industries (`https://github.com/PacktPublishing/Cloud-Computing-for-Beginners/tree/main/Allfiles/Chapter6`).

Microsoft 365 OneDrive

Microsoft 365 is the quintessential example of a SaaS offering. It offers a pay-as-you-go payment model, also referred to as a subscription, where the customer agrees to pay either monthly or annually, and, in turn, gets a suite or bundle of services, which are apps (software). For example, Volvo required services to drive efficiencies across disparate teams to improve how their employees collaborated to design innovative vehicles that improve how we live. Volvo chose Microsoft 365 services and utilized OneDrive for Enterprise to support secure internal and external content sharing and collaboration.

OneDrive for Enterprise, also referred to as OneDrive for Business, helps organizations streamline storage and accessibility securely, regardless of whether the end user is inside or outside the private corporate network. And like Amazon WorkDocs, Microsoft 365 OneDrive for Enterprise adheres to well-known compliance standards needed in today's threat landscape to conduct business securely.

OneDrive for Enterprise supports accessing files from any device, including mobile, and through popular and modern web browsers such as Chrome or Microsoft Edge. It also provides optimized collaboration features that offer coauthoring both online mobile apps. And organizations can use OneDrive's interoperability with native Microsoft 365 services such as Microsoft Teams to further extend coauthoring capabilities by using real-time communications.

As SaaS products, Microsoft 365 services such as OneDrive for Enterprise inherit all the benefits of cloud computing. It's fully managed and hosted by Microsoft, who utilize their world-renowned resilient global infrastructure:

Figure 6.2 – Microsoft 365 OneDrive

The following are common cloud configuration recommendations:

- Identity and access management administrators should grant least privilege access and never assume trust, requiring authentication and authorization for each user before granting access.

- Security teams need to go beyond network controls and into protecting the data access layer. They must make sure the right people have access to the right data.

Tip

If a file is accidentally deleted, you can restore the file using the website or command-line tools.

Google Workspace docs

Google Workspace provides several services that can work together or apart to improve how end users collaborate. Google's suite of SaaS services helps teams connect anywhere, on any device. And they include services with features designed to optimize project management and productivity. Moreover, data is accessible from anywhere and it's secured resiliently by Google Cloud.

Like the other cloud providers, Google Workspace supports a pay-as-you-go model. Google Workspace services are well known, such as Gmail, which delivers email, chat, and more. Gmail is a mature email service that has been improving how personal and business end users send emails, organize mail, and instantly connect with business partners or loved ones using chat or video meetings without requiring administrative assistance to install any software because it's accessible online from any device or platform.

Another great service within its suite of services is Google Docs, which supports creating content using your favorite web browser. It has features such as coauthoring, so you and a friend can work together on a project outline in real time. Additionally, Google Docs can import files as is and convert files to acceptable formats before formatting the data so that it can interoperate with services such as Sheets or Slides to complete the *wow factor* when concluding or initiating your key project meeting.

SaaS services such as Google Docs have been key solutions in helping start-ups and enterprise organizations brainstorm ideas. Why? Because it's simpler when the company culture encourages sharing information. Create a doc and make it the canvas that you and your business use to illustrate ideas. Collaborate by editing as a team and getting the iterative feedback you need to deliver value. And that's why SaaS products from Amazon, Microsoft, and Google Cloud are great examples of SaaS offerings done right – because they improve the way we work and they keep it simple.

Without cloud computing, these turnkey software services could not exist and provide value that we can count on. Google Cloud's infrastructure, platform, and software are accessible online as a subscription service:

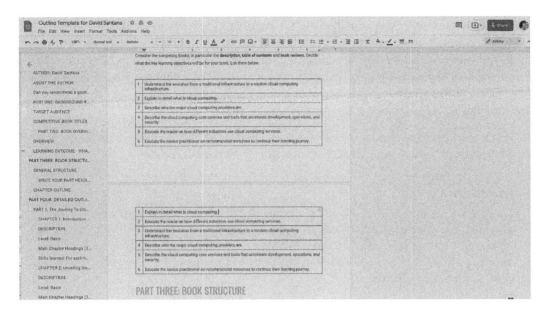

Figure 6.3 – Google Docs

> **Did you know?**
>
> With Google Docs, you can dictate your notes using the Chrome browser and a configured microphone. Amazing!

Highly available

Customers today shift to cloud computing for several business outcomes that serve as justification for transformation. This includes things such as resiliency, speed, savings, abundant options, and more. Customers assume services are highly available by default, no questions asked. And your business, no matter the size, must deliver. SaaS is not just a purchasing option or an app – it's much more. Its model provides a holistic solution, wherein products are fully managed. In this context, it is implied that a level of service, agreed upon by the consumer and the provider, ensuring the product is up to date, secure, and highly available is offered.

Service-level agreements

Cloud computing providers such as Amazon, Microsoft, and Google provide high availability by default for SaaS products. Availability refers to the level of service that the SaaS product type provides to customers and their end users, and it's expressed as the percentage of time that a service is available. Each service has a unique **service-level agreement** (**SLA**) documented and shared by the cloud computing provider at the time of purchase and throughout the product's term of use.

Every customer and seller should understand the availability expectations for any SaaS product. For example, if an enterprise organization requires an SLA of 99.9%, this must be denoted and transparent during procurement. And if there are changes to the level of service, there must be documentation describing what to expect. The cloud computing leaders described within this book provide detailed information and expectations regarding each service's SLA and how to monitor the health of said service, ensuring customers and sellers are on the same page.

It's very important for any business to define its required target SLA, so it can then decide whether the SaaS product's features, limits, and SLA meet its current business needs.

> **Information**
>
> The cloud computing leaders provide online articles that address SLA at `https://aws.amazon.com/workdocs/sla/`, `https://docs.microsoft.com/en-us/office365/servicedescriptions/office-365-platform-service-description/service-level-agreement`, and `https://workspace.google.com/terms/sla.html`.

Managing

Organizations that use the public cloud benefit from a wide range of services and tools to efficiently manage SaaS products. There are many native administrative and developer-friendly resources. These tools help organizations manage and govern SaaS products efficiently. These cloud-native tools and services allow you to automate managing your products throughout their terms of use.

> **Tip**
>
> Customers can use **infrastructure as code** (**IaC**) strategies to help administrators and development teams automate management processes consistently and reliably. Amazon, Microsoft, and Google SaaS products may support API calls, **software development kits** (**SDKs**), and command-line tools. Please note that this API access is limited and varies from service to service.

Health status

Administrative tasks such as deploying and managing infrastructure sites, network infrastructure, and racking and stacking physical servers are a thing of the past for organizations that have adopted cloud computing. And based on the type of service model purchased, SaaS customers are not even responsible for managing the underlying infrastructure in the cloud. However, this does not mean a customer isn't responsible for the service it offers to its end user.

Whether it's IaaS or SaaS, some issues can potentially arise, including misconfigurations, SLA misconceptions, and even outages. That is why it's important to monitor services and their resources, even in the public cloud.

Cloud computing providers Microsoft, Amazon, and Google offer monitoring services that centralize analyzing your SaaS products, end user devices, and end users.

These monitoring services ingest metrics and logs from your SaaS products. All activities or interactions with your digital estate are recorded. From here, organizations can view, search, and even elect to share this data with third-party auditors to meet compliance requirements.

AI services are also optionally leveraged and may be included implicitly or must be explicitly configured with cloud monitoring services. Monitoring reports are included and provide past or present near-real-time data insights, which give businesses of any size the capability to analyze performance, operations, identity and access management, and the current health of said service.

> **Common cloud configuration recommendations**
> We recommend enabling and enforcing multi-factor authentication for all privileged accounts.

Sharing responsibility

In this section, you will learn how to describe and understand the cloud computing Shared Responsibility Model.

Shared Responsibility Model

It is very important that each customer or business, no matter the size, review and understand the Shared Responsibility Model in cloud computing. Moreover, they must understand which tasks are managed by the cloud provider and which tasks are managed by the customer and end user. Responsibilities vary, depending on the cloud computing service model, such as IaaS, PaaS, and SaaS, and even then, some services and their resources that fall under these categories may include or exclude additional administrative tasks. I recommend everyone review each cloud computing provider's services and resources limits, as well as their SLAs, in depth to grasp any unique variance in responsibilities.

An example of this is building an internal corporate website by using PaaS resources, such as Elastic Beanstalk, App Services, or App Engine in comparison to SaaS pre-configured apps, which are already hosted and managed by Amazon, Microsoft, and Google, and may have subtle similarities in identity and access management. However, if the customer chose a SaaS product, such as Microsoft 365 SharePoint, to build and host the internal web app, then the customer is only responsible for managing and governing access to the data and application.

In the public cloud, cloud computing leaders are responsible for procuring, architecting, installing, maintaining, and securing the physical infrastructure that runs all the services offered in the public cloud. This infrastructure is comprised of servers, virtualization hosts, and networking infrastructure, and includes managing the data center.

As mentioned previously, the customer's responsibility will be determined by the cloud computing service model they select. This choice determines the amount of work the customer must perform as part of their responsibilities but still varies from service to service:

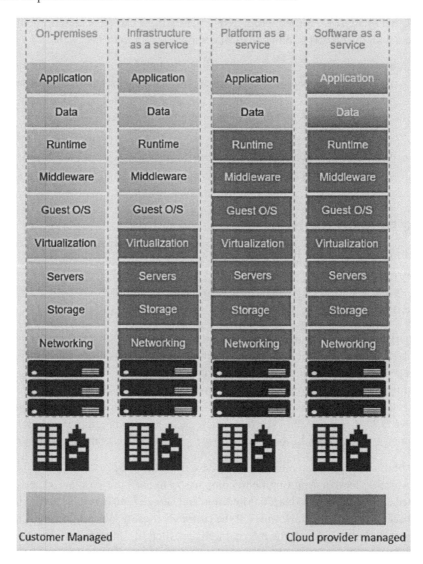

Figure 6.4 – Shared Responsibility Model

In the graphic illustrated in *Figure 6.4*, you can see that SaaS provides the greatest agility. The customer using this service model is responsible for managing the SaaS product settings and application data layer and governing identity and access management.

In short, the customer is responsible for ensuring the service they are using is managed and governed as per the business requirements and best practices. In stark contrast, IaaS requires the most customer management of all cloud computing service models. This is because the customer is responsible for implementing and managing the core cloud infrastructure services such as virtual machines, middleware, APIs, the runtime environment, data, and the application.

Summary

In this chapter, you learned about the essential concept of SaaS and its managed services, namely the well-known online services. You also learned factors to consider when managing and governing these SaaS products derived from the public cloud leaders' well-architected framework of best practices.

In the next few chapters, we will take you on an in-depth journey through how to implement fundamental AWS, Azure, and GCP services step by step.

Questions

Answer the following questions to test your knowledge of this chapter:

1. What does SaaS stand for?

    A. Software available anywhere systems

    B. Services available anywhere systems

    C. Serverless available anywhere systems

    D. Software as a service

2. What can I buy from cloud computing providers' marketplace?

    A. Hardware

    B. Phone plans

    C. Data centers

    D. Software

3. What can I sell on the cloud computing providers' marketplace?

    A. Applications

    B. Infrastructure

    C. Cisco hardware

    D. None of the above

4. Which of the following describes SaaS?

    A. Customer managed

    B. Fully managed

    C. Made up of virtual machine instances

    D. None of the above

5. SaaS is which of the following?

    A. Highly available

    B. Not secure

    C. Does not support MFA

    D. None of the above

6. Which of the following are examples of SaaS? (Choose all that apply)

    A. Google Docs

    B. Microsoft 365

    C. Serverless

    D. Linux GNOME

Part 3: Cloud Infrastructure Services in Action

This part of the book will take you on an in-depth journey in how to implement AWS, Azure, and GCP fundamental infrastructure services.

This part comprises the following chapters:

- *Chapter 7, Implementing Virtual Network Resources for Security*
- *Chapter 8, Launching Compute Service Resources for Scalability*
- *Chapter 9, Configuring Storage Resources for Resiliency*

Implementing Virtual Network Resources for Security

This chapter will take you through implementing various essential networking services. You will also learn how to set up a public load balancer and a site-to-site (hybrid) **virtual private network** (**VPN**), and you will reinforce concepts and configuration procedures by completing review questions.

The following concepts will be covered in this chapter:

- Virtual networking
- Load balancing
- Site-to-site VPNs

Virtual networking

In this section, you will learn how to configure and implement virtual networking services. You will also learn helpful tips and about potential pitfalls that encumber beginners.

First, allow me to define **virtual networks** (**VNets**), which are components of a process known as **network virtualization**. The process combines software and hardware networking devices—including networking features—into what is named a VNet. And important components such as **virtual local area networks** (**VLANs**) and VLAN switches can be used to combine or divide many networks efficiently as a singular software-based administrative object. VNets support connectivity between end users, networks, servers, and applications, and interconnect operating system-level virtualization environments, better known as **containers**.

The previous paragraph should give you an idea of network virtualization, but truly, it's only scratching the surface. Nevertheless, my mission here is not to expound on VLAN technology but to ensure you understand its importance to VNets. This may also lead you to research not only VLANs but software-defined networking, which we do not define or elaborate on in this book. But let us move forward with at least an understanding that virtual networking is not just components but, due to its roots, a process that conjoins components and processes to optimize network management.

Cloud computing leaders leverage network virtualization to optimize managing **infrastructure-as-a-service** (**IaaS**), **platform-as-a-service** (**PaaS**), and **software-as-a-service** (**SaaS**) resource types and centralize or even decentralize local to **wide area networks** (**WANs**) spanning the world.

Cloud computing providers offer a method to simplify configuring a VNet **classless inter-domain routing** (**CIDR**) range that you define initially within a cloud computing region of your choice that is by default isolated from other networks. And you can deploy your cloud service resource types, such as **virtual machine** (**VM**) instances— also known as **Elastic Compute Cloud** (**EC2**) instances or Google Cloud Compute Engine instances and more, into your VNet. Your VNet closely resembles a traditional network that your organization owns and operates in a data center.

The following screenshot illustrates **Amazon Web Services** (**AWS**), Azure, and **Google Cloud Platform** (**GCP**) networking service resource type names classified as VNets:

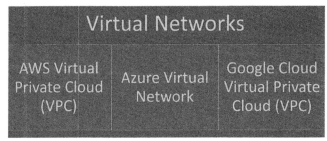

Figure 7.1 – VNets

Follow me as I create each cloud computing provider's VNet step by step, as the lab gods intended— thus, learn by doing.

First, let's start with the AWS **virtual private cloud** (**VPC**), which enables us to quickly define a VPC in an AWS region within the AWS cloud. Remember—you can implement resources such as EC2 instances into a VPC. However, in the following tasks, I will elect to exclude EC2 creation.

Allow me to immerse you in the world of cloud computing by delivering this subject matter as I would to a student.

Implementing AWS VPC overview

In these tasks, you will learn how to create and configure VPC resources in AWS. You will also learn about the other VPC components, and finally, we will review several principles associated with cloud networking.

Objectives

After completing these tasks, you will be able to achieve the following:

- Describe and configure a VPC
- Describe and configure a CIDR
- Describe and configure subnets
- Describe and configure an internet gateway
- Describe and configure routing

Prerequisites

These are the recommended requirements for completing all tasks:

- An updated version of the Windows 8.1 or later, macOS 10.15 or later, or Linux Ubuntu 18.04 or later computer operating system
- An up-to-date and secure internet browser (Chrome or Edge is recommended)
- Instructions are located in the following places:
  - In this chapter, in the *Virtual networking* section
  - At `https://github.com/PacktPublishing/Cloud-Computing-for-Beginners/tree/main/Instructions/Chapter7/VNET/AWS`
- Access to an AWS account with the required privileges to create and manage all VPC resources and dependencies
  - Here's how to create an AWS trial account for training purposes only: `https://aws.amazon.com/free`

> **Note**
> I am using a Windows 10 OS, and both Chrome or Edge browsers.

Whether your role correlates with either architecting, system administration, or development, every project, no matter the size or industry, must perform some modicum of risk analysis. For every organization described in *Chapters 4, 5,* and *6*, companies such as PayPal, Volvo, and Moderna must evaluate their network's vulnerability to adhere to regulatory and non-regulatory compliance. So, the question is: *How vulnerable is your network, and what is the importance of the asset that could be damaged or made unavailable?* Assets include but are not limited to data and, in this context, your network topology.

One of the main tasks before migrating to the cloud or expanding your preexisting cloud service is analyzing controls—controls that are either in place or in some planning phase—and both technical and non-technical controls can be analyzed. In this case, we started our tasks by understanding the importance of examining the cloud networking service resources before further development and testing. If approved, implement them in production to securely host your organization's **line-of-business (LOB)** application or service.

> **Important note**
>
> You should fork, clone, or download, and follow along with the step-by-step tasks in GitHub or described herein. I recommend using GitHub in conjunction with the book because any snippets of code are more clearly defined in GitHub. However, that's my preference—you may prefer the book format.

Ready?

Let us start the tasks to implement an AWS VPC:

To do 0: Subscribe to AWS

Task 1: Sign in to AWS. The steps are as follows:

1. Select the Edge or Chrome browser on your computer and go to `https://aws.amazon.com/free`.

2. After the website loads, select **Create a Free Account**.

3. On the `portal.aws.amazon.com` website, populate the fields labeled **Root user**, **Email address**, and **AWS account name**, and enter a valid and readily accessible email account name and AWS account name for training purposes. Here are some email accounts and AWS account name examples:

    - `Example.lastname@gmail.com`

    - `Example.lastname@outlook.com`

    - `Cloud Practitioner`

4. Follow the remaining prompts and populate all required fields to complete the new account creation process.

> **Note**
>
> I have elected to exclude any guidance pertaining to billing details that include **personally identifiable information (PII)**.

There are several resources to help you create and manage your AWS Free Tier to ensure you don't incur substantial costs:

- `https://aws.amazon.com/premiumsupport/knowledge-center/create-and-activate-aws-account/`

- `https://aws.amazon.com/premiumsupport/knowledge-center/what-is-free-tier/`

To do 1: Implement an AWS VPC

> **Important**
>
> The instructions listed are accurate if you are using the new VPC experience, which is optional.

Task 1: Describe and configure a VPC

In this task, you will implement a VPC by using the AWS Management Console.

Amazon provides a preconfigured VPC in every AWS geographical region. The VPC is labeled **Default VPC**, and it is already configured with a subnet to host your resources, a gateway to the internet, and more. The default VPC is recommended for less significant and temporary projects. For example, hypothetically, I need to deploy a **minimum viable product** (**MVP**) to test my **proof-of-concept** (**POC**) solution to internal stakeholders before considering the product or service for general availability.

The steps are as follows:

1. Sign in to the AWS Management Console (`https://console.aws.amazon.com/console/`).

2. In the console, navigate and select **Services**, and in the **Services** section, navigate and select **Networking & Content Delivery**.

3. In the **Networking & Content Delivery** section, select **VPC**.

4. In the **VPC Dashboard** window, navigate and select **Launch VPC Wizard**.

> **Insight**
>
> Do not modify any fields or sections unless explicitly instructed. For example, if we circumvent an option that appears as a button, box, name field, or metadata, it's intentional. These options or settings are already configured by the system, and I will refer to them as the default settings.

5. Review the VPC dashboard, and create VPC wizard sections labeled **VPC settings**, **VPC**, **Subnets**, and **Route tables**.

> **Insight**
>
> The VPC dashboard configuration section labeled **Create a VPC** streamlines the manual configuration by automatically proposing overall VPC settings, which include subnets and fault-tolerant services leveraging Amazon's global infrastructure and simplifying routing network traffic publicly and privately, both inbound and outbound.

Task 2: Describe and configure CIDR

In this task, you will define CIDR by using the **Launch VPC Wizard** functionality.

In cloud computing, VNets require network administrators to define the starting IP and the size of the VPC using CIDR notation. Here is an example: 10.0.0.0/16. The CIDR size must be between a /16 netmask and a /28 netmask. It's assumed that you have basic networking fundamentals; therefore, you should understand what an **Internet Protocol (IP)** address and netmask are and how to calculate how many IPs are available before and after allocation. Remember, cloud compute VMs require valid IP addresses, so knowing how many IPs helps organizations plan for how many VMs can deploy in a VPC.

> **Note**
>
> You can find various CIDR calculators online, but cloud computing leaders have included VPC or VNet built-in calculators to simplify the IP address calculation process.

The steps are as follows:

1. In the **IPv4 CIDR block** field, review the default settings. Analyze the IPs available—65,536 IPs are listed.
2. The calculation was performed automatically.
3. Update the **IPv4 CIDR block** field to 10.0.0.0/18. Analyze the IPs available—how many are listed?
4. Review the **Availability Zones** options. Analyze the recommendation denoted—at least two **availability zones (AZs)** for **high availability (HA)**.
5. Remember—in *Chapter 3*, we described the fault-tolerant infrastructure, which explained AZs.

Task 3: Describe and configure subnets

In this task, you will define and configure your VPC subnets.

Now that you have defined a starting IP and size for your VPC, you are required to further define subnets from your CIDR. The maximum subnets available are based on the specified CIDR mask prefix. Here is an example: 10.0.0.0/16. The CIDR mask prefix is /16, and the maximum subnets are 65536. Please note that cloud computing leaders have optimized this manual tedious process by automating the subnet calculation and proposing how to assign them. However, you are responsible for the subnet configuration and have the capability to define how subnets are assigned in your VPC.

Cloud computing leaders such as Amazon recommend defining a subnet as public or private based on several factors, such as workload access patterns, endpoint network topology, and security best practices such as **defense in depth (DiD)**.

The steps are as follows:

1. On the **Create a VPC** page, the number of public subnets default settings display two public subnets and denote four web applications that need to be publicly accessible over the internet. If you interpreted it accurately, you understand publicly accessible resources such as web applications need a subnet that allows for public access.

2. If we follow best practices in terms of resiliency, recall that we elected at minimum two AZs. Theoretically, we should distribute a web application or service across two different AZs to improve resiliency. Therefore, we will leave the default settings unmodified.

3. And because we are adhering to best practices, we should also have at minimum two private subnets for resiliency and to secure backend resources that should not be accessible over the public internet. Hence, private IP addresses are sufficient, and internal VPC routing for the private subnet should only allow inbound traffic from VPC-isolated services and service ports explicitly defined after one or more rigorous risk analysis tests are concluded and approved by all stakeholders.

4. Review the **Customize subnets CIDR blocks** section. Notice that you can customize the subnets, and the calculated IPs available are listed automatically.

> Insight
>
> Cloud computing leaders' VNets do not support overlapping IP addressing. Notice the network bits in the subnets displayed are different.

Task 4: Describe and configure routing

In this task, you will define and configure routing.

Cloud computing uses routers such as on-premises data centers and route tables to control where network traffic is routed, and every subnet in your VNet has a route table, controlling the subnets' routing. Cloud computing providers include their own route tables. In this context, Amazon's VPC has a main route table that by default is assigned to each subnet.

> Insight
>
> Customers can define their own custom routes in a new route table to modify the default subnet routing behavior. Here is an example: rerouting all inbound traffic to a specific isolated intrusion prevention device hosted on one of your subnets.

The steps are as follows:

1. Review the **Route tables** section located on the **Create VPC** page. Identify the route table suffix labeled **<place holder>-rtb-public**. This route table was automatically generated and assigned to your public subnets. As with the other route tables, this table has a destination and a target. This route table enables the public subnets to access the public internet (which is the destination) via an internet gateway (which is the target).

2. Lastly, select **Create VPC**, and review the details upon successfully creating an AWS VPC.

In these tasks, you have implemented an AWS VPC with public and private subnets distributed across multiple AZs. In the next section, we venture into Microsoft Azure's ecosystem.

Microsoft Azure VNet helps organizations define a VNet in an Azure region within the public cloud. As with AWS, you can implement IaaS resource types, such as VMs, in a VNet. In this step-by-step task, we will elect to exclude deploying a VM.

Implementing an Azure VNet overview

In these tasks, you will learn how to create and configure VNet resources in Azure. You will also learn about the other VNet components, and finally, we will review several principles associated with cloud networking.

Objectives

After completing these tasks, you will be able to achieve the following:

- Describe and configure a VNet
- Describe and configure an address space
- Describe and configure subnets
- Describe and configure an internet gateway
- Describe and configure routing

Prerequisites

These are the recommended requirements for completing all tasks:

- An updated version of the Windows 8.1 or later, macOS 10.15 or later, or Linux Ubuntu 18.04 or later computer operating system
- An up-to-date and secure internet browser (Chrome or Edge is recommended)

- Instructions are located in the following places:

  - In this chapter, in the *Virtual networking* section

  - At `https://github.com/PacktPublishing/Cloud-Computing-for-Beginners/tree/main/Instructions/Chapter7/VNET/Azure`

- Access to an Azure subscription with the required privileges to create and manage all VPC resources and dependencies

  - Here's how to create an Azure trial subscription for training purposes only: `https://azure.microsoft.com/en-us/free/`

> **Note**
>
> I am using a Windows 10 OS and a Chrome or Edge browser.

You should fork, clone, or download, and follow along with the step-by-step tasks in GitHub or described herein. I recommend using GitHub in conjunction with the book because any parts written in code are more clearly defined in GitHub. However, that's my preference—you may prefer the book format.

Ready?

Let's start the tasks to implement an Azure VNet.

To do 0: Subscribe to Microsoft Azure

Task 1: Sign in to Azure. The steps are as follows:

1. Select the Edge or Chrome browser on your computer and search for `https://azure.microsoft.com/en-us/free/`.

2. After the website loads, select **Start free**.

3. On the `login.microsoftonline.com` website, select **Create one!** Here are a couple of email account name examples:

   - `Example.lastname@outlook.com`

   - `Example98765@outlook.com`

4. Follow the remaining prompts and populate all required fields to complete the new account creation process.

> **Note**
>
> I have elected to exclude any guidance pertaining to billing details that include PII.

There are several resources to help you create and manage your Azure Free Tier to ensure you don't incur substantial costs. You can refer to `https://azure.microsoft.com/en-us/free/free-account-faq/`.

Tasks

To do 2: Implement an Azure VNet

Task 1: Describe and configure a VNet

In this task, you will implement a VNet by using the Azure portal.

Microsoft, as with the Amazon and Google Cloud computing leaders, includes transport and network layer **distributed denial-of-service (DDoS)** protection, which improves protection from multi-layer attacks in every Azure geographical location. Cloud computing leaders understand that DDoS attacks are very common, and because of their frequency, all cloud networks offer DDoS protection features and provide at an additional cost optimized DDoS support to adapt and mitigate against attacks designed to exhaust resource capacity. For example, what if your current cloud computing budget is impacted due to unplanned additional data transfer and consistent scaling-out costs because of DDoS attacks? No need to fret—Microsoft will *credit* your organization because of DDoS attacks.

> **Insight**
>
> Cloud computing leaders provide numerous features to defend against DDoS attacks, and each cloud computing provider recommends using these in conjunction with their cloud architecting principles sourced from the well-architected frameworks.

Let us begin with the steps:

> **Note**
>
> As I describe some of each provider's cloud resources, such as VNet/VPC, I'll add attributes and features that are similar across Azure, AWS, and GCP. However, I'll describe them separately to support describing as many incredible cloud computing features as possible in one book.

1. Sign in to the Azure portal (`https://portal.azure.com/`).

2. In the portal, navigate and select **Create a resource**, and on the **Create a resource** page, navigate to the **Categories** section and select **Networking**.

3. On the **Create a resource** page, select **Virtual network**.

4. On the **Create virtual network** page, on the **Basics** tab, review and populate the following empty fields—use the table entries from the *Value* column:

Project details/instance details	Value	Additional instructions
Resource group	ccebnetworkRG	Select Create new
Name	Vnet0	None
Region	East US	Select drop-down menu

Table 7.1 – Table with data and values to be entered for reference

5. Select **IP Addresses**.

Task 2: Describe and configure an address space

In this task, you will define and configure an IP address space.

As with AWS, Microsoft Azure administrators must define the starting IP and size of the VNet using CIDR notation. Here's a similar example: 10.0.0.0/16. Azure CIDR size can be between a /08 netmask and a /32 netmask. Remember—cloud compute VMs require valid IP addresses, so knowing how many IPs helps organizations architect future expansion.

Insight

Azure supports the 10/8 and 10/32 prefixes; however, current Microsoft articles denote that VNet constraints are like AWS with respect to the VNet IP address limit of 65,536. So, in brief, the number of IP addresses you can use is similar to AWS VPC, and cloud providers (including Google Cloud) use the IP address ranges specified in **Request for Comments (RFC)** *1918*.

The steps are as follows:

1. In the **IP Addresses** tab, review the default IPv4 address space field value automatically generated, displaying 10.0.0.0/16.

2. This IPv4 address space can be modified, and the empty field below supports additional address spaces. Remember—IP address spaces cannot overlap.

Task 3: Describe and configure subnets

In this task, you will define and configure an IP address space subnet.

In cloud computing, you are responsible for the subnet configuration and have the capability to define how subnets are assigned in your VNet. Microsoft recommends defining your subnets by considering various factors, such s workload access patterns and security best practices such as DiD. Notice the similarities between AWS and Azure, and both cloud providers include guidance on how to design your network to comply with your governance and compliance documentation.

The steps are as follows:

1. In the **IP address** tab, select the subnet name labeled **default**, then replace the subnet name field value named **default** by entering `public_1`, and then select **Save**.

2. In the **IP address** tab, select **Add subnet**, and in the **Add subnet** page, enter `private_1` in the **Subnet name** field.

3. On the **Add subnet** page, enter `10.0.1.0/24` in the **Subnet address range** field, and then select **Add**.

4. In the **IP address** tab, select **Add subnet**, and on the **Add subnet** page, enter `public_2` in the **Subnet name** field.

5. On the **Add subnet** page, enter `10.0.2.0/24` in the **Subnet address range** field, and then select **Add**.

6. In the **IP address** tab, select **Add subnet**, and in the **Add subnet** page, enter `private_2` in the **Subnet name** field.

7. On the **Add subnet** page, enter `10.0.3.0/24` in the **Subnet address range** field, and then select **Add**.

8. In the **IP address** tab, navigate and select **Review + create**. Then, in the **Review + create** tab, select **Create**.

Task 4: Describe and configure routing and an internet gateway

In this task, you will understand Azure routing and its built-in internet gateway.

Cloud computing providers such as Azure include their own route tables. Microsoft Azure has a system route table that by default is assigned to each subnet. Furthermore, internet-destined traffic defined by default in the system route table labeled 0.0.0.0/0 address prefix does not require an administrator to explicitly define a gateway for Azure to route traffic to the public internet. This differs from an AWS VPC implementation, which requires you to define an internet gateway or another service to support outbound internet traffic. Nevertheless, Azure, AWS, and GCP support overriding outbound internet traffic defined as the 0.0.0.0/0 address prefix.

Insight

Azure customers can define their own custom routes named **User-defined** in a new route table to modify the default subnet routing behavior.

In these tasks, you have implemented an Azure VNet with public and private subnets. In the next section, we explore Google Cloud VPC.

Google Cloud VPC supports creating VNets in the Google cloud. As with Azure, you can launch compute resource types—such as Kubernetes, VMs, and more—in a VPC. In the following tasks, we will not deploy Kubernetes.

Implementing Google Cloud VPC overview

In these tasks, you will learn how to create and configure VPC resources in Google Cloud. You will also learn about the other VPC components, and lastly, we will review several principles associated with cloud networking.

Objectives

After completing these tasks, you will be able to achieve the following:

- Describe and configure a VPC
- Describe and configure IP addresses
- Describe and configure subnets
- Describe and configure an internet gateway
- Describe and configure routes

Prerequisites

These are the recommended requirements for completing all tasks:

- An updated version of the Windows 8.1 or later, macOS 10.15 or later, or Linux Ubuntu 18.04 or later computer operating system
- An up-to-date and secure internet browser (Chrome or Edge is recommended)
- Instructions are located in the following places:
  - In this chapter, in the *Virtual networking* section
  - At `https://github.com/PacktPublishing/Cloud-Computing-for-Beginners/tree/main/Instructions/Chapter7/VNET/GoogleCloud`
- Access to a GCP account with the required privileges to create and manage all VPC resources and dependencies
  - Here's how to create a GCP free account for training purposes only:
    - `https://cloud.google.com/free/`
    - `https://cloud.google.com/resource-manager/docs/manage-google-cloud-resources`

> **Note**
> I am using a Windows 10 OS and the Chrome or Edge browser.

You should fork, clone, or download, and follow along with the step-by-step tasks in GitHub or described herein. I recommend using GitHub in conjunction with the book because any parts written in code are more clearly defined in GitHub. However, that's my preference –you may prefer the book format.

Ready?

Start the tasks to implement a Google Cloud VPC.

To do 0: Subscribe to GCP

Task 1: Sign in to GCP

1. Select the Edge or Chrome browser on your computer and go to `https://cloud.google.com/free/`.

2. After the website loads, select **Get started for free**.

3. On the `accounts.google.com` website, select **Create account**, and then select **Create a new Gmail address instead**. Here are a couple of email account name examples (replace **Example** with your name or alias):

    *   `Example.lastname@gmail.com`

    *   `Example98765@gmail.com`

4. Follow the remaining prompts and populate all required fields to conclude the new account creation process.

> **Note**
>
> I have elected to exclude any guidance pertaining to billing details that include PII.

There are several resources to help you create and manage your free GCP account to ensure you don't incur substantial costs. You can refer to `https://cloud.google.com/free/`.

Tasks

To do 2: Implement a Google Cloud VPC

Task 1: Describe and configure a VPC

In this task, you will implement a VPC by using the Google Cloud console.

Google Cloud, as with AWS, includes a preconfigured VPC, but the VPC is a global resource instead of a regional one. The VPC is labeled **Default network**, and it is already configured with a subnet to host your resources, and more.

The steps are as follows:

1. Sign in to the Google Cloud console (`https://console.cloud.google.com/`).

2. In the *search* field, enter the search parameter value `VPC`, and then select **VPC network**.

3. On the **VPC networks** page, select **CREATE VPC NETWORK**.

4. On the **Create a VPC network** page, enter `vnet0` in the **Name** field.

Task 2: Describe and configure IP addresses and subnets

In this task, you will define and configure VPC IP addresses and subnets.

Google Cloud VPC administrators define the starting IP and size of a VPC subnet using CIDR notation. Here's an example: 10.0.0.0/08. The GCP CIDR size can be between a /08 netmask and a /29 netmask. In GCP, you define subnet IP addresses, not VPC address spaces.

Insight: Google Cloud VPC supports custom and automatic subnet IP address creation mode. The automatic mode will create a subnet in every region. Regardless of your choice, cloud computing providers, including Google Cloud, use the IP address ranges specified in RFC *1918*; however, Google allows you to use a range not in RFC 1918 if you confirm that the range does not conflict with any existing network topology. I was able to use a 10/07 prefix; nevertheless, I would not use this in production. As the age-old adage proclaims, just because you can, doesn't mean you should.

Follow these steps:

1. On the **Create a VPC network** page, in the **New subnet** section, enter `public-1` in the **Name** field.

2. On the **Create a VPC network** page, in the **New subnet section**, select `us-east1` in the **Region** field.

3. On the **Create a VPC network** page, in the **New subnet** section, enter `10.0.0.0/24` in the **Name** field.

4. On the **Create a VPC network** page, select **ADD SUBNET**.

5. On the **Create a VPC network** page, in the **New subnet** section, enter `private-1` in the **Name** field.

6. On the **Create a VPC network** page, in the **New subnet** section, select `us-east1` in the **Region** field.

7. On the **Create a VPC network** page, in the **New subnet** section, enter `10.0.1.0/24` in the **Name** field.

8. On the **Create a VPC network** page, select **ADD SUBNET**.

9. On the **Create a VPC network** page, in the **New subnet** section, enter `public-2` in the **Name** field.

10. On the **Create a VPC network** page, in the **New subnet** section, select us-east1 in the **Region** field.

11. On the **Create a VPC network** page, in the **New subnet** section, enter 10.0.2.0/24 in the **Name** field.

12. On the **Create a VPC network** page, select **ADD SUBNET**.

13. On the **Create a VPC network** page, in the **New subnet** section, enter private-2 in the **Name** field.

14. On the **Create a VPC network** page, in the **New subnet** section, select us-east1 in the **Region** field.

15. On the **Create a VPC network** page, in the **New subnet** section, enter 10.0.3.0/24 in the **Name** field.

16. On the **Create a VPC network** page, select **CREATE**.

Task 3: Describe and configure routes and an internet gateway

With this task, you will come to understand Google Cloud routes and their built-in internet gateway.

GCP VPCs include their own system-generated route tables that by default are assigned to the VPC network, and they include a route for internet-destined traffic defined by default in the system-generated default routes labeled 0.0.0.0/0. And as with Microsoft Azure, it does not require an administrator to explicitly define a gateway to route traffic to the public internet. This too differs from the AWS VPC implementation, which requires you to define an internet gateway or another service to support outbound internet traffic.

Load balancing

In this section, you will learn about AWS, Azure, and Google Cloud load balancers. Load balancers receive inbound and outbound network traffic from clients and services to a target group of resources, such as IaaS resource type-labeled VMs, more commonly referred to as compute instances.

Load balancers by type

Cloud computing providers offer various resources to improve scale and availability, such as load balancers. Cloud load balancers are built to scale and are resilient due to the cloud infrastructure, and cloud load balancers support distributing inbound traffic across AZs.

Cloud computing leaders offer different types of load balancers, typically classified by the **Open Systems Interconnection** (**OSI**) layer. Here is an example: application load balancers are typically layer 7. And here is a client request example: a client requests a website that includes a **Domain Name System** (**DNS**) hostname such as trucksmart.com, which typically starts with http or https. That incoming request will be passed through (or proxied, in layman's terms), distributed by a layer 7 load balancer, sometimes referred to as **application load balancing**.

Here is a table listing cloud load balancers by type and supported protocol:

AWS	Elastic Load Balancers: • Gateway Load Balancers • Layer 3: • IP *NVA	Elastic Load Balancers: • Network Load Balancers: Private/Public • Layer 4: • TCP, UDP	Elastic Load Balancers: • Application Load Balancer • Layer 7 • HTTP, HTTPS
Azure	Azure Load Balancers: • Gateway Load Balancer • Layer 3: • IP *NVA	Azure Load Balancers: • Load Balancer • Layer 4: • TCP, UDP	Azure Load Balancers: • Application Gateway • Layer 7: • HTTP, HTTPS
GCP	*Google Cloud Load Balancers: • Internal TCP/UDP load balancer • Layer 4: • *NVA	Google Cloud Load Balancers: • Network Load Balancing • Layer 4 • TCP, UDP	Google Cloud Load Balancers: • Global Load Balancing • Layer 7 • HTTP, HTTPS

Table 7.2 – AWS, Azure, and GCP load balancers by type and protocol

Cloud computing leaders offer a variety of load balancer types by protocol and traffic (including resource-specific) and for **network virtual appliances** (**NVAs**) and DNS, which are not explored within this book. Providers may offer alternatives for specific workloads through advanced configurations, combining architecture and internal load balancers, as Google Cloud did to support highly available NVAs. In brief, this table is not an exhaustive list and is only up to date with any cloud computing resources in preview or generally available from April 2022.

Amazon, as with Microsoft and Google, is aware of the need to continuously improve fault tolerance, **business continuity** (**BC**), and scalability. It has gone as far as defining best practices centered around the principles of resiliency that correlate with fault tolerance, recoverability, and scalability. And in this journey toward perfecting high availability processes and services such as load balancing are crucial to optimizing HA.

Implementing AWS Elastic load balancers

Amazon Elastic load balancers automatically distribute incoming traffic across multiple AZs to target groups of EC2 instances.

Its purpose is to improve fault tolerance in your workloads, effortlessly providing the load-balancing capacity needed for incoming traffic. Amazon's load balancing detects unhealthy EC2 instances and can redirect traffic to one or more healthy instances.

The following is an example of Amazon Elastic load balancers:

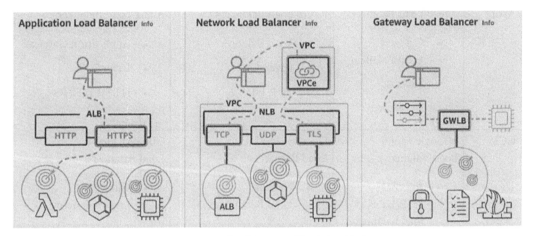

Figure 7.2 – Example of Amazon Elastic load balancers

In these tasks, you will learn how to create and configure an Elastic load balancer in AWS. You will also learn how to efficiently deploy the service.

Objectives

After completing these tasks, you will be able to achieve the following:

- Describe and configure an Elastic load balancer
- Configure a CloudFormation template

Prerequisites

These are the recommended requirements for completing all tasks:

- An updated version of the Windows 8.1 or later, macOS 10.15 or later, or Linux Ubuntu 18.04 or later computer operating system
- An up-to-date and secure internet browser (Chrome or Edge is recommended)

- Instructions are located at `https://github.com/PacktPublishing/Cloud-Computing-for-Beginners/tree/main/Instructions/Chapter7/VNET/AWS`

- Access to an AWS account with the required privileges to create and manage all VPC resources and dependencies

  - Here's how to create an AWS trial account for training purposes only: `https://aws.amazon.com/free`

Tasks

To do 1: Implement an AWS Elastic load balancer

Important

The instructions listed are accurate if you are using the New VPC Experience, which is optional. Furthermore, to help you successfully implement a service, I have elected to utilize **infrastructure-as-code (IaC)**-like tools and services to streamline creation. However, this may impact your experience mastering all the components and features of the cloud computing service in this chapter.

Additionally, this book is not intended to replace an instructor-led course that allocates the time required to learn all the components of a service. I do elaborate on instructor-led courses in *Chapter 13*.

Task 1: Describe and configure an Elastic load balancer

In this task, you will implement an Elastic load balancer by using AWS CloudFormation:

1. Sign in to the AWS Management Console (`https://console.aws.amazon.com/console/`).

Insight

You will need to create an AWS key pair for the task in *step 13*.

---

2. In the console, navigate and select **Services**, and in the **Services** section, navigate and select **Management & Governance**.

3. In the **Management & Governance** section, select **CloudFormation**.

4. In the **CloudFormation** dashboard, navigate and select **Designer**.

5. On the **CloudFormation Designer** page, navigate and select the *file* icon, and then select **Open**.

6. In the **Open a template** dialog box or prompt, select **Local file**.

> **Note**
>
> If you followed the previous recommendations to fork, clone, or download the GitHub repository directory and files to your local machine, you can upload any files to help complete tasks.

7. After selecting the **Local file** option, you'll have access to your local machine directory and files using your local machine filesystem. For example, File Explorer opens and displays my directories.

8. Using File Explorer, I navigate to the ~ `Cloud-Computing-Essentials-Beg\ Allfiles\Chapter7\VNET\AWS`. directory. And then, I select `awsloadbalancer. json`.

9. On the **CloudFormation Designer** page, navigate and select the *validate template* icon. The output should display **Template is valid**.

10. On the **CloudFormation Designer** page, navigate and select the create stack icon.

11. Select **Next**.

12. On the **Specify stack details** page, enter a stack name—for example, `stack01`.

13. On the **Specify stack details** page, review the instance type, `KeyName`, and `SSHLocation` parameters. Then, select a key name preexisting value—for example, `KeyPairCh7`—and then select **Next**.

14. Select **Next**.

15. On the **Review <place holder for your stack name>** page—for example, **Review stack01**—navigate and select **I acknowledge that AWS CloudFormation might create IAM resources**, and then select **Create stack**.

Stack creation can take some time.

16. Review the AWS resources created by using the search feature in the AWS Management Console.

17. Delete the stack of resources to prevent incurring further charges:

   • Launch the cloud shell in the AWS Management Console.

   • At the cloud shell command-line prompt, enter the following to delete the stack of resources:

```
aws cloudformation delete-stack \
--stack-name <enter your stack name here>.
```

Implementing Azure load balancers

The modular data center looks like a container, and inside there are blade servers that are contained in racks. Additionally, there is a multitude of powerful fans that force heated air generated by the blade servers to go through equipment designed to exchange heat for cool air, which consequently cools the blade servers. The modular data center was motivated by a demand for lowering energy and cooling costs, which are also managed using environmental controls. Furthermore, the modular data center compute system utilizes custom commodity hardware, which is a business practice with cloud computing providers' equipment replacement methods to control costs.

The following is an example of an Azure load balancer:

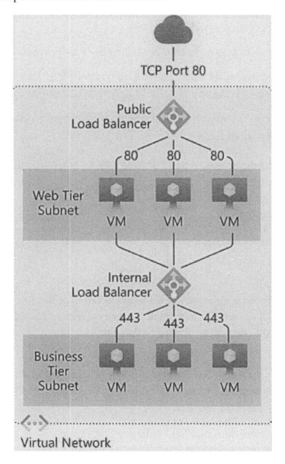

Figure 7.3 – Azure load balancer

In these tasks, you will learn how to create and configure a load balancer in Azure. You will also learn how to efficiently deploy the service.

Objectives

After completing these tasks, you will be able to achieve the following:

- Describe and configure an Azure load balancer
- Configure one or more resources, including an availability set, VMs, and an Azure load balancer

Prerequisites

These are the recommended requirements for completing all tasks:

- An updated version of the Windows 8.1 or later, macOS 10.15 or later, or Linux Ubuntu 18.04 or later computer operating system
- An up-to-date and secure internet browser (Chrome or Edge is recommended)
- Instructions are located at `https://github.com/PacktPublishing/Cloud-Computing-for-Beginners/tree/main/Instructions/Chapter7/VNET/Azure`
- Access to an Azure subscription with the required privileges to create and manage all VPC resources and dependencies
  - Here's how to create an Azure trial subscription for training purposes only: `https://azure.microsoft.com/en-us/free/`

Tasks

To do 1: Implement an Azure load balancer.

> **Important note**
> To help you successfully implement a service, I have elected to utilize IaC-like tools and services to streamline creation. However, this may impact your experience mastering all the components and features of the cloud computing service in this chapter.

Additionally, this book is not intended to replace an instructor-led course that allocates the time required to learn all the components of a service. I do elaborate on instructor-led courses in *Chapter 13, Enhancing the Continuous Learning Journey*.

Task 1: Describe and configure an Azure load balancer

In this task, you will implement an Azure load balancer by using AWS CloudFormation:

1. Sign in to the Azure portal (`https://portal.azure.com/`).
2. In the portal, navigate and select **Create a resource**, and on the **Create a resource** page, enter `template` in the **Search services and marketplace** field. Then, select **Template deployment**.

3. On the **Template deployment (deploy using custom templates)** page, select **Create**.

4. On the **Custom deployment** page, select **Build your own template in the editor**.

5. On the **Edit template** page, select **Load file**.

> **Note**
>
> If you followed the previous recommendations to fork, clone, or download the GitHub repository directory and files to your local machine, you can upload any files to help complete tasks.

6. Select the file named `azureloadbalancer.json` located in the `~ /Cloud-Computing-Essentials-Beg\Allfiles\Chapter7\VNET\Azure` directory. Then, select **Save** on the **Edit template** page.

7. On the **Custom deployment** page, enter the following parameter values:

   - **Resource group**: `azurelbrg`

   - **Region**: `East US` (any region with available resource capacity)

   - **Admin Username**: `<place holder for your name>`

   - **Admin Password**: `Pa55w0rd12345` (This is not a strong password and is only an example. Create a strong password instead.)

8. On the **Custom deployment** page, select **Review + create**.

9. After validation has passed, select **Create**.

   Azure template creation can take some time.

10. Review the Azure resources created by using the search feature in the Azure portal.

11. Delete the resources to prevent incurring further charges:

    - Launch the cloud shell in the Azure portal.

    - At the cloud shell command-line prompt, enter the following to delete the resources:

      ```
      Az group delete -name <Enter your resource group name
      here>
      ```

12. And then, enter `y` at the next prompt.

Implementing Google Cloud load balancers

The continuous influx of digital information dubbed data in today's era is staggering. The massive volumes of data include structured, semi-structured, and unstructured data from different data origins, and in different sizes that range from gigabytes to petabytes.

The following is an example of a Google Cloud load balancer:

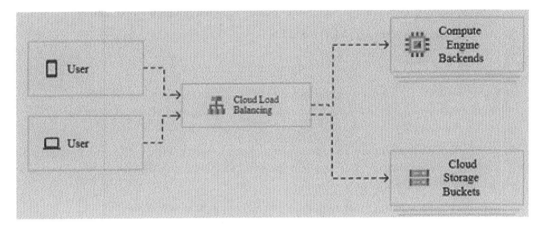

Figure 7.4 – Google Cloud load balancer

In these tasks, you will learn how to create and configure a cloud load balancer in Google. You will also learn how to efficiently deploy the service.

Objectives

After completing these tasks, you will be able to achieve the following:

- Describe and configure a Google Cloud load balancer
- Configure one or more resources such as Cloud Run including a Google Cloud load balancer

Prerequisites

These are the recommended requirements for completing all tasks:

- An updated version of the Windows 8.1 or later, macOS 10.15 or later, or Linux Ubuntu 18.04 or later computer operating system
- An up-to-date and secure internet browser (Chrome or Edge is recommended)
- Instructions are located at `https://github.com/PacktPublishing/Cloud-Computing-for-Beginners/tree/main/Instructions/Chapter7/VNET/GoogleCloud`
- Access to a Google Cloud account with the required privileges to create and manage all resources and dependencies
  - Here's how to create a Google Cloud trial account for training purposes only: `https://aws.amazon.com/free`

Tasks

To do 1: Implement a Google Cloud load balancer

To help you successfully implement a service, I've elected to utilize IaC tools and patterns to streamline creation.

Task 1: Describe and configure a Google Cloud load balancer

In this task, you will implement a Google Cloud load balancer by using AWS CloudFormation. Follow these steps:

1.   Sign in to the Google Cloud console (`https://console.cloud.google.com/`).

2.   In the console, enter `Cloud Run API` in the *search* field, and then select **Cloud Run API**.

3.   On the **Cloud Run API** page, select **ENABLE**.

4.   In the console, select **Activate Cloud Shell**.

> **Note**
>
> If you followed the previous recommendations to fork, clone, or download the GitHub repository directory and files to your local machine, you can upload any files to help complete tasks. For example, you can clone your GitHub forked copy in *step 6*, listed next. In *step 6*, you can change directory (`cd`) to the folder/directory where the Terraform files are located.

5.   In the cloud shell, at the prompt, enter `git clone <Enter Your GitHub repo URL>`.

> **Important note**
>
> Please provide your unique GitHub URL. Utilize that URL in *steps 5* and *6*. In *step 6*, use the change directory command (denoted as `cd`), and include the path to the directory ending in `/LoadBalancer/GoogleCloud`. If your path name is different, then enter the path directory containing files such as `main.tf`, `outputs.tf`, `variables.tf`, and `versions.tf`.

6.   Next, enter `cd ~/Allfiles/Chapter7/LoadBalancer/GoogleCloud` to change to the directory containing the Terraform files.

7.   Set the project by entering `PROJECT=YOUR_PROJECT`.

8.   Next, enter `gcloud config set project ${PROJECT}`.

9.   Configure the Terraform environment by entering the following:

```
[[ $CLOUD_SHELL ]] || gcloud auth application-default
login
export GOOGLE_PROJECT=$(gcloud config get-value project)
```

10. Initialize Terraform by entering `terraform init`.

11. And then, implement the resources defined in the Terraform files such as the load balancer by entering the following:

```
terraform apply -var=project_id=$PROJECT \
-var=ssl=false -var=domain=null.
```

Resource creation may take several minutes.

12. If you encounter any prompts, enter `yes` to continue.

13. After successful resource creation, review the resources/assets governed by your Google Cloud project.

Here are some essential Google Cloud load balancer resources, and characteristics of import:

• Internet-facing or internal—self-explanatory, no?

• Global or regional—it doesn't get any simpler.

• The backend configuration is made up of Google Cloud resources such as VMs, named instance groups, and the protocol and port the load balancer uses to communicate with the instances. Logging and security features are included—for example, help against DDoS.

• All load balancers need rules to follow to direct traffic flow, which varies depending on your choice of load balancer type.

• And let's not forget the frontend IP configuration. This IP is the frontend for your client's requests.

14. After reviewing the load balancer resources, I recommend you delete all resources to prevent incurring additional charges.

15. At the cloud shell prompt (if not active, activate it), change directory back to the folder containing the Terraform files, then run `terraform init` again, and then, at the prompt, enter `terraform destroy`.

Site-to-site VPN

In this section, you will learn about the essential site-to-site VPN options available across the cloud computing leaders AWS, Azure, and Google Cloud.

Developing hybrid solutions where services reside—such as on-premises and in the cloud—is strategic for many customers, and it's simple to configure using network hybrid options such as VPNs. This strategy helps organizations develop cutting-edge, resilient, and secure hybrid solutions by delivering private or public accessibility.

What is a VPN? VPNs support sending encrypted traffic between a cloud computing network and an on-premises local network over the public internet. One of the main benefits of a VPN is the security and management of one or more private subnetworks. Typically, administrators use VPN clients to establish an encrypted session with a private network from anywhere around the globe.

AWS VPN

In AWS, your VPC resources cannot communicate with your on-premises network resources and services by default, and this is similar across the other cloud computing leaders. What if your cloud-hosted API ran in an isolated VPC network and required communicating with an on-premises data management system securely? Well, with AWS site-to-site VPN, organizations can enable resources and services such as a VPC-hosted API to route traffic securely over the public internet to a private local network resource.

Virtual private gateways

Amazon provides a **virtual private gateway** (**VPG**), a VPN endpoint hosted in AWS, attached to a single VPC, offering more connectivity options, such as a site-to-site VPN connection—meaning connecting a network site to a distinct network site using a VPN.

Customer gateways and devices

A customer gateway device is your enterprise organization's device, such as a Cisco CSR 1000—a physical device or software on your local network. Furthermore, the information about your physical gateway device is stored in AWS as a customer gateway, which is a logical object that you configure.

VPN tunnels and connections

Once the VPG and the customer gateway are configured securely, a connection is established that supports VPN tunnels. The VPN gateway supports one or more encrypted tunnels for traffic to pass through from your on-premises network to the AWS VPC.

Azure VPN

Cloud computing leaders such as Microsoft Azure, AWS, and Google Cloud VPN resources can be used to route encrypted traffic from on-premises and between distinct VNets, even if a VNet is in a different region.

VPN gateways

In Azure, a VPN gateway is also referred to as a VNet gateway, and as with Amazon's VPG object, it's also an endpoint.

VPN devices

As with Amazon, Microsoft Azure site-to-site VPN requires a supported VPN device, configured on the customer's on-premises site. And the customer gateway device, which is referred to as the VPN device in Azure, is where you define the customer's gateway device information in Azure.

> **Did you know?**
> Cloud computing providers offer numerous resource guides to help with VPN device configuration.

Local network gateways

Another similarity is the Azure local network gateway object, which resembles the AWS customer gateway object. If you recall, the object represents the customer's on-premises configuration, including the local network IP address of the VPN device.

VPN tunnels and connections

Both Azure and AWS support more than one tunnel. Furthermore, you can connect to multiple on-premises network sites from the same Azure VNet or AWS VPG. Don't forget, however, that IP addresses cannot overlap.

Google Cloud VPN

Cloud computing leaders such as Google offer low-volume connections traversing the public internet securely between the public cloud and your enterprise on-premises networks. And as with the other providers, Google Cloud offers highly available VPN solutions that are not only secure but also resilient.

VPN gateways

Much as with AWS and Microsoft Azure, Google Cloud's VPN is an endpoint target for on-premises and other cloud networks hosting customer-managed VPN devices. The Google Cloud VPN gateway supports not one but multiple tunnels and connections to offer highly available site-to-site VPN connectivity.

Peer VPN gateways

In Google Cloud, when you define a peer VPN gateway, which is a customer gateway device located on-premises, you configure a peer VPN gateway interface. The configuration information defined includes an external IP address for that peer gateway device's interface.

Cloud Router

Google Cloud Router works much like your own router but at a cloud scale. The main purpose of Cloud Router is to dynamically exchange network routing information from your on-premises network to your VPC where your VPN gateway endpoint resides in this context. If not applicable to your organization's requirements, static routing is optional. Nevertheless, to configure a highly available site-to-site VPN in Google Cloud, Cloud Router is recommended.

VPN tunnels and connections

In Google Cloud, when you have finished creating the VPN gateway and defining the peer VPN gateway interface, then you create your tunnels and establish your connection.

HA VPN connections

Resiliency is crucial, even more so when implementing network hybrid connectivity. Cloud computing providers' virtual network gateway objects represent cloud-scaled VPN devices and support active-standby and active-active HA.

With active-standby, there are two tunnels, except that only one is active, but if one were to fail, then the standby would automatically enable and route traffic. Each cloud computing leader recommends redundant customer gateway devices on-premises, with one or more interfaces, in support of multiple tunnels, which increases HA.

If your organization requires greater HA without downtime, which is inevitable with active-standby, organizations can elect an active-active configuration, which has two tunnels that are always on, consequently ensuring no downtime if one tunnel were to fail.

I elected to exclude step-by-step instructions for the site-to-site VPN due to various factors. The most evident and important from my perspective for beginning practitioners is the costs incurred with procuring and implementing an actual customer gateway device on-premises.

However, each cloud computing leader mentioned herein has instructor-led courses that include labs that provide the initial setup required to immerse oneself in a real-world task. Unfortunately, I wouldn't recommend a video tutorial. A human trainer in real time, not a video playback, should guide you through those precarious steps to ensure you understand what it is you are doing, and what to expect when things don't immediately work as planned.

Summary

In this chapter, you learned about implementing various essential cloud networking resources, including network virtualization, cloud load balancers, and site-to-site VPN services.

In the next chapter, we explore launching scaled cloud compute.

Questions

1. What is a VPC?

    A. VM

    B. Container

    C. VPC

    D. None of these

2. What is a VNet?

    A. Virtual network

    B. VM image

    C. VPN

    D. None of these

3. Which of the following is a known characteristics of a VPC?

    A. Public

    B. Private

    C. Hardware

    D. On-premises

4. Which of the following is a known characteristic of a VNet?

    A. Private

    B. Public

    C. Hardware

    D. On-premises

5. Which of the following is a known characteristic of a VPC and a VNet?

    A. Public

    B. Virtual box

    C. Default route table

    D. OSI model layer 1

6. Which of the following is a known characteristic of a load balancer?

    A. Scales

    B. Isolates failure

    C. Distributes ingress traffic to targets

    D. Provides intrusion prevention

7. Which of the following options is common for load balancers across AWS, Azure, and GCP?

    A. Layer 4

    B. Layer 1

    C. Code analysis

    D. Content delivery networks (CDNs)

8. Site-to-site VPN is used in which of the common scenario options?

    A. Public

    B. Hybrid

    C. VLAN

    D. None of these

9. Which of the following is a known characteristic of cloud VPN gateways?

    A. Single-tunnel

    B. Multi-tunnel

    C. Unlimited tunnels per gateway

    D. Default service-level agreement (SLA) 99.9999999999

10. Which of the following cloud VPN configuration tools are supported across AWS, Azure, and GCP?

    A. Management portal

    B. Bash shell

    C. CLI

    D. None of these

8
Launching Compute Service Resources for Scalability

This chapter will take you through implementing various essential compute services. You will also learn how to set up a **virtual machine** (**VM**), web application services, and serverless function resources, and you will reinforce concepts and configuration procedures by completing review questions.

The following concepts will be covered in this chapter:

- VMs
- Web applications
- Container services
- Serverless functions

VMs

In this section, you will learn how to configure and implement VMs. You will also learn helpful tips and potential pitfalls that encumber beginners.

It's practical for most businesses to require a modicum of control over the infrastructure, such as the operating system configuration, compute disk performance, and the ability to install and configure not just modern but legacy software. These typical needs are addressed by utilizing either **Amazon Web Services** (**AWS**), Azure, or **Google Cloud Platform** (**GCP**) compute services. One of the most widely used services to date is **infrastructure-as-a-service** (**IaaS**) VMs.

A cloud computing VM is one of the core infrastructures as a service resource, in conjunction with network virtualization, also known as **virtual networking**. Cloud compute offers near-total control over the configuration of the VM, and cloud computing leaders offer numerous ways to configure and create compute instances quickly and efficiently. They also support various operating system images such as Windows, Linux, Microsoft original licensed software, Microsoft preconfigured licensed software, third-party licensed software from companies such as CISCO, **open source software** (**OSS**), and more.

One of the many strategic reasons organizations leverage cloud computing is its known capability to optimize compute elasticity through scaling. The capability to resize compute capacity or add compute capacity on demand is a valuable commodity. Improving customer experience and controlling costs by scaling out or in are two of the many benefits derived from modern cloud compute instances, also known as VMs.

The following figure illustrates AWS, Azure, and GCP VM service names:

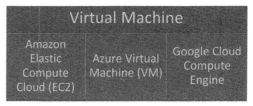

Figure 8.1 – VMs

Let us learn by creating each cloud computing provider's VM instance step by step, in the hope of reinforcing the well-known cloud computing characteristics such as rapid elasticity and on-demand self-service.

We begin by utilizing Amazon's **Elastic Compute Cloud** (**EC2**) (see *Figure 8.2*), which enables us to quickly configure and create a VM instance in an AWS region within the AWS cloud. You can implement resources such as custom **Amazon Machine Images** (**AMIs**) of popular licensed products such as Microsoft SQL Server and open source Linux distros such as Ubuntu, and more, into a **virtual private cloud** (**VPC**).

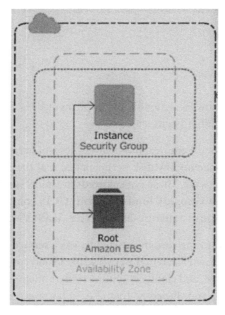

Figure 8.2 – Amazon EC2 instance

Launching AWS EC2 instances

In these tasks, you will learn how to configure and create VM cloud resources in AWS. You will also learn helpful tips and potential pitfalls that encumber beginners.

Objectives

After completing these tasks, you will be able to achieve the following:

- Describe and configure an instance and AMI
- Describe and configure an instance type
- Describe and configure network settings
- Describe and configure an **Elastic Block Store** (**EBS**) storage volume

Prerequisites

The recommended requirements for completing all tasks are as follows:

- An updated version of Windows 8.1 or later, macOS 10.15 or later, or Linux Ubuntu 18.04 or later computer operating system.
- An up-to-date and secure internet browser (Chrome or Edge is recommended).
- Instructions are located in either of the following places:

  - In this chapter
  - At `https://github.com/PacktPublishing/Cloud-Computing-for-Beginners/tree/main/Instructions/Chapter8/VM`

- Access to an AWS account with the required privileges to create and manage all EC2 resources and dependencies. Head over to `https://aws.amazon.com/free` on how to create an AWS trial account for training purposes only.

> **Note**
> I am using a Windows 10 operating system and the Chrome or Edge browser.

Migrating to the cloud has become a strategic motivation for all businesses in every sector, and performance and reliability are key business outcomes. It is important that every organization ensures that data is never lost, and **line-of-business** (**LOB**) services always remain available regardless of server failures, electrical outages, and even in the face of natural disasters.

Cloud computing compute services offer intuitive backup solutions that decrease infrastructure costs and provide holistic **business continuity (BC)**, with advanced mechanisms for resiliency to optimize the recovery process, such as supporting capabilities to frequently test **disaster recovery (DR)** efficiently across your workloads, whether they are all-in cloud or in a hybrid architecture.

But we must first learn how to efficiently configure and create EC2 instances at cloud scale utilizing the cloud's known agility.

> **Important note**
> You should fork, clone, or download and follow along with the step-by-step tasks in GitHub or described herein. I recommend using GitHub in conjunction with the book because any text of code is more clearly defined in GitHub. However, that's my preference; you may prefer the book format.

Ready?

Start the tasks to create an AWS EC2 instance.

To do 0: Subscribe to AWS

Task 1: Sign in to AWS

1. Select the Edge or Chrome browser on your computer and go to `https://aws.amazon.com/free`.

2. After the website loads, select **Create a Free Account**.

3. On the `portal.aws.amazon.com` website, populate the fields labeled **Root user email address** and **AWS account name**, and enter a valid, and readily accessible email account name and AWS account name for training purposes. Here are several email accounts and AWS account name examples:

    - `Example.lastname@gmail.com`

    - `Example.lastname@outlook.com`

    - `Cloud Practitioner`

4. Follow the remaining prompts and populate all required fields to complete the new account creation process. Note that I have elected to exclude any guidance pertaining to billing details that include **personally identifiable information (PII)**.

> **Insight**
>
> Here are several resources to help you create and manage your AWS Free Tier to ensure you don't incur substantial costs. You can visit `https://aws.amazon.com/premiumsupport/knowledge-center/create-and-activate-aws-account/` and `https://aws.amazon.com/premiumsupport/knowledge-center/what-is-free-tier/`.

To do 1: Launch an AWS EC2 instance

Real-world examples:

Moderna **Drug Design Studio (DDS)** is an application that uses several (clustered) AWS EC2 instances to handle compute-intensive jobs, loosely coupled with other AWS services to drive research and development.

> **Helpful tip or trick**
>
> To understand how AWS services meet Moderna's needs, you must first learn how to efficiently create an EC2 instance, also known as a **VM**.

Task 1: Describe and configure instances and AMI

> **Important note**
>
> The instructions listed match the AWS management portal version available in May 2022. AWS is always updating the interface to improve the user experience.

In this task, you will launch an EC2 instance using the AWS Management Console. Follow these steps:

1. Sign in to the AWS Management Console (`https://console.aws.amazon.com/console/`).

2. In the console, navigate and select **Services**, and on the **Services** section, navigate and select **Compute**.

3. In the **Compute** section, select **EC2**.

4. In the **EC2 Dashboard** pane, select **Instances**, and then select **Launch instances**.

> **Insight**
>
> Do not modify any fields or sections unless explicitly instructed. For example, if the author passes over an option that appears as a button, box, name field, or metadata, it's intentional. These options or settings are already configured by the system, and I will refer to them as the default settings.

5. Review the **Launch an instance** page, and enter `<Example: WebApp >` in the **Name** field.

> **Insight**
>
> The EC2 dashboard configuration section labeled **Launch an instance** improves the manual configuration process by centralizing overall VM settings, which include application and operating system configuration, VM sizing, disk storage, and network settings.

6. In the **Application and OS Images (Amazon Machine Image)** section, select **Windows** from the **Quick Start** options of the AMIs listed, and then select **Confirm Changes** once prompted.

> **Insight**
>
> Amazon provides AMIs, which describe the data required to launch an instance. An AMI contains many things such as the source AMI, also referred to as an image, which is an image of an operating system. The AMI helps you launch multiple instances with a similar configuration and denotes a template for the root volume containing your operating system, privileges required to allow your AWS account or others to use the AMI, and the information required to attach a block storage device to your EC2 instance when created.

7. Review your AMI, description, architecture, and the unique AMI ID associated with your image within the current region.

Task 2: Describe and configure an instance type

In this task, you will define a **classless inter-domain routing (CIDR)** instance by using the **Launch VPC Wizard** functionality.

In AWS, *instance type* refers to the compute capacity size selections for your applications. They include CPU architecture such as **Advanced Micro Devices (AMD)**, CPU virtual core count, amount of disk storage, RAM, and estimated **network interface controller (NIC)** network performance for ingress and egress.

> **Insight**
>
> Cloud computing leaders including Amazon, Microsoft, and Google provide various categories based on different types of workloads, such as general purpose, which supports a general balance between CPU and memory.

Follow these steps:

1. In the **Instance type** section, select **Compare instance types**, and then review the **Compare instance types** page. Once you are done, select **Select instance type**.

2. In the **Key pair (login)** section, either select a preexisting key pair or select **Create new key pair**.

Task 3: Describe and configure network settings

In this task, you will define and configure your VPC network settings.

Recall what you learned in *Chapter 7* regarding AWS VPC, which is, you are responsible for the subnet configuration and have the capability to define how subnets are assigned in your VPC. Amazon's best practices recommend defining a public or private subnet based on factors such as workload, network topology, and **defense in depth (DiD)**.

Proceed as follows:

1. In the **Network settings** section, review the following settings:

    *   The default VPC has already been selected and the CIDR IP address auto-populated.

    > **Insight**
    >
    > Recall what we mentioned regarding the default VPC in *Chapter 7*.

    *   The subnet setting displays **No preference**, meaning the system will automatically configure a subnet from the CIDR IP address

    *   The **Auto-assign public IP** setting is set to **Enable**, meaning the system will automatically assign a public IP

2. In the **Firewall (security groups)** section, review the firewall rules that control traffic for your EC2 instance:

    *   **Create security group** is pre-selected

    *   The **Security group name** field displays `launch-wizard-1`

    *   The inbound security group rules list the following:

        *   **Type**: **rdp**

        *   **Protocol**: **TCP**

        *   **Port range**: `3389`

        *   **Source type**: **Anywhere**

        *   **Source**: Add CIDR, prefix list, or security—`0.0.0.0/0`

        *   **Description** (*optional*): For example, **SSH for admin desktop**

3. And you will see an AWS best practice suggestion such as **We recommend setting security group rules to allow access from known IP addresses only.**

Task 4: Describe and configure an EBS storage volume

In this task, you will configure EC2 disk storage.

AWS supports block-level storage for EC2 instance disks, known as EBS. EBS disks, also referred to as EBS volumes, are resilient network-attached disks that can be attached to any instance located in the same AZ.

> **Insight**
>
> For fast local or direct attached disk storage, AWS EC2 supports instance storage as an alternative to EBS, but it's a temporary disk option, while its benefits are high throughput and cost savings.

Proceed as follows:

1. Review the **Configure storage** section settings:

    - **Root volume**: gp2—General-purpose **solid-state drive** (**SSD**):

        - SSDs are known for their performance

        - General-purpose disk types are practical for a range of workloads, development, testing, and for base operating system volumes

    - **GiB (Gigabyte)**: 30

2. Review the **Summary** section, and then select **Launch instance**.

    This may take several minutes.

3. After the successful creation of your EC2 instance, I recommend you review your instance by utilizing the EC2 dashboard.

In these tasks, you have launched an AWS EC2 instance with EBS and VPC. In the next section, we venture into Microsoft Azure's ecosystem.

Microsoft Azure **Virtual Network** (**VNet**) helps organizations define a **virtual network** (**VNet**) in an Azure region within the public cloud. As with AWS, you can implement infrastructure as a service resource types, such as VMs, into a VNet. In this step-by-step task, I will elect to exclude deploying a VM.

Launching Azure VM instances

In these tasks, you will learn how to configure and create VM instances in Azure. You will also learn helpful tips and potential pitfalls that encumber beginners.

Objectives

After completing these tasks, you will be able to achieve the following:

- Describe and configure a VM instance
- Describe and configure the VM image and size
- Describe and configure network settings
- Describe and configure a VM-managed disk

Prerequisites

Recommended requirements for completing all tasks:

- An updated version of a Windows 8.1 or later, macOS 10.15 or later, or Linux Ubuntu 18.04 or later computer operating system.
- An up-to-date and secure internet browser (Chrome or Edge is recommended).
- Instructions are also located at `https://github.com/PacktPublishing/Cloud-Computing-for-Beginners/tree/main/Instructions/Chapter8/VM`

> **Note**
> I am using a Windows 10 operating system and a Chrome or Edge browser.

- Access to an Azure subscription with the required privileges to create and manage all VNet resources and dependencies. Go to `https://azure.microsoft.com/en-us/free/` on how to create an Azure trial subscription for training purposes only.

> **Important**
> You should fork, clone or download and follow along with the step-by-step tasks in GitHub or described herein. I recommend using GitHub in conjunction with the book because any parts written in code are more clearly defined in GitHub. However, that's my preference; you may prefer the book format.

Ready?

Start the tasks to launch an Azure VM.

To do 0: Subscribe to Microsoft Azure

Task 1: Sign in to Azure

1. Select the Edge or Chrome browser on your computer and go to `https://azure.microsoft.com/en-us/free/`.

2. After the website loads, select **Start free**.

3. In the `login.microsoftonline.com` website select **Create one!** Here are several email account name examples:

    *   `Example.lastname@outlook.com`

    *   `Example98765@outlook.com`

4. Follow the remaining prompts and populate all required fields to complete the new account creation process. Note that I have elected to exclude any guidance pertaining to billing details that include PII.

> **Insight**
>
> Here are several resources to help you create and manage your Azure Free Tier to ensure you don't incur substantial costs. Visit `https://azure.microsoft.com/en-us/free/free-account-faq/`.

To do 1: Launch an Azure VM

Real-world examples:

Retailers such as Albertsons' e-commerce sites are hosted on Azure VM instances and other LOB solutions are utilizing not only IaaS but **platform-as-a-service** (**PaaS**) as well.

> **Helpful tip or trick**
>
> To understand how Azure services support Albertsons' e-commerce site needs, you must first learn how to create a **VM**.

Task 1: Describe and configure a VM instance

In this task, you will create a VM using the Azure portal.

Microsoft, as with Amazon and GCP, offers IaaS VM resources.

Insight

Cloud computing leaders provide numerous features to automate scaling efficiently and support a variety of built-in and open source tools to optimize managing scaling in and scaling out and support advanced scaling, such as leveraging **machine learning** (**ML**) algorithms to predict scaling and further control costs.

As I describe each provider's resources, such as VNet/VPC, I'll add some features that are similar across Azure, AWS, and GCP.

Proceed as follows:

1. Sign in to the Azure portal (`https://portal.azure.com/`).

2. In the portal, select **Create a resource**, and on the **Create a resource page**, navigate to the **Categories** section and select **Compute**.

3. In the **Create a resource** page, select **Virtual machine**.

   In the **Create virtual machine** page, on the **Basics** tab, review and populate the following settings listed in the **Project details** section:

Project details	Value	Additional instructions
Subscription	`<Your subscription>`	None
Resource group	`computerg`	Create new

Table 8.1 – Project details settings

Insight

In Azure, your subscription, and logical containers known as resource groups, are used to manage cloud computing projects. Every cloud computing leader has something similar organizations can use for planning and managing governance policies.

4. On the **Basic** tab, review and populate the following settings listed in the **Instance details** section:

Instance details	Value	Additional instructions
VM name	`winvm0`	None
Region	`<Select a region near you>`	None
Availability options	`Availability zone`	None
AZ	`Zones 1, 2`	Select Zones 1 and 2

Table 8.2 – Instance details settings

> **Insight**
>
> AZs were described in *Chapter 3*. After selecting two different AZs, Azure notifies you that it will place two VMs, one in each selected zone, thereby improving your application architecture resiliency by configuring fault tolerance.

Task 2: Describe and configure the VM image and size

In this task, you will configure a VM image and size.

The Azure VM image contains several things, such as the base or updated image version of an operating system—for example, Ubuntu Server 10.04 LTS – Gen2. The VM image helps you create multiple instances with a similar operating system configuration. VM size is the compute capacity of your VM. It includes CPU architecture information, such as Intel, CPU virtual core count, amount of disk storage, RAM, and NIC performance.

> **Insight**
>
> Cloud computing leaders support a cloud marketplace, a modern-day technical bazaar of base, custom, third-party, and open source images. You can select from the marketplace and launch the compute image seamlessly within your cloud ecosystem of choice.

Proceed as follows:

1. In the **Instance details** section, review the image setting, select the **Context** menu, and then select **Windows Server 2022 Datacenter: Azure Edition – Gen2**.
2. Review the **Size** setting, and leave the default selection, but notice the **virtual CPU (vCPU)** core quantity, the memory allocation, and the estimated monthly cost.

> **Insight**
>
> Optionally, you can select **See all sizes** and review additional size offerings in more granularity.

3. Populate the **Administrator account** section with a strong username and password.

Task 3: Describe and configure network settings

In this task, you will review and configure VNet settings.

In the cloud computing service model IaaS, you are responsible for the network configuration and have the capability to customize your VNet. Microsoft recommends defining your VNet by considering various factors, such as workload access patterns and security best practices such as DiD. Notice the similarities between AWS and Azure—both cloud providers include guidance on how to design your network to comply with best practices.

Proceed as follows:

1. In the **Inbound port rules** section, review and select **Allow selected ports**, and then, in the **Select inbound ports** context menu, select **HTTP (80)**.

2. Review both **HTTP (80)** and **RDP (3389)** inbound ports.

> **Insight**
>
> Notice that Microsoft recommends this configuration only be used for testing.

3. Select the **Networking** tab, and then review the **Network interface** and the **Load balancing** sections. Select **None** for the **Load balancing** options.

> **Note**
>
> Microsoft Azure has a system route table that by default is assigned to each subnet.

4. Select the **Disks** tab.

> **Insight**
>
> Azure automatically populates the VNet, subnet, public IP, NIC network security group, public inbound ports, and load balancing settings. For example, the VNet is a VM dependency and must be created or exist to launch a VM instance.

Task 4: Describe and configure a VM-managed disk

In this task, you will configure managed disks.

Cloud computing providers such as Azure include highly durable and available block-level storage volumes managed by Microsoft Azure. Azure-managed disks by default integrate with built-in **high availability** (**HA**) and fault tolerance services such as AZ.

> **Insight**
>
> Azure customers can transfer their on-premises VM disk, known as **vhd**, to a managed disk seamlessly using command-line tools.

Proceed as follows:

5. In the **Disk** tab, in the **Disk options** section, review the following settings:

    *   **OS disk type**, which supports different types of disks, such as **Premium SSD**, and the disk is locally redundant by default, improving availability

    *   You can alternatively delete the disk when the VM instance is deleted, or elect to support an unattached disk, which persists independently of the VM

    *   You can also encrypt the host

    *   **Encryption type** is defaulted to **Encrypt at rest**, and Microsoft Azure manages the key for you

6. In the **Data disk for VM** section, you can add data disks for your VM or attach existing disks.

7. Select **Review + create**, and then select **Create**.

In these tasks, you have implemented an Azure VM resource and its dependencies. In the next section, we explore Google Cloud Compute Engine.

Google Cloud optimizes creating VM instances. As with Azure, you can launch compute resource types, such as instances—and more—into a VPC.

Launching Google Cloud Compute Engine

In these tasks, you will learn how to configure and create VM cloud resources in Google Cloud. You will also learn helpful tips and potential pitfalls that encumber beginners.

Objectives

After completing these tasks, you will be able to achieve the following:

*   Describe and configure a VM instance

*   Describe and configure a machine type

*   Describe and configure the boot disk

*   Describe and configure networking

Prerequisites

These are the recommended requirements for completing all tasks:

*   An updated version of a Windows 8.1 or later, macOS 10.15 or later, or Linux Ubuntu 18.04 or later computer operating system.

*   An up-to-date and secure internet browser (Chrome or Edge is recommended).

- Instructions are also located at `https://github.com/PacktPublishing/Cloud-Computing-for-Beginners/tree/main/Instructions/Chapter8/VM`

> **Note**
>
> I am using a Windows 10 operating system and a Chrome or Edge browser.

- Access to a GCP account with the required privileges to create and manage all VPC resources and dependencies. Go to `https://cloud.google.com/free` and `https://cloud.google.com/resource-manager/docs/manage-google-cloud-resources` on how to create a GCP free account for training purposes only.

> **Important**
>
> You should fork, clone or download and follow along with the step-by-step tasks in GitHub or described herein. I recommend using GitHub in conjunction with the book because any parts written in code are more clearly defined in GitHub. However, that's my preference; you may prefer the book format.

Ready?

Start the tasks to launch a Google Cloud Compute Engine VM instance.

To do 0: Subscribe to GCP

Task 1: Sign in to GCP

Proceed as follows:

1. Select the Edge or Chrome browser on your computer and go to `https://cloud.google.com/free/`.

2. After the website loads, select **Get started for free**.

3. In the `accounts.google.com` website, select **Create account**, and then select **Create a new Gmail address instead**. Here are several email account name examples (replace `Example` with your name or alias):

   - `Example.lastname@gmail.com`

   - `Example98765@gmail.com`

4. Follow the remaining prompts and populate all required fields to conclude the new account creation process. Note that I have elected to exclude any guidance pertaining to billing details that include PII.

> **Insight**
>
> There are several resources to help you create and manage your GCP free account to ensure you don't incur substantial costs. Visit `https://cloud.google.com/free/` to find out more.

Tasks

To do 3: Launch a Google Cloud VM instance

Real-world examples:

PayPal uses Google Compute Engine instances to add capacity to its infrastructure in minutes to meet growing customer demands due to the rise of e-commerce, which requires digital forms of payment.

> **Helpful tip or trick**
>
> To understand how Google Compute Engine meets PayPal's scalability requirements, you must learn how to create a **VM**.

Task 1: Describe and configure a VM instance

In this task, you will launch a VM instance using Google Cloud Compute Engine.

Google Cloud Compute Engine helps you create and run resilient, performant, and scalable VM instances, supporting various industry workloads for start-ups and enterprise organizations.

Proceed as follows:

1. Sign in to the Google Cloud Console (`https://console.cloud.google.com/`).
2. In the Google Cloud console, on the **Project selector** page, select or create a Google Cloud project.
3. Make sure that billing is enabled for your Google Cloud project.
4. In the search field, enter VM as a search parameter, and then select **VM instances**.
5. On the **Compute Engine** page, select **CREATE INSTANCE**.
6. Update the following settings:

    - **Name**: `instance-1`
    - **Region**: Select a region from the list
    - **Zone**: **us-central1-a**
        - Zone refers to an AZ location in a region

Task 2: Describe and configure a machine type

In this task, you will configure a machine type.

Google Cloud Compute Engine offers a variety of machine types supporting different compute capacity requirements. Machine configurations are comprised of vCPU cores, memory, and more, and as with Azure, Google Cloud provides machine-family categories to assist customers by selecting common workload compute sizes. For example, Google Cloud Compute Engine offers GPU types that are optimized for ML and visualization workloads.

Proceed as follows:

1. In the **Machine configuration** section, review the series that correlates with the machine family, and the machine type that denotes the compute capacity size.

Task 3: Describe and configure a boot disk

In this task, you will configure a boot disk.

Google Cloud Compute Engine offers a network-attached boot disk. A boot disk is derived from operating system images or snapshots. You can select public or custom images such as Linux and Windows for your boot disk operating system, and boot disks come in different performance types based on your IOPS and disk volume size requirements.

Proceed as follows:

1. In the **Machine configuration** section, review the series that correlates with the machine family, and the machine type that denotes the compute capacity size.

Task 4: Describe and configure networking

In this task, you will review and configure the network settings.

The Google Cloud Compute Engine dashboard facilitates VPC and firewall rules management, during VM creation. While configuring your VM instance, customers can manage API access, inbound firewall rules, hostnames, and the Google Cloud Compute Engine network interface settings.

Insight

Cloud computing leaders such as Amazon, Microsoft, and Google support additional security features to shield VM instances using unique security technologies and ensuring dedicated hosts such as VM offerings are available to help organizations' workloads with complex compliance needs.

---

1. Review the **Firewall** section, and then select **Allow HTTPS traffic**, which in turn configures an inbound rule. Deselect **Allow HTTPS traffic**.

2. Access the context menu in the **Networking** section, and then review the settings that support custom hostnames and network interfaces.

3. Select **Create** and wait for the instance status.

In these tasks, you have created a Google Cloud Compute Engine VM instance and dependencies. In the next lesson, we explore PaaS.

Web applications

In this section, you will learn about cloud computing-managed PaaS for web applications and mobile backend services. We will explore one of the many AWS, Azure, and Google Cloud web application deployment and agile hosting services.

Application services

Cloud computing provides application deployment and hosting of managed services, which improve the processes of planning, maintaining, and carrying out the delivery of software. Cloud leaders' PaaS unique resources help automate the app infrastructure, runtime, API and middleware, and dependencies required to run your custom application.

Application services also support the process of integrating new code frequently throughout the life cycle of the application and support automating testing frequent code releases, preceding **continuous deployment** (CD) onto prebuilt infrastructure tagged as production environments. Alternatively, cloud computing leaders Google, Microsoft, and Amazon cloud platforms offer features that even simplify testing in production by instantiating a clone of your production environment, which you can pilot in the hope of improving the overall customer experience.

Here is a non-exhaustive table listing some of the cloud computing application services:

Cloud computing provider	Application services
AWS	Elastic Beanstalk
Azure	App Service
Google Cloud	App Engine

Table 8.3 – AWS, Azure, and GCP application services

Application services are hosting platforms that are intuitive, agile, and support almost any programming language and most modern framework and runtime versions. And each cloud computing provider's services support scaling and security through unique features; although there are subtle similarities, the administration does vary from one to another. Objectively, all application services in the cloud are simpler to create and use than IaaS VM.

Implementing with AWS Elastic Beanstalk

Let's start with AWS Elastic Beanstalk, which truly lives up to its name, wherein customers can accelerate application deployment and management without all the complexity and responsibility of an IaaS.

The following screenshot provides an example view of Amazon Elastic Beanstalk:

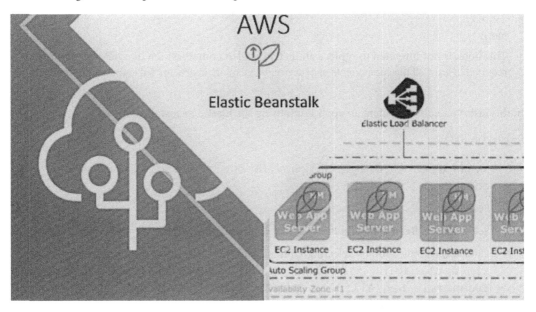

Figure 8.3 – Elastic Beanstalk

In these tasks, you will learn how to configure and deploy an application with Elastic Beanstalk in AWS, and you will also learn helpful tips and potential pitfalls that encumber beginners.

Objectives

After completing these tasks, you will be able to achieve the following:

- Describe and implement an application with Elastic Beanstalk

To do 1: Implement an application using Elastic Beanstalk

Real-world examples:

Social media service Snapchat uses AWS PaaS to drive development.

> **Helpful tip or trick**
>
> To understand how AWS helps Snapchat, you should learn how to efficiently develop apps using **PaaS**.

Task 1: Deploy an application using Elastic Beanstalk

> **Note**
>
> This book is not intended to replace an instructor-led course, which does allocate the time required to learn all the components of a service. I do explore instructor-led courses in *Chapter 14*.

In this task, you will implement an application using the Elastic Beanstalk platform.

Proceed as follows:

1. Sign in to the AWS Management Console (`https://console.aws.amazon.com/console/`).

2. Search for `Elastic Beanstalk`.

3. Select **Elastic Beanstalk**, and then select **Create an application**.

4. Upload the application by selecting **Upload**, and then select the `dotnet-core-linux.zip application zipped` files and folder located in the `~/Cloud-Computing-Essentials-Beg/Allfiles/Chapter8/WebApp` directory.

> **Insight**
>
> Did you know that Elastic Beanstalk supports Docker containers for web applications?

Implementing with Azure App Service

A modular data center looks like a container, and inside there are blade servers that are contained in racks. Additionally, there is a multitude of powerful fans that force heated air generated by the blade servers to go through equipment designed to exchange heat for cool air, which consequently cools the blade servers. The modular data center design was motivated by the demand for lowering energy and cooling costs, which are also managed using environmental controls. Furthermore, the modular data center compute system utilizes custom commodity hardware, which is a business practice for cost effective equipment replacement method by cloud computing providers

The following screenshot provides an example of an Azure load balancer:

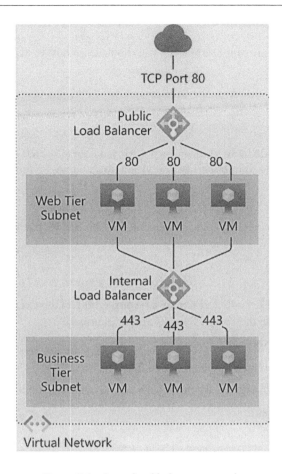

Figure 8.4 – Azure load balancer example

In these tasks, you will learn how to create and configure a load balancer in Azure. You will also learn how to efficiently deploy the service.

Objectives

After completing these tasks, you will be able to achieve the following:

- Describe and implement an application with App Services

Tasks

To do 1: Implement an application using App Services

Real-world examples:

Transportation **service provider** (**SP**) Maersk uses Azure PaaS to accelerate development.

> **Helpful tip or trick**
>
> To understand how Azure supports Maersk, you should learn how to develop apps using **PaaS**.

Task 1: Deploy an application using App Service

> **Note**
>
> This book is not intended to replace an instructor-led course, which does allocate the time required to learn all the components of a service. I do elaborate on instructor-led courses in *Chapter 14*.

In this task, you will implement an application using the App Service platform.

Proceed as follows:

1. Sign in to the Azure portal (`https://portal.azure.com/`).
2. In the portal, navigate and select **Create a resource**, and on the **Create a resource** page, enter `App Services` in the **Search services and marketplace** field.
3. Select **Create App Services**.
4. In the **Basics** tab, populate all the required information.
5. Select **Container**, and then leave the default sample container application.
6. Select **Review + create**.
7. Select **Create**.

> **Insight**
>
> Did you know that Azure App Service integrates with VNets, enabling web applications to enforce access in or through a private network?

Implementing with Google Cloud App Engine

The continuous influx of digital information dubbed data in today's era is staggering. The massive volumes of data include structured, semi-structured, and unstructured data from different data origins, and in different sizes that range from gigabytes to petabytes of whole countries' digital information.

The following diagram provides an example of Google Cloud load balancers:

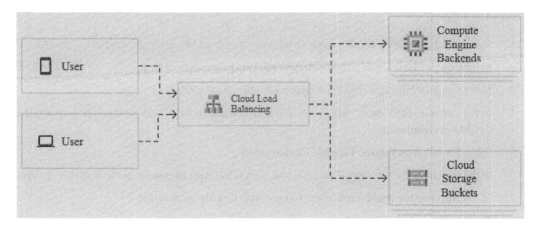

Figure 8.5 – Google Cloud load balancers example

In these tasks, you will learn how to create and configure a cloud load balancer in Google. You will also learn how to efficiently deploy the service.

Objectives

After completing these tasks, you will be able to achieve the following:

- Describe and implement an application with App Engine

To do 1: Implement an application using Google Cloud App Engine

Real-world examples:

Pizza Hut uses Google PaaS to push development to drive innovation.

> **Helpful tip or trick**
>
> To understand how Google helps Pizza Hut, you should learn how to efficiently develop apps using **GCP PaaS**.

Task 1: Deploy an application using App Engine

> **Note**
>
> This book is not intended to replace an instructor-led course. Instructor-led courses allocate the time recommended to learn all the components of a service. I do provide recommendations on how to improve your learning experience with instructor-led courses in *Chapter 14*.

In this task, you will implement an application using the App Engine platform.

Proceed as follows:

1. Sign in to the Google Cloud console (`https://console.cloud.google.com/`).

2. In the Google Cloud console, on the **Project selector** page, select or create a Google Cloud project.

3. Make sure that billing is enabled for your Google Cloud project

4. In the console, enter `App Engine API` in the search field, and then select **App engine flexible environment**.

5. Select **Enable App Engine Flexible Environment**.

6. In the search field, enter `App Engine`, and then select **App engine** from the available options.

7. In the **App Engine** dashboard, select **Create App Engine application**.

8. Download and install the following resources to your local machine:

    *   Install the Google Cloud SDK (`https://cloud.google.com/sdk/`)

    *   Install the .NET Core SDK, version 2.0 (`https://github.com/dotnet/core/blob/master/release-notes/download-archives/2.0.5-download.md`)

9. Using your local machine's command-line tools, change directory to `~/Cloud-Computing-Essentials-Beg/Allfiles/Chapter8/WebApp/dotnetappengine/`.

    Here's an example of how to do this:

    ```
    cd ~/Cloud-Computing-Essentials-Beg/Allfiles/Chapter8/
    WebApp/dotnetappengine/
    dotnet restore
    dotnet publish -c Release
    gcloud app deploy .\bin\Release\netcoreapp2.1\publish\
    app.yaml
    ```

> **Insight**
>
> Did you know that you can configure custom domain names to host an App Engine application using Google Domains?

Container services

In this section, you will learn about cloud computing-managed PaaS containers. We will explore one of the many AWS, Azure, and Google Cloud container deployment and hosting services that run Docker containerized applications.

Docker containers

Cloud computing leaders support containers or, more accurately, put containerization methods and tools that streamline operations and development teams' ability to manage, automate, and package software with portable distribution services such as Docker. Containers are also known for their architecture, which makes it feasible to package an application and its dependencies in a unit referred to as a container, which can run in any environment, and—more importantly—can be optimized and scaled by cloud computing.

Here is a non-exhaustive table listing some of the cloud computing container services:

Cloud computing provider	Container services
AWS	Elastic Kubernetes Service
Azure	Azure Kubernetes Service (AKS)
Google Cloud	Kubernetes Engine

Table 8.4 – AWS, Azure, and GCP application services

Kubernetes is a simple-to-use platform to orchestrate the deployment, scale, and administration of multiple Docker container instances in a network-secure elastic cluster.

Implementing container applications with AWS Kubernetes Service

Amazon's EKS is a fully managed Kubernetes platform that empowers developers to deploy containers without the IaaS responsibilities.

The following diagram provides an example of Amazon Elastic Beanstalk:

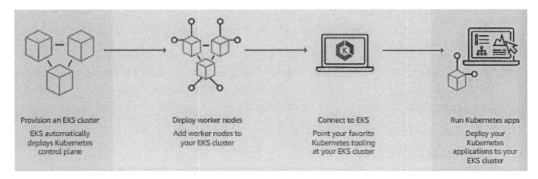

Figure 8.6 – Amazon Elastic Beanstalk example

In these tasks, you will learn how to create an EKS cluster and deploy a container on AWS, and you will also learn helpful tips and potential pitfalls that encumber beginners.

Objectives

After completing these tasks, you will be able to achieve the following:

- Describe and configure an application with EKS

To do 1: Implement a container application with a Kubernetes service

Real-world examples:

Social media service Snapchat uses the AWS Kubernetes service to rapidly orchestrate sustainable container application development.

> **Helpful tip or trick**
>
> To understand how AWS helps Snapchat, you should learn how to efficiently develop apps using **Kubernetes**.

Task 1: Describe and implement a container application with a Kubernetes service.

> **Note**
>
> This book is not intended to replace an instructor-led course, which allocates the time required to learn all the components of a service. I do elaborate on instructor-led courses in *Chapter 14*.

In this task, you will learn to implement a container application with a Kubernetes service.

Proceed as follows:

1. Sign in to the AWS Management Console (`https://console.aws.amazon.com/console/`).

   Use this quickstart guide provided by Amazon that uses a launch wizard to build an EKS cluster (available at `https://us-east-2.console.aws.amazon.com/launchwizard/home?region=us-east-2#firstRun`).

2. Select **Amazon EKS**.

3. Select **Create deployment**.

4. Select **Deploy into a new VPC**.

5. Complete **Step 2**, **Configure application settings**.

6. Populate all required fields. Do not populate the optional settings.

7. Complete **Step 3**, **Configure infrastructure settings**.

8. Populate all required fields. Do not populate the optional settings.

9. Complete **Step 4**, **Review and deploy**.

10. Populate all required fields. Do not populate the optional settings.

> Insight
>
> Creating an Amazon EKS cluster may take 30 minutes or more. I chose the launch wizard to create the cluster nodes and services because of its ease of use over utilizing command-line tools and CloudFormation templates, which I believe are more complex for beginning practitioners. However, I recommend using CloudFormation templates for development and production environments because the tool is utilized in **Infrastructure as Code** (**IaC**) patterns.

Implementing container applications with AKS

Azure's managed Kubernetes service helps your developers by managing Kubernetes clusters' scaling and maintenance operations, thereby helping your organization's operations members and developers focus on what matters most: creating and deploying container applications.

The following diagram provides an example of AKS:

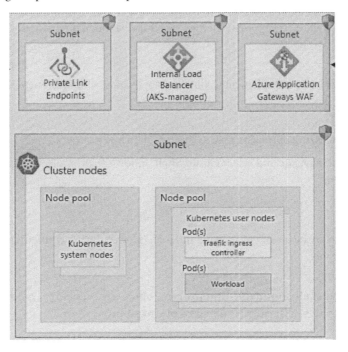

Figure 8.7 – AKS example

In these tasks, you will learn how to implement a container application with AKS, and you will also learn helpful tips and potential pitfalls that encumber beginners.

Objectives

After completing these tasks, you will be able to achieve the following:

- Describe and configure an application with AKS

To do 1: Implement a container application with a Kubernetes service

Real-world examples:

Transportation SP Maersk uses AKS to securely orchestrate resilient container application development.

Helpful tip or trick

To understand how Azure supports Maersk, you should learn how to develop apps using **Kubernetes**.

Task 1: Describe and implement a container application with a Kubernetes service

---

Note

This book is not intended to replace an instructor-led course, which does allocate the time required to learn all the components of a service. I do elaborate on instructor-led courses in *Chapter 14*.

In this task, you will learn to implement a container application with Kubernetes Engine.

Proceed as follows:

1. Sign in to the Azure portal (`https://portal.azure.com/`).

2. In the portal, navigate and select **Cloud Shell**, follow the prompts, and complete the cloud shell creation.

Insight

You will need to create a storage account and a file service during configuration to support cloud shell creation.

---

3. In the cloud shell command-line prompt, enter `az group create --name pharmaResourceGroup --location eastus`.

4. Then, create an **Azure Container Registry** (**ACR**) instance. Enter the `az acr create --resource-group pharmaResourceGroup --name <YourAcrName> --sku Basic` command.

> **Insight**
>
> Docker container images can be stored in the ACR, and version controlled. The ACR integrates with AKS to deploy container applications to AKS.

5. Create an AKS cluster using the following command:

```
az aks create \
    --resource-group pharmaResourceGroup \
    --name pharmaAKSCluster \
    --node-count 2 \
    --generate-ssh-keys \
    --attach-acr <EnterYourAcrName>
```

6. Install the `kubectl` client by entering the following command:

```
az aks install-cli
```

7. To connect to AKS, enter the following command:

```
az aks get-credentials --resource-group
pharmaResourceGroup --name pharmaAKSCluster
```

Implementing container applications with Google Kubernetes Engine

Many businesses from start-ups to enterprise organizations (including the public sector) use **Google Kubernetes Engine** (**GKE**) to eliminate operational overhead with its known capabilities, such as auto-scaling, and take advantage of its improvements over on-premises protection with modern security features that optimize vulnerability scanning of container images, all while your business leverages the portability and efficiencies derived from modern containers.

The following diagram provides an example of GKE:

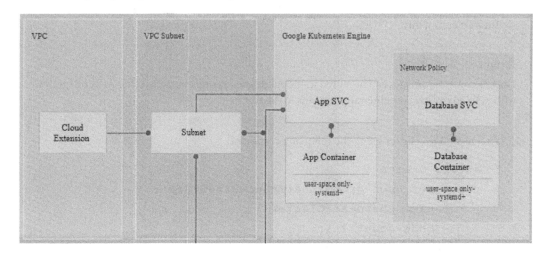

Figure 8.8 – GKE example

In these tasks, you will learn how to implement a container application with GKE, and you will also learn helpful tips and potential pitfalls that encumber beginners.

Objectives

After completing these tasks, you will be able to achieve the following:

- Describe and configure an application with GKE

To do 1: Implement a container application with GKE

Real-world examples:

Pizza Hut uses GKE to orchestrate container application development to deliver niche customer experiences.

> **Helpful tip or trick**
> To understand how Google helps Pizza Hut, you should learn how to build apps using **Kubernetes**.

Task 1: Describe and implement a container application with GKE

> **Note**
>
> This book is not intended to replace an instructor-led course. Instructor-led courses allocate the time recommended to learn all the components of a service. I do provide recommendations on how to improve your learning experience with instructor-led courses in *Chapter 14*.

In this task, you will implement a container application with GKE.

Proceed as follows:

1. Sign in to the Google Cloud console (`https://console.cloud.google.com/`).

2. In the Google Cloud console, on the **Project selector** page, select or create a Google Cloud project.

   Make sure that billing is enabled for your Google Cloud project.

3. In the console, select **Activate Cloud Shell**.

> **Insight**
>
> Cloud Shell comes preinstalled with the Google Cloud CLI and `kubectl` command-line tool. The `kubectl` client is used to connect and manage the GKE platform.

4. In cloud shell, enter the following commands:

```
gcloud config set project EnterYourProjectName
gcloud config set compute/zone us-east1-a
gcloud config set compute/region us-east1
```

5. Create a GKE cluster by entering the following commands:

```
gcloud container clusters create-auto hello-cluster
```

6. To connect and manage the cluster, you'll need credentials, so enter the following commands:

```
gcloud container clusters get-credentials hello-cluster
```

7. And to deploy an application, enter the following commands:

```
kubectl create deployment hello-server \
--image=us-docker.pkg.dev/google-samples/containers/gke/
hello-app:1.0
```

> **Insight**
>
> Cloud computing clusters consist of a cluster control plane and one or more worker nodes. The nodes are VM instances. The container applications are deployed to and run on the nodes. This is true for Amazon's EKS, Microsoft's AKS, and Google's GKS.

Serverless functions

In this section, you will learn about cloud computing serverless resources—in particular, their function. We will explore one of the many AWS, Azure, and Google Cloud serverless resources.

Serverless services

Cloud computing provides fully managed serverless services that host and run your code. The function service, which goes by many names, lets you run any code for various workloads such as the application tier, or even the data access logic tier, with little to no administration. And the cloud computing provider manages everything, including HA, and dynamically scales when you need on demand.

Here is a non-exhaustive table listing some of the cloud computing serverless services:

Cloud computing provider	Serverless services
AWS	Lambda
Azure	Functions
Google Cloud	Cloud Functions

Table 8.5 – AWS, Azure, and GCP serverless functions

Serverless functions are fully managed hosting platforms that run any programming language, and each cloud computing provider supports auto-scaling, but the administration does vary from one provider to another.

Implementing AWS Lambda functions

Run code when you want, how you want, efficiently with zero overhead. Amazon's Lambda functions can support almost any workload and are used in scenarios from data processing to API GET methods, mobile backend API data access logic methods, and more. Lambda functions handle any event; therefore, they truly can be used in any event-driven scenario.

The following diagram provides an example of Amazon Lambda functions:

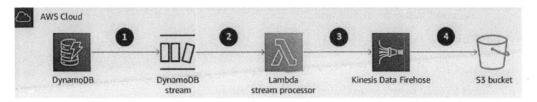

Figure 8.9 – AWS Lambda functions

In these tasks, you will learn how to configure and run a Lambda function in AWS, and you will also learn helpful tips and potential pitfalls that encumber beginners.

Objectives

After completing these tasks, you will be able to achieve the following:

- Describe and configure a Lambda function

To do 1: Implement an AWS Lambda function

Real-world examples:

Social media service Snapchat can use AWS Lambda to programmatically process mobile API event-driven requests such as offloading customer search queries, in turn decreasing the need to scale out additional container nodes.

> **Note**
> This book is not intended to replace an instructor-led course, which does allocate the time required to learn all the components of a service. I do elaborate on instructor-led courses in *Chapter 14*.

Task 1: Implement an AWS Lambda function

In this task, you will learn to implement an AWS Lambda function.

Proceed as follows:

1. Sign in to the AWS Management Console (`https://console.aws.amazon.com/console/`).
2. In the search field, enter `lambda`, then select **Lambda**.
3. In the **Lambda** dashboard, select **Create function**.

4. Under **Basic information**, fill in the following values:

    *   **Function name**: `pharmafunction`

    *   **Runtime**: **Python**

5. Select **Create function**.

6. Select **Upload from context menu**, then select **.zip file**.

7. Select **Upload**, then access the `~/Cloud-Computing-Essentials-Beg/Allfiles/ Chapter8/Serverless/AWS and select lambda_function.zip file` directory path.

8. Select **Save**.

9. Select **Test**, then enter `test` in the **Event name** field.

10. Review the **Event JSON** input data.

11. Select **Save**.

12. Select **Test**, and then review the **Execution results** response. The status code displays **200** and returns a body of output, **Welcome to cloud computing!**.

Implementing Azure function apps

Organizations use cloud computing functions because of the business requirement to develop services that react to events and have the capability to access data, process data, and manage telemetry, messages, smart device input, and more in real time.

And as the events grow, so too does Azure's cloud-scaled function to meet the ever-growing demands of reactive processing. It's simple to use, requires zero VM administration, and you can integrate it with almost any service across the cloud landscape to be invoked and provide business logic that can accomplish almost any task.

The following diagram provides an example of an Azure function app:

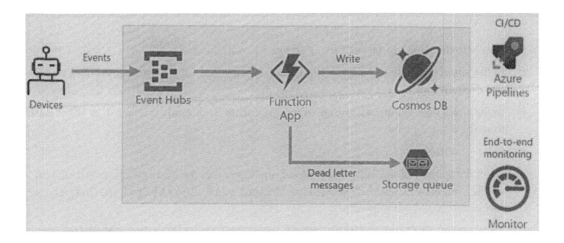

Figure 8.10 – Azure function app example

In these tasks, you will learn how to implement an Azure function app, and you will also learn helpful tips and potential pitfalls that encumber beginners.

Objectives

After completing these tasks, you will be able to achieve the following:

- Describe and configure an Azure function app

To do 1: Implement an Azure function app

Real-world examples:

Transportation SP Maersk has the capability to use Azure Functions to optimize event-driven tasks throughout its supply chain and logistics services APIs.

> **Note**
>
> This book is not intended to replace an instructor-led course, which does allocate the time required to learn all the components of a service. I do elaborate on instructor-led courses in *Chapter 14*.

Task 1: Implement an Azure function app

In this task, you will learn to implement an Azure function app.

Proceed as follows:

1. Sign in to the Azure portal (`https://portal.azure.com/`).

2. In the portal, navigate and select **Cloud Shell**. If prompted, create a storage account and file share requirements.

3. In the cloud shell command-line environment, ensure **Bash mode** is enabled, or select **Bash** from the context menu.

4. Enter `code .`

5. Select the upload setting, then select **Upload**, and then select the `azurePythonFunction.sh` file from the `~/Cloud-Computing-Essentials-Beg/Allfiles/Chapter8/Serverless/Azure` directory.

6. Update the `azurePythonFunction.sh` Bash file by replacing the subscription and storage account values with unique values.

> **Insight**
>
> Be careful to not change or delete the `$randomIdentifier` string value.

7. In the cloud shell CLI, enter `bash azurePythonFunction.sh`.

8. In the Azure portal search field, enter `function app`, and then select **Function app**.

9. Select your function app.

10. Select **Functions**, then select **Create**, and select **Time trigger**.

11. Select **Create**.

12. Select **Code + Test**, and then select **Upload**.

13. Select the `azureTimerFunction.py` file from the `~/Cloud-Computing-Essentials-Beg/Allfiles/Chapter8/Serverless/Azure` directory.

14. Select **Test/Run**, then select **Run**, and finally, select **Close** and review the logs.

> **Insight**
>
> It may take up to several minutes to see the logs from Application Insights.

Implementing Google Cloud functions

The rise of serverless has innovated many solutions, but none quite so powerful as functions, which provide the capability to do almost anything upon input, event action, and event condition being met and output.

Functions can also be scheduled and used to optimize daily tasks from analyzing to processing, and cloud functions are program language-agnostic, so they are flexible and familiar. Functions can be used to support advanced integrations between legacy workloads and back your APIs as HTTP methods. They can support workloads such as resizing data, web applications, ML feature engineering, ML classification jobs, and more.

Run code, not servers; handle any event, invoke other functions, and—if needed—replace your job with scheduled functions. The real question is what a function can't do.

The following diagram provides an example of Google Cloud functions:

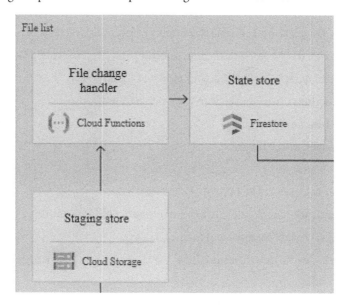

Figure 8.11 – Google Cloud functions example

In these tasks, you will learn how to implement Google Cloud functions, and you will also learn helpful tips and potential pitfalls that encumber beginners.

Objectives

After completing these tasks, you will be able to achieve the following:

- Describe and configure Google Cloud functions

To do 1: Implement a Google Cloud function

Real-world examples:

Pizza Hut utilizes Google Cloud Functions to process customer cart orders by integrating order cart APIs.

> **Note**
>
> This book is not intended to replace an instructor-led course. Instructor-led courses allocate the time recommended to learn all the components of a service. I do provide recommendations on how to improve your learning experience with instructor-led courses in *Chapter 14*.

Task 1: Describe and configure a Google Cloud function.

In this task, you will learn to implement a Google Cloud function.

Proceed as follows:

1. Sign in to the Google Cloud console (`https://console.cloud.google.com/`).
2. In the Google Cloud console, on the **Project selector** page, select or create a Google Cloud project.
3. Make sure that billing is enabled for your Google Cloud project.
4. Open the **Functions Overview** page in the Google Cloud console.
5. Click **Create function**.
6. For **Environment**, select **1st gen**.
7. Name your function `http-function`.
8. In the **Trigger** field, select **HTTP**.
9. In the **Authentication** field, select **Allow unauthenticated invocations**.
10. Select **Save** to save your changes, and then click **Next**.
11. In the **Source code** field, select **Inline editor**. Use the default `Hello World` function provided in the editor.
12. Use the **Runtime** dropdown to select your desired language runtime.
13. Select **Deploy**.
14. Select the context menu beside your function, and then select **Test function**.
15. Review the logs by selecting **View logs** on the **Cloud Functions overview** page.

Summary

In this chapter, you learned about creating core essential cloud computing services, including VMs, web applications, container services, and serverless functions using different APIs and tooling native to cloud computing.

In the next chapter, we explore creating cloud storage resources that are inherently resilient to single-server scaling limitations, server outages, and performance constraints.

Questions

1. Which of the following options is accurate when creating a VM instance?

   A. Hardware procurement

   B. Configuring the Linux Kernel-based VM (KVM) host

   C. Scaling

   D. None of the above

2. Which option is configurable during the EC2 launch configuration process?

   A. AMI

   B. Graphics card installation

   C. I/O port installation

   D. None of the above

3. Microsoft Azure VM images and AMIs currently support which of the following (choose all that apply)?

   A. Windows

   B. Linux

   C. iOS

   D. Chromebooks

4. Google Cloud Compute Engine supports which of the following options?

   A. Windows

   B. Chromebooks

   C. iOS

   D. None of the above

5. Does Amazon's Elastic Beanstalk require administrators to manually implement EC2 instances before creating an application environment?

   A. Yes

   B. No

6. Does Azure App Service require administrators to manually implement the Docker container configuration before creating an App Service plan, which acts as a host and supports capacity management?

    A. Yes

    B. No

7. Which of the following object-oriented programming (OOP) languages is supported by Google App Engine?

    A. Python

    B. .NET

    C. JSON

    D. None of the above

8. Which cloud computing provider supports Docker containers?

    A. AWS

    B. Azure

    C. GCP

    D. None of the above

9. Traditional organizations have concerns with creating new VNets due to IP addressing constraints. Can you select a preexisting VPC during EKS configuration?

    A. Yes

    B. No

10. Which of the following options are recommended for accelerating EKS configuration and creation?

    A. AWS Management portal

    B. Bash shell

    C. CloudFormation

    D. ARM templates

11. Which of the following options are recommended for version control with AKS configuration?

    A. AKS

    B. Local host Git repo

    C. ACR

    D. GKS

12. GKE, AKS, and EKS support which of the following management options?

    A. JavaScript

    B. kubectl

    C. Zonal

    D. None of the above

13. Which of the following VM maintenance options are you responsible for with AWS, Azure, and GCP functions?

    A. Hardware

    B. Guest operating system

    C. Implementing the runtime environment

    D. None of the above

14. Which of the following coincides with serverless resource types?

    A. Auto-scaling

    B. Tightly coupled

    C. On-premises

    D. HTML websites

15. Which of the following are supported across AWS, Azure, and GCP functions?

    A. Events

    B. Big data storage

    C. Bash shell

    D. None of the above

9
Configuring Storage Resources for Resiliency

This chapter will take you through implementing various essential storage services. You will learn how to set up object-level, file share, key-value, and queue storage services, and you will reinforce the concepts and configuration procedures learned by completing review questions.

The following concepts will be covered in this chapter:

- Configuring object-level storage
- Configuring file share storage
- Configuring key-value storage
- Configuring queue storage

Configuring object-level storage

In this section, you will learn how to configure and create object-level storage services. You will also learn helpful tips and potential pitfalls that encumber beginners.

It is a cloud computing best practice to store static objects and large data types in object-level storage services. AWS, Azure, and Google Cloud's storage services are delivering unparalleled performance and resiliency in cloud computing today. Object-level storage is used not only as a data backup and restore solution, including for archiving, but also in practical applications.

The following table illustrates AWS, Azure, and GCP object-level storage services:

Object-Level Storage Services	Type
AWS	Simple Storage Service
Azure	Blob Storage
GCP	Cloud Storage

Table 9.1 – Virtual machines

Join me as I configure each cloud computing provider's object-level storage service, and, in turn, discover how easy it is to create and store massive amounts of data with inherent redundancy. We will start by looking at Amazon **Simple Storage Service (S3)**.

It may be labeled **Simple Storage Service** but its benefits to your workloads are far from simple. Review the following figure illustrating an AWS S3 bucket:

Figure 9.1 – Amazon S3 bucket

Creating an Amazon S3 bucket

In this section, you will learn how to configure an AWS S3 bucket resource in AWS.

Those who have adopted cloud computing in many ways can attest that Amazon S3 delivers utility. For example, various workloads use S3, from unstructured media files to data lake patterns, static web hosting, EC2 backups, and overall data redundancy, all of which are managed by Amazon.

> **Insight**
>
> If you have forgotten what EC2 is, review *Chapter 8*.

Objective

After completing these tasks, you will be able to achieve the following:

- Describe and deploy S3

Prerequisites

The following are the requirements for completing all tasks:

- An updated version of Windows 8.1 or later, macOS 10.15 or later, or Linux Ubuntu 18.04 or later.
- An up-to-date and secure internet browser (Chrome or Edge is recommended).

> **Note**
>
> I am using a Windows 10 **operating system (OS)** and Chrome and Edge as my browser.

- The instructions are located at `https://github.com/PacktPublishing/Cloud-Computing-for-Beginners/tree/main/Instructions/Chapter9/Object`

- Access to an AWS account with the required privileges to create and manage S3 resources and dependencies. You can head over to `https://aws.amazon.com/free` to create an AWS trial account for training purposes only.

> **Important**
>
> You should fork, clone, or download, and then follow along with, the step-by-step tasks in GitHub or those described herein. I recommend using GitHub in conjunction with this book because the code text is more clearly defined in GitHub. However, that's my preference; you may prefer the book format.

Ready?

Complete these tasks to create an S3 account.

To do 0: Subscribe to AWS.

Task 1: Sign in to AWS. The steps are as follows:

1. Select the Edge or Chrome browser on your computer and search for `https://aws.amazon.com/free`.

2. After the website loads, select **Create a Free Account**.

3. On the `portal.aws.amazon.com` website, populate the fields labeled **Root user email address** and **AWS account name**; enter a valid and readily accessible email account name and AWS account name for training purposes. Here are several email accounts and AWS account name examples:

   - `Example.lastname@gmail.com`

   - `Example.lastname@outlook.com`

   - `Cloud Practitioner`

> **Note**
>
> I have elected to exclude any guidance on billing details, which includes **personally identifiable information** (**PII**).

4. Follow the remaining prompts and populate all required fields to complete the new account creation process.

> **Insight**
>
> You can find several resources to help you create and manage your AWS Free Tier account to ensure you don't incur substantial costs; for example, you can go to `https://aws.amazon.com/premiumsupport/knowledge-center/create-and-activate-aws-account/` and `https://aws.amazon.com/premiumsupport/knowledge-center/what-is-free-tier/`.

To do 1: Create an S3 bucket.

> **Important**
>
> The instructions listed match the AWS management portal version available in May 2022. AWS is always updating the interface to improve the user experience, so the interface be set out differently when you're working through the steps.

Task 1: Describe and create an S3 bucket.

In this task, you will create an S3 bucket using the AWS management console:

1. Sign in to the AWS Management Console (`https://console.aws.amazon.com/console/`).
2. Launch AWS CloudShell, select a region, and then select **Shell**.
3. (*Optionally*) Upload a file to CloudShell.
4. In the CloudShell command line, create an S3 bucket (container) by entering the following command:

    ```
    aws s3api create-bucket --bucket <enter-unique-bucket-name> --region us-east-1
    ```

5. (*Optionally*) If you uploaded a file to CloudShell, you could upload that file to the S3 bucket you created by entering the following command:

    ```
    aws s3api put-object --bucket <enter-unique-bucket-name> --key <EnterfileName> --body <EnterfileName>
    ```

> **Insight**
>
> Did you know that you can copy multiple files between CloudShell or even your local machine destined for S3?

In these tasks, you have created an Amazon S3 bucket with CloudShell and the AWS CLI. In the next section, we journey into Azure's cloud to review binary large object storage at scale.

Creating Azure Storage Blobs

In this section, you will learn how to efficiently create Storage Blobs in Azure.

Microsoft Azure's object-level storage is optimized for storing large volumes of data. The Azure Storage account, as it's known, is a storage service for supporting unstructured and semi-structured data types. And like AWS and GCP, all kinds of workloads can efficiently get and put data using its public API.

> **Insight**
>
> Review the section regarding APIs in *Chapter 5*.

Objective

After completing these tasks, you will be able to achieve the following:

- Describe and deploy Azure Storage Blobs

Prerequisites

The following are the requirements for completing all tasks:

- An updated version of Windows 8.1 or later, macOS 10.15 or later, or Linux Ubuntu 18.04 or later.

- An up-to-date and secure internet browser (Chrome or Edge is recommended).

> **Note**
>
> The author is using a Windows 10 OS and Chrome and Edge browser.

- The instructions are also located at `https://github.com/PacktPublishing/Cloud-Computing-for-Beginners/tree/main/Instructions/Chapter9/Object`

- Access to an Azure subscription with the required privileges to create and manage all resources and dependencies. You can head over to `https://azure.microsoft.com/en-us/free/` to create an Azure trial subscription for training purposes only.

> **Important**
>
> You should fork, clone, or download and follow along with the step-by-step tasks in GitHub or those described herein. I recommend using GitHub in conjunction with this book because any parts written in code are more clearly defined in GitHub. However, that's my preference; you may prefer the book format.

Ready?

Start these tasks to create an Azure Storage Blob.

To do 0: Subscribe to Microsoft Azure.

Task 1: Sign in to Azure The steps are as follows:

1. Select the Edge or Chrome browser on your computer and search for `https://azure.microsoft.com/en-us/free/`.

2. After the website loads, select **Start free**.

3. On the `login.microsoftonline.com` website, select **Create one!**. Here are several email account name examples:

    *   `Example.lastname@outlook.com`

    *   `Example98765@outlook.com`

> **Note**
>
> I have elected to exclude any guidance on billing details, which includes PII.

4. Follow the remaining prompts and populate all required fields to complete the new account creation process.

> **Insight**
>
> There are several resources to help you create and manage your Azure Free tier account to ensure you don't incur substantial costs. You can also go to `https://azure.microsoft.com/en-us/free/free-account-faq/`.

To do 2: Create an Azure Storage Blob.

Task 1: Describe and create an Azure Storage Blob.

In this task, you will create an Azure Storage Blob using the Azure portal.

Microsoft, like Amazon and Google, simplifies creating inherently redundant storage services to maximize resiliency in almost any workload. It also supports web management, **CLI**, **software development kits (SDKs)**, and public APIs, which improve access, administration, and empower innovation:

1. Sign in to the Azure portal (`https://portal.azure.com/`).

2. In the portal, select and launch CloudShell.

> **Insight**
>
> Try using the CloudShell editor by entering the `Code` command and then using the untitled file to write code and efficiently update parameters and arguments. Save the file as either a shell script – for example, `file.sh` – or a PowerShell script – for example, `file.ps`. Then, execute your script using the command from the command line.

3. In the CloudShell command line, enter the following command to create a project container, known as a resource group:

    ```
    az group create --name <enter-resource-group> --location
    <region location>
    ```

4. Create a storage account service that can be used to support object-level storage, known as a **blob**, by entering the following command:

    ```
    az storage account create \
    --name <storage-account> \
    --resource-group <resource-group> \
    --location <location> \
    --sku Standard_ZRS \
    --encryption-services blob
    ```

5. Now, let's create a container to store our blobs, also known as objects, by entering the following commands:

    ```
    az storage container create \
    --account-name <storage-account> \
    --name <container>
    ```

6. Create a file and then upload the file using the following commands:

    ```
    touch cloudrocks.txt
    ```

7. Then, enter the following command to upload the blobs:

    ```
    az storage blob upload \
    --account-name <enter-storage-account> \
    --container-name <enter-container> \
    --name cloudrocks \
    --file cloudrocks.txt
    ```

8. After successfully creating and uploading the data, review the storage account.

With that, you have created and configured an Azure Storage blob container. In the next section, we will explore the Google Cloud Storage service.

Creating Google Cloud Storage

In this section, you will learn how to configure and create virtual machine cloud resources in Google Cloud. Google Cloud streamlines creating cloud storage and, like Azure, you can quickly create and manage massive storage services at scale.

Google Cloud Storage is a developer-friendly cloud storage that supports numerous APIs. Additionally, it's known for its redundancy and global availability, and it's used widely by many machine learning experts that require a data lake-like service.

> **Insight**
>
> If you are not familiar with the concept of a data lake, I highly recommend researching data lakes and machine learning after reading this book.

Objective

After completing these tasks, you will be able to achieve the following:

- Describe and deploy Google Cloud Storage

Prerequisites

The following are the requirements for completing all tasks:

- An updated version of Windows 8.1 or later, macOS 10.15 or later, or Linux Ubuntu 18.04 or later.

- An up-to-date and secure internet browser (Chrome or Edge is recommended).

> **Note**
>
> I am using a Windows 10 OS and Chrome and Edge browser.

- The instructions are located at `https://github.com/PacktPublishing/Cloud-Computing-for-Beginners/tree/main/Instructions/Chapter9/Object`

- Access to a GCP account with the required privileges to create and manage all VPC resources and dependencies. You can go to `https://cloud.google.com/free` and `https://cloud.google.com/resource-manager/docs/manage-google-cloud-resources` to create a free GCP account for training purposes only.

> **Important**
>
> You should fork, clone, or download and follow along with the step-by-step tasks in GitHub or those described herein. I recommend using GitHub in conjunction with this book because any parts written in code are more clearly defined in GitHub. However, that's my preference; you may prefer the book format.

Ready?

Start these tasks to deploy Google Cloud Storage.

To do 0: Subscribe to GCP.

Task 1: Sign in to GCP The steps are as follows:.

1. Select the Edge or Chrome browser on your computer and search for `https://cloud.google.com/free/`.

2. After the website loads, select **Get started for free**.

3. On the `accounts.google.com` website, select **Create account**. Then, select **Create a new Gmail address instead**. Here are several email account name examples (replace `Example` with your name or alias):

    -   `Example.lastname@gmail.com`

    -   `Example98765@gmail.com`

> **Note**
>
> I have elected to exclude any guidance on billing details, which includes PII.

4. Follow the remaining prompts and populate all required fields to conclude the new account creation process.

> **Insight**
>
> There are several resources to help you create and manage your GCP free account to ensure you don't incur substantial costs. `https://cloud.google.com/free/` is one.

To do 3: Deploy Google Cloud Storage.

Task 1: Describe and deploy Google Cloud Storage.

In this task, you will create and configure a Google Cloud Storage service.

The Google Cloud Storage service can be used by any industry to provide more than just a backup solution. Alternatively, companies have been using its massive scale and resiliency to support big data workloads. Here are the steps to create and configure a Google Cloud Storage service:

1. Sign in to the Google Cloud console (`https://console.cloud.google.com/`).

2. In the Google Cloud console, on the project selector page, select or create a Google Cloud project.

3. Use Cloud Shell and open a terminal window.

4. Enter the following commands to create a Google Cloud Storage bucket:

    ```
    gsutil mb -b on -l us-east1 gs://<enter-unique-name>/
    ```

5. Enter the following command to create a file, also known as a blob (object), and then upload it to the destination Cloud Storage bucket:

    ```
    touch cloudrocks.txt
    gsutil cp cloudrocks.txt gs://<enter-unique-name>
    ```

6. After successfully creating and uploading the data, review your Google Cloud Storage.

In this section's tasks, you created cloud-scaled object-level storage. In the next section, we will explore the resilient cloud computing network file share storage services.

Configuring file share storage

In this section, you will learn about PaaS for file shares. We will explore one of the various AWS, Azure, and Google Cloud file share services.

Cloud computing supports network-attached storage services, commonly referred to as a file server or file share. File shares allow multiple users to store, retrieve, and share files securely on your local network. Traditional and modern cloud file share appliances are also offered by numerous vendors as **network-attached storage** (**NAS**) devices or servers. Some vendors you may be familiar with that are used on-premises include NetApp, Pure Storage, Dell, and QNAP. While this is not an exhaustive list, it should be obvious that file share services are widely used, and an important service utilized in any computing environment.

Here is a non-exhaustive table listing some of the cloud computing file share services:

Cloud Computing Provider	Application Services
AWS	Elastic File System
Azure	File Share
GCP	Cloud Filestore

Table 9.2 – AWS, Azure, and GCP file share services

Cloud computing providers deliver not only file share services but also the capabilities inherent to cloud computing. Cloud computing file share services are simple to configure, accessible via APIs, secured by resources modeled using defense in depth such as identity and access management and network access control optional features, inherently redundant, and backed by each cloud computing leader's impressive service-level agreement, ensuring a highly available service. And each cloud provider supports connectivity options that allow you to connect either using a local network interconnected to the cloud by way of a VPN or supporting a **wide area network** (**WAN**) interconnected using dedicated connections. Some clouds even support connectivity over the public internet.

Creating an Amazon Elastic File System instance

AWS **Elastic File System** (**EFS**) is a simple-to-use serverless resource that supports services hosted in either the VPC or your on-premises local network. Amazon fully manages the service while you configure your resources, such as EC2 instances or virtual machines, that are running in your local network to mount to AWS EFS. The connection configuration is referred to as a mount point or target. Then, you must install AWS DataSync to conclude configuring a source and destination; AWS DataSync will keep your filesystems in sync, all while you centrally manage one or more EFS mount targets, such as a virtual machine on-premises using a VPN or Direct Connect connected to an AWS VPC, or resources hosted and isolated on your VPC.

In this section, you will learn how to create and configure EFS in AWS.

Objective

After completing these tasks, you will be able to achieve the following:

- Describe and configure EFS

> **Note**
>
> The instructions are also located at `https://github.com/PacktPublishing/Cloud-Computing-Demystified-for-Aspiring-Professionals/tree/main/Instructions/Chapter9/FileShare/AWS`

To do 1: Create and configure EFS.

> **Note**
>
> This book is not intended to replace an instructor-led course, which allocates the time required to learn all the components of a service. However, I do explore instructor-led courses in *Chapter 14*.

Task 1: Create and configure an EFS.

In this task, you will learn how to create and configure EFS in AWS:

1. Sign in to the AWS Management Console (`https://console.aws.amazon.com/console/`).

2. Launch AWS CloudShell.

3. In the CloudShell command line, enter the following command to create an AWS EFS instance:

```
aws efs create-file-system \
--encrypted \
--creation-token FileSystemToken \
--tags Key=Name,Value=tag1 \
--region us-west-2 \
--profile adminuser
```

4. Copy the filesystem ID output.

5. Create a mount target for your EFS in a subnet on your AWS Availability Zone where you've deployed an EC2 instance by entering the following command:

```
aws efs create-mount-target \
--file-system-id <enter-file-system-id> \
--subnet-id  <enter-subnet-id> \
--security-group <enter-securityId-group-created-for-
mount-target> \
--region us-west-2 \
--profile adminuser
```

> **Insight**
>
> If you want to implement EFS with your AWS VPC and EC2 resources, you'll need to create and configure security group inbound rules, as well as create an EC2 instance in a VPC. Read *Chapter 7* and *Chapter 8*, which describe how to implement and launch an AWS VPC and EC2 instance.

6. You will need to collect some information, namely the **Domain Name System (DNS)** name of your EC2 instance; for example, `ec2-xx-xxx-xxx-xx.us-east-1.compute.amazonaws.com`.

7. You will also require the DNS name of your filesystem; for example, `<enter-file-system-id>.efs.us-east-1.amazonaws.com`.

8. Furthermore, you will need to connect to your EC2 instance to install a client (agent). While this book covers the essentials, it does not detail how to remotely access and manage EC2 instances. However, there is a chapter that describes the resources you will need to continue your learning journey and thus learn how to connect to an EC2 instance post-launch: *Chapter 14*.

9. After you have connected to the EC2 instance, we recommend updating the system and installing `nfs-utils` by entering the following command:

    ```
    sudo yum -y install nfs-utils
    ```

10. Use the following commands to mount EFS on one or more EC2 instances:

    ```
    mkdir ~/efs-mount-point
    sudo mount -t nfs -o
    nfsvers=4.1,rsize=1048576,wsize=1048576,hard,timeo=600,
    retrans=2,noresvport <enter-mount-target-DNS>:/  ~/
    efs-mount-point
    ```

11. After successfully configuring the mount point, you can review the directory and create files.

> Insight
>
> You can also use DataSync to automatically sync files between two or more EFS filesystems efficiently.

With that, you have created an AWS EFS. In the next section, we will explore the Azure Storage service's file share resource type.

Creating an Azure Files

Azure Files share, like Amazon EFS, is known for its performance and redundancy options. And as it supports centralized filesystem management for cloud and hybrid workloads, it also supports the **Network File System (NFS)** and **Server Message Block (SMB)** protocols for Windows and Linux systems. You can use Azure Files share with a site-to-site connection using a VPN or connect over the public internet from anywhere and leverage Azure Active Directory services to control identity and access management to one or more file shares.

The following is an example of Azure Files architecture:

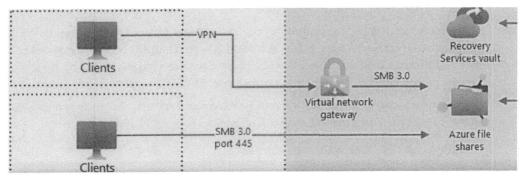

Figure 9.2 – Example of Azure Files architecture

In this section, you will learn how to configure and create an Azure file share. You will also learn how to efficiently deploy the service.

Objective

After completing these tasks, you will be able to achieve the following:

- Describe and configure an Azure file share

> **Note**
> The instructions are also located at `https://github.com/PacktPublishing/`
> `Cloud-Computing-Demystified-for-Aspiring-Professionals/tree/`
> `main/Instructions/Chapter9/FileShare/Azure`

To do 1: Create and configure an Azure file share.

Task 1: Create and configure an Azure file share.

In this task, you will create and configure an Azure file share using Cloud Shell:

1. Sign in to the Azure portal (`https://portal.azure.com/`).

2. In the portal, launch Cloud Shell.

3. In the Cloud Shell command line, enter the following commands to create a resource group to manage this project:

   ```
   az group create --name fileshareRG --location <region
   location>
   resourceGroupName="fileshareRG"
   ```

```
storageAccountName="<enter-unique-name>$RANDOM"
region="eastus"
```

4. Enter the following commands to create an Azure Storage account that supports a file share:

```
az storage account create \
--resource-group $resourceGroupName \
--name $storageAccountName \
--kind StorageV2 \
--sku Standard_ZRS \
--enable-large-file-share \
--output none
```

5. Enter the following commands to create the Azure file share:

```
shareName="cloudfileshare"

az storage share-rm create \
--resource-group $resourceGroupName \
--storage-account $storageAccountName \
--name $shareName \
--access-tier "TransactionOptimized" \
--quota 1024 \
--output none
```

Mounting an Azure file share on Windows or Linux is as simple as navigating to the Azure portal and managing your Azure Storage account's file share.

1. Simply select the file share, and then select **Connect**

2. Review all the important information detailed on the **Connect** page for mounting Windows, Linux, and macOS.

Insight

Azure includes a downloadable setup script that will do all the heavy lifting, so to speak, regarding configuration.

With that, you have created an Azure file share. In the next section, we will explore the Google Cloud file share services.

Creating a Google Cloud Filestore instance

Google Cloud offers managed network file share servers at cloud scale. Workloads running in **VPCs** such as client applications on Compute Engine instances can access the Filestore services.

In this section, you will learn how to configure and create a Google Cloud Filestore instance. You will also learn how to efficiently deploy the service.

Objective

After completing these tasks, you will be able to achieve the following:

- Describe and configure a Google Cloud Filestore

> **Note**
>
> The instructions are also located at `https://github.com/PacktPublishing/Cloud-Computing-Demystified-for-Aspiring-Professionals/tree/main/Instructions/Chapter9/FileShare/GoogleCloud`

TO DO 1: Configure and create a Google Cloud Filestore instance.

Task 1: Configure and create a Google Cloud Filestore instance.

In this task, you will configure and create a Google Cloud Filestore instance:

1. Sign in to the Google Cloud console (`https://console.cloud.google.com/`).

2. In the Google Cloud console, on the project selector page, select or create a Google Cloud project.

3. Launch Cloud Shell.

4. Create the project container to manage our resources by entering the following command:

    ```
    gcloud projects create <enter-project-name>
    ```

5. Next, create a virtual machine instance to be used as the client by entering the following commands:

    ```
    gcloud compute instances create nfs-client -zone=us-
    central1-c -image-project=debian-cloud -image-
    family=debian-10 -tags=http-server
    ```

6. Create a Filestore instance by entering the following command:

    ```
    gcloud beta filestore instances create nfs-server
    -zone=us-central1-c -tier=BASIC_HDD -file-
    share=name="vol1",capacity=1TB -network=name="default"
    ```

7. Retrieve the Filestore instance's IP address by entering the following command:

```
gcloud filestore instances describe nfs-server --zone=us-
central1-c
```

8. Connect to the Compute Engine instance, install NFS, and create the mount directory by entering the following commands:

```
gcloud compute ssh nfs-client
sudo apt-get -y update &&
sudo apt-get -y install nfs-common
sudo mkdir /mnt/cceb
```

9. Enter the following command to mount the file share:

```
sudo mount <enter-IP>:/vol1 /mnt/cceb
```

> **Insight**
>
> You will need to make the file share accessible, so change its permissions using `sudo  chmod`.

10. After you have successfully created and configured your Google Cloud Filestore, review the resource.

In this section, you created cloud file share services. In the next section, we will explore the cloud computing event storage architecture.

Configuring discrete event data storage services

In this section, you will learn about cloud computing fully managed event-driven services. We'll explore the topic together and review one each of the many AWS, Azure, and Google Cloud event storage and routing services.

Cloud computing leaders have designed numerous microservices to support various scenarios and patterns, such as event architectures, which typically consist of an event or occurrence from a cloud or hybrid source that generates event data from systems and services. This event data is generated almost immediately after an occurrence – or in layman's terms, something has changed. That change or event creates data that can be collected and delivered in near real time so that an application, or if you prefer, a workload, can receive the event data and respond either immediately or at a later point in time based on how we develop our workload to handle the incoming event data. What you and your team of developers decide to do once the event data is received is up to your imagination. The data that's extrapolated can be analyzed to locate data that typically displays a state change. Typically, an event can be something as simple as incrementing or decrementing an integer or floating-point value – for example, your thermostat system decrementing the numerical value for your room temperature in Fahrenheit because the room is getting warmer.

To support this event-driven architecture, you will need a place to store and route the data being generated in real time. Therefore, cloud computing delivers event-driven microservices without you having to implement, customize, or maintain the underlying infrastructure.

Here is a non-exhaustive table listing some of the cloud computing event services:

Cloud Computing Provider	Application Services
AWS	EventBridge
Azure	Event Grid
GCP	Eventarc

Table 9.3 – AWS, Azure, and GCP event services

Event services are storage and routing platforms that are intuitive to use, highly available, and can scale to handle millions of data events being generated from disparate sources. They can also route data events to trigger any number of cloud computing services to handle the event.

Configuring events using EventBridge

AWS provides a serverless event routing and integration service that can support real-time event data delivery to one or more workloads running in your public cloud by connecting to the workload's endpoint.

In this section, you will learn how to create and configure EventBridge in AWS.

Objective

After completing these tasks, you will be able to achieve the following:

- Describe and configure EventBridge

> **Note**
> The instructions are also located at `https://github.com/PacktPublishing/Cloud-Computing-Demystified-for-Aspiring-Professionals/tree/main/Instructions/Chapter9/EventStorage/AWS`

To do 1: Create and configure EventBridge.

Task 1: Create and configure the target event handler.

In this task, you will create and configure EventBridge using the AWS management console:

1. Sign in to the AWS Management Console (`https://console.aws.amazon.com/console/`).

2. In the search field, enter `lambda`, and then select **Lambda** to access the Lambda dashboard.

3. Select **Create function**.

4. Select **Author from scratch**.

5. Enter a unique name for the Lambda function.

6. Select **Create function**.

7. On the function page, select **index.js**.

8. Select **Upload from .zip file**, then **Upload**. Then, select the `index.zip` file from the `~/Cloud-Computing-Essentials-Beg/Allfiles/Chapter9/EventStorage/AWS` directory path.

9. Select **Deploy**.

Task 2: Create and configure the event archive and rule. Take the following steps:.

1. Sign in to the EventBridge management console using the following link: `https://console.aws.amazon.com/events/`.

2. Select **Archives**.

3. Select **Create archive**.

4. Enter a unique archive name.

5. Select **Create archive**.

6. Select **Rules**.

7. Select **Create rule**.

8. Enter a unique rule name.

9. Select the default event bus. If it's preselected, then disregard it.

10. Select **Rule with an event pattern** for **Rule type**.

11. Select **Next**.

12. Select **Other** for the event source.

13. Enter the following for the event pattern:

```
{
    "detail-type": [
       "customerCreated"
    ]
}
```

14. Select **Next**.

15. Select **AWS service** for **Target types**.

16. Select **Lambda function** for **Select a target**.

17. Select the Lambda function you created previously.

18. Select **Next**, and then **Next** again.

19. Select **Create a rule** and then review your EventBridge resources.

In this section, you have created an AWS EventBridge instance, resources, and a target Lambda function. In the next section, we will explore Azure event services.

Configuring events using Event Grid

Microsoft Azure Event Grid resource capabilities support configuring endpoints, known as topics, that you can send custom events to, empower business partners to create partner-purposed topics, and have built-in features to integrate with SaaS. Furthermore, Event Grid offers a unified authentication service that allows you to manage identity and access for multitenant businesses and their partners.

The following is an example of an Azure Event Grid architecture:

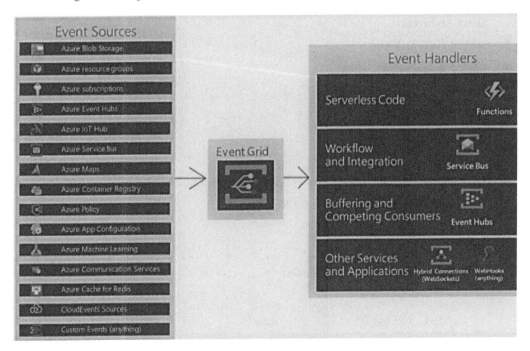

Figure 9.3 – Azure Event Grid

In this section, you will learn how to create and configure an Event Grid Topic in Azure.

Objective

After completing these tasks, you will be able to achieve the following:

- Describe and configure an Azure Event Grid Topic

> **Note**
>
> The instructions are also located at `https://github.com/PacktPublishing/`
> `Cloud-Computing-Demystified-for-Aspiring-Professionals/tree/`
> `main/Instructions/Chapter9/EventStorage/Azure`

To do 1: Create and configure an Event Grid Topic in Azure.

Task 1: Create and configure an Event Grid Topic in Azure.

In this task, you will create and configure an Event Grid Topic in Azure. Additionally, you will use a Queue message storage service to view the event data. A queue is a destination or handler in this context. Event data is sent to an endpoint, which will trigger Event Grid to route the event data to one or more queues for further analysis:

1. Sign in to the Azure portal (`https://portal.azure.com/`).

2. In the Azure portal, select and launch CloudShell.

3. In the Cloud Shell command line, enter the following command:

   Code .

4. In the Cloud Shell editor, select **Upload**, and upload the files named `CreateQueue.sh`, `CreateEventGrid.sh`, and `PostEventData.sh` from the `~/Cloud-Computing-Essentials-Beg/Allfiles/Chapter9/EventStorage/Azure` directory path.

5. Review each file and replace the placeholders and the string value enclosed. For example, the following is a placeholder with a string value:

   `<EnterUniqueName>`

6. Save each file after you've replaced all the placeholders.

7. In the Cloud Shell editor, enter the following commands:

   bash CreateQueue.sh
   bash CreateEventGrid.sh
   bash PostEventData.sh

> **Insight**
>
> If you encounter errors, try replacing the placeholder string value with a different string value. If the problem persists, execute the commands found in the shell script files individually from the command line.

8. After you have executed the shell scripts successfully, review the Azure Storage Queue event data routed by the Event Grid Topic.

> **Insight**
>
> If you don't know your way around, try using the search field located in the Azure portal.

With that, you have created an Azure Event Grid service and queue resources and used the Azure CLI to produce events routed by Event Grid to the Queue Storage service. In the next section, we will explore Google Cloud Eventarc.

Configuring events using Eventarc

Like AWS and Azure, Google Cloud Eventarc supports event-driven architectures, wherein one or more event producers, which are the originating event sources, send events to be filtered and routed by Eventarc, which acts as a router. Eventarc routes the incoming event data to one or more event consumers. The main objective remains the same across the cloud computing leaders: to route event data to downstream event handlers efficiently.

The following diagram shows examples of Google Cloud Eventarc depicted as the event router:

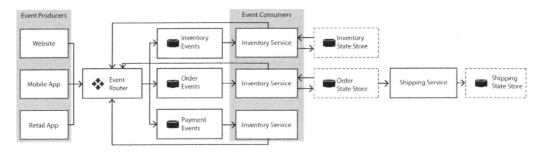

Figure 9.4 – Google Cloud Eventarc

In this section, you will learn how to create and configure Eventarc in Google.

Objective

After completing these tasks, you will be able to achieve the following:

- Describe and configure Google Cloud Eventarc

> **Note**
>
> The instructions are also located at `https://github.com/PacktPublishing/Cloud-Computing-Demystified-for-Aspiring-Professionals/tree/main/Instructions/Chapter9/EventStorage/GoogleCloud`

To do 1: Create and configure Eventarc in Google.

Task 1: Create and configure Eventarc in Google.

In this task, you will create and configure Eventarc in Google using the Google Cloud CLI:

1. Sign in to the Google Cloud console (`https://console.cloud.google.com/`).

2. In the Google Cloud console, on the project selector page, select or create a Google Cloud project.

3. Enable the **Cloud Run**, **Cloud Logging**, **Cloud Build**, **Pub/Sub**, and **Eventarc** APIs.

4. In the Google Cloud console, activate Cloud Shell. Enter the following commands:

```
gcloud components update
gcloud config set project <EnterPROJECT_ID>
gcloud config set run/region us-central1
gcloud config set run/platform managed
gcloud config set eventarc/location us-central1
```

5. Next, enable audit logs to read and write by entering the following commands:

```
gcloud projects get-iam-policy <EnterPROJECT_ID > /tmp/
policy.yaml
```

6. Edit the YAML file by only adding the following information:

```
auditConfigs:
- auditLogConfigs:
   - logType: ADMIN_READ
   - logType: DATA_WRITE
   - logType: DATA_READ
  service: storage.googleapis.com
```

7. Next, set your YAML policy by entering the following command:

```
gcloud projects set-iam-policy PROJECT_ID /tmp/policy.
yaml
```

8. Assign the `eventarc.eventReceiver` role permission to the Compute Engine service by entering the following commands:

```
gcloud projects add-iam-policy-binding PROJECT_ID \
    --member=serviceAccount:PROJECT_NUMBER-compute@
developer.gserviceaccount.com \
    --role='roles/eventarc.eventReceiver'
```

9. Create the storage bucket event source by entering the following command:

```
gsutil mb -l us-central1 gs://events-cceb-EnterPROJECT_
ID/
```

10. Create a Cloud Run service that handles the events routed by Eventarc by entering the following commands:

```
git clone https://github.com/GoogleCloudPlatform/python-
docs-samples.git
cd python-docs-samples/eventarc/audit-storage
```

11. Build and deploy the container image by entering the following commands:

```
gcloud builds submit --tag gcr.io/PROJECT_ID/helloworld-
events
gcloud run deploy helloworld-events \
    --image gcr.io/PROJECT_ID/helloworld-events \
    --allow-unauthenticated
```

12. Configure the Eventarc trigger that will route events from the storage to the Cloud Run service by entering the following commands:

```
gcloud eventarc triggers create events-cceb-trigger \
        --destination-run-service=helloworld-events \
        --destination-run-region=us-central1 \
        --event-filters="type=google.cloud.audit.log.
v1.written" \
        --event-filters="serviceName=storage.googleapis.
com" \
        --event-filters="methodName=storage.objects.create"
```

```
\
        --service-account=<EnterPROJECT_NUMBER>-compute@
developer.gserviceaccount.com
```

13. If you upload a file to the Google Cloud Storage bucket, the event will generate event data that will send event messages to the Cloud Run service.

With that, you have configured Google Cloud Eventarc, Cloud Storage, and Cloud Run. Using Eventarc, you routed event data from Cloud Storage to Cloud Run. In the next section, we will explore the cloud computing queue messaging services.

Configuring queue messaging storage

In this section, you will learn about cloud computing message queue services. We will explore one of the many AWS, Azure, and Google Cloud resources.

Message queue services are fully managed resources that temporarily store messages. These queue or queue-like services can be accessed from cloud and hybrid deployment models. These services can store millions of messages and are typically used to log messages used in a task or work process.

The cloud queue services do not require upfront installation or ongoing infrastructure management. They are inherently scalable and highly available services, so they provide alternatives to message delivery.

Here is a non-exhaustive table listing some of the cloud computing serverless services:

Cloud Computing Provider	Serverless Services
AWS	SQS
Azure	Queue
Google Cloud	Cloud Tasks queues

Table 9.4 – AWS, Azure, and GCP serverless functions

These queue-like resources help you decouple distributed workload components by offloading a critical piece in your solution – that is, resilient message delivery. It also allows your other components to continue processing asynchronously, hence freeing them from waiting for other components to respond to every message sent.

Configuring AWS Simple Queue Service

Amazon's **Simple Queue Service** (**SQS**) helps organizations decouple distributed applications that require resilient message delivery. It's in the name – the service is simple to use. Simply create a queue service that provides a public endpoint; from there, you can connect, send, and retrieve messages from anywhere with confidence.

The following diagram shows an example of AWS SQS:

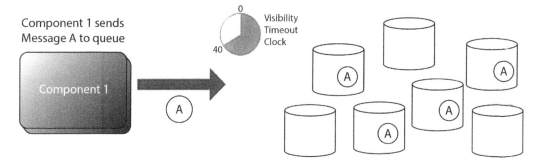

Figure 9.5 – Example of AWS SQS

In this section, you will learn how to configure SQS in AWS.

Objective

After completing these tasks, you will be able to achieve the following:

- Describe and configure SQS in AWS

Note

The instructions are also located at `https://github.com/PacktPublishing/Cloud-Computing-Demystified-for-Aspiring-Professionals/tree/main/Instructions/Chapter9/QueueStorage/AWS`

To do 1: Configure SQS in AWS.

Task 1: Configure SQS in AWS.

In this task, you will learn how to configure SQS in AWS:

1. Sign in to the AWS Management Console (`https://console.aws.amazon.com/console/`).

2. In the AWS management console, enter `Queue` in the search field, and then select **Queue**.

3. Select **Create queue**.

4. On the **Create queue** page, select **FIFO**.

5. Enter a unique name for your queue with the `.fifo` suffix.

6. Select **Create Queue**.

7. Once your queue has been created, select **Queues**, and then select your queue.

8. Select **Actions** from the top menu, and then select **Send and receive messages**.

9. Enter `message1` in the message body, and enter a message group ID.

10. Select **Send message**.

11. Upon success, select **View details** to display the sent message.

With that, you have configured AWS SQS and sent a message into the queue. In the next section, we will learn about Azure Queue Storage.

Configuring Azure Queue Storage

Azure offers a managed queue PaaS for persisting millions of messages from any platform and supports a multitude of programming languages. Microsoft's storage account queue service is simple to use, similar to AWS SQS. It is used to loosely couple microservices such as Azure App Service workloads by messaging a backend API such as an Azure Functions app, which can poll messages from Azure's resilient queue resource type.

The following diagram illustrates an example of Azure Queue storage:

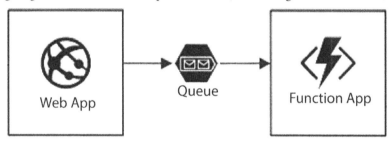

Figure 9.6 – Azure Queue Storage

> **Insight**
> Did you know that you can configure private endpoints for your Azure Storage account queue service to allow workloads on a VNet to securely access messages over a private link IP address to avoid accessing the Queue native public endpoint?

In this section, you will learn how to configure Azure Queue Storage.

Objective

After completing these tasks, you will be able to achieve the following:

*   Describe and configure Azure Queue Storage

> **Note**
>
> The instructions are also located at `https://github.com/PacktPublishing/`
> `Cloud-Computing-Demystified-for-Aspiring-Professionals/tree/`
> `main/Instructions/Chapter9/QueueStorage/Azure`

To do 1: Configure Azure Queue Storage.

Task 1: Configure Azure Queue Storage.

In this task, you will learn how to configure Azure Queue storage:

1. Sign in to the Azure portal (`https://portal.azure.com/`).

2. In the Azure portal, select **Create a resource**. Then, select **Storage**, and then **Create**.

3. On the **Create a storage account** page, populate the **Basics** tab with unique values.

> **Insight**
>
> If you need assistance creating an Azure Storage account, I recommend reviewing the *Configuring object-level storage* section in this chapter.

4. Select **Review + create**, and then select **create**.

5. Navigate to your storage account.

6. In the left menu for the storage account, select **Queue Storage**, then select **Queues**.

7. Select the **+ Queue** button.

8. Enter a unique name for your queue.

9. Select **OK** to create the queue.

10. Once the queue has been created, select the queue in the storage account.

11. Select **+ Add** to add a message. Enter `message1` in the **Message** field.

12. Select **OK** to add the message.

13. After adding the message, the console will display the messages in your queue.

With that, you have configured Azure Queue storage and sent a message into the queue. In the next section, we will explore the Google Cloud queue-like services.

Configuring a Google Cloud Tasks queue

The strategic benefit of offloading isolated processes or tasks by utilizing a queue is of great interest to cloud computing leaders such as Google Cloud. Google Cloud delivers Cloud Tasks, which adds a queue to persist one or more distinct tasks. And like Amazon, it is simple to create a queue managed by a Cloud Tasks service. Workers or workloads running in IaaS and PaaS connect to the queue's endpoint to process the message or payload.

The following is an example of a Google Cloud Tasks queue:

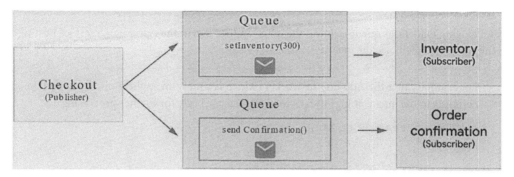

Figure 9.7 – Example of a Google Cloud Tasks queue

In this section, you will learn how to configure a Google Cloud Tasks queue.

Objective

After completing these tasks, you will be able to achieve the following:

- Describe and configure a Google Cloud Tasks queue

> **Note**
> The instructions are also located at https://github.com/PacktPublishing/
> Cloud-Computing-Demystified-for-Aspiring-Professionals/tree/
> main/Instructions/Chapter9/QueueStorage/GoogleCloud

To do 1: Configure a Google Cloud Tasks queue.

Task 1: Configure a Google Cloud Tasks queue.

In this task, you will learn how to configure a Google Cloud Tasks queue:

1. Sign in to the Google Cloud console (https://console.cloud.google.com/).

2. In the Google Cloud console, on the project selector page, select or create a Google Cloud project.

3. In the Google Cloud console, select **Activate Cloud Shell**.

4. In the Cloud Shell command line, enter the following command to create a Cloud Tasks queue:

```
gcloud tasks queues create <EnterUniqueName>
--location=<EnterLocation>
```

5. Review the queues in your current project by entering the following command:

```
gcloud tasks queues list --location=<EnterLocation>
```

> **Insight**
>
> A Google Cloud Tasks queue requires the name and version of the App Engine service hosting the worker that will use the queue.

For example, after the App Engine worker (which is simply an application, if you prefer code) connects to the queue, it logs the payload or message body for further processing:

```
class CreateHttpTask
{
    public string CreateTask(
        string projectId = "YOUR-PROJECT-ID",
        string location = "EnterLocation",
        string queue = "EnterUniqueName",
        string url = "http://taskqueue.com/taskhandler",
        string payload = "CCEB Rocks!",
        int inSeconds = 0)
    {
        CloudTasksClient client = CloudTasksClient.
Create();
        QueueName parent = new QueueName(projectId,
location, queue);

        var response = client.CreateTask(new
CreateTaskRequest
        {
            Parent = parent.ToString(),
            Task = new Task
            {
                HttpRequest = new HttpRequest
                {
                    HttpMethod = HttpMethod.Post,
                    Url = url,
// The example code below is separate from above.
            routeBuilder.MapPost("log_payload", context
    =>
```

```
            {
                // Log the request payload
                var reader = new StreamReader(context.
Request.Body);
                var task = reader.ReadToEnd();

                logger.LogInformation($"Received task
with payload: {task}");
                return context.Response.
WriteAsync($"Printed task payload: {task}");
            });
```

With that, you have configured a Google Cloud Tasks queue, and you've had an opportunity to review the code logic used by workers hosted on PaaS such as App Engine to connect and process your queue message payload.

Summary

In this chapter, you learned how to configure storage resources for resiliency, including object-level, file share, discrete event, and queue messaging storage services.

In the next chapter, we will explore developing database service resources for scale.

Questions

Answer the following questions to test your knowledge of this chapter:

1. Which of the following options are optimized with object-level storage services?

    A. Dynamic files

    B. Static files

    C. 1 KB attributes

    D. Metadata

2. Which of the following options are optimized by Amazon S3?

    A. Block files

    B. NFS file shares

    C. Object-level attributes

    D. Item attributes

3. Which of the following options are optimized by Azure Storage Blobs?

    A. Object-level attributes

    B. Item attributes

    C. SMB file shares

    D. None of the above

4. Which of the following options are optimized by Google Cloud Storage?

    A. Item attributes

    B. PNG files

    C. Messages

    D. None of the above

5. What is a bucket or container in cloud computing?

    A. A legal hold

    B. Something that provides access control

    C. A location to store objects

    D. None of the above

6. Amazon S3, Azure Storage Blobs, and Google Cloud Storage can support which of the following?

    A. IoT device storage

    B. AI compute

    C. Machine learning compute

    D. Big data workloads

7. Cloud object-level storage is categorized as which of the following?

    A. SaaS

    B. Infrastructure

    C. IaaS

    D. PaaS

8. Amazon EFS, Azure Files, and Google Cloud Filestore are categorized as which of the following?

    A. Serverless

    B. Compute

    C. Virtual networks

    D. None of the above

9. Connecting or mounting a cloud file share service is supported in which of the following scenarios?

    A. On-premises

    B. Hybrid

    C. Hypervisor

    D. None of the above

10. Which of the following commands are used to create and configure an Azure Storage Blob?

    A. `touch storageblob.blob`

    B. `aws efs`

    C. `gcloud beta filestore`

    D. `az storage account`

11. Which of the following resembles an event?

    A. Inbound traffic

    B. Continuously running program

    C. Change in state

    D. None of the above

12. Which of the following services are supported by native targets for cloud EventBridge, Event Grid, and Evantarc services?

    A. Serverless

    B. SaaS

    C. On-premises

    D. None of the above

13. Which of the following options are optimized using cloud EventBridge, Event Grid, and Eventarc?

    A. Events

    B. Raw data messages

    C. Item attributes

    D. Large files

14. Which of the following options is best suited for cloud queue-like services?

    A. Large files

    B. Inbound traffic

    C. IP addresses

    D. Messages

Part 4:
Administrating Database and
Security on the Cloud

This part will help you create database tables and build data management analysis resources by implementing AWS, Azure, and GCP data services.

The part comprises the following chapters:

- *Chapter 10, Developing Database Services for APIs*
- *Chapter 11, Building Data Warehouse Services for Scalability*
- *Chapter 12, Implementing Native Cyber Security Controls for Protection*
- *Chapter 13, Managing API Tools for Agility*

10
Utilizing Database Service Resources for Agility

This chapter will describe utilizing key database services, including relational databases and non-relational database resources.

The following concepts will be covered in this chapter:

- Utilizing relational databases
- Utilizing non-relational databases

Utilizing relational databases

In this section, you will learn how to configure and implement **relational database services** (**RDSs**). You will also learn helpful tips and about potential pitfalls that encumber beginners.

Most organizations require purpose-built databases organized in a relational model. We explored relational models, also known as **relational databases**, in *Chapter 5*, in the *Data services* section. If your organizational needs require managing structured data that is predefined by a schema and normalization is a business requirement cloud **RDSs** will help enforce a schema and improve performance for relational table-to-table lookups using predominantly **Structured Query Language** (**SQL**) statements at cloud scale.

Let's consider a real-world example. The format of a Microsoft Office 365 Excel or Google Sheets worksheet is categorized as a relational and structured dataset. These structured services are used in industries such as finance and across business verticals for report analysis. The following is an example of a structured dataset:

PROBLEM AREA	OCCURRENCES	PERCENT OF TOTAL	CUMULATIVE PERCENT
Databases	35	23.18%	23.18%
License	25	16.56%	39.74%
Environment	21	13.91%	53.64%
Operating System	18	11.92%	65.56%

Figure 10.1 – Excel worksheets are in a table format

The following table provides examples of AWS, Azure, and **Google Cloud Platform** (**GCP**) RDSs.

Cloud Service Providers	Relational Database Services
AWS	Amazon Aurora
Azure	Azure SQL Database
Google Cloud Platform	Cloud SQL

Table 10.1 – RDSs

Stick with me as I expand on each cloud computing provider's RDS, and in turn, you will learn how to utilize RDSs in the cloud.

Review the following figure illustrating an Amazon Aurora architecture, depicting its native resiliency in the eventuality of failure:

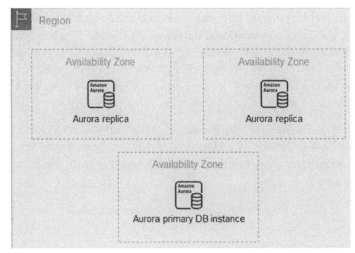

Figure 10.2 – Amazon Aurora

> **Note**
>
> Here's something that will impress you. Consider this: it takes several minutes to create what is displayed in the preceding figure. I can tell you from experience that before the rise of cloud computing, it would take enterprise organizations several years to plan, prepare, and deploy a similar infrastructure on-premises. Impressed?

Utilizing Amazon Aurora database tables

In this section, you will learn how to develop Aurora database table resources in AWS. You will also learn helpful tips and about potential pitfalls that encumber beginners.

The AWS Aurora database service is a fully managed database engine. Aurora supports MySQL and PostgreSQL database workloads. Aurora empowers developers to repurpose data access logic (code) used in on-premises applications to target Aurora as the primary database engine endpoint without requiring extensive code refactoring, which in turn helps you move efficiently to the cloud and leverage its inherent high-availability and performance benefits.

> **Insight**
>
> Did you know that Amazon's RDS offers a special region for the US government?

Objective

After completing these tasks, you will be able to do the following:

- Describe and develop an Amazon Aurora Database instance

Prerequisites

The following are the requirements for completing all the tasks:

- An updated version of Windows 8.1 or later, macOS 10.15 or later, or Linux Ubuntu 18.04 or later.

- An up-to-date and secure internet browser (Chrome or Edge is recommended).

> **Note**
>
> I am using the Windows 10 operating system and the Chrome and Edge browsers.

- Access to the instructions that are located at `https://github.com/PacktPublishing/Cloud-Computing-Demystified-for-Aspiring-Professionals/tree/main/Instructions/Chapter10`.

- Access to an AWS account with the required privileges to create and manage resources and dependencies. Go to `https://aws.amazon.com/free` to create an AWS trial account for training purposes only.

> **Important**
>
> You should fork, clone, or download and follow along with the step-by-step tasks on GitHub or as described in the chapter. I recommend using GitHub in conjunction with the book because the code text is more clearly defined on GitHub. However, that's my preference; you may prefer the book format.

To do 0: Subscribe to AWS.

Task 1: Sign in to AWS.

The steps are as follows:

1. Open the Edge or Chrome browser on your computer and go to `https://aws.amazon.com/free`.

2. After the website loads, select **Create a Free Account**.

3. On the `portal.aws.amazon.com` website, populate the fields labeled **Root user email address** and **AWS account name**, then enter a valid and readily accessible email account name and AWS account name for training purposes. Here are several examples of email accounts:

   - `Example.lastname@gmail.com`

   - `Example.lastname@outlook.com`

   Here is an example of an AWS account name:

   - `Cloud Practitioner`

> **Note**
>
> I have elected to exclude any guidance pertaining to billing details that include **personally identifiable information (PII)**.

4. Follow the remaining prompts and populate all the required fields to complete the new account creation process.

> **Insight**
>
> There are several resources to help you create and manage your AWS Free Tier to ensure you don't incur substantial costs. You can go to https://aws.amazon.com/premiumsupport/ knowledge-center/create-and-activate-aws-account/ and https://aws. amazon.com/premiumsupport/knowledge-center/what-is-free-tier/.

Tasks

To do 1: Develop an Amazon Aurora database table.

> **Important**
>
> The instructions listed match the AWS management portal version available as of May 2022. AWS is always updating the interface to improve the user experience.

Task 1: Develop an Amazon Aurora database table.

In this task, you will develop an Amazon Aurora database table using the AWS Management Console:

1. Sign in to the AWS Management Console (https://console.aws.amazon.com/ console/).

Practical applications:

Let's start our journey by understanding how utilizing cloud SQL and NoSQL database services and their resources helps different industries drive agility, which in turn decreases ongoing operational costs incurred through developing practical applications, testing them, and publishing them to production.

> **Note**
>
> I recommend reviewing what an API is, which is described in the *API endpoints* section in *Chapter 5*.

Healthcare companies and service providers such as Humana, Blue Cross, UnitedHealthcare, and Pfizer, which are among the most prominent, all utilize APIs to support and enrich their customer service, which consequently improves their health. Don't agree? Consider the web and mobile health services you have at your fingertips. Ask anyone between the ages of 45 and 80 what services were available 10 years earlier. The response is usually less than adequate.

Healthcare customers need readily available access to health services data and rich services to improve their quality of life, whether for non-emergency or life-threatening events. Patients should have the capability to access said services from home and abroad. Mobile devices empower patients to quickly find and use these services.

Mobile platforms offer SaaS applications or apps through mobile marketplaces such as Apple's App Store or Google Play Store. For example, you can install the MyHumana app, which is a healthcare app that supports secure sign-in services and access to data, including user profiles; transactional, sensitive, and non-sensitive PII data; frequently overwritten or extended data; preview features that support dynamic updates; and areas that support patient notes, healthcare provider compliance documents, and storage for large image files. As you can imagine, there are many requirements, and healthcare providers are constantly innovating.

Envision using a mobile healthcare app. You must first sign in, and that request is handled by either your device or an online service such as AWS, Azure, or GCP. Once you are signed in, you're greeted by the mobile app's default home screen. However, the data displayed on the home screen is derived from a database service. Note that there are scenarios where the session state data is on the client side, meaning on the mobile app. But by default or due to security concerns, most healthcare mobile apps adhering to PCI, HIPPA, and other regulatory compliance requirements segregate their presentation, API and business logic, and data model in modern development. What if you wanted to review your previous in-patient and out-patient transactions with your primary medical doctor efficiently without having to enter your local clinic? Let's expand on the situation. You need to review the transactions because you were overcharged and currently, you're suffering from breathlessness and chest pains. In other words, time is against you. Your mobile app integrates with the API through endpoints, and the API in turn gets the data from a transactional data management service.

Healthcare companies continuously redesign and develop their systems to improve the overall service. So, as you can imagine, these companies need to be able to continuously create the infrastructure on demand using tried and true methods. This is only feasible in cloud computing. This tutorial describes a well-known infrastructure as code service using AWS CloudFormation that helps you design, deploy, and manage AWS service resources in minutes. Utilizing the templates, you can reuse and quickly amend template details and thus resource configurations iteratively, which supports continuous development patterns:

1. Using the search field, enter `cloudformation`, and then select **CloudFormation**.

2. Select **Create stack** and then choose **Select with new resources** from the menu.

3. Select **Upload a template file | Choose file**, and then select `auroraDB.yml` from the `~ Cloud-Computing-for-Beginners/blob/main/Allfiles/Chapter10/RDS/ AWS/` directory path.

> **Note**
>
> **YAML**, or **Yet Another Markup Language**, is often used in infrastructure as code configuration management tools and resource files. This is an example of a template file.

4. Select **View in designer**, and on the **CloudFormation designer** dashboard, locate and update the YAML template's **Description** property value.

> **Note**
> The designer gives you a visual presentation of your resources.

5. Select the create stack icon.

6. On the **Create stack** page, select **Next**, enter unique password and username values in the **Parameters** section, and then select **Next**.

7. Select **Next**, and then select **Create stack**.

8. Enter RDS in the search field, and then select **RDS**.

9. On the **Amazon RDS** dashboard, select **Databases** and review the database instance you created utilizing Amazon CloudFormation's template and designer.

Once your infrastructure resource, namely the database, is available, you can continue to design and develop the mobile backend API that manages large concurrent client requests.

Here's a suggestion to develop your skills further, but it will require some heavy lifting on your part. May I suggest attending a *Developing on AWS* training class? There is more about instructor-led training in *Chapter 14*. I am assuming you have intermediate to advanced knowledge of AWS **software development kits (SDKs)** and APIs. The following code example interacts with the Amazon Aurora Data API using the AWS SDK for Python (Boto3). *Chapter 13* describes SDKs, so you can skip ahead to that chapter if you need a proper introduction.

To connect, read, and write to a relational table, you will need to do the following. Create a table, and during creation, enable the HTTP endpoint, similar to the API endpoint. You must grant the necessary permissions to use the data API. You can use an AWS-managed policy such as **AmazonRDSDataFullAccess** or define a custom policy. I recommend the former. You will also find the word secret in the code that follows. When calling the data API, you pass credentials using Secrets Manager.

> **Note**
> Secrets Manager helps you store and manage thousands of secrets, such as password strings used in database connections.

The following Python code inserts a row of data in the patient_users table:

```
Import boto3
dataapi = boto3.client('aurora-data')
aurora_arn =
'arn:aws:rds:<region>:<awsaccountid>:cluster:enteryourcluster'
secret_arn = 'arn:aws:secretsmanager:<region>:<awsaccoun-
tid>:secret:enteryoursecret'
tr = dataapi.begin_transaction
```

```
(
     serviceArn = aurora_arn,
     secretArn = secret_arn,
     database = 'enteryourdatabase'
)
response3 = dataapi.execute_statement
(
     serviceArn = aurora_arn,
     secretArn = secret_arn,
     database = 'enteryourdatabase'
     sql = 'insert into patient_users(firstname, lastname) val-
ues('John', 'Tukey')',
     transactionId = tr['transactionId']
)
cr = dataapi.commit_transaction(
     serviceArn = aurora_arn,
     secretArn = secret_arn,
     transactionId = tr['transactionId'])
```

The preceding Python application example can be installed and developed using EC2 instances, Elastic Beanstalk applications, Kubernetes, or as a lambda function invoked by your mobile client and the REST API HTTP POST method.

The conclusion of this practical application is that the patient mobile app backend can be built utilizing Amazon Aurora database tables to accelerate the creation of a database model for patients. Meanwhile, app development teams harness the cloud computing API and resources to implement a web or mobile API to create or get patient data, including transaction data history, optimized by RDMSs in the cloud to drive agility.

> **Note**
> Control costs incurred when creating the database by immediately deleting resources. Enter the `aws cloudformation delete-stack --stack-name EnterStackName` command into AWS Cloud Shell.

In these tasks, you've developed an Amazon Aurora database instance with CloudFormation. In the next section, we will investigate Azure's fully managed Microsoft SQL database at cloud scale.

> **Insight**
>
> Did you know that Amazon RDS provides a query editor online but presently, it only supports Amazon's Aurora Serverless databases?

Utilizing Azure SQL database tables

In these tasks, you will learn how to develop a SQL database in Azure. You will also learn helpful tips and about potential pitfalls that encumber beginners.

Microsoft Azure offers native RDSs, fully managed by Microsoft. Simply select the capacity required to meet your business needs and create an easy-to-use Azure SQL database at cloud scale.

> **Insight**
>
> Review the configurable data classification options available that can help any business of any size plan what data entities are deemed confidential.

Objective

After completing these tasks, you will be able to do the following:

- Describe and develop an Azure SQL database

Prerequisites

The following are the recommended requirements for completing all the tasks:

- An updated version of Windows 8.1 or later, macOS 10.15 or later, or Linux Ubuntu 18.04 or later.

- An up-to-date and secure internet browser (Chrome or Edge is recommended).

- Access to the instructions that are located at `https://github.com/PacktPublishing/Cloud-Computing-Demystified-for-Aspiring-Professionals/tree/main/Instructions/Chapter10`.

- Access to an Azure subscription with the required privileges to create and manage all resources and dependencies. Go to `https://azure.microsoft.com/en-us/free/` to create an Azure trial subscription for training purposes only.

To do 1: Subscribe to Microsoft Azure.

Task 1: Sign in to Azure.

The steps are as follows:

1. Open the Edge or Chrome browser on your computer and go to `https://azure.microsoft.com/en-us/free/`.

2. After the website loads, select **Start free**.

3. On the `login.microsoftonline.com` website, select **Create one**. Here are several email account name examples:

    - `Example.lastname@outlook.com`

    - `Example98765@outlook.com`

> **Note**
>
> I have elected to exclude any guidance pertaining to billing details that include PII.

4. Follow the remaining prompts and populate all the required fields to complete the new account creation process.

> **Insight**
>
> There are several resources to help you create and manage your Azure Free Tier to ensure you don't incur substantial costs. You can refer to `https://azure.microsoft.com/en-us/free/free-account-faq/`.

Tasks

To do 3: Develop an Azure SQL database table.

Task 1: Describe and develop an Azure SQL database table.

In this task, you will create an Azure Storage Blob using the Azure portal.

Microsoft, like Amazon and Google, simplifies creating inherently redundant storage services to maximize resiliency in almost any workload and supports web management, **command-line interfaces (CLIs)**, SDKs, and public APIs, which improves access and administration and empowers innovation. The steps are as follows:

1. Sign in to the Azure portal (`https://portal.azure.com/`).

Practical applications:

Similar to the Amazon Aurora database, Azure SQL Database supports transactional data. Most companies commonly use Microsoft SQL Server on-premises to support OLTP workloads. It's also a best practice for organizations with product familiarity to control costs by using known services that can support cost-efficient lift-and-shift strategies designed to reduce the operational expenditures incurred through many factors, such as training or hiring new talent for temporary projects, such as adopting cloud services.

As mentioned previously, companies must continuously innovate on demand. Infrastructure-as-code tools and strategies utilize templates, also known as configuration files. The following steps describe using **Azure Resource Manager** (**ARM**) templates to help design, deploy, and manage Azure infrastructure resources, such as a highly available SQL database, efficiently without the capital required to invest in racking and stacking more physical infrastructure:

2. In the portal, navigate to the search field and type `deploy a custom template`, and then select **Deploy a custom template**.

3. Select **Build your own template** in the editor.

4. Select **Load file**, and then select `azuredeploy.json` from the `~Cloud-Computing-for-Beginners/blob/main/Allfiles/Chapter10/RDS/Azure/azuresqlDB/` directory path.

5. Select **Save**, and on the **Custom deployment** page, enter the following values for each field:

    • **Subscription**: Select your subscription

    • **Region**: Select your region

    • **Server Admin Login**: Enter your unique username

    • **Server Admin Login Password**: Enter your unique password

    • **Ccebdb Name**: `sqldb`

> **Note**
> Leave default values unless explicitly instructed to modify them.

6. Select **Review + create**, and then select **Create**.

7. Enter `azure sql` in the search field, and then select **Azure SQL**.

8. Select the Azure SQL database you created in the previous task and review the database settings.

Once the database is available, you can continue to design the mobile backend API that queries client requests. You will need to create the database table. Use the `patient_users.csv` data located on GitHub. Using the Azure SQL Database query editor, create the table using SQL.

I recommend attending a *Developing Solutions for Microsoft Azure* training class. More about instructor-led training can be found in *Chapter 14*. I am assuming you have intermediate to advanced knowledge of Azure SDKs and APIs. The code example that follows interacts with the Azure SQL Data API using the Azure C# SDK. *Chapter 13* describes SDKs, so you can skip ahead to that chapter if you need more information.

You will need the following data for this task: the client ID, the client secret, the tenant ID, and the connection string to your Azure SQL database.

To add the properties, create an application settings JSON file and enter the property values. The values or information can be found in Azure Active Directory. Either register the application or use managed identities to generate the preceding property information. Note, the managed identity and registration create a new principal object, such as a Google service account, which is used in lieu of our credentials. The tenant ID is derived from the current Azure Active Directory domain. As a refresher, review the configure services method and members such as `.AddMvc`, `Configure`, and `.AddSingleton` used in the majority of C# `startup.cs` files. It's recommended that you implement an authentication helper class to handle authentication by getting the access token. Review the `.httpcontextaccessor` methods and members. Note that class types include members such as methods. Think of a method as a local Python function.

Here is an example of a `Get` method in a model view:

```
[HttpGet]
public JsonResult Get()
{
    JsonResult retVal = null;

    AuthenticationResult authResult = AuthenticationHelper.
GetAuthenticationResult(httpContextAccessor, authSettings);

    if (authResult != null) {
        string queryString = "SELECT patientid FROM dbo.
patient_users";

        using (SqlConnection connection = new
SqlConnection(authSettings.ConnectionString)) {
            connection.AccessToken = authResult.AccessToken;
            try {
                connection.Open();
                SqlCommand command = new
SqlCommand(queryString, connection);
                SqlDataAdapter adapter = new
```

```
SqlDataAdapter(command);

            DataTable table = new DataTable();
            adapter.Fill(table);

            retVal = new JsonResult(table);

        }
        catch (SqlException ex)
        {
        }
    }
}
    return retVal;
}
```

In conclusion, a patient mobile app can use the Azure SDK and API to integrate with your Azure SQL Database model for patients. Unbeknownst to your customers, the API, not the mobile client app, is securely retrieving their data, including their transaction history.

> **Insight**
>
> Try using the built-in query editor using your Azure SQL username and password. You need to add a firewall rule for your client IP and allow all Azure services to connect to your database.

In these tasks, you have developed an Azure SQL database using an ARM template. In the next section, we will explore developing an Google Cloud RDS.

> **Note**
>
> To control incurring costs, we recommend deleting all resources by deleting the resource group you created while developing your ARM template online.

Utilizing Google Cloud SQL tables

In this section, you will learn how to develop Cloud SQL resources in Google Cloud. You will also learn helpful tips and about potential pitfalls that encumber beginners.

Google Cloud SQL is intuitive, predictable, and developer friendly. Google Cloud SQL facilitates architecting fault-tolerant RDSs backed by Google Cloud's massive infrastructure.

> **Insight**
>
> To bolster high availability, we recommend making a secondary database available in a secondary region. Eventually, when a failure occurs, you can fail over to a secondary region and make the secondary region the new primary database.

Objective

After completing these tasks, you will be able to do the following:

- Describe and develop Google Cloud SQL

Prerequisites

The following are the recommended requirements for completing all tasks:

- An updated version of Windows 8.1 or later, macOS 10.15 or later, or Linux Ubuntu 18.04 or later.

- An up-to-date and secure internet browser (Chrome or Edge is recommended).

- Access to the instructions that are located at `https://github.com/PacktPublishing/ Cloud-Computing-Demystified-for-Aspiring-Professionals/tree/ main/Instructions/Chapter10`.

- Access to a GCP account with the required privileges to create and manage all resources and dependencies. Go to `https://cloud.google.com/free/` and `https://cloud. google.com/resource-manager/docs/manage-google-cloud-resources` to create a free GCP account for training purposes only.

To do 0: Subscribe to GCP.

Task 1: Sign in to GCP.

The steps are as follows:

1. Open the Edge or Chrome browser on your computer and go to `https://cloud.google. com/free/`.

2. After the website loads, select **Get started for free**.

3. On the `accounts.google.com` website, select **Create account**. Then, select **Create a new Gmail address instead**. Here are several email account name examples (replace `Example` with your name or alias):

   - `Example.lastname@gmail.com`

   - `Example98765@gmail.com`

> **Note**
>
> I have elected to exclude any guidance pertaining to billing details that include PII.

4. Follow the remaining prompts and populate all required fields to conclude the new account creation process.

> **Insight**
>
> Here are several resources to help you create and manage your free GCP account to ensure you don't incur substantial costs. You can go to `https://cloud.google.com/free/`.

Tasks

To do 1: Develop with Google Cloud SQL.

Task 1: Describe and develop with Google Cloud SQL.

In this task, you will develop a Google Cloud SQL database:

1. Sign in to the Google Cloud console (`https://console.cloud.google.com/`).
2. In the Google Cloud console, on the project selector page, select or create a Google Cloud project.
3. Use Google Cloud Shell and open a terminal window.
4. Enter the following command:

    ```
    mkdir cceb && cd cceb
    nano main.tf
    ```

5. Copy the contents of the file named `googleCloudSql.tf` located in the `~/ Cloud-Computing-for-Beginners/blob/main/Allfiles/Chapter10/RDS/ GoogleCloud/` directory path.
6. Paste the content you copied from the previous task into the Cloud Shell command line using nano.

Practical applications:

Like the other cloud providers, Google Cloud offers not only native infrastructure as code tooling but also well-known configuration management services such as Terraform. HashiCorp's configuration management tool is known throughout open source communities for its declarative syntax and templates:

Enter the following commands from the Cloud Shell command line:

```
terraform init
terraform plan
terraform apply
```

7. Enter yes to confirm the Terraform apply command.

8. Using the search field, enter sql, and then select **Cloud SQL**.

9. Review your **Cloud SQL instance** properties.

Mobile APIs can use Google Cloud functions to connect and query MySQL Cloud SQL database tables on Google Cloud to retrieve structured patient data.

After creating the Cloud SQL instance, ensure it has been assigned a public IP. For this brief tutorial, create a cloud function and configure a service account. Assign the service account to your function. Set up the service account with Cloud SQL roles such as SQL Client, Editor, and Admin to establish a connection.

Review the following Python code example:

```python
import os
from google.cloud.sql.connector import Connector, IPTypes
import pymysql
import sqlalchemy
def connect_with_connector() -> sqlalchemy.engine.base.Engine:
    """
    Initializes a connection pool for a Cloud SQL instance of
MySQL.

    Uses the Cloud SQL Python Connector package.
    """
    instance_connection_name = os.environ["INSTANCE_CONNECTION_
NAME"]  # e.g., 'project:region:instance'
    db_user = os.environ.get("DB_USER", "")  # e.g., 'my-db-
user'
    db_pass = os.environ["DB_PASS"]  # e.g., 'my-db-password'
    db_name = os.environ["DB_NAME"]  # e.g., 'my-database'
```

You can conclude the app development. But to get the patient_users table, implement the following Python code example:

```python
  exports.helloSql = functions.https.onRequest((request,
response) => {
  console.log('connecting...');
  try {
    client.connect(function(err) {
```

```
      if (err) throw err;

      console.log('connection success');
      console.log('querying...');

      client.query('SELECT patientid FROM patient_users;',
function(err, result){
          if (err) throw err;
```

> **Insight**
>
> Did you know that Google Cloud Shell has your favorite tools, such as Bash, kubectl, Docker, the gcloud command-line tool, and Terraform? They're all pre-installed, always up to date and ready to go!

In these tasks, you have developed Google Cloud SQL using Terraform. In the next section, we will review cloud computing non-RDSs.

Review the following Google Cloud SQL service illustration:

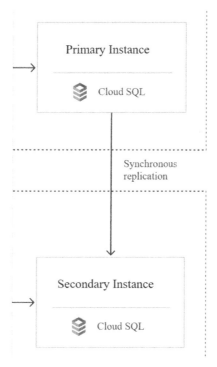

Figure 10.3 – Google Cloud SQL

> **Note**
> To control costs incurred, immediately delete everything that you created by entering the following command into the Cloud Shell command line: `terraform destroy`.

Utilizing non-relational databases

In this section, you will learn about fully managed non-RDSs in cloud computing. We will explore some of the many non-RDSs in AWS, Azure, and Google Cloud.

The cloud computing leaders support non-RDSs, also referred to as NoSQL—meaning not only SQL.

Let's consider a real-world example.

Non-relational data services are somewhat like relational ones because there are key names, also known as partition keys, which are used to help identify parts of a dataset. A key distinction in the formats is, unlike relational data, non-relational data does not conform to a traditional table, as in the example that follows, which depicts a JSON dataset, typically optimized by NoSQL (non-relational) database management services, such as DynamoDB, Azure Cosmos DB, and Google Cloud Firestore.

Companies such as **Maersk**, a global leader in transportation, and **Onomondo**, an **Internet of Things** (**IoT**) software organization, utilize cloud computing services such as Cosmos DB to support the frequently generated IoT device semi-structured data being sent and received bidirectionally from the cloud to client applications and APIs to operators and business end users' mobile apps.

The following code depicts a JSON dataset. JSON-structured data is optimized using NoSQL database management services:

```
"Items":{
    "Authors":{
        "SS":[
            "Author1",
            "Author2"
        ]
    }
    "Dimensions":{
        "S":"8.5 x 11.0 x 1.5"
    }
    "ISBN":{
        "S":"333-3333333333"
    }
    "ID":{
```

```
            "N":"103"
        }
    "InPublication":{
        "BOOL":false
    }
    "PageCount":{
        "N":"600"
    }
    "Price":{
        "N":"2000"
    }
```

Here is a non-exhaustive table listing some of the cloud computing NoSQL services:

Cloud Computing Provider	Container Services
AWS	DynamoDB
Azure	Cosmos DB
Google Cloud Platform	Cloud Firestore

Table 10.2 – AWS, Azure, and GCP NoSQL services

NoSQL database management services are known for their performance, scalability, and ease of use. More and more dynamic services, whether mobile, gaming, or static web and microservice architectures, use the dynamic nature of non-RDMSs to support varying data type structures and flexible schemas that can adapt to nuanced features needed in modern workloads that are constantly in flux.

Utilizing an AWS DynamoDB table

Amazon's DynamoDB is a fully managed NoSQL service that helps developers efficiently develop and manage scalable non-relational database tables backed by Amazon's global infrastructure.

In these tasks, you will learn how to develop DynamoDB tables on AWS. You will also learn helpful tips and about potential pitfalls that encumber beginners.

Objective

After completing these tasks, you will be able to do the following:

- Describe and develop an Amazon DynamoDB table

Tasks

To do 1: Develop an Amazon DynamoDB table.

This book is not intended to replace an instructor-led course, which accounts for the time required to learn all the components of a service. I elaborate on instructor-led courses in *Chapter 14*.

Task 1: Describe and develop an Amazon DynamoDB table.

In this task, you will learn how to develop an Amazon DynamoDB table:

1. Sign in to the AWS Management Console (`https://console.aws.amazon.com/console/`).

2. Select the Cloud Shell icon, and in the Cloud Shell CLI, enter the following commands to create a DynamoDB table and put items into the table:

```
aws dynamodb create-table \
    --table-name cceb \
    --attribute-definitions \
        AttributeName=CloudComputing,AttributeType=S \
        AttributeName=IaaS,AttributeType=S \
    --key-schema \
        AttributeName=CloudComputing,KeyType=HASH \
        AttributeName=IaaS,KeyType=RANGE \
    --provisioned-throughput \
        ReadCapacityUnits=5,WriteCapacityUnits=5 \
    --table-class STANDARD
```

3. Review the status of your table by entering the following command:

```
aws dynamodb describe-table --table-name cceb | grep
TableStatus
```

4. Put an item in the table by entering the following command:

```
aws dynamodb put-item \
    --table-name cceb  \
    --item \
        '{"CloudComputing": {"S": "AWS"}, "IaaS": {"S":
"VM"}, "Compute": {"S": "EC2"}, "Managed": {"N": "0"}}'
```

5. After successfully creating your DynamoDB table, review the DynamoDB properties by navigating to the dashboard on the AWS Management Console.

Practical applications:

Think back to what we described in the preceding sections about RDMSs. Recall that healthcare apps must support access to a variety of data, including profile data, PII data, frequently overwritten data, preview features that support dynamic updates, and patient notes and documents. The data structure and dynamic nature are best optimized using NoSQL database solutions.

After creating your DynamoDB table, you can create a lambda function as a backend API to query the table data:

```
        /// <summary>
        /// Gets information about an existing the table.
        /// </summary>
        /// <param name="client">An initialized Amazon DynamoDB
client object.</param>
        /// <param name="tableName">The name of the table
containing the items.</param>
        /// <returns>A Dictionary object containing information
about the item
        public static async Task<Dictionary<string,
AttributeValue>> GetItemAsync(AmazonDynamoDBClient client,
Patient newPatient, string tableName)
        {
            var key = new Dictionary<string, AttributeValue>
            {
                ["patientid"] = new AttributeValue { S =
newPatient.Title },
                ["userid"] = new AttributeValue { N =
newPatient.Userid.ToString() },
            };
```

```
var request = new GetItemRequest
{
    Key = key,
    TableName = tableName,
};

var response = await client.GetItemAsync(request);
return response.Item;
}
```

> **Insight**
>
> Did you know that DynamoDB can dynamically adjust the initial provisioned throughput capacity units automatically in response to millions of table read requests and decrement when utilization decreases? Research DynamoDB On-Demand mode and Autoscaling DynamoDB.

In these tasks, you have developed Amazon DynamoDB tables. In the next section, we will review an Azure non-RDS at a cosmic level.

> **Note**
>
> To control costs incurred, immediately delete the resource created by entering aws dynamodb delete-table --table-name cceb.

Utilizing an Azure Cosmos DB container

Azure Cosmos DB is a fully managed non-RDS. It delivers serverless and autoscaling capacity management. Cosmos DB is well known for its native multi-API capability; that is, Cosmos DB supports APIs such as Gremlin, Cassandra, Table, and MongoDB. This greatly accelerates user adoption because developers can use tools and skills they have acquired to continue data modeling and querying without having to learn a new programming language and rebuild the data access logic.

The following is an example of Azure Cosmos DB:

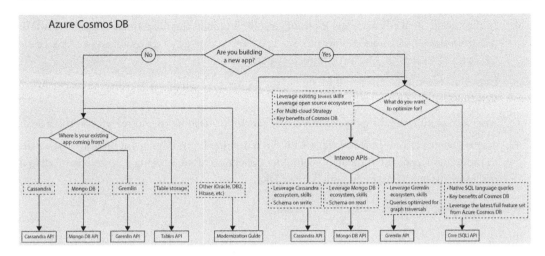

Figure 10.4 – Azure Cosmos DB

In these tasks, you will learn how to implement an Azure Cosmos DB account. You will also learn helpful tips and about potential pitfalls that encumber beginners.

Objective

After completing these tasks, you will be able to do the following:

- Describe and develop an Azure Cosmos DB account

Tasks

To do 1: Develop an Azure Cosmos DB account.

This book is not intended to replace an instructor-led course, which accounts for the time required to learn all the components of a service. I elaborate on instructor-led courses in *Chapter 14*.

Task 1: Describe and develop an Azure Cosmos DB account.

In this task, you will learn how to develop an Azure Cosmos DB instance:

1. Sign in to the Azure portal (`https://portal.azure.com/`).

2. In the portal, find and select **Cloud Shell**, follow the prompts, and complete the Cloud Shell creation.

3. In the Cloud Shell CLI, type the following:

```
Code .
```

4. In the Cloud Shell editor, select **Upload**, and then upload the file named **azureCosmoDB. ps1** from the · /Cloud-Computing-for-Beginners/tree/main/Allfiles/ Chapter10/NoSQL/Azure/ directory path.

5. Copy the PowerShell commands located in the file and enter them separately to create an Azure Cosmos DB account.

6. After successfully creating the resource, navigate to the dashboard and review its properties.

7. Azure Cosmos DB supports multiple APIs. So, a developer can implement programmatic calls to the Azure Cosmos DB database container collection of items using a serverless or virtual machine instance configured with Azure SDKs.

The following snippet of code uses a REST client:

```
POST https://placeholder.placeholder.azure.com/placeholder/docs
HTTP/1.1
x-ms-documentdb-isquery: True
x-ms-date: Day, 18 Aug XXXX XX:XX:49 EDT
authorization: <placeholder>
x-ms-version: 2015-12-16
x-ms-query-enable-crosspartition: True
Accept: application/json
Content-Type: application/query+json
Host: <placeholder>.documents.azure.com
Content-Length: 50

{
    "query": "SELECT patientid FROM patient_users",
    "parameters": []
}
```

> **Insight**
>
> Did you know that you can create and manage Cosmos DB containers and items using built-in Jupyter notebooks? For example, you can use the %%sql magic command to run a SQL query against any container in your account.

In these tasks, you have developed Azure Cosmos DB. In the next section, we will explore Google non-RDSs.

> **Note**
>
> To control costs incurred, immediately delete all resources by deleting the resource group.

Utilizing a Google Cloud Firestore database

Any business, no matter the size, needs to accelerate mobile, web, and IoT app development by leveraging document databases. Google Cloud Firestore is just that, a serverless, fully customizable, simple-to-integrate non-RDS.

The following is an example of Google Cloud Firestore:

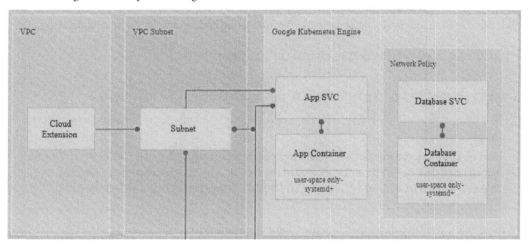

Figure 10.5 – Google Cloud Firestore

In these tasks, you will learn how to develop a Google Cloud Firestore database. You will also learn helpful tips and about potential pitfalls that encumber beginners.

Objective

After completing these tasks, you will be able to do the following:

- Describe and develop a Google Cloud Firestore database.

Tasks

To do 1: Develop a Google Cloud Firestore database.

Task 1: Develop a Google Cloud Firestore database.

In this task, you will develop a Google Cloud Firestore database:

1. Sign in to the Google Cloud console (`https://console.cloud.google.com/`).

2. In the Google Cloud console, on the project selector page, select or create a Google Cloud project.

3. Make sure that billing is enabled for your Google Cloud project.

4. Select **Activate CloudShell**, and then in the Cloud Shell CLI, enter the following command:

    ```
    gcloud firestore databases create
    ```

5. After successfully creating your Firestore database, navigate to the dashboard and review its properties.

Similar to the other NoSQL database offerings, we can easily create and put items into a Firestore table and, after creation, query the database table. The following code example queries the database table:

```
patients_ref = db.collection(u'patient_users')

query = patients_ref.where(u'patientid', u'==', True)
```

> **Insight**
>
> Did you know you can interact with your Firestore database using C#, that is, .NET? Review the file named `googleFirestore.cs` located in the `~/Cloud-Computing-for-Beginners/tree/main/Allfiles/Chapter10/NoSQL/GoogleCloud/` directory path.

In these tasks, you have developed Google Cloud NoSQL services.

> **Note**
>
> To control costs incurred, immediately delete the Firestore database, for example, with the `gcloud firestoreoperations delete` command.

Summary

In this chapter, you learned about utilizing cloud-native data management services, for relational databases and non-relational database resources.

In the next chapter, we will explore implementing native fundamental cloud security features.

Questions

1. What is an RDS?

    A. An analytical database service

    B. NoSQL

    C. A relational database service

    D. None of the above

2. Which of the following data formats is optimized by RDSs?

    A. HTML

    B. Python

    C. JSON

    D. Tabular

3. Say you're working with a small table of data in one location, but you need to support a managed highly available service. What would you use?

    A. Azure Cosmos DB

    B. Google Cloud SQL

    C. AWS Lake Formation

    D. None of the above

4. Which of the following best categorizes cloud-native managed RDSs?

    A. IaaS

    B. SaaS

    C. PaaS

    D. On-demand instances

5. Which of the following best categorizes non-relational database management services?

    A. NoSQL

    B. SQL

    C. RDBMS

    D. No local secondary indexes

6. What data format can be optimized with DynamoDB, Cosmos DB, and Cloud Firestore?

    A. Large unstructured media files

    B. JSON

    C. JavaScript

    D. Java

7. Multimedia and social media text communication formats from Instagram, Twitter, and Snapchat are best serviced by using which of the following database services?

A. Amazon EBS, Azure Managed Disks, Google Cloud Persistent Disk

B. Amazon Aurora, Azure SQL, Google Cloud SQL

C. Python, .NET, Go

D. Amazon DynamoDB, Azure Cosmos DB, Google Cloud Firestore

11
Building Data Warehouse Services for Scalability

This chapter will describe how to build instrumental data warehouse databases and data lake storage resources.

The following will be covered in this chapter:

- Building data warehouse services
- Building big data lake services

Building data warehouse services

In this section, you will learn about cloud computing data warehouse management services. We will explore some AWS, Azure, and Google Cloud non-relational database management services.

The cloud computing leaders provide managed data warehouse services that enable you to deploy clustered data warehouse resources that can perform **online analytical processing (OLAP)** on massive amounts of data in parallel, while integrating with business intelligence services and tools.

In todays world, every industry, including **multimedia**, **transportation**, and **hospitality**, periodically needs to analyze current and historical data for reporting and to garner data insights. The volume of historical data alone can be daunting, and it may need to be formatted, validated, and organized based on business needs to help with decision making. What if we needed to make an informed decision based on a comparison week-to-date or month-to-date, due to the trajectory or path of the data values, rise or plummet? That would help us to make informed decisions about the future. Such a service would be valuable to any organization that needs to make decisions based on data observations, and companies around the world are using such services in conjunction with machine learning to adapt and improve current and new customers' experiences.

Here is a non-exhaustive table listing some of the cloud computing data warehouse services:

Cloud Computing Provider	Application Services
AWS	Redshift
Azure	Synapse Analytics
GCP	BigQuery

Table 11.1 – AWS, Azure, and GCP data warehouse services

In cloud computing, data warehouse services are resources used for storing historical datasets, reporting, and data analysis. For example, data warehouse resources are used in various batch-processing solutions.

Building Amazon Redshift resources

AWS Redshift is an Amazon-managed data warehouse that supports large volumes of data and integrates with numerous BI tools, such as RStudio.

In the following tasks, you will learn how to configure and develop Amazon Redshift resources. You will also pick up helpful tips and learn about some potential pitfalls that beginners can encounter.

Objectives

After completing these tasks, you will be able to achieve the following:

- Develop Amazon Redshift resources

Tasks

To do 1: Develop an Amazon Redshift database

Note that this book is not intended to replace an instructor-led course, which would allocate the time required to learn about all the components of a service. I do explore instructor-led courses in *Chapter 14*.

Task 1: Develop an Amazon Redshift data warehouse

In this task, you will develop a data warehouse using Amazon Redshift:

1. Sign in to the AWS Management Console (`https://console.aws.amazon.com/console/`).

Practical applications:

This is a continuation of our healthcare app from *Chapter 10*. If you recall, we needed to support various data types for different patient features, such as transactions and patient documents. Our solution used relational database and non-relational database services.

As mentioned, healthcare companies must be able to innovate. If a patient walked into a clinic, a nurse or non-accredited clinic member might perceive that the patient's symptoms were common among groups diagnosed with obesity and they might recommend exercise and a healthier diet. What if that meant heart disease went undiagnosed? Patients with heart disease display similar symptoms to those with obesity. The heart disease could have been diagnosed accurately if further analysis was performed.

Trusting one individual's diagnosis could lead to more than just patient misinformation; it could open the healthcare company up to litigation and further liability, eventually impacting customer loyalty and diminishing the brand name.

Data science techniques access abundant information from multiple data sources to help us make better decisions. Historical data for patients reporting symptoms can help us discover data that was perhaps overlooked. Data warehouse services are perfect resources for storing large datasets to identify obscure trends using additional tooling designed for transformation.

2. Search for `Redshift`, and then select **Redshift**.

3. On the **Redshift dashboard** page, select **Clusters**, and then select **Create cluster**.

4. In the **Cluster configuration** area, enter a unique value for the cluster identifier.

5. Select **Free Trial**.

6. Review the calculated configuration summary section, specifically the node type and the quantity of nodes.

> **Insight**
>
> Did you know that sample data is included with your data warehouse? The sample data labeled **Tickit** contains individual sample data files.

7. Enter unique values into the database configuration section.

8. Select **Create cluster**.

Practical applications:

Concerns arise when data is aggregated from disparate external sources, generated at high volumes, and include unique analysis requirements that vary for each business; for instance, analyzing batched data or near-real-time streams of data. Consequently, a business must architect a hot or cold path to manage the ingested data. Inferring the correct data type from the original source is arduous, to say the least. Data engineers and scientists need to extrapolate that information. To do so, they need flexible data pipelines that can organically change on demand for unpredictable workloads or provisioned for predictable workloads.

Such pipelines are used in practical applications today to drive product growth across various industries and require the correlation of historical trends to infer market trajectories. While pundits might consider feature engineering and other techniques, it's essential to consider cloud-scaled resources that are utilized in data warehousing patterns and offer on-demand storage, processing power, and memory at scale, as well as ease of use.

9. Next, you will need to connect to your cluster and run queries to create a table and load data from Amazon Simple Storage Service.

> **Helpful tips or tricks**
>
> Analysts and data-scientist-centric roles may use either a third-party query editor or Amazon Redshift's built-in query editor for agility.

Apache products are the most widely used framework in optimizing Big Data solutions. Apache and non-Apache data warehouse services are adopted today by pharmaceutical and financial institutions. Marketing is a key pillar in any business model and should be capable of building data warehouse services and underlying resources quickly and economically. Marketing leaders and their analysts, with structured query language aptitude, should be capable of querying vast amounts of data and building intuitive models without outsourcing to externally managed service providers. They should not negatively affect the company's bottom line by recruiting talent en masse for temporary projects designed to campaign cutting-edge products and services for the general market. While SaaS apps for data engineering and analytics are all the rage, you should consider how your data is to be ingested and how to efficiently extrapolate your data before data mining and further excavation.

To complete the following tasks, you will need access to the query editor. I presume you are using the root account. In production environments, you will need to attach an AWS-managed policy to the IAM user utilizing the query editor. Note that these instructions do not describe how to manage IAM policies for Redshift:

10. Select your created Amazon Redshift cluster.

11. On the Amazon Redshift dashboard, select **Go to query editor v2**. For additional guidance, see the following figure.

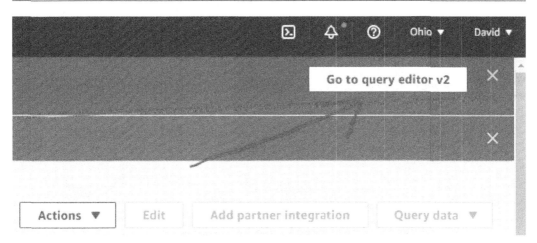

Figure 11.1 – Amazon Redshift dashboard – query editor button

Because you elected to create a free trial Redshift cluster, AWS included a sample database named DEV and loaded a sample dataset with tables.

12. In the Redshift query editor window, expand the node labeled with your unique Redshift cluster name. Select the DEV database node.

13. In the Redshift query editor work pane, enter the following code and select **Run**:

```
create table patient_users(
    userid integer not null distkey sortkey,
    patientid integer not null,
    firstname varchar(100),
    lastname varchar(100),
    email varchar(100)
);
```

Practical applications:

It's important to learn what SQL commands and functions are supported in RedShift. The partition key strategy is still a best practice; without prior knowledge of supported keys and Amazon recommendations, DBAs, analysts, and developers can create inefficient and costly tables. Review the service and architecting best practices on designing tables to avoid any pitfalls.

14. Create or repurpose an Amazon S3 bucket.

For further guidance, please review the information in *Chapter 9*.

15. To ingest data from S3, you will require an accessible bucket and data. I recommend that you configure the bucket as public, not private, by disabling ACLs and developing a bucket policy that allows all actions to decrease the probability of authorization errors, just for training purposes.

    The following code is an example of a bucket policy that meets the preceding requirements:

    ```
    {
        "Version": "2012-10-17",
        "Statement": [
            {
                "Sid": "ccdap1",
                "Effect": "Allow",
                "Principal": "*",
                "Action": "*",
                "Resource": "arn:aws:s3:::<enterbucketname>"
            }
        ]
    }
    ```

16. Find and download the `patient_users.csv` file from the following GitHub directory path: `~/Cloud-Computing-Demystified-for-Aspiring-Professionals/tree/main/Allfiles/Chapter11`.

17. Upload the file to your Amazon S3 bucket.

18. Select the object and review the properties. Copy the object URI. Note that **URIs**, or **uniform resource indicators**, resemble a URL.

19. DBAs, analysts, data scientists, and machine learning practitioners can use the Amazon Redshift `copy` command to ingest data into a table from AWS services such as S3. You can also copy data from external systems that are not native to AWS.

Helpful tips or tricks

The information included in this part of the task is insufficient to fully learn the intricacies of querying data with Amazon Redshift. This information is at the intermediate-to-expert level and will require an enhanced instructor-led training course with live guidance to ensure full comprehension of this technology and how to query effectively. Nevertheless, I am providing you with the basics of creating and running the service.

20. If needed, navigate back to your Amazon Redshift dashboard and access the query editor.

21. In the query editor work pane, enter the following code and select **Run**:

```
copy patient_users from 's3://<s3bucketname>/patient_
users.csv'
iam_role default
delimiter ',' region '<aws region>';
```

The following screenshot is for reference:

Figure 11.2 – Query editor reference for step 21

22. After you have successfully created the table and ingested the data using the `copy` command, review the newly created table.

23. If you are done admiring your work, we recommend deleting the Amazon Redshift cluster, including the database tables and S3 bucket, to stop incurring costs.

In these tasks, you have built a data warehouse resource using Amazon Redshift. In the next section, we will review Microsoft Azure data warehouse services.

Building Azure Synapse Analytics resources

Microsoft Azure offers massive data warehouse storage and built-in analytics resources that can manage even big data. Azure Synapse Analytics is a popular SQL and Apache Spark data warehouse that supports built-in data integration pipelines to **Extract Transform Load** (**ETL**) or **Extract Load Transform** (**ELT**) at scale. It has data and compute analytical resources from hybrid and multi-cloud services. Like its competitors, it supports BI tools and programming language protocols such as **Open Database Connectivity** (**ODBC**) and **Java Database Connectivity** (**JDBC**).

The following is an example of how Azure Synapse Analytics is used:

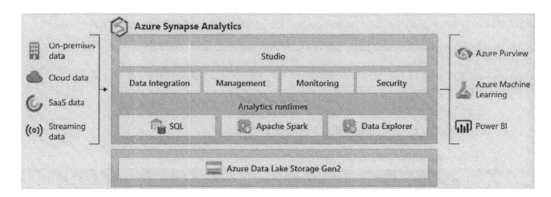

Figure 11.3 – An Azure Synapse Analytics framework

In these tasks, you will learn how to configure and develop Azure Synapse Analytics. You will also learn how to efficiently deploy the service.

Objectives

After completing these tasks, you will be able to do the following:

- Develop Azure Synapse Analytics resources

Tasks

To do 1: Develop Azure Synapse Analytics resources

Task 1: Develop an Azure Synapse Analytics data warehouse service

In this task, you will implement a data warehouse solution using Azure Synapse Analytics. The steps are as follows:

1. Sign in to the Azure portal (`https://portal.azure.com/`).

Practical applications:

Like Amazon, Azure supports data science protocols to help us make informed decisions. Historical data for patients' symptoms can be stored and accessed using data warehouse services.

2. In the portal, search for `Azure Synapse`, and then select **Azure Synapse Analytics**.

3. Select **Add**, then in the **Basics** tab, enter the following and leave the other values as their defaults unless explicitly instructed otherwise:

    - **Subscription**: Select your subscription.

    - **Resource group**: Create a new one or select a preexisting one.

- **Workspace name**: Enter a unique name.

- **Region**: Select a region.

- **Data Lake**: Create a new one and enter a unique name.

- **File system name**: Enter a unique name.

This book assumes you are using a root account, in the current context, a subscription owner role combined with a global administrator directory role. It is important to note that it is best practice to create new Active Directory users with the least privileged role. You will need to delegate certain roles in development environments. Select **Assign myself the storage blob data contributor role** to delegate the necessary privileges.

4. Select **Review + create**, and then select **Create**.

Practical application:

If you have experience with Oracle or Microsoft SQL Server, including Apache Hive, you'll know that the time it takes to plan and prepare a suitable environment to handle big data challenges is not feasible for start-ups and small businesses due to various factors, capital being chief among them.

IoT product distributors and managed service providers need to quickly develop minimum viable products by efficiently create a proof of concept to deliver new services to thrive in their market space by efficiently building data warehouse solutions that can ingest and infer large volumes of telemetry data in the early stage of development. Also needed is support for familiar query languages like SQL that empower developers and analysts alike. The complex creation of a massive parallel processing data warehouse in minutes to control costs is unthinkable for on-premises. ETL or ELT strategies tried on on-premises, like on a fleet of Linux, PC, or Mac personal computer devices, do not currently offer the power and extensibility available in comparison to cloud services like Amazon Redshift and Azure Synapse Analytics.

> **Note**
> It may take several minutes to complete the creation process in *step 4*.

5. After successfully creating the data warehouse service, select **Overview**.
6. In the **Overview** section, select **Open Synapse Studio**.
7. On the dashboard, select **Manage** and then select **SQL pools**.
8. Select **New**.
9. Populate the SQL pool name with a unique string.
10. Do not modify the default performance levels.
11. Select **Review + create**. It will take several minutes for your dedicated SQL pool to be ready.

12. Select the dedicated SQL pool resource.

13. In the dashboard, select the option to open Synapse Studio.

14. On the **Synapse Analytics workspace** home page, select **Ingest**.

15. On the **Properties** page, select **Next** to use the convenient copy data tool to ingest files to query.

16. On the **Source data store** page, set **Source type** to **Azure Data Lake Storage Gen2**. Configure the connection to your workspace default storage.

Source data store

Specify the source data store for the copy task. You can use an existing data store connection or specify a new data

Source type | Azure Data Lake Storage Gen2 ⌄ |

Connection * | ccap-WorkspaceDefaultStorage ⌄ | ✎ Edit   ＋ New connection

Integration runtime * | ✔ AutoResolveIntegrationRuntime ⌄ | ✎ Edit

File or folder

If the identity you use to access the data store only has permission to subdirectory instead of the entire account, specify the path to browse

| | ▢ Browse

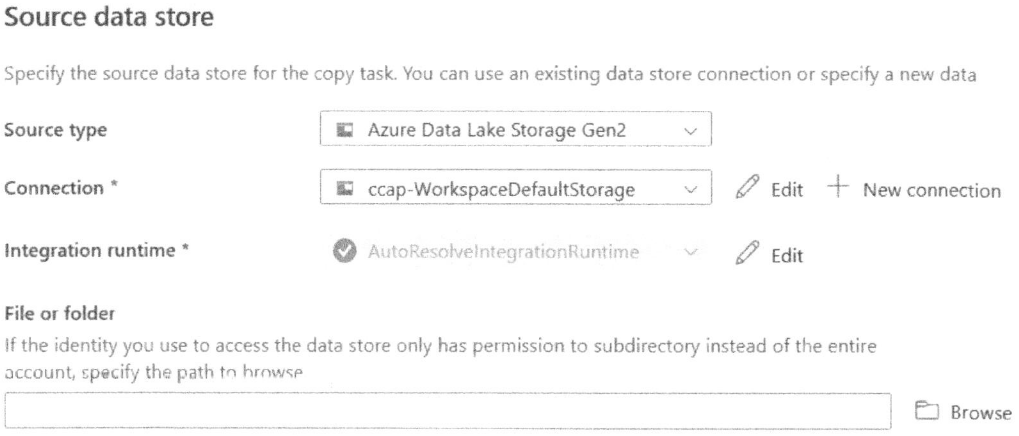

Figure 11.4 – Source data store page for Azure Data Lake

17. Browse to the file or folder area and select the file you previously copied into your Azure Data Lake data folder when you initially created the Azure Synapse Analytics resource, named `patient_users.csv`.

18. Review the configuration settings and select **Next**.

19. Review the destination data store. Notice you can select Azure and non-Azure services, including **REST** (short for **representational state transfer**), as a destination and establish a connection. For training purposes, I recommend using Azure Data Lake Storage resources.

20. Select the folder path area and browse to the data folder, but enter a unique filename so that you can distinguish the copy from the original file.

21. Review both the configuration and settings, and then select **Review and finish** to successfully copy the data.

22. Navigate to the **Synapse Analytics** home page, select the **New** dropdown, and then select **New SQL script**.

23. In the **SQL script editor** pane, enter the following code to create a database table:

```
CREATE TABLE dbo.patient_users
    (
```

```
    [userid] int NOT NULL,
    [patientid] int NOT NULL,
    [firstname] varchar(100) COLLATE SQL_Latin1_General_
CP1_CI_AS NULL,
    [lastname] varchar(100) COLLATE SQL_Latin1_General_
CP1_CI_AS NULL,
    [email] varchar(100) COLLATE SQL_Latin1_General_CP1_
CI_AS NULL
    )
WITH

    (

    DISTRIBUTION = ROUND_ROBIN,
    CLUSTERED COLUMNSTORE INDEX
    )
```

Practical applications:

As explained while describing Amazon Redshift, it's apparent that the SQL syntax in Azure is dissimilar in certain aspects to that of Amazon and will require further review before querying Azure Synapse Analytics database tables.

In the era of APIs, business users and other non-IT users can use a client app or web app that handles events to call a get or post method via HTTP (using REST) to an Azure-hosted backend API that performs **create, read, update, and delete** (**CRUD**) queries against data warehouse tables. This happens using Azure SDK library programming classes, which use **Language Integrated Query** (**LINQ**) or ADO.NET to programmatically query the data warehouse using SQL syntax.

24. After successfully creating the table, review the tables by selecting the **Data** option. Expand the dedicated SQL pool, go to **Tables**, and lastly, click on the table named dbo.patient_users to review your result set.

25. If you are done reviewing your work, we recommend deleting all resources to stop incurring costs.

> **Helpful tips or tricks**
>
> Did you know that you can load data into Azure Data Lake Storage from Azure Synapse Studio? After ingesting the data, you can manage it from Azure Synapse Studio and then grant access to multiple analysts to further process and review your data.

In these tasks, you have built a data warehouse resource using Azure Synapse Analytics. In the next section, we will review Google Cloud's data warehouse services.

> **Note**
> To stop incurring costs, immediately delete the resource group.

Building Google Cloud BigQuery resources

Google Cloud's serverless data warehouse architecture, known as BigQuery, offers zero infrastructure management. Its scalable and distributed analytics engine processes large volumes of data in seconds.

In these tasks, you will learn how to configure and develop Google Cloud BigQuery resources. You will also learn how to efficiently deploy the service.

Objectives

After completing these tasks, you will be able to do the following:

- Develop Google Cloud BigQuery resources

Tasks

To do 1: Develop Google Cloud BigQuery resources

Task 1: Develop a Google Cloud BigQuery Data warehouse

In this task, you will implement a serverless data warehouse using Google Cloud BigQuery:

1. Sign in to the Google Cloud console (`https://console.cloud.google.com/`).
2. In the Google Cloud console, on the project selector page, select or create a Google Cloud project.
3. Enable the BigQuery API.
4. Search for `BigQuery`, and then select **BigQuery**.
5. In the **type to search** field, enter `bigquery-public-data`.

Practical applications:

More and more data scientists use public datasets because of their value in different use cases. Querying and sharing data from applications and multiple collaborators for reuse in non-enterprise and enterprise scenarios enables information to be accessed from a variety of sources, systems, and APIs, while also providing value in the form of feedback. Old and new protocols are breaking down data silos and enhancing this aspect of inclusivity by sharing data that may be advantageous to people, processes, and tools. Ultimately, the data becomes useful through this iterative process. So, the moral of this story is that you should appreciate your public data.

6. Select **More Actions**, and then select **Open**.
7. On the **BigQuery** page, select + **Compose new query** and review the **Editor** field.

8. In the **Editor** field, enter the following commands:

```
SELECT
    name, gender,
    SUM(number) AS total
FROM
    `bigquery-public-data.usa_names.usa_1910_2013`
GROUP BY
    name, gender
ORDER BY
    total DESC
LIMIT
        10
```

9. After you enter the preceding code syntax, select **Run**.

Practical applications:

The cross-industry BI service organization btProvider has supported industries such as banking, oil, transportation, and government by way of visualizing unique trends that have staved off market irregularities and helped companies across different business verticals to build end-to-end BI solutions. Practical applications developed in collaboration with btProvider integrate data warehouse services such as BigQuery that deliver end-to-end ETL with tried-and-true visualization platform Tableau. This is done in order to discover actionable insights through exploratory data analysis of long-term historical datasets.

10. If you are done reviewing your work, we recommend deleting all resources to stop incurring costs.

Helpful tips or tricks

Did you know that you can load, preview, and process data all by utilizing Google Cloud's BigQuery console? Also, BigQuery automatically encrypts data at rest.

In these tasks, you have developed Google Cloud data warehouse services. In the next section, we will review some cloud computing data lake storage services for big data.

Note

To stop incurring costs, immediately delete the project.

Building data lake services for big data

In this section, you will learn about cloud computing data lake resources, in particular, big data storage services. We will explore some AWS, Azure, and Google Cloud resources.

Big data

Collecting and analyzing exabytes of data with traditional strategies and processing tools is challenging. These large volumes of data can include a variety of data types, and velocity can vary from streams of social media data to batches of transactional history data, from millions of services and resources around the globe.

The cloud has optimized how we plan, prepare, and implement technologies that manage big data. Cloud computing leaders deliver cloud-scale services that allow us to store and analyze big data.

Here is a non-exhaustive table listing some cloud computing big data storage services:

Cloud Computing Provider	Serverless Services
AWS	Lake Formation
Azure	Data Lake
Google Cloud	BigQuery BigLake tables

Table 11.2 – AWS, Azure, and GCP data lake services

Cloud computing data lake services enable you to ingest large volumes of data, no matter the structure or type, from almost anywhere, and they support processing the data using an array of analytics engines via integration in either hybrid or multi-cloud scenarios.

Building AWS Lake Formation resources

Amazon's Lake Formation is a cloud-scale service that streamlines building, securing, and managing big data. Lake Formation focuses on helping to collect, mine, move, and catalog big data efficiently.

The following is an example of AWS Lake Formation in use:

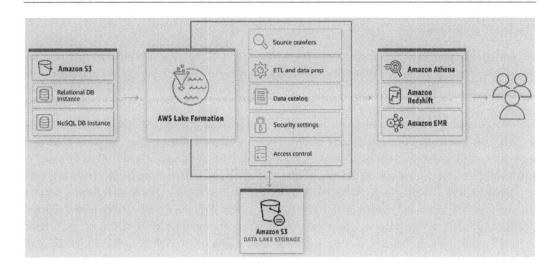

Figure 11.5 – AWS Lake Formation in use

In these tasks, you will learn how to develop AWS Lake Formation resources. You will also pick up helpful tips and learn about some potential pitfalls that beginners can encounter.

Objectives

After completing these tasks, you will be able to achieve the following:

- Develop AWS Lake Formation resources

Tasks

To do 1: Develop AWS Lake Formation resources

Task 1: Develop an AWS Lake Formation resource

In this task, you will learn how to develop AWS Lake Formation resources:

1. Sign in to the AWS Management Console (`https://console.aws.amazon.com/console/`).

Practical applications:

To conclude our journey with respect to the patient mobile app, what if we could do more with the data we collected from our patients? When I say more, I'm referring to extending or further optimizing the app's capabilities. We will need more data and new data models. The data model's initial transactional records fit into a tabular normalized SQL database, and the semi-structured documents were supported by denormalized systems to eventually be transformed into several normalized columnar datasets that are to be stored and batch processed using modern relational data warehouse services. But we're leaving some data on the table, so to speak, such as the patient notes that are frequently submitted by patients and healthcare professionals using the mobile app, as well as data entries from clinic personnel. Let's try classifying the data by structure or type. The notes submitted include, but are not limited to, text with various delimiters and images of all sizes (size varies based on the mobile device manufacturer, make, and model). Say we want to deliver a new feature that improves patients' healthcare. If we have already provided better diagnoses using historical data, what's next? Well, if we have identified an ailment with high probability, then the next course of action is to predict what will happen in the next several days if it's not treated, and more importantly, what treatment should be prescribed (the prognosis). So, our patient healthcare app will diagnose and then deliver a prognosis. Let us take a break here. Before moving on to the next step, try reflecting on our journey.

2. Create and configure an S3 location for the data lake.

Where can we aggregate data from multiple disparate data sources with variability in terms of structure and type? I almost forgot to mention: we will need to analyze the data, including text and mobile images, in real time. Additionally, we must correlate the data with historical batched records and document content. Sounds like a big job, doesn't it? You must store these aggregated datasets in unlimited storage before using the same storage hierarchically to stage the clustered data that correlates based on patient attributes and symptoms and persistently set aside uncorrelated data for compliance requirements. The ingested data should be extracted, loaded, and then transformed or modeled. Take a moment to consider what is happening. Continue to the next step.

3. You can repurpose an S3 bucket or create a new one. If you need guidance, refer to the information in *Chapter 9*.

Please ensure that your S3 bucket policies are configured to support the following actions. If you don't recall, review *Chapter 9*.

4. Get started creating your AWS Lake Formation resource. Upon choosing to create the service, you will be greeted with the following. Select **Get started**:

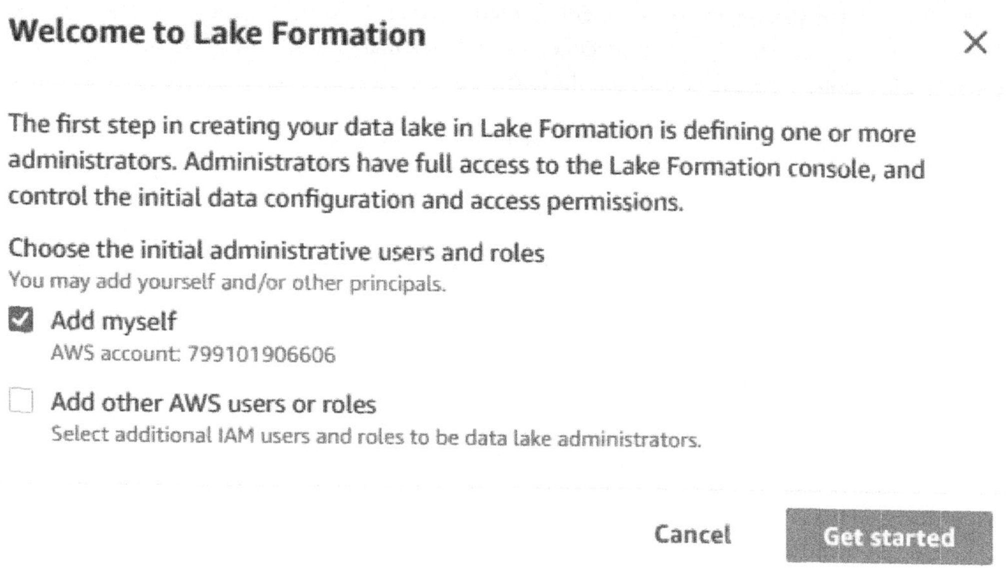

Welcome to Lake Formation

The first step in creating your data lake in Lake Formation is defining one or more administrators. Administrators have full access to the Lake Formation console, and control the initial data configuration and access permissions.

Choose the initial administrative users and roles
You may add yourself and/or other principals.

☑ **Add myself**
AWS account: 799101906606

☐ **Add other AWS users or roles**
Select additional IAM users and roles to be data lake administrators.

Cancel   **Get started**

Figure 11.6 – Lake Formation home page

> **Note**
> Do not modify the default setting.

5. On the AWS Lake Formation dashboard, select **Data lake locations**.

6. In the **Data lake locations** area, select **Register location**.

7. Review the **Register location** page information regarding the Lake Formation IAM role. Then, select **Register location**.

> **Helpful tips or tricks**
> In production environments, I recommend following the principle of least privileges to ensure any data engineering roles have only the permissions needed to complete a task.

8. Create a second Amazon S3 bucket and upload the `patient_users.csv` file.

In this tutorial, the second S3 bucket might emulate a business partner account's storage, a fleet of EC2 instances, an internal log agent, or a daemon sink destination, including but not limited to hot or cold path storage for big data storage solutions.

9. You can use Cloud 9, a local compute IDE configured with the AWS SDK, or use the AWS CLI to copy the files from the second bucket to the Amazon S3 bucket you registered with AWS Lake Formation. Type the following command:

```
# Replace with your bucket name:
YOUR_1BUCKET=EnterBucketName
YOUR_2BUCKET=EnterBucketName
aws s3 cp s3://$YOUR_2BUCKET/patient_users.csv
s3://$YOUR_1BUCKET/
```

Your initial bucket is the data lake backend.

We need to create a database and table to map to the objects in your Amazon S3 bucket. The Lake Formation tables include searchable metadata, and data engineers and analysts can design the tables to include columns and key-value-paired data items.

10. Select **Databases** on your AWS Lake Formation dashboard.

11. Select **Create database** and then populate the following database properties:

  • **Name**: Enter a unique name and add the `Prod` suffix. For example, `BigData-Prod`

  • **Location**: `s3://<EnterBucketName>/BigData-Prod`

12. Select **Create table using crawler**.

13. In the AWS Glue console, follow the intuitive prompts to type a crawler name.

> **Note**
>
> AWS Glue crawlers can efficiently automate searching through your data and infer a database table schema, including metadata. You can manually design and create a table schema using the AWS CLI or the graphical management console, but these methods are manual and therefore error prone.

14. Continue clicking **Next** in each prompt and select the Amazon S3 folder where your data is located so the crawler can complete its inference.

Practical applications concluded:

We extract, load, and then transform or process the data. We can infer the schema from our various datasets and start to optimize the data into useful data models that can be trained continuously to ensure that we have the necessary information to provide a prognosis. By using data lakes and data warehouse solutions, you not only help healthcare professionals by decreasing diagnosis timelines but also eliminate the need for second opinions, which may delay the provision of an efficient prognosis. These services are the backbone of our patient mobile app, which can help fast-track the healthcare that your patients need.

15. Select your AWS Glue crawler and then select **RUN**. The execution process takes several minutes.

16. After the crawler has finished successfully, AWS Glue generates a new database table and schema. You can select the table and view the schema.

Figure 11.7 – AWS Glue: the Database properties page

If you are done reviewing your work, we recommend deleting all resources to stop incurring costs.

> **Insight**
>
> Did you know that you can analyze data with **Elastic Map Reduce** (**EMR**) clusters? EMR is an Amazon big data analytics service.

In these tasks, you have developed an AWS Lake Formation solution. In the next section, we will review Azure Data Lake.

Building Azure Data Lake resources

Microsoft, like Google and Amazon, understands how critical it is to offer enterprises big data analytical services in today's digital world. Azure utilizes Azure Storage as the foundation for its cloud-scale data lake resources on Azure. Azure's Data Lake supports massive volumes of data and integrates easily with many of Azure's analytics services, such as Azure Databricks.

In these tasks, you will learn how to develop Azure Data Lake resources. You will also pick up helpful tips and learn about some potential pitfalls that beginners can encounter.

Objectives

After completing these tasks, you will be able to do the following:

- Develop Azure Data Lake resources

Tasks

To do 1: Develop Azure Data Lake resources

Task 1: Develop an Azure Data Lake service

In this task, you will learn how to implement big data storage by building Azure Data Lake resources.

Practical applications:

Data lakes can efficiently store semi-structured and unstructured data, such as patient notes and documents that contain text, which can be extracted and loaded before transforming the data into useful data models for backend applications. Future innovations to patient services can use these same data lakes to help healthcare organizations to use machine-learning-infused, AI-driven, mobile app chatbots to manage patients at scale, without the assistance of medical professionals, for non-critical scenarios or for patients that require transportation assistance and have unique accessibility needs.

The steps for this task are as follows:

1. Sign in to the Azure portal (`https://portal.azure.com/`).
2. Create a storage account as the backend for the Azure Data Lake solution.
3. Configure Azure Data Lake Storage Gen2 on the storage account. I recommend using the latest version of any cloud service's resources, whether that's Microsoft, Amazon, or Google Cloud. It's a well-known fact that the latest versions provide the best performance and cost savings.
4. Download **AzCopy**. This utility is yet another great cloud tool used in scenarios such as big data ingestion, data migration, and data movement. Most impressive are its streamlined CLI commands.
5. Download the Bureau of Transportation Statistics files. Optionally, you can generate your own data and upload your files to the data lake storage target. I recommend uploading the `patient_users.csv` file located on GitHub.
6. Optionally, upload the files using the Azure management portal API to Azure Data Lake. Preferably, if you have installed AzCopy, type the following CLI command to get help:

   ```
   azcopy -h
   ```

Here is an example of how to ingest files to Azure Blob Storage or Data Lake:

```
azcopy copy '<local-file-path>' 'https://<storage-
account-name>.<blob or dfs>.core.windows.net/<container-
name>/<blob-name>'
```

7. Create or reuse an Azure Synapse Analytics resource from the *Building data warehouse services* section.

   Synapse Analytics can be used to query the dataset you have stored in Azure Data Lake.

8. Lastly, explore your data using SQL queries such as the following:

```
SELECT
    TOP 100 *
FROM
    OPENROWSET(
        BULK 'https://<storage-account-name>.dfs.core.
windows.net/<container-name>/folder1/patient_users.csv',
        FORMAT='CSV',
        PARSER_VERSION='2.0'
    ) AS [result]
```

9. If you are done reviewing your work, we recommend deleting all resources to stop incurring costs.

Insight

Did you know that you can integrate Azure Data Lake with Azure Databricks via Spark?

In these tasks, you have developed an Azure Data Lake resource. In the next section, we will explore Google Cloud BigQuery.

Building BigLake tables in BigQuery

As the name implies, Google Cloud's BigQuery queries and processes big data using BigLake tables and extrapolates data from native storage services to external, and even multi-cloud, data resources, all while you monitor your data from the serverless BigQuery service. At its core, BigLake abstracts access to the underpinning cloud storage resource.

The following is an example of Google Cloud BigQuery BigLake tables in use:

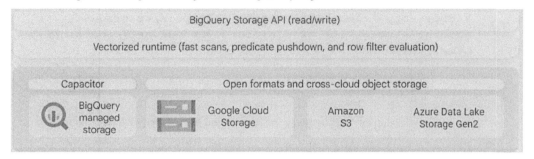

Figure 11.8 – Google Cloud BigQuery BigLake table example

In these tasks, you will learn how to develop BigQuery BigLake tables. You will also pick up helpful tips and learn about some potential pitfalls that beginners can encounter.

Objectives

After completing these tasks, you will be able to do the following:

- Develop BigQuery BigLake tables

Tasks

To do 1: Develop BigQuery BigLake tables

Task 1: Develop a BigQuery BigLake table service

In this task, you will learn how to implement access to Google Cloud Storage designed as a BigData resource, by building BigQuery BigLake tables:

1. Sign in to the Google Cloud console (`https://console.cloud.google.com/`).

2. In the Google Cloud console, on the project selector page, select or create a Google Cloud project.

3. Make sure that billing is enabled for your project.

4. You can repurpose a Google Cloud Storage bucket or create a new one. If you need guidance, refer to the information in *Chapter 9*.

5. Find and download the `patient_users.csv` file from the GitHub directory at `~/Cloud-Computing-Demystified-for-Aspiring-Professionals/tree/main/Allfiles/Chapter11`.

6. Upload the file to your Google Cloud Storage bucket.

> **Note**
>
> For tutorial purposes and to control costs, efficiently configure the bucket to support public access. However, development and QA environments should never support unrestricted public access to a Google Cloud Storage bucket. Tutorial environments are not development environments that will eventually mirror production.

7. Enable **BigQuery Connection API**.

8. This tutorial assumes that you are using the owner role. However, if you are delegating access and following least-privilege best practices, I recommend you consider these built-in roles prior to assigning roles: Data Lake administrator, Data Warehouse administrator, and Data Analyst.

9. Using the BigQuery service, configure an external connection resource by selecting + **Add data**. See *Figure 11.9* as a reference for what happens next.

> **Note**
>
> Google Cloud services provide native integration options for multi-cloud big data solutions.

Practical applications:

What if our big data workloads were initially developed as minimum viable proof-of-concepts, and we needed to quickly review the advantages and disadvantages of multi-cloud or compare the query and storage costs of the three major cloud providers? Google Cloud's services help us move forward by supporting streamlined methods for integration without all the heavy lifting involved in migrating data lake resources, including dependencies, from one provider to another.

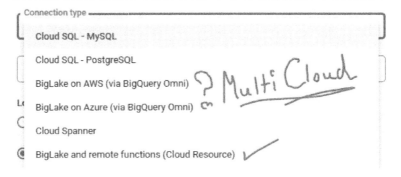

Figure 11.9 – The BigQuery External data source page

10. After successfully creating a connection, make note of the connection properties.

11. Create a dataset, populate the dataset properties with a unique name, and select the region where your Google Cloud Storage bucket data resides to control costs and improve latency.

12. Next, create a table using the newly generated dataset object.

   During table creation, select the storage bucket you created in one of the preceding task steps.

Practical applications:

Data ingestion, or copying data in layman's terms, is common in logical data pipelines and used widely across all business verticals in all industries. It is used to input new observations before transformation or processing occurs for server or serverless workloads. We could even say that the majority of, if not all, online retailers have to copy data from private and public networks and stage it before moving data to other phases of their pipelines.

13. Continue populating the table properties by choosing the data object you stored in the Google Cloud Storage bucket. Review the format and understand its constraints. Ensure you've selected the correct delimiter. Enter a unique name for your table.

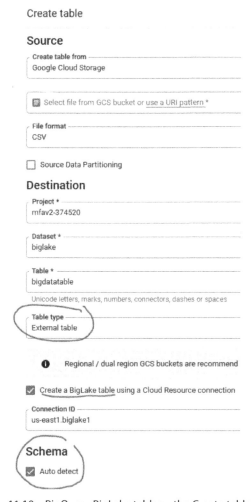

Figure 11.10 – BigQuery BigLake tables – the Create table page

14. Prior to completing your table creation request, review the preceding figure and identify several important properties. A BigLake table is an external table in the Google Cloud table storage options, and it supports cross-account and federated access to tables. The service connection is granted access and gets data from external sources on your behalf, improving security by ensuring that your principal and its role permissions are not utilized.

Practical applications:

After the staged data moves into a data lake, multiple analysts will require access to the data efficiently, without using owner access, to establish a connection to the dataset.

15. Select the BigLake table you created in the preceding tasks. Review the newly created table schema. Identify the **patientid** field.

16. Select the **BigLake table query** option. In the menu, select the **In-split** tab, to allow you to view the schema and the query editor window. In the query editor window, type the following SQL code:

```
SELECT patientid FROM
`<projectid>.<BigLakedatasetname>.<BigLaketablename>`
LIMIT 25

Example: SELECT patientid FROM `mfav2-374520.BigLake.
bigdatatable` LIMIT 25
```

For further visual guidance regarding querying the table, see the following screenshot:

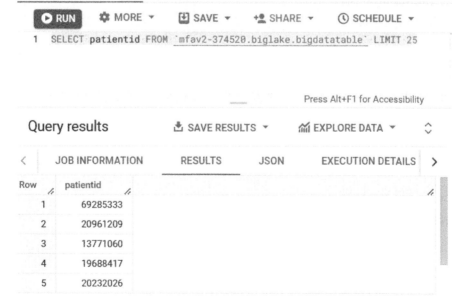

Figure 11.11 – The BigLake table query editor

17. If you are done reviewing your work, we recommend deleting all resources to stop incurring costs.

> **Helpful tips or tricks**
>
> Did you know that you can integrate Google Cloud BigQuery with Azure Data Lake?

In these tasks, you have developed Google Cloud BigQuery BigLake tables.

> **Note**
>
> To stop incurring costs, immediately delete the project.

Summary

In this chapter, you learned about building cloud-native data management services, specifically, data warehouse resources and big data storage services.

In the next chapter, we will explore implementing native fundamental cloud security features.

Questions

1. What is commonly stored in a data warehouse?

    A. Pictures

    B. Unstructured data

    C. Historical data

    D. Frequently accessed IoT telemetry logs

2. Which of the following options are supported with cloud data warehouse services such as AWS Lake Formation, Azure Data Lake, and Google Cloud BigQuery BigLake tables?

    A. OLTP

    B. OLAP

    C. Archival

    D. None of the above

3. What does BI stand for?

    A. Business intermediary

    B. Better information

    C. Business intelligence

    D. None of the above

4. Which delimiter is supported in CSV files?

    A. |

    B. /

    C. \

    D. ,

5. You can manage Azure dedicated SQL pool database table clusters.

    A. True

    B. False

6. In a SQL select statement, what does the FROM clause refer to?

    A. The database connection

    B. The partition

    C. The table

    D. The namespace

12

Implementing Native Cyber Security Controls

This chapter will take you through descriptions of the native cloud cyber security features. You will learn how to configure the built-in database, storage, compute, and network security features. You'll also learn about the concepts of defense in depth in the cloud, which involve the data, app, host, network, and authentication security capabilities native to Amazon, Microsoft, and Google.

The following topics will be covered in this chapter:

- Security and compliance
- Implementing built-in data security
- Implementing built-in app security
- Implementing built-in host security
- Implementing built-in network security
- Implementing zero trust (authentication and authorization)

Security and compliance

As organizations from every industry expand to the cloud because of various fiscal, agile, and global reach benefits, they must adapt and combine security technologies and strategies to stay one step ahead of the cyber threats that target on-premises, public, and hybrid infrastructure resources.

First, industries such as **information technology (IT)** are some of the most well-known sectors with critical infrastructure. Other industries, such as finance, energy, and healthcare are also important, but if a sector such as IT is compromised, it can incur significant damage to every industry because product lines are supported by IT infrastructure and resources. The impacts can negatively affect companies, their stakeholders, and employees due to decreases or significant loss in revenue and reputation can even put public safety at risk.

Sectors such as energy and healthcare now more than ever are increasingly integrated with IT. It is safe for you to presume that if one or more of these sectors are breached due to their dependency on IT, it can negatively impact our lives.

It is critical to understand compliance and security. Compliance relates to rules, policies, or laws, which can be regulatory or non-regulatory. Let's focus on regulations, such as the FISMA for US federal agencies, where the FISMA requires formal reviews that assess risk and provides oversight. The FISMA's well-known risk assessment categorizes information and validates a system's security control to determine whether additional controls are required to protect operations, including data and even physical assets.

Here is an example of compliance. **System and Organization Controls** (**SOC**) is a report that you use to audit controls. The report focuses on security controls such as firewalls, availability, confidentiality, quality assurance, and privacy. Each cloud computing leader provides resources to help organizations in varying industries adhere to compliance controls. While each is fully accredited and provides publicly attested documentation, it is important to note that they help you by providing the resources and guidance, but you do not inherit their accreditations. Please research and collaborate with your organization's compliance leadership for further insight into your company's unique requirements. Now, let's address security.

Security or security standards refer to reducing the risks, including preventing or remediating attacks, by using the best practices and technologies to establish secure communications, identify vulnerabilities, and prevent threats by following security frameworks. Frameworks help us understand what technologies, policies, security concepts, guidelines, risk management patterns, actions, and training can help reduce risk and deter known and unknown threats.

One of the most prominent frameworks is defense in depth, which we will use throughout this entire chapter. You'll notice that we start this chapter with data, and end with networking and **identity and access management** (**IAM**), which I've labeled zero trust (authentication and authorization).

It is essential to understand how the defense-in-depth security framework can be utilized to improve cloud security. In general, the defense-in-depth framework for cyber security uses multiple layers of security controls, thereby providing redundancy in the eventuality of a layer being breached because of a security control vulnerability. In summary, the more layers of security, the better!

Implementing built-in data security

In this section, you will learn how to configure cloud-native database security features. You will learn how simple it is to implement a secure AWS, Azure, and Google Cloud data platform and infrastructure service. You will also learn about helpful tips and potential pitfalls that encumber beginners.

The objective is simple – we will describe and configure the built-in data security features from AWS, Azure, and Google Cloud. Consequently, you will learn how to implement the key security features used to protect data at rest across the leaders of cloud computing. This is but one of the defense-in-depth security control layers in our multi-layered strategy.

The following table lays out the AWS, Azure, and GCP database and block storage disk services.

Data Service Resources	Relational Database Management Services and Disk Block Storage
AWS	DynamoDB, **Elastic Block Storage (EBS)**
Azure	Azure SQL Database, managed disk
Google Cloud	Cloud SQL, boot disk

Table 12.1 – PaaS and IaaS database and disk storage resources

Follow me as I implement each cloud computing provider's built-in data security features, thereby learning how to configure data security.

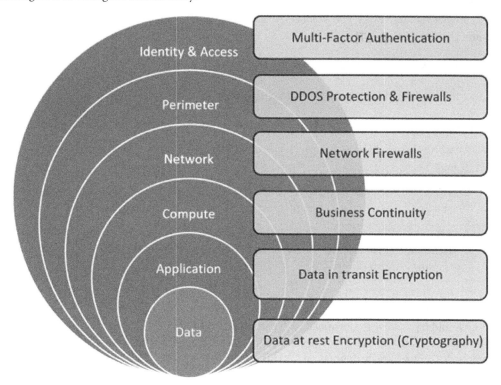

Figure 12.1 – Defense-in-depth data security layers

Configuring Amazon EBS and DynamoDB data security

In these tasks, you will learn how to implement data security in AWS. You will also learn about helpful tips and potential pitfalls that encumber beginners.

Amazon provides numerous services that can natively host and secure your data at rest efficiently. EBS is one of the managed disk options supporting IaaS **Elastic Compute Cloud (EC2) virtual machine (VM)** instances. While EBS can be used in various compute storage scenarios, such as storing operating system files, it can also be used to store relational and non-relational database management services software and its data files. However, if you read the previous chapters, you will have learned that PaaS relational and non-relational database management services are optimized to deliver resiliency and performance at the cloud scale. With that in mind, we can use, for example, DynamoDB to support our non-relational data. And like EC2 EBS disks, DynamoDB can host data and natively secure data at rest.

In addition, Amazon EBS and DynamoDB both support customer-managed keys for encrypting data at rest.

Objectives

After completing these tasks, you will be able to describe and implement built-in data security for EBS and DynamoDB.

Prerequisites

Here are the recommended requirements for completing all tasks:

- An updated version of Windows 8.1 or later, macOS 10.15 or later, or Linux Ubuntu 18.04 or later.

- An up-to-date and secure internet browser. I recommend using Chrome or Edge.

- The instructions for the steps in this chapter can also be found at `https://github.com/PacktPublishing/Cloud-Computing-Demystified-for-Aspiring-Professionals/tree/main/Instructions/Chapter12`.

- Access to an AWS account with the required privileges to create and manage resources and dependencies. Go to `https://aws.amazon.com/free` to create an AWS trial account for training purposes only.

Helpful tips or tricks

You should fork, clone, or download and follow along with the step-by-step tasks on GitHub or the ones described herein. I recommend using GitHub in conjunction with the book because any code is more clearly defined on GitHub. However, that's my preference; you may prefer the book format.

Tasks

To do 0: Subscribe to AWS

Task 1: Sign in to AWS

1. Select the Edge or Chrome browser on your computer and go to `https://aws.amazon.com/free`.

2. After the website loads, select **Create a Free Account**.

3. At `portal.aws.amazon.com`, populate the fields labeled **Root user email address** and **AWS account name**, and enter a valid and readily accessible email account name and AWS account name for training purposes. Here are several email accounts and AWS account name examples:

   - `Example.lastname@gmail.com`

   - `Example.lastname@outlook.com`

   - `Cloud Practitioner`

Note

I have elected to exclude any guidance pertaining to billing details that include **personally identifiable information (PII)**.

---

4. Follow the remaining prompts and populate all required fields to complete the new account creation process.

Helpful tip or trick

There are several resources to help you create and manage your AWS Free tier to ensure you don't incur substantial costs. You can go to `https://aws.amazon.com/premiumsupport/knowledge-center/create-and-activate-aws-account/` and `https://aws.amazon.com/premiumsupport/knowledge-center/what-is-free-tier/`.

To do 1: Implement built-in data security for EBS and DynamoDB

Helpful tips or tricks

The instructions listed match the AWS management portal version available in May of 2022. AWS frequently updates the interface to improve the user experience.

Task 1: Implement built-in data security for EBS

In this task, you will implement built-in data security for EBS and DynamoDB using the AWS Management Console:

1. Sign in to the AWS Management Console (`https://console.aws.amazon.com/console/`).

After signing into the management console, let us take a step aside from our step-by-step tutorial and expound on the practical applications as it relates to data security with a focus on encrypting data at rest and provider-managed keys and key infrastructure.

Start-ups and enterprise organizations market and manage products and services internally and externally. Internally, end users administratively access resources and use services. End users include leadership, stakeholders, partners, and employees that must adhere to compliance guidelines. And businesses have a responsibility to implement security controls to decrease and, if possible, eliminate risk. This also applies to external end users, commonly referred to as consumers of the company's products and services. These products and services make use of data classified as either public or private. Product and service data classifications are crucial to an organization's success in defending its assets, which are data, including the people who hold information. Whether your organization hosts its assets on-premises, with a hybrid cloud solution, or entirely in the cloud, you share responsibility with your cloud provider, and you both share similar security goals, which are to ensure assets such as your data are secured and that the protection you administer meets or exceeds your requirements. Data security demands data confidentiality and integrity, the data is expected to be highly available per the agreements defined by a company's security protocols, and it must adhere to the regulatory compliance standards mandated by government agencies.

Consider, fundamentally, that when we discuss securing something, we mean protecting the underlying data of a network or system. Organizations are responsible for processing and storing your data, and therefore must protect the data and processes used to generate or store information.

You must not only administratively control access to assets by implementing policies, procedures, and standards through compliance controls but also administer technical controls, such as perimeter and host firewalls and encryption!

Threats exist everywhere, whether you are on-premises or in the cloud. A threat exploits a vulnerability. Therefore, decreasing or eliminating vulnerabilities is essential. If you reduce the number of vulnerabilities, you consequently reduce risk. Inquire in any business setting or engineering environment and you will find that all organizations and their divisions aim to be risk-averse. So, IT administrators use best practices and security controls such as encrypting data at rest to utilize encryption to make sure that data is incomprehensible to ensure its confidentiality. As you may recall, confidentiality is one of our security goals.

Encrypting and the application of cryptography is a business requirement for reducing risk. However, while they're important, you don't have to master cryptography and delve into the learning permutations and biased views on what is considered the perfect form of encryption yourself. Why? Because modern cryptographic systems and applications natively use encryption to generate the encryption keys used to encrypt data as your system writes to storage. Storing and managing your keys in a secure location with access controls and systems that audit events related to encryption keys is more important. It is more important that you scale and optimize availability to people and processes that are explicitly authorized with minimum privileges.

Cloud leaders', such as AWS, Azure, and Google Cloud, services, streamline encrypting VM disk data at rest. Utilizing EC2 instance and EBS volume encryption features do not require security specialists to master cryptography. Let's stop there and continue to the next task:

2. Using the search field, enter `EC2`, and then select **EC2** to navigate to the EC2 dashboard.

    You will need to create an EC2 instance backed by an EBS-managed disk. To create a compute instance backed by an EBS, use the instructions detailed in *Chapter 8*.

Helpful tip or trick

AWS EBS disks use AWS **Key Management Service** (**KMS**) keys to encrypt EBS volumes and the snapshots used as backups.

---

3. Select **Account Attributes**, and then **EBS encryption**.
4. Select **Manage**.
5. Select **Enable**.
6. Set the AWS-managed key to `alias/aws/ebs`, created as the default encryption key for future auditing purposes.
7. Select **Update EBS encryption**.

Before moving on to the next task, allow me to further expound on our subject matter. Amazon encryption runs on the AWS infrastructure that hosts EC2 instances and its disk, EBS, making certain the data in transit between VM instances and its network-attached EBS is encrypted as well.

I would go as far as providing a visual, but the data (or more accurately put, the cyphertext) is incomprehensible.

By enabling encryption by default, your AWS account will enforce the encryption of new EBS volumes and snapshots that you create.

You will need to create an EC2 instance backed by an EBS-managed disk. To create a compute instance backed by an EBS, use the instructions detailed in *Chapter 8*.

You can create an encrypted EBS root volume during EC2 configuration if you select an instance type that supports EBS encryption.

Task 2: Implement built-in data security for DynamoDB:

1. Using the search field, enter DynamoDB, and then select **DynamoDB** to navigate to the DynamoDB dashboard.

> **Helpful tip or trick**
>
> AWS DynamoDB encryption at rest integrates with AWS KMS for managing the encryption key used to secure your data in an encrypted table.

2. You will need to create a DynamoDB table. To create a table, use the instructions detailed in *Chapter 10*.

3. If you prefer, use the following AWS CLI command to create a table:

```
aws dynamodb create-table \
    --table-name patients \
    --attribute-definitions \
        AttributeName=PatientId,AttributeType=S \
        AttributeName=FirstName,AttributeType=S \
    --key-schema \
        AttributeName=PatientId,KeyType=HASH \
        AttributeName=FirstName,KeyType=RANGE \
    --provisioned-throughput \
        ReadCapacityUnits=5,WriteCapacityUnits=5 \
    --table-class STANDARD
```

4. If you used the default settings upon table creation, the tables will be encrypted at rest using AWS-owned keys.

You can also create a customer-managed key using KMS instead of using an AWS-owned key to meet unique security requirements for client-side encryption.

In these tasks, you've implemented built-in data security for EBS and DynamoDB. In the next section, we will explore Azure's built-in data security.

Configuring Azure-managed disk and Azure SQL Database data security

In this section, you will learn how to implement data security in Azure. You will also learn about helpful tips and potential pitfalls that encumber beginners.

Microsoft Azures offers built-in security features, such as encryption of your data at rest. Azure VM instance persistent volumes, known as managed disks, can be encrypted. But if the data type and structure are best served by a PaaS relational database service I recommend using a Azure SQL Database, instead of implementing and maintaining an IaaS compute VM instance that hosts SQL server relational database. With Azure SQL Database, the data at rest can also be encrypted to provide a layer of security.

Objectives

After completing these tasks, you will be able to achieve the following:

- Describe and implement built-in data security for managed disks and Azure SQL Database

Prerequisites

Here are the recommended requirements for completing all tasks:

- An updated version of Windows 8.1 or later, macOS 10.15 or later, or Linux Ubuntu 18.04 or later.

- An up-to-date and secure internet browser. I recommend using Chrome or Edge.

- The instructions for the steps in this chapter can also be found at `https://github.com/PacktPublishing/Cloud-Computing-Demystified-for-Aspiring-Professionals/tree/main/Instructions/Chapter12`.

- Access to an Azure subscription with the required privileges to create and manage all resources and dependencies. You can go to `https://azure.microsoft.com/en-us/free/` to create an Azure trial subscription for training purposes only.

Helpful tips or tricks

You should fork, clone, or download the step-by-step tasks in GitHub. I recommend using GitHub in conjunction with the book because any parts written in code are more clearly defined in GitHub. However, that's my preference; you may prefer the book format.

Tasks

To do 0: Subscribe to Microsoft Azure

Task 1: Sign in to Azure

1. Select the Edge or Chrome browser on your computer and go to `https://azure.microsoft.com/en-us/free/`.

2. After the website loads, select **Start free**.

3. At `login.microsoftonline.com`, select **Create one!**. Here are several email account name examples:

    -   `Example.lastname@outlook.com`

    -   `Example98765@outlook.com`

> **Note**
>
> I have elected to exclude any guidance pertaining to billing details that include PII.

4. Follow the remaining prompts and populate all required fields to complete the new account creation process.

> **Helpful tips or tricks**
>
> There are several resources to help you create and manage your Azure Free tier to ensure you don't incur substantial costs. You can go to `https://azure.microsoft.com/en-us/free/free-account-faq/` for more information.

To do 2: Implement built-in data security for managed disks and Azure SQL Database

Task 1: Implement built-in data security for managed disks

In this task, you will implement built-in data security for managed disks and Azure SQL Database using the Azure portal:

1. Sign in to the Azure portal (`https://portal.azure.com/`).

    You will need to create an Azure VM instance backed by a managed disk. To create a compute instance backed by managed disk, use the instructions detailed in *Chapter 8*.

2. Optionally, create an Azure VM using the AZ CLI command:

    ```
    az vm create \
        --resource-group EnterResourceGroupName \
        --name vm007 \
    ```

```
--image Win2022AzureEditionCore \
--public-ip-sku Standard \
--admin-username EnterVMAdminName
```

3. In the portal, use the search field and enter `virtual machine`, and then select **Virtual machine** to navigate to the dashboard.

4. Select **Disks** from the settings.

Let us stop for a moment while I elaborate on data security, including encrypting data at rest, factoring in managing keys at scale, and the key infrastructure.

Whether a business is hosted in the cloud or owns and operates a data center on-premises, it will use cryptographic systems and applications to encrypt data as it is written to storage. Storing and managing keys is paramount and defending this key infrastructure with identity controls and auditing systems improves the level of protection. Azure Disk Encryption is integrated with Azure Key Vault. Key Vault is a key management service used in this context to create and control the encryption key. Key Vault can use asymmetric **data encryption key** (**DEK**) and supports symmetric encryption to protect the DEK using **key encryption key** (**KEK**) envelopment as the wrapper for the DEK. This cloud based key infrastructure scales to support thousands of keys and key requests and is inherently highly available.

It's important to note that enabling and using encryption should not be complex but quite the opposite. And if someone tells you otherwise, it's because they are still working on-premises or running a start-up from several MacBooks and Linux instances on a shared, private, locally distributed network and have yet to embrace cloud computing so they are unaware that there is a better way. Cloud encryption optimizes key management for small to enterprise organizations that are continuously expanding their services through innovation, which, in turn, increases resources and consequently creates more keys to manage due to market growth.

Here is something to note – key encryption command-line operations in Linux Bash shell, gcloud CLI, or PowerShell, while helpful in certain scenarios, are prone to errors when repurposed or automated at large scale, such as managing 50-100 systems on multiple LANs across WANs that span multiple regions. Manually using a command line to generate and manage thousands of keys is not a best practice, but it does call the attention of a few scripting aficionados:

1. Select **Encryption settings**, then select **Disks to encrypt**, and then select **OS and data disks** from the menu.

2. Select a key vault and key for encryption.

3. Select **Create New** to create a key vault, which is the Azure key management service.

4. Select a key, and then select **Create new** under the **Key Vault** field area.

5. Enter a unique name for your key vault.

6. Select **Access Policies**, and then select **Azure Disk Encryption** for volume encryption.

7. Select **Review + create** and then select **Create**.

8. Select the **Select** option.

9. Select **Save**, and when prompted, select **Yes**.

You have successfully configured your VM-managed disk to use Azure Disk Encryption to encrypt the operating system and data disks inside your VM using Windows Bitlocker or Linux DM-Crypt features. Azure Key Vault is used to manage the disk encryption keys.

Task 2: Implement built-in data security for Azure SQL Database:

1. Select the search field and enter `Azure SQL Database`.

    You will need to create an Azure SQL Database. To create an Azure SQL Database, use the instructions detailed in *Chapter 10*.

2. Alternatively, you can create an Azure SQL Database with the following AZ CLI command:

    ```
    az sql db create –resource-group <EnterResourceGroupName>
    --server <EnterSQLServerName> --name <EnterDatabaseName>
    --sample-name AdventureWorksLT –edition GeneralPurpose –
    family Gen5 –capacity 1 –zone-redundant false
    ```

3. Select your Azure SQL Database resource.

    By default, **transparent data encryption** (**TDE**) is enabled for all Azure SQL Databases and TDE is set at the logical server level, which, in turn, is inherited by all logical server databases.

4. Review your Azure SQL Database resource security settings. As noted previously, encryption is set by default.

Dynamic data masking is different from TDE. Data masking will limit exposing sensitive data by obfuscating part of the data from the viewer in a result set from a query – for example, masking PII such as a veteran's social security number using this example format: `xxx-xx-1234`.

In these tasks, you implemented built-in data security for managed disks and Azure SQL Database. In the next section, we will go over implementing built-in data security in Google Cloud.

Configuring Google Cloud boot disk and Cloud SQL data security

In these tasks, you will learn how to implement data security in Google Cloud. You will also learn about helpful tips and potential pitfalls that encumber beginners.

Google Cloud SQL is not only developer-friendly – it's also resilient and secure. And Google Cloud persistent disks support encrypting data at rest, too.

Objectives

After completing these tasks, you will be able to achieve the following:

- Describe and implement data security in Google Cloud

Prerequisites

Here are the recommended requirements for completing all tasks:

- An updated version of Windows 8.1 or later, macOS 10.15 or later, or Linux Ubuntu 18.04 or later.

- An up-to-date and secure internet browser (Chrome or Edge is recommended).

- The instructions for the steps in this chapter can also be found at `https://github.com/PacktPublishing/Cloud-Computing-Demystified-for-Aspiring-Professionals/tree/main/Instructions/Chapter12`.

- Access to a Google Cloud Platform account with the required privileges to create and manage all resources and dependencies. You can go to `https://cloud.google.com/free/` and `https://cloud.google.com/resource-manager/docs/manage-google-cloud-resources` to see more details on how to create a Google Cloud Platform free account for training purposes only.

Tasks

To do 0: Subscribe to Google Cloud Platform

Task 1: Sign in to Google Cloud Platform

1. Select the Edge or Chrome browser on your computer and go to `https://cloud.google.com/free/`.

2. After the website loads, select **Get started for free**.

3. At `accounts.google.com`, select **Create account**. And then select **Create a new Gmail address instead**. Here are several email account name examples (replace `Example` with your name or alias):

   - `Example.lastname@gmail.com`

   - `Example98765@gmail.com`

> **Note**
>
> I have elected to exclude any guidance pertaining to billing details that include PII.

4. Follow the remaining prompts and populate all required fields to conclude the new account creation process.

> **Helpful tips and tricks**
>
> Here are several resources to help you create and manage your Google Cloud Platform free account to ensure you don't incur substantial costs. `https://cloud.google.com/free/`

To do 3: Implement data security in Google Cloud

Task 1: Implement data security in Google Cloud Compute Engine disks

In this task, you will implement data security in Google Cloud Compute Engine disks and Cloud SQL:

1. Sign in to the Google Cloud console (`https://console.cloud.google.com/`).

2. In the Google Cloud console, on the project selector page, select or create a Google Cloud project.

   You will need to create a Compute Engine instance backed by a disk. To create a Compute Engine instance, use the instructions detailed in *Chapter 8*.

3. You can also use the following command to quickly create an instance:

   ```
   gcloud compute instances create examplevm-instance
   --image-family=rhel-8 --image-project=rhel-cloud
   --zone=<enter_region_zone>
   ```

4. Use the Google Cloud search field and enter `Compute Engine`.

5. Select your instance and review the security default settings.

Google Cloud, by default, encrypts all data at rest. Google manages this encryption on your behalf.

Task 2: Implement data security in Google Cloud SQL:

1. Sign in to the Google Cloud console (`https://console.cloud.google.com/`).

2. In the Google Cloud console, on the project selector page, select or create a Google Cloud project.

3. Use Google CloudShell and open a terminal window.

4. Copy the contents of the file named `googleCloudSql.tf` located in the `~/ Cloud-Computing-for-Beginners/blob/main/Allfiles/Chapter10/RDS/ GoogleCloud/` directory path.

5. Use Terraform to create a Google Cloud SQL instance.

6. Select your Cloud SQL instance and review the default properties.

If you choose to use the Google Cloud key infrastructure service known as Cloud KMS. you can design and configure service accounts and KMS using the console or gcloud CLI. Here is an example of creating a Google Cloud SQL instance with KMS:

```
export KEY_NAME=$(gcloud kms keys describe $KMS_KEY_ID \
    --keyring=$KMS_KEYRING_ID --location=$REGION \
```

```
    --format 'value(name)')
export CLOUDSQL_INSTANCE=<entername>
gcloud sql instances create $CLOUDSQL_INSTANCE \
    --project=$PROJECT_ID \
    --authorized-networks=${AUTHORIZED_IP}/32,$CLOUD_SHELL_
IP/32 \
    --disk-encryption-key=$KEY_NAME \
```

Google Cloud SQL encrypts data backups, temporary files, and database tables. Data keys are also encrypted and managed by Google. Since the cloud provider manages the keys and the key infrastructure, you have less operational overhead.

In these tasks, you have implemented built-in data security across the cloud computing leaders. In the next section, we will review the built-in application platform security features in cloud computing.

Implementing built-in app security

In this section, you will learn how to configure cloud-native application security features. And we will explore one each of the many AWS, Azure, and Google Cloud application platform services. You will also learn about helpful tips and potential pitfalls that encumber beginners.

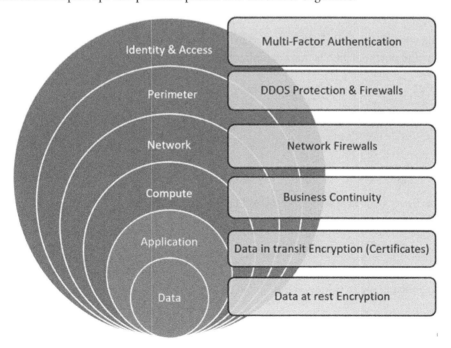

Figure 12.2 – Defense-in-depth application security layers

Here is a non-exhaustive table listing the cloud application platform hosting services:

Cloud Computing Provider	Container services
AWS	**Elastic Beanstalk**
Azure	App Service
Google Cloud	App Engine

Table 12.2 – AWS, Azure, and GCP application platform services

Configuring application security with Amazon Elastic Beanstalk

Amazon Elastic Beanstalk accelerates application development and improves the overall administration of your application. Administrative tasks include managing permissions and versioning, tagging, and protecting the application and its data. The Elastic Beanstalk feature makes administrating compliance standards and security controls simpler.

Elastic Beanstalk environments include load balancers that can be configured to support HTTPS. Therefore, Elastic Beanstalk applications can enforce clients to establish HTTPS secure connections. And the service supports instance-level firewalls, known as security groups.

In this task, you will configure built-in app security using TLS on AWS, and you will also learn about helpful tips and potential pitfalls that encumber beginners.

Objectives

After completing this task, you will be able to describe and configure built-in app security.

Tasks

To do 1: Configure built-in app security using TLS

Task 1: Configure built-in app security using TLS:

1. Sign in to the AWS Management Console (`https://console.aws.amazon.com/console/`).

2. Select the Elastic Beanstalk instance you created in a previous chapter. If required, recreate it using the instructions located in *Chapter 8*.

3. Elastic Beanstalk includes interactive command-line tools to help you quickly create an environment and launch an application, but you'll need the tooling. You can install the Elastic Beanstalk CLI with `pip`. Use the following command:

```
pip install awsebcli --upgrade –user
```

4. Use the following command to enter an interactive mode to create the environment that hosts your app:

```
eb create
```

The interactive mode also helps launch a sample app for this tutorial. Don't worry about the app for now. We only need the sample app to implement application security.

Practical applications

Once the environment and application are running and healthy, you should secure the connection to your application by encrypting it using the **Secure Socket Layer** (**SSL**) protocol, which protects data sent or received by the users or application.

To facilitate HTTPS using SSL, you'll need to assign a certificate to Elastic Beanstalk's load balancer. A certificate in this context is a cryptographic public key certificate, known as a digital certificate. Certificates are used to encrypt data in transit.

You can create a self-signed or procure a certificate from a **certificate authority** (**CA**). It is recommended that you purchase your certificates from a CA service provider if the application or service is publicly available and used in a production environment. After obtaining your certificate, you'll need to upload the certificate and then configure it.

To assign a certificate to your Elastic Beanstalk load balancer, review the following task:

1. Edit the Elastic Beanstalk load balancer.
2. Select **Add listener**.
3. Update the following properties:

   - **Listener port**: 443
   - **Listener protocol**: Select **HTTPS**
   - **Instance port**: 80
   - **Instance protocol**: Select **HTTP**
   - **SSL certificate**: Select the certificate you uploaded in the preceding tasks

In this task, you have configured built-in app security using TLS. In the next section, we review Azure's built-in app security features.

> **Helpful tips and tricks**
>
> You will incur costs when procuring certificates. I recommend researching SSL/TLS certificates.

Configuring App Service application security in Azure

Azure App Service supports secure custom domain names using TLS/SSL bindings.

In this task, you will configure built-in app security by restricting access, and you will also learn helpful tips and potential pitfalls that encumber beginners.

Objectives

After completing this task, you will be able to describe and configure built-in app security.

Tasks

To do 1: Configure built-in app security using TLS

Task 1: Configure built-in app security using TLS:

1. Sign in to the Azure portal (`https://portal.azure.com/`).

2. In the portal, navigate and select your App Service.

    If you need step-by-step guidance deploying Azure App Service, use the information in *Chapter 8*.

3. Alternatively, use the following commands to create the application's host named `EnterAppServicePlan` and to create and deploy the application to the host:

    ```
    az appservice plan create --name <EnterAppServicePlanName>
    --resource-group EnterResourceGroupName --sku FREE
    az webapp create --resource-group
    <EnterResourceGroupName> --plan <EnterAppServicePlanName>
    --name <EnterUniqueAppName> --deployment-local-git
    ```

Practical applications

For an on-premises or hybrid-cloud solution, continuous integration, used widely in DevOps, leverages source control resources such as Git technology and frameworks. The `deployment-local-git` parameter, denoted in the preceding example, enables a local Git repositories for use, and the `az webapp deployment user set` operation optimizes publishing code from local machines in a publicly distributed network to the cloud.

4. In Azure, you'll need to map an existing domain name to your custom domain name in Azure Active Directory or on the Azure App Service page. You will need to assign the custom domain to your Azure App Service.

5. Next, select **App Service Managed Certificate**. Then, set the **Binding type** property to TLS/SSL. Do not modify the default setting.

A private certificate thumbprint option is used in production scenarios. This option is not free, and I would encourage you to research CA costs before taking that path. Development and non-production scenarios can use a free managed certificate by selecting the custom domain setting. For managing **domain name systems (or services) (DNS)**, I recommend additional research – for example, on editing the DNS record sets, such as AAAA, SRV, TXT, and CNAME, also referred to as record sets.

6. Check your **Add Custom domain** page and ensure you copy the domain validation hostname records.

7. If you reviewed DNS as recommended, add the records you copied.

8. Return to the **Add Custom domain** page and select **Validate**.

In this task, you have configured built-in app security using TLS. In the next section, we will explore Google's built-in app security.

Configuring Google App engine application security

Google App Engine is fully managed, which means less work for you. Configuring security has never been easier.

In this task, you will learn how to configure built-in app security, and you will also learn about helpful tips and potential pitfalls that encumber beginners.

Objectives

After completing this task, you will be able to describe and configure built-in app security.

Tasks

To do 1: Configure built-in app security using SSL

Task 1: Configure built-in app security using SSL:

1. Sign in to the Google Cloud console (`https://console.cloud.google.com/`).

2. In the Google Cloud console, on the project selector page, select or create a Google Cloud project.

3. Make sure that billing is enabled for your Google Cloud project.

Practical applications

I am pleased to inform you that Google and its cloud arm, Google Cloud, including App Engine, among other services, provide managed SSL certificates at no cost to you. Let me expound. In real-world scenarios, planning, creating, publishing, and managing certificates is a full-time job. Research about certificate revocation when time permits. You'll be aghast at the results. Simply put, with App Engine, you select the custom domain, click **Enable managed security**, and in a short span of time, usually minutes, Google will create and assign a certificate to encrypt data in transit from App Engine to your web and mobile clients.

Otherwise, use your own SSL certificates and consider using Google Cloud Load Balancing to terminate SSL traffic.

In this task, you have configured built-in app security using SSL/TLS. In the next section, we will review native compute security controls in cloud computing.

Implementing built-in compute security

In this section, you will learn about implementing built-in compute security controls. We will explore one each of the many AWS, Azure, and Google Cloud compute security control services to protect data at rest and improve the overall data recovery process using built-in compute features.

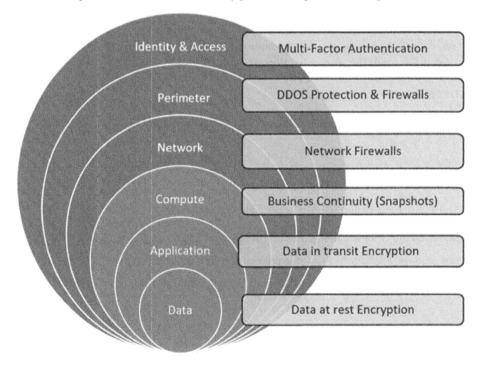

Figure 12.3 – The defense-in-depth compute security layer

Cloud computing's built-in host security features have matured over the years to the point that we can argue that the cloud is more secure than on-premises services. There are numerous real-world examples in which businesses either did not migrate to the cloud or did not use cloud security frameworks and security updates to improve their security posture and those businesses, which shall remain unnamed, were impacted severely. Nevertheless, this can happen to anyone if they do not adhere to and adopt compliance controls and security best practices.

In *Table 11.3*, you will find several compute services across AWS, Azure, and GCP that natively support the capability to comply with various compliance controls and utilize mature security controls to protect your most valuable assets.

Here is a non-exhaustive table listing some of the cloud compute services:

Cloud Computing Provider	Computing Services
AWS	EC2 instances
Azure	VM instances
Google Cloud	Compute Engine instances

Table 12.3 – AWS, Azure, and GCP IaaS VMs

In cloud computing, compliance and security controls for VM instances and disks are easy to implement and manage throughout the use of the compute and its workload. However, remember that you share a responsibility with your cloud provider. Therefore, you are responsible for implementing security controls in adherence to regulatory compliance edicts such as SOC and cyber security best practices.

Configuring built-in compute security with EC2

AWS offers numerous host-level security controls such as using EBS snapshots for VM disk backup and controlling network access on an EC2 instance using security groups a feature, which allows you to manage firewall rules. You can install or procure an Amazon machine image that has a preconfigured IDS/IPS or anti-malware software built in from Amazon Marketplace.

In this task, you will learn how to configure built-in compute security for EC2, and you will also learn about helpful tips and potential pitfalls that encumber beginners.

Objectives

After completing this task, you will be able to describe and configure EC2 built-in compute security using EBS snapshots.

Tasks

To do 1: Configure EC2 built-in compute security using EBS snapshots

Task 1: Configure EC2 built-in compute security using EBS snapshots:

1. Sign in to the AWS Management Console (`https://console.aws.amazon.com/console/`).

2. Search for `EC2` and then select the **EC2** instance that you created earlier in this chapter.

3. Select **Snapshots | Create snapshot**.

4. Select **Choose volume**.

5. For **Volume ID**, select the volume from which to create the snapshot.

6. Choose **Create snapshot**.

Practical applications

Implementing a backup and restore strategy is crucial to IT and business operations. These patterns are an important part of the business continuity framework.

Cloud leaders such as Amazon, Microsoft, and Google continuously innovate and optimize the practice of data restoration and resiliency and therefore the framework for business continuity. AWS streamlines creating snapshots and backups of your EBS disks. In AWS, you are capable of copying, deleting, and restoring from a point-in-time snapshot to a new volume. Backups and snapshots are used to extend data protection beyond encryption. For example, you can use your backup solution as a control or protection from ransomware attacks that aim to control or delete your data or DEK, encrypted or not.

Use best practices such as defense in depth and augment security by using instance-level security group rules to deny inbound threats of network traffic targeting your vulnerable EC2 instances – for example, denying inbound non-secured HTTP traffic over port 80. It's unfathomable that this port is still used by threat actors, but studies show that it is commonly exploited by malicious actors.

In this task, you have configured EC2 built-in compute security using EBS snapshots. In the next section, we will review Microsoft Azure's built-in compute security controls to protect data with snapshots.

Configuring VM built-in compute security

Azure includes built-in host-level security controls, such as managed disk incremental snapshots or Azure Disk Backup for data protection, including instance-level firewall rules known as **network security groups** (**NSGs**). And Microsoft delivers a fully integrated intrusion detection and anti-malware service named Microsoft Defender for Cloud. An NSG here is subtly different from AWS in that an Azure NSG can be used either at the network level or instance level; I refer to the latter. Microsoft Defender is a suite of services including endpoint and cloud protection that can be integrated.

In this task, you will learn how to configure VM built-in compute security. And you will also learn about helpful tips and potential pitfalls that encumber beginners.

Objectives

After completing this task, you will be able to describe and configure VM built-in compute security using incremental snapshots.

Tasks

To do 1: Configure VM built-in compute security using incremental snapshots

Task 1: Configure VM built-in compute security using incremental snapshots:

1. Sign in to the Azure portal (`https://portal.azure.com/`).

    You will need a VM instance. Search for and select the Azure VM instance you created earlier in this chapter. You'll require the VM property values in the following CloudShell tasks.

2. In the portal, search for and activate CloudShell.

3. In the CloudShell command-line interface, enter the following commands and replace all *placeholders* with unique values:

    ```
    # Create variables
    diskName="<placeholder>"
    resourceGroupName="<placeholder>"
    snapshotName="<placeholder>"
    # Select the disk to backup
    yourDiskID=$(az disk show -n $diskName -g
    $resourceGroupName --query "id" --outputtsv)
    # Create the snapshot
    az snapshot create -g $resourceGroupName -n $snapshotName
    --source $yourDiskID --incremental true
    ```

Practical applications

Protecting your data with encryption and implementing a backup and restore strategy using backups or snapshots, while important, is not the only method to defend against threats to decrease risk. You can also use NSGs, which are similar to Amazon EC2 security groups to create host firewall rules, hence defending your host from threats with additional layers. This security pattern is well known. If you read earlier sections of this chapter, we described the framework known as defense in depth. The key takeaway here is that it's a layered form of defense, so combining host-level firewalls and encryption improves security.

Furthermore, Microsoft Defender for Cloud checks for vulnerabilities across your digital estate, integrates not only with IaaS VMs but also AWS EC2 instances too, thus providing multi-cloud benefits.

In this task, you configured VM built-in compute security using incremental snapshots. In the next section, we review Google Cloud's built-in compute security.

Configuring built-in security for Compute Engine instances

Google Cloud's Compute Engine VM instances support snapshots and instance-level access controls and can be preconfigured with anti-malware, like AWS and Azure compute resources.

In this task, you will learn how to configure built-in compute security for a Compute Engine instance. You will also learn how to efficiently deploy the service.

Objectives

After completing this task, you will be able to describe and configure Compute Engine instance built-in compute security using snapshots.

Tasks

To do 1: Configure built-in compute security for a Compute Engine instance using snapshots

Task 1: Configure built-in compute security for a Compute Engine instance using snapshots:

1. Sign in to the Google Cloud console (`https://console.cloud.google.com/`).

2. In the Google Cloud console, on the project selector page, select or create a Google Cloud project.

    You will need a VM instance. Search for and select the instance you created earlier in this chapter. You'll require instance property values, such as the source disk information, in the following CloudShell tasks.

3. Select, **Activate CloudShell**.

4. In the CloudShell command-line interface, enter the following command and replace any *placeholders* with unique values:

    ```
    gcloud compute snapshots create <placeholder> \
        --source-disk <placeholder> \
        --source-disk-zone <placeholder>
    ```

Practical applications

Business continuity is all-encompassing, meaning defense against data infiltration is but one of many scenarios factored into the framework. What about unplanned natural disasters? These continue to grow over the years due to known and unknown climate factors. Google Cloud is known for driving resiliency in all its work, which includes optimizing business continuity by supporting cross-region disaster recovery services and frameworks. So, you can copy snapshots to another region and then utilize them for disaster recovery.

In this task, you have configured built-in compute security for a Compute Engine instance using snapshots. In the next section, we will review implementing built-in network security controls in cloud computing.

Implementing built-in network security

In this section, you will learn about cloud computing's virtual network security controls. We will explore one each of the many AWS, Azure, and Google Cloud network security resources.

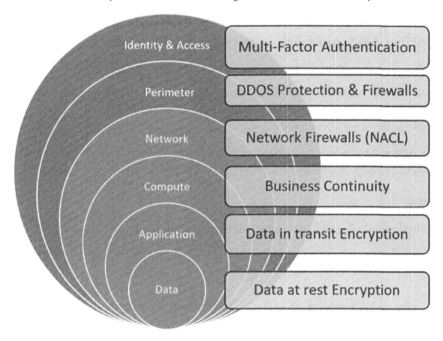

Figure 12.4 – The defense-in-depth network security layer

The cloud has truly optimized how we plan, prepare, and implement networking technologies and support compliance initiatives by using agile network security controls that are easy to configure and robust enough to govern one or multiple networks, even if the network resides on-premises or across one or more cloud providers.

Here is a non-exhaustive table listing some of the cloud computing network services that support built-in security controls.

Cloud Computing Provider	Networking Services
AWS	VPC
Azure	VNet
Google Cloud	VPC

Table 12.4 – AWS, Azure, and GCP networking services

Cloud computing virtual network and edge components provide various security controls, from the perimeter to the internal network, and cloud computing leaders support known network topologies such as hub-and-spoke, among others, to provide additional layers of control to protect your data.

Let's look at each cloud provider's network access control services.

Configuring AWS network access control lists for built-in network security

AWS network **access control lists** (**ACLs**) are rules that you can configure at the subnet level, thus controlling ingress and egress traffic. For example, you can either deny or allow all traffic or specific traffic by defining its source IP, port, and protocol, including its destination or target, among other things.

In this task, you will learn how to configure AWS network ACLs for built-in network security, and you will also learn about helpful tips and potential pitfalls that encumber beginners.

Objectives

After completing this task, you will be able to describe and configure AWS network ACLs for built-in network security.

Tasks

To do 1: Configure AWS network ACLs for built-in network security

Task 1: Configure AWS network ACLs for built-in network security:

1. Sign in to the AWS Management Console (`https://console.aws.amazon.com/console/`).

2. Search for `VPC` and then access the VPC dashboard.

3. Select **Network ACLs**.

4. Select **Create Network ACL**.

5. When prompted by the **Create Network ACL** dialog box, enter a unique name for your network ACL, and select the ID of your VPC from the VPC list. Select **Yes | Create**.

6. Select your network ACL.

7. Select **Details**, then select **Inbound Rules**, and then select **Edit**.

8. Add the rule number, type, protocol, port, source, or destination, and either allow or deny based on your security control requirements.

It's important to note that Amazon's default network ACL allows all inbound and outbound traffic. You can create a VPC security group rule assigned to an EC2 instance. This provides an additional layer of protection at the host level.

In this task, you have configured AWS Network access control lists for built-in network security. In the next section, we review an Azure built-in network security control.

Configuring NSGs for built-in network security

Microsoft Azure, like Google and Amazon, supports inbound and outbound firewall rules that can be assigned either at the network or instance level.

In this task, you will learn how to configure NSGs for built-in network security. And you will also learn about helpful tips and potential pitfalls that encumber beginners.

Objectives

After completing this task, you will be able to describe and configure NSGs for built-in network security.

Tasks

To do 1: Configure NSGs for built-in network security

Task 1: Configure NSGs for built-in network security

In this task, you will learn to configure NSGs for built-in network security:

1. Sign in to the Azure portal (`https://portal.azure.com/`).
2. Select **Create a resource**.
3. Select **Networking** and then select **Network security groups**.
4. In the **Basics** tab, set values for the following settings: **Subscription**, **Resource group**, **Name**, and **Region**.
5. Select **Review + create** and then select **Create**.
6. Select the NSG you created.
7. Select **Inbound security rules**.
8. Select **Add**, and then populate the following settings – **Source**, **Source IP**, **Source service tag**, **Source application security group**, **Source port ranges**, **Destination**, **Destination IP**, **Destination service tag**, **Destination application security group**, **Destination port ranges**, **Protocol**, **Allow or Deny**, **Priority**, **Name**, and **Description**.
9. On the **Network security group** dashboard, select **Subnets**.
10. Select **+ Associate**
11. Select your VNet and then select **OK**.

A key difference between AWS and GCP is that Azure's NSGs can be associated with a VM NIC, meaning it can be assigned at the instance level too, so you can use the NSG as a firewall for either the network or host.

In this task, you have configured NSGs for built-in network security. In the next section, we explore Google Cloud's built-in network security control.

Configuring VPC firewall rules for built-in network security

Google Cloud's VPC firewalls does exactly what it implies, facilitates creating firewall inbound and outbound rules as with AWS and Azure.

In this task, you will learn how to configure VPC firewall rules for built-in network security, and you will also learn about helpful tips and potential pitfalls that encumber beginners.

Objectives

After completing this task, you will be able to describe and configure VPC firewall rules for built-in network security.

Tasks

To do 1: Configure VPC firewall rules for built-in network security

Task 1: Configure VPC firewall rules for built-in network security:

1. Sign in to the Google Cloud console (`https://console.cloud.google.com/`).
2. In the Google Cloud console, on the project selector page, select or create a Google Cloud project.
3. Make sure that billing is enabled for your Cloud project.
4. Activate CloudShell.
5. In the CloudShell command-line interface, enter the following commands replacing all *placeholders*:

```
gcloud compute firewall-rules create NAME \
    [--network <placeholder>; default="default"] \
    [--priority < placeholder >;default=1000] \
    [--direction (<placeholder >); default="ingress"] \
    [--action (deny | allow )] \
    [--target-tags < placeholder >] \
    [--target-service-accounts=<IAM_SERVICE_ACCOUNT>] \
    [--source-ranges <CIDR_RANGE>] \
    [--source-tags <TAG,TAG>,] \
    [--source-service-accounts=<IAM_SERVICE_ACCOUNT>] \
```

```
[--destination-ranges <CIDR_RANGE>] \
[--rules (PROTOCOL[:PORT[-PORT]],[PROTOCOL[:PORT[-
PORT]],...]] | all ) \
[--disabled | --no-disabled] \
[--enable-logging | --no-enable-logging] \
[--logging-metadata LOGGING_METADATA]
```

> **Helpful tips and tricks**
>
> Did you know that you can manage firewall rules using firewall policies? Firewall policies are hierarchical. Unlike VPC firewall rules, they must have a unique priority and can be assigned at the organizational or folder level.

In this task, you configured VPC firewall rules for built-in network security.

Implementing zero trust (authentication and authorization)

In this section, you will learn about the IAM multi-layered approach using **multi-factor authentication** (**MFA**) services in cloud computing. We will explore one each of the many AWS, Azure, and Google Cloud MFA security resources.

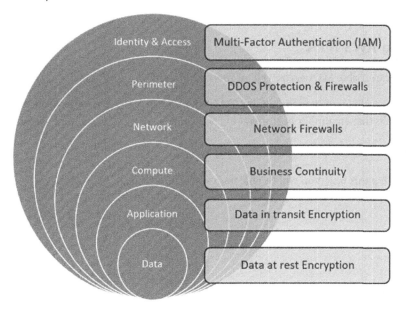

Figure 12.5 – The defense-in-depth IAM security layer

We live in an age where networked devices are assumed to be breached. Thus, we require a new security model that assumes a breach and verifies every authentication and authorization request. The new model is known as **zero trust**, wherein we always authenticate based on all available information and limit user access using adaptive policies and data protection controls. And even then, we assume a breach and monitor for vulnerabilities, detect threats, and ensure protection end to end throughout the workload's life cycle. It's key to incorporate zero trust into your defense-in-depth strategy. Cloud computing leaders understand and embrace this strategy using different identity controls to enforce the Zero Trust model.

Here is a non-exhaustive table listing some of the cloud computing IAM services that support MFA:

Cloud Computing Provider	Authentication and Authorization Services
AWS	IAM
Azure	Azure AD
Google Cloud	Cloud Identity

Table 12.6 – AWS, Azure, and GCP IAM services

Cloud computing supports MFA… so, what is MFA? MFA is a layered approach to protecting your assets by securing your accounts. When utilizing MFA, organization members require a combination of two or more authentication methods to verify the user's identity explicitly before they are authorized or allowed access.

Managing AWS MFA

In AWS, you can enable MFA across one or more IAM users.

In this task, you will learn how to manage IAM MFA and you will also learn about helpful tips and potential pitfalls that encumber beginners.

Objectives

After completing this task, you will be able to describe and manage AWS MFA.

Tasks

To do 1: Managing AWS MFA

Task 1: Managing AWS MFA

In this task, you will learn how to manage AWS IAM MFA services:

1. Sign in to the AWS Management Console (`https://console.aws.amazon.com/console/`).

Practical applications

We live in a world fractured by unknown and known upheaval, such as a pandemic that consequently forced companies to support millions of remote workers with less-than-secure networks. Every industry requires comprehensive visibility on the who, why, what, and where of resource access and management. We're told to use strong passwords, no passwords, or even told that keys are better than passwords, and so on to ensure the right people or services have access and appropriate authorization and, if possible, only for a limited time. The well-known two-factor authentication, now known as MFA, has been used in ATMs and for online banking access by financial institutions and is among the most widely accepted layered protocol used in IAM across data, apps, and computes, including networks as a control plane. For example, you frequent a public site, that site is hosted on a network, and that site is trusted through your network client. Consequently, you don't have to authenticate the next time you visit. Sounds great, right? What if it is not you? Not so great anymore! Networks that were once private are now hybrid wherein the network supports public access as well. The cloud was not the catalyst, contrary to popular belief. Services and products are distributed digitally, so your company or the company you use has services available on public networks. We need to use MFA globally – while this is frustrating, it has become a norm in most businesses no matter the size. I use it daily, as I did even when I was writing this book. Be aware there are different permutations of MFA from third parties, but the underlying framework is the same.

2. Log in to the IAM console (`https://console.aws.amazon.com/singlesignon`).

3. Select **Settings** and then select **Authentication**.

4. In the **Multi-factor authentication** section, select **Configure**, and you will get the following screenshot:

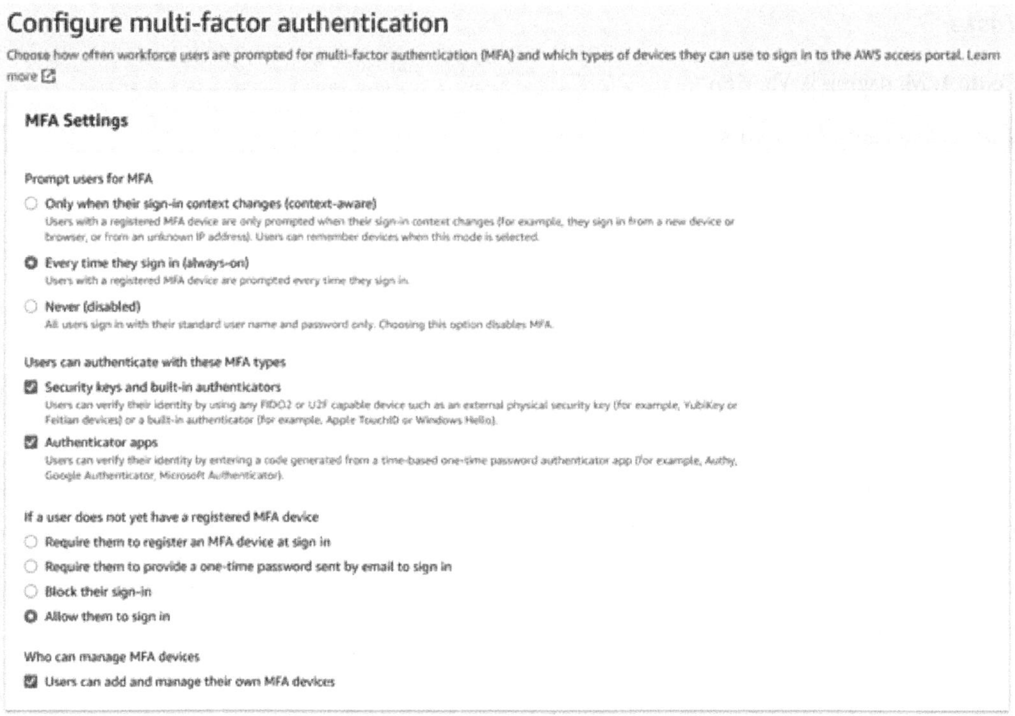

Figure 12.6 – MFA settings page

5.   Configure the MFA settings as shown in the preceding screenshot.

Managing Azure Active Directory MFA

Azure supports MFA across one or more IAM users.

In this task, you will learn how to manage MFA, and you will also learn about helpful tips and potential pitfalls that encumber beginners.

Objectives

After completing this task, you will be able to describe and manage Azure Active Directory MFA.

Tasks

To do 1: Managing Azure Directory MFA

Task 1: Managing Azure Active Directory MFA:

1. Sign in to the Azure portal (`https://portal.azure.com/`).

2. Select **Azure Active Directory**.

3. Select **Security**.

4. Select **Conditional Access**.

5. Select **New Policy** and create a new policy.

6. Enter a unique name for your policy. Enter the following text: `MultiFactorAuth`.

7. Select **Users or workload**.

8. Select the option labeled **Select users and groups**.

9. Enter your username in the search field and then click **Select**.

10. Next, select **Cloud apps or actions**.

11. Select **All cloud apps**.

12. Select **Grant**, and then select **Grant access**.

13. Select **Require multi-factor authentication**.

In this task, you have configured Azure MFA. In the next section, we will configure GCP MFA.

Managing GCP MFA

GCP enables support for MFA across one or more IAM users.

In this task, you will learn how to manage IAM MFA, and you will also learn about helpful tips and potential pitfalls that encumber beginners.

Objectives

After completing this task, you will be able to describe and manage GCP MFA.

Tasks

To do 1: Managing GCP MFA

Task 1: Managing GCP MFA:

1. Sign in to the Google Cloud console (`https://console.cloud.google.com/`).

2. In the Google Cloud console, on the project selector page, select or create a Google Cloud project.

3. Make sure that billing is enabled for your Cloud project.

4. Search for `identity platform MFA`.

5. Enable the identity platform if required.

6. Select **ADD A PROVIDER**.

7. For the purposes of training, populate the web client ID and web client secret with placeholder syntax, such as `111122223333`, and enter the text `secrete` in the **Web Client Secrete** field.

8. Select **Save**.

9. Select **MFA**.

10. Select **ENABLE** on the **Multi-Factor Authentication** page.

In this task, you have reviewed how to configure GCP MFA.

Summary

In this chapter, you learned about protecting cloud services, data, application platforms, compute instances, networks, and managing IAM MFA.

In the next chapter, we will explore the awesome agile tools used to create and manage cloud resources.

Questions

1. Which of the following is a security strategy?

    A. NIST

    B. SSH

    C. Defense in depth

    D. The HIPAA

2. Which of the following is an example of compliance?

    A. The ARPA

    B. The HIPAA

    C. Defense in depth

    D. None of the above

3. Which of the following options do EBS volumes use to secure data at rest?

   A. Key Vault

   B. KMS

   C. SSH

   D. None of the above

4. Which of the following options do managed disks use to secure data at rest?

   A. KMS

   B. RDP

   C. SSH

   D. Key Vault

5. Does a Google Cloud boot disk natively secure data at rest?

   A. Yes

   B. No

6. Which of the following options can be configured to secure data in transit for EB, Azure App Service, and App Engine web applications?

   A. REST

   B. HTTP

   C. A load balancer

   D. Certificates

7. What options are available to support backup and restore scenarios to protect volume data?

   A. Regional replication

   B. Immutability

   C. Snapshots

   D. Live migration

8. Which of the following cloud virtual network security controls are natively supported across AWS, Azure, and GCP?

   A. NSGs

   B. VLANs

   C. IDS

   D. None of the above

9. Which of the following services is managed using MFA?

   A. Authorization

   B. Compliance policies

   C. CIA

   D. Authentication

13
Managing API Tools for Agility

This chapter will teach you how you can use cloud-native API management tools. You will also learn how these tools manage resources. As well as understanding the web-based portal/interfaces and CLI, you'll learn how some of the different cloud-native **infrastructure as code** (**IaC**) tools make building IaaS and PaaS solutions more efficient.

The following concepts will be covered in this chapter:

- Utilizing API web portals for agility
- Utilizing the cloud CLI
- Utilizing IaC templates
- Utilizing software engineering resources

Utilizing API web portals for agility

In this section, you will learn about the cloud computing administrative website interface. You will also learn helpful tips and discover the potential pitfalls that encumber beginners.

Every great service needs an intuitive, customizable, and helpful graphical user interface to streamline the creation and administration of resources. Cloud computing providers include some of the most robust but simple-to-use web portals. These web portals are supported by numerous browsers, such as Google Chrome, Edge, and Firefox. Cloud providers are always updating their graphical user interfaces to improve the overall user experience.

Cloud computing web portals include powerful search tools and resource documentation to support learning and administrative guidance. These portals provide access to resources on topics such as architecting, governance, compliance, and security, in addition to helping you to create and manage all cloud-native resources.

> **Insight**
> Did you know that the AWS, Azure, and Google cloud providers' web portals support hybrid and multi-cloud governance? That's right, you can centralize management for your entire digital estate.

The following table identifies AWS, Azure, and GCP administrative website portals:

Cloud providers	Management portals
AWS	The AWS Management Console
Azure	The Azure portal
GCP	The Google Cloud console

Table 13.1 – Administrative website interfaces

Review the following screenshot, which displays the AWS Management Console:

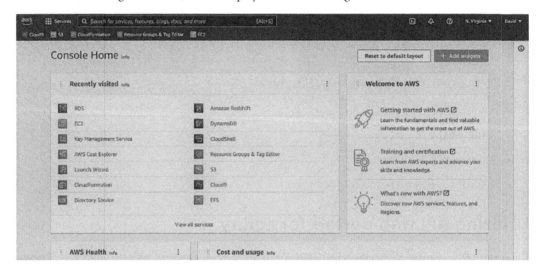

Figure 13.1 – The AWS Management Console

Utilizing the AWS Management Console

In this section, you will learn about the AWS Management Console. You will also learn helpful tips and discover the potential pitfalls that encumber beginners.

The AWS Management Console is a browser-accessible graphical user interface, where you can build and operate AWS and its resources, such as using the AWS Management Console to create and monitor compute instances from the EC2 dashboard. For an example of this, review the *Launching AWS EC2 instances* section in *Chapter 8*.

Objectives

After completing these tasks, you will be able to utilize the AWS Management Console.

Prerequisites

The requirements for completing the tasks in this section are as follows:

- An updated version of Windows 8.1 or later, macOS 10.15 or later, or Linux Ubuntu 18.04 or later.

- An up-to-date and secure internet browser (Chrome or Edge is recommended).

- The instructions of these tasks are also located at `https://github.com/PacktPublishing/Cloud-Computing-Demystified-for-Aspiring-Professionals/blob/main/Instructions/Chapter13/AWS-Tools/aws_console_apitools.md`.

- Access to an AWS account with the required privileges to create and manage resources and dependencies. Learn how to create an AWS trial account at `https://aws.amazon.com/free`, for training purposes only.

> **Important**
>
> You should fork, clone, or download, and follow along with the step-by-step tasks in GitHub or described herein. I recommend using GitHub in conjunction with the book because any code text is more clearly defined in GitHub. However, that's just my preference; you may prefer the book format.

Ready?

Let's start the tasks to utilize the AWS Management Console.

To do 0: Subscribe to AWS

Task 1: Sign in to AWS. The steps are as follows:

1. Open your Edge or Chrome on your computer and go to `https://aws.amazon.com/free`.

2. After the website loads, select **Create a Free Account**.

3. On the `portal.aws.amazon.com` website, populate the fields labeled **Root user email address** and **AWS account name** by entering a valid and readily accessible email account name and AWS account name for training purposes. Here are several examples of email account and AWS account names:

   - `Example.lastname@gmail.com`

   - `Example.lastname@outlook.com`

   - `Cloud Practitioner`

> **Note**
>
> I have elected to exclude any guidance pertaining to billing details that include personally identifiable information.

4. Follow the remaining prompts and populate all required fields to complete the new account creation process.

> **Insight**
>
> Here are a couple of resources to help you create and manage your AWS Free Tier account to ensure you don't incur substantial costs:
>
> `https://aws.amazon.com/premiumsupport/knowledge-center/create-and-activate-aws-account/`
>
> `https://aws.amazon.com/premiumsupport/knowledge-center/what-is-free-tier/`

Tasks

To do 1: Utilize the AWS Management Console

> **Important**
>
> The instructions listed match the AWS Management Console version available in May of 2022. AWS is always updating the interface to improve the user experience.

Task 1: Utilize the AWS Management Console

In this task, you will familiarize yourself with the AWS Management Console:

1. Sign in to the AWS Management Console (`https://console.aws.amazon.com/console/`).
2. Click on the **Services** icon in the top-left corner and then select **Services**.
3. After selecting **Services**, review the **All services** section.

    Review the following figure, which displays service categories.

Figure 13.2 – All the service categories

4. Exit by closing the **All services** area.

5. Locate the search field and enter EC2.

6. In the search results section, review the service categories. If you navigate over to the **EC2** services search results, you will notice additional options such as **Top features** to utilize when creating EC2 resources.

Insight

Did you know that you can find tutorials to help you learn while you use the AWS Management Console? Use the search field and enter EC2, but this time locate **Tutorials** in the search results.

---

7. Exit the search results section and review the icons listed in the top-right corner of the Management Console. Select the support icon and review the options, such as **Support Center** or **Training**.

    Review the following figure, which displays the support icons:

Figure 13.3 – The AWS Management Console support options

Insight

Did you know that the Support Center includes features such as AWS support cases, the AWS Health Dashboard, and the AWS Knowledge Center?

---

8. If you select **Training**, you will be redirected to the **AWS training and certification** portal.

Note

We will explore training and certification in the next two chapters.

---

9. If you navigate further down the AWS home page, you will see more helpful resources such as **Explore AWS**. There, you can explore AWS products, services, resources, events, and more.

    If you have not had an opportunity to learn how to use the AWS Management Console to create a resource, then I recommend revisiting *Chapter 8*.

Helpful tips and tricks

For self-paced quick-start online tutorials and intermediate-to-expert technical details on the AWS Management Console, I recommend visiting the following online resource: `https://docs.aws.amazon.com/awsconsolehelpdocs/latest/gsg/working-with-console.html`.

In this task, you've familiarized yourself with the AWS Management Console interface and learned that the AWS Management Console helps users to create and manage resources. But, more importantly, you have learned how to get the most out of using AWS. In the next section, we will review the look and feel of the Azure portal.

Utilizing the Azure portal

In this section, you will learn about the Azure portal. You will also learn helpful tips and discover the potential pitfalls that encumber beginners.

Review the following figure, which displays the Azure portal:

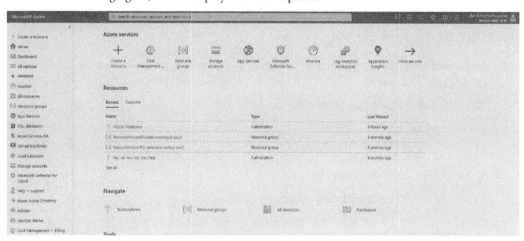

Figure 13.4 – The Azure portal home page

Microsoft Azure's web portal is robust and intuitive. Some practitioners consider the site to be overwhelming. However, you'll come to understand that it's a common misconception. The web portal is very user-friendly. Like the AWS Management Console, the Azure portal is built for learning.

Objectives

After completing these tasks, you will be able to utilize the Azure portal.

Prerequisites

The requirements for completing the tasks in this section are as follows:

- An updated version of Windows 8.1 or later, macOS 10.15 or later, or Linux Ubuntu 18.04 or later.

- An up-to-date and secure internet browser (Chrome or Edge is recommended).

- The instructions for this section are located at `https://github.com/PacktPublishing/Cloud-Computing-Demystified-for-Aspiring-Professionals/blob/main/Instructions/Chapter13/Azure-Tools/azure_console_apitools.md`.

- Access to an Azure subscription with the required privileges to create and manage all resources and dependencies. Learn how to create an Azure trial subscription at `https://azure.microsoft.com/en-us/free/`, for training purposes only.

Ready?

Let's start the task to utilize the Azure portal.

To do 2: Utilize the Azure portal

Task 1: Sign in to Azure. The steps are as follows:

1. Open your Edge or Chrome on your computer and go to `https://azure.microsoft.com/en-us/free/`.

2. After the website loads, select **Start free**.

3. On the `login.microsoftonline.com` website, select **Create one!**. Here are a couple of examples of potential email account names:

   - `Example.lastname@outlook.com`

   - `Example98765@outlook.com`

Note

I have elected to exclude any guidance pertaining to billing details that include personally identifiable information.

---

4. Follow the remaining prompts and populate all required fields to complete the new account creation process.

Insight

For resources to help you create and manage your Azure Free Tier account to ensure you don't incur substantial costs, visit the following site: `https://azure.microsoft.com/en-us/free/free-account-faq/`.

Tasks

To do 3: Utilize the Azure portal

Task 1: Utilize the Azure portal

In this task, you will familiarize yourself with the Azure portal:

1. Sign in to the Azure portal (`https://portal.azure.com/`).

2. In the portal, locate and select the **Menu** icon.

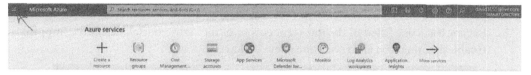

Figure 13.5 – The Azure portal's menu icon

3. Identify and select the **All services** option.

4. Locate the **Categories** section and review the Azure services by category.

Figure 13.6 – The Azure portal | All services

5. After reviewing the categories, locate the search field and type `Virtual Machines`.

6. In the search results area, review the filter options, such as **Services** and **Documentation**. Like AWS, Azure not only helps you accelerate development but also empowers the end user to learn while doing. Take note of the **Documentation** section in the search results. The **Documentation** section includes resource links to educate you on Azure Virtual Machines.

7. Review the icons listed in the top-right corner of the Azure portal. Select the **Support + troubleshooting** icon and review the menu options.

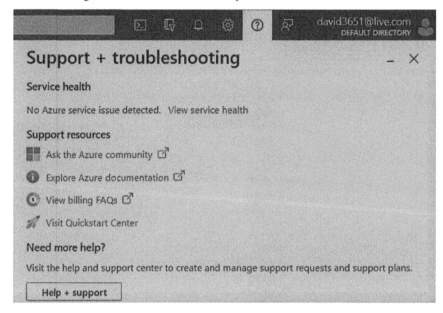

Figure 13.7 – The Azure portal's support options

8. Like the AWS Management Console, the Azure portal's **Support + troubleshooting** feature includes an area where you can create and review your support requests in addition to reviewing overall service health and learning resources.

   If you have not had an opportunity to learn how to use the Azure portal to create a resource, then I recommend revisiting *Chapter 8*.

> **Helpful tips and tricks**
>
> For self-paced and intuitive online tutorials and expert-level technical content on the Azure portal, I recommend visiting the following online resource: `https://docs.microsoft.com/en-us/azure/azure-portal/set-preferences`.

In this section, you have reviewed the Azure portal and you've learned that it is user-friendly. In the next section, we will explore the Google Cloud console.

Utilizing the Google Cloud console

In this section, you will learn about the Google Cloud console. You will also learn helpful tips and discover the potential pitfalls that encumber beginners.

Review the following figure, which displays the Google Cloud console:

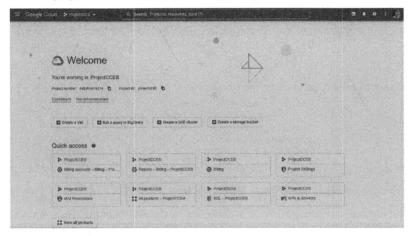

Figure 13.8 – The Google Cloud console home page

The Google Cloud console is a graphical management tool used to develop and manage web service resources such as Compute Engine and virtual machine instances. It's supported by modern web browsers. The console, like AWS and Azure, includes features such as Cloud Shell and web service dashboards and is customizable.

> **Helpful tip**
>
> Did you know when you create resources using the Google Cloud console, it generates an equivalent CLI command, which in turn can be used by practitioners who want to continue their learning journey utilizing the Google Cloud CLI?

Objectives

After completing these tasks, you will be able to utilize the Google Cloud console.

Prerequisites

The requirements for completing the tasks in this section are as follows:

- An updated version of Windows 8.1 or later, macOS 10.15 or later, or Linux Ubuntu 18.04 or later.

- An up-to-date and secure internet browser (Chrome or Edge is recommended).

- The instructions for this section are located at `https://github.com/PacktPublishing/Cloud-Computing-Demystified-for-Aspiring-Professionals/blob/main/Instructions/Chapter13/GCP-Tools/google_console_apitools.md`.

- Access to a GCP account with the required privileges to create and manage all resources and dependencies. Visit `https://cloud.google.com/free/` and `https://cloud.google.com/resource-manager/docs/manage-google-cloud-resources` for more information on how to create a free GCP account for training purposes only.

Ready?

Let's start the task to utilize the Google Cloud console.

To do 4: Subscribe to GCP

Task 1: Sign in to GCP. The steps are as follows:

1. Select Edge or Chrome on your computer and go to `https://cloud.google.com/free/`.

2. After the website loads, select **Get started for free**.

3. On the `accounts.google.com` website, select **Create account**. Then, select **Create a new Gmail address**. Here are several examples of email account names (replace `Example` with your name or alias):

    - `Example.lastname@gmail.com`

    - `Example98765@gmail.com`

> **Note**
>
> I have elected to exclude any guidance pertaining to billing details that include personally identifiable information.

4. Follow the remaining prompts and populate all required fields to conclude the new account creation process.

> **Insight**
>
> For resources to help you create and manage your free GCP account to ensure you don't incur substantial costs, visit the following site: `https://cloud.google.com/free/`.

Tasks

To do 5: Utilize the Google Cloud console

Task 1: Utilize the Google Cloud console

In this task, you will familiarize yourself with the Google Cloud console:

1. Sign in to the Google Cloud console (`https://console.cloud.google.com/`).

2. On the project selector page of the Google Cloud console, select or create a Google Cloud project.

3. Using the Google Cloud project from the previous step, select the **Google Cloud** icon located in the top-left corner.

Figure 13.9 – The Google Cloud console – menu

4. Select the **Menu** icon.

5. Select **View all products** and review the categories, such as **Compute**.

6. After reviewing, find the search field and type in `virtual machine`.

7. Like in Azure and AWS, you will notice that the search results display learning materials too, located in a section labeled **DOCUMENTATION & TUTORIALS**.

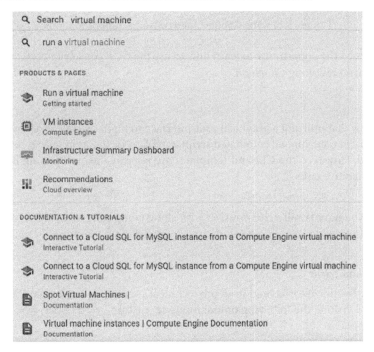

Figure 13.10 – The Google Cloud console – menu options

8. You can also locate similar support options by selecting the **Support** icon.

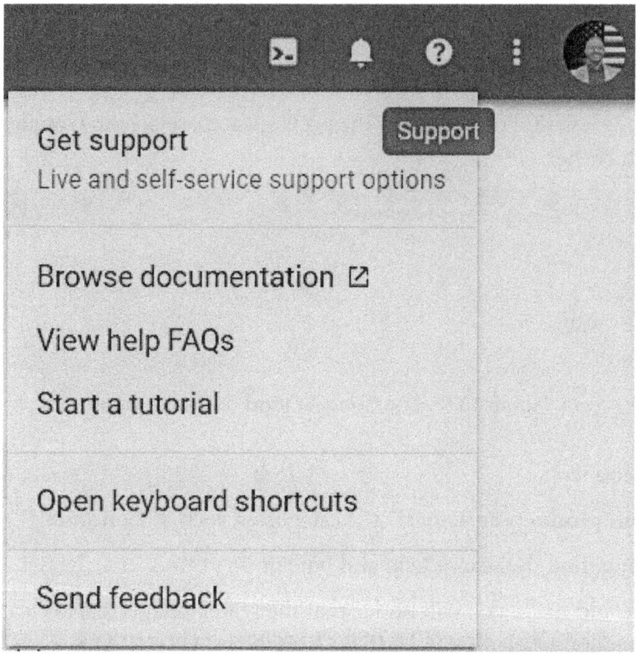

Figure 13.11 – The Google Cloud console – support options

If you missed the opportunity to learn how to use the GCP console to create a resource, then I recommend revisiting *Chapter 8*.

Insight

Did you know that utilizing a graphical user interface to build or scale is deemed a manual process? You can configure an automated script, template, or function task to be on-demand or scheduled. However, the CLI and templates are regarded as performing bulk tasks or automating iterative tasks.

In this section, you have familiarized yourself with cloud computing administrative web graphical user interfaces. In the next section, we will review cloud-native CLI services.

Helpful tips and tricks

For self-paced online tutorials and in-depth technical content on the Google Cloud console, I recommend visiting the following online resource: `https://cloud.google.com/cloud-console`.

Utilizing cloud CLIs

In this section, you will learn about CLIs. We will explore one of each of the AWS, Azure, and Google Cloud CLI tools.

Cloud computing providers support CLI tools that can build and manage resources at scale. Like many other CLI tools, a cloud-native CLI is used typically to automate administrative tasks and is also referred to as a scripting tool. That is, utilizing CLI syntax, you can develop a block of commands that is commonly referred to as a script block or script.

You will also come to find that a cloud service provider's native CLI is supported by a programming language framework; think of this as its underpinnings. Each cloud computing provider offers online detailed information on not only how to install the CLI on your local machine but also any additional prerequisite services, such as programming frameworks that are required to support the CLI.

Another important fact is that when using the CLI from any device or browser-based CLI, every operation executed must make an API call to a cloud provider's API endpoint and must be authenticated.

Additionally, each cloud provider's online browser-based **integrated development environment (IDE)** supports a cloud-first CLI and these online cloud shells or IDEs are already preconfigured to support CLI commands. We will not delve into Cloud Shell in this chapter, but we will use Cloud Shell to run CLI commands. By using Cloud Shell, we can explore CLIs efficiently.

Here is a non-exhaustive table listing some of the cloud computing CLIs:

Cloud computing provider	Container services
AWS	AWS CLI
Azure	Azure CLI
GCP	Google Cloud CLI

Table 13.2 – The AWS, Azure, and GCP CLI tools

Utilizing the AWS CLI

Amazon's CLI interacts with AWS API services and can be used to create and manage resources.

Review the following figure, which displays the AWS CLI running on CloudShell.

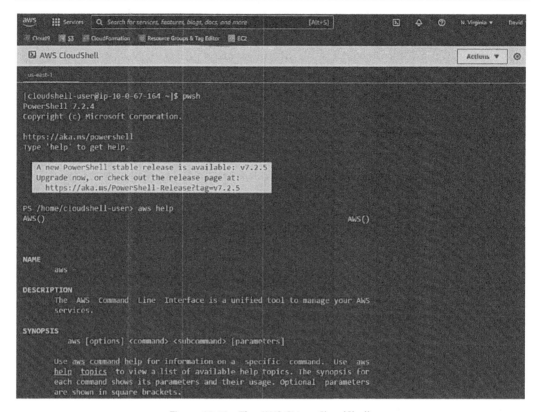

Figure 13.12 – The AWS CLI on CloudShell

In this section, you will learn about the AWS CLI fundamentals. You will also learn helpful tips and discover the potential pitfalls that encumber beginners.

Objectives

After completing these tasks, you will have learned about the AWS CLI fundamentals.

> **Note**
> The instructions are also located at `https://github.com/PacktPublishing/`
> `Cloud-Computing-Demystified-for-Aspiring-Professionals/blob/`
> `main/Instructions/Chapter13/AWS-Tools/aws_CLI_apitools.md`.

Tasks

To do 6: Learn about the AWS CLI fundamentals

Task 1: Learn about the AWS CLI fundamentals

In this task, you will learn about the AWS CLI fundamentals:

1. Sign in to the AWS Management Console (`https://console.aws.amazon.com/console/`).

2. Start by selecting the **CloudShell** icon.

Figure 13.13 – The AWS Management Console

> **Helpful tips and tricks**
>
> Review the documentation regarding how to use AWS CloudShell: `https://docs.aws.amazon.com/cloudshell/latest/userguide/working-with-cloudshell.html`.

3. Once AWS CloudShell is active, you'll notice the output displays syntax such as **Preparing your terminal…** as well as other useful information to get you started, such as using the AWS help commands.

4. Notice that you are at the CLI prompt.

> **Helpful tips**
>
> Cloud computing providers' Cloud Shell CLI initializes a Bash prompt, meaning the Bash shell is the initial CLI running. If required, you can switch to a different CLI, also referred to herein as a shell, by typing the following commands:
>
> `pwsh`
>
> `bash`
>
> Typing `pwsh` will initialize the PowerShell CLI, which supports PowerShell syntax. If you wish to switch back to Bash shell syntax support, enter `bash`.

5. If you did switch to PowerShell, please switch back to the Bash shell for the remainder of this task.

6. Understanding the syntax is essential for any CLI. Let's start by typing the following command:

```
aws help
```

7.   Observe the output and review the **NAME**, **DESCRIPTION**, and **SYNOPSIS** fields.

Right below the **SYNOPSIS** field, identify the syntax output that resembles the following:

```
aws [options] <command> <subcommand> [parameters]
```

> **Note**
>
> The previous line is commonly referred to as the **syntax**. Think of this as the command structure.

AWS CLI commands are comprised of a call to AWS and one of its services, such as EC2. This is known as a top-level command. The subcommand corresponds to an operation. Each operation has specific options and parameters that are either required or optional during an operation's execution. This seems fairly common practice if you have experience with either the bash shell or PowerShell.

> **Helpful tips or tricks**
>
> I recommend researching bash shell and PowerShell commands, also known as scripting languages or shells. These two shells are widely used across cloud computing and are currently supported on Linux, Windows, and macOS. They also run both on-premises and in-cloud computing virtual machine instances.

The AWS CLI includes an extensive help guide, which comprises CLI `aws help` and `aws <command> help` commands. For example, `aws EC2 help`, wherein EC2 is the command—meaning the top-level command, which is an AWS service. Recall that the subcommand is the operation and the online reference guide, which currently is the exhaustive `help` file.

> **Insight**
>
> I recommend reviewing each command's help file in the **SYNTAX** and **EXAMPLES** areas because it displays typical usage examples that are important. Learning the implementation will require hands-on experience.

If you did not have an opportunity to learn how to use the AWS CLI to create a resource, then I recommend revisiting *Chapter 8*.

> **Helpful tips and tricks**
>
> For self-paced online tutorials and detailed technical content on the AWS CLI, I recommend reviewing the following online resource: `https://awscli.amazonaws.com/v2/documentation/api/latest/index.html`.

In this section, you have learned about the AWS CLI fundamentals. In the next section, we will review the Azure CLI.

Utilizing the Azure CLI

The Azure CLI facilitates creating and managing Azure resources utilizing a CLI.

Review the following figure, which displays the Azure CLI running on Cloud Shell:

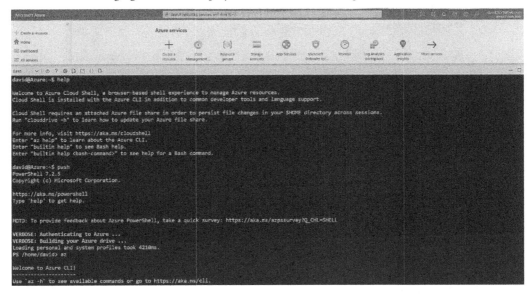

Figure 13.14 – The Azure CLI on Cloud Shell

In this section, you will learn the Azure CLI essentials. You will also learn helpful tips and discover the potential pitfalls that encumber beginners.

Objectives

After completing these tasks, you will have learned the Azure CLI essentials.

> **Note**
>
> The instructions are also located at `https://github.com/PacktPublishing/Cloud-Computing-Demystified-for-Aspiring-Professionals/blob/main/Instructions/Chapter13/Azure-Tools/azure_CLI_apitools.md`.

Tasks

To do 7: Learn the Azure CLI essentials

Task 1: Learn the Azure CLI essentials

In this task, you will learn the Azure CLI essentials:

1. Sign in to the Azure portal (`https://portal.azure.com/`).

2. In the portal, navigate to and select the **Cloud Shell** icon, follow the prompts, and create the Cloud Shell storage resources.

Figure 13.15 – The Azure portal

3. Upon selecting Azure Cloud Shell, you'll be prompted to create a file share using an Azure storage account. You are required to create the storage resource. Select **Create storage**.

> **Helpful tips**
>
> If you encounter an error after selecting **Create storage**, select **Additional settings** and enter unique values for the **Storage Account** name and **File Share** name fields. Then, select **Create**.

Notice that you are at the CLI prompt. The Azure and AWS CloudShell CLI Bash shell is the initial CLI running. However, like AWS, you can switch to a different CLI scripting language by typing the following commands:

- `pwsh`

- `bash`

Typing `pwsh` will initialize the PowerShell CLI, which in turn supports PowerShell syntax. If you wish to switch back to Bash shell syntax support, enter `bash`.

4. Switch to PowerShell for the remainder of this task.

> **Insight**
>
> You can call and thereby use the Azure CLI by typing `az` if you are in PowerShell or Bash shell mode in Azure Cloud Shell.

5. You must learn the Azure CLI syntax: it's essential for creating and managing resources. Let's start by typing the following command:

    ```
    az help
    ```

6. Observe the output and review the **Group** and **Subgroups** areas.

    The group syntax is az or az vm.

    The subgroups correspond to Azure services.

Helpful tips and tricks

Alternatively, consider groups and subgroups as a group. For example, az vm is a group so we will use a group command.

---

7. Type the az vm –help command and review the output. (- -help is an argument in this context.)

8. Observe the output, and review the **Group**, **Subgroup**, and **Commands** areas.

9. In the **Commands** area, review the operations listed.

10. Type the az vm list –help groups command with an argument and review the output.

11. Review the **Arguments** and **Examples** sections.

    Now, let's try the PowerShell CLI via Cloud Shell.

12. Type the get-command get-azvm -Syntax command and review the output.

13. The syntax displays the structure of the get-azvm PowerShell commandlet or command. Like the AWS, Azure, and Google CLIs, the PowerShell commands supported in Azure Cloud Shell can also be mastered by learning the syntax. Review the following syntax:

```
Get-AzVM [[-ResourceGroupName] <string>] [[-Name]
<string>] [-Status] [-UserData] [-DefaultProfile
<IazureContextContainer>] [<CommonParameters>]
```

Each command has specific parameters and arguments that are either required or optional during a command's execution.

Note: The Bash shell and PowerShell are supported in Azure.

Helpful tips or tricks

I recommend researching Bash shell and PowerShell commands, also known as scripting languages or shells. These two shells are widely used across cloud computing and are currently supported on Linux, Windows, and macOS. They run both on-premises and in cloud computing virtual machine instances.

The Azure CLI includes a help guide that is available from the CLI via help commands, such as az help, and Microsoft includes an online reference guide too.

If you did not have an opportunity to learn how to use the Azure CLI to create a resource, then I recommend revisiting *Chapter 8*.

> **Helpful tips and tricks**
>
> For self-paced online tutorials and technical content on the Azure CLI, I recommend reviewing the following online resource: `https://docs.microsoft.com/en-us/cli/azure/reference-index?view=azure-cli-latest`.

In this section, you have learned the Azure CLI essentials. In the next section, we will explore the Google Cloud CLI.

Utilizing the Google Cloud CLI

The Google Cloud CLI is part of the Google Cloud SDKs. We will explore SDKs later in this chapter. Nevertheless, the Google Cloud CLI is used for managing Google Cloud products and services. The Google Cloud CLI is better known as gcloud. The Google Cloud CLI is used when orchestrating administrative tasks as well as improving software development.

Review the following figure, which displays the Google Cloud CLI on Cloud Shell:

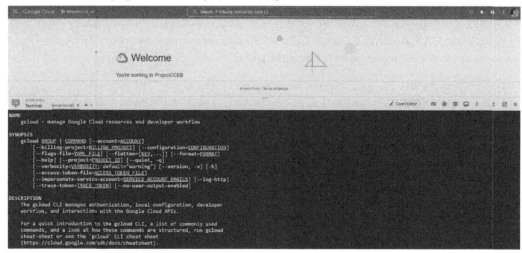

Figure 13.16 – The Google Cloud CLI on Cloud Shell

In this section, you will learn the Google Cloud CLI essentials. You will also learn helpful tips and discover the potential pitfalls that encumber beginners.

Objectives

After completing these tasks, you will have learned the Google Cloud CLI essentials.

> **Note**
>
> The instructions are also located at `https://github.com/PacktPublishing/Cloud-Computing-Demystified-for-Aspiring-Professionals/blob/main/Instructions/Chapter13/GCP-Tools/google_CLI_apitools.md`.

Tasks

To do 1: Learn the Google Cloud CLI essentials

Task 1: Learn the Google Cloud CLI essentials

In this task, you will learn the Google Cloud CLI essentials:

1. Sign in to the Google Cloud console (`https://console.cloud.google.com/`).

2. On the project selector page of the Google Cloud console, select or create a Google Cloud project.

3. Make sure that billing is enabled for your Google Cloud project.

4. Select the **Cloud Shell** icon to activate Cloud Shell.

Figure 13.17 – The Google Cloud console

5. Notice that you are at the CLI prompt.

> **Helpful tips**
>
> Cloud computing providers' Cloud Shell CLI initializes a Bash prompt by default; this behavior is similar across AWS, Azure, and Google Cloud. If you elect to switch modalities, type the following commands:
>
> `pwsh`
>
> `bash`
>
> Typing `pwsh` will initialize the PowerShell CLI, which supports PowerShell syntax.

6. If you did switch to PowerShell, please switch back to the Bash shell for the remainder of this task.

7. Start by typing the `gcloud -help` command.

8. Observe the output and review the **NAME**, **SYNOPSIS**, and **DESCRIPTION** fields.

9. In the **SYNOPSIS** area, identify the syntax output that resembles the following code snippet:

```
gcloud GROUP | COMMAND [--account=ACCOUNT]
```

> **Note**
>
> The preceding line is commonly referred to as syntax. Think of this as the command structure.

The Google Cloud CLI commands comprise a call to GCP services, such as `iam`, and a command. Here is an example: `gcloud iam roles create`. The subcommand corresponds to an operation. Each command has specific parameters or flags that are either required or optional during execution.

> **Insight**
>
> I recommend reviewing each command's **SYNTAX** and **EXAMPLES** area. Reviewing typical usage examples is key to learning.

If you did not have an opportunity to learn how to use the Google Cloud CLI to create a resource, then I recommend revisiting *Chapter 8*.

> **Helpful tips and tricks**
>
> For self-paced online tutorials and technical content on the Google Cloud CLI, I recommend the following online resource: `https://cloud.google.com/sdk/gcloud/reference`.

In these tasks, you have learned about the cloud-native CLI tools that can build and manage resources at scale. In the next section, we will review IaC tools.

Utilizing IaC templates

In this section, you will learn about unique cloud computing IaC tools. We will explore one each of the AWS, Azure, and Google Cloud configuration management services.

IaC tools are used heavily in cloud computing today. This is because organizations can define *what* an environment requires as opposed to indicating how to configure the environment, which is typical when using scripting languages such as PowerShell or the Bash shell. By defining *what*, you can expect to create a consistent experience using a configuration file and one or more templates. This strategy and use of templates can help create a reusable file, thus improving repeatable, consistent deployments.

IaC allows for greater agility because team members from different departments can work together, utilizing a core framework and tooling to create and manage cloud resources at scale and reliably. This is in contrast to the error-prone nature of creating or changing global resources using a manual pattern, such as using an administration website to create thousands of resources that all must adhere to similar configuration standards.

Here is a non-exhaustive table listing some of the cloud computing IaC template services:

Cloud computing provider	Automation services
AWS	CloudFormation
Azure	ARM templates
GCP	Cloud Deployment Manager

Table 13.3 – AWS, Azure, and GCP IaC services

Defining resources with AWS CloudFormation

The AWS CloudFormation service supports IaC features. System operation representatives and developers use human-readable templates to define stacks of cloud resources that comprise your cloud infrastructure in a repeatable fashion with minimal to no configuration deviation. An AWS CloudFormation template is a JSON or YAML text file.

Learning about the CloudFormation template anatomy is very important. The anatomy of the CloudFormation template consists of the following:

- The format version element is used to ensure conformity to AWS versions
- The description element is optional but can be used to provide a brief description or custom version number
- The metadata element is also optional but can provide additional information
- The parameters element is optional but can be used to impart values to pass during deployment
- The mappings element is also optional and can be used to control conditional values, such as mapping Amazon Regions to explicitly allowed unique Amazon image values for deployment
- The conditions element is optional but can be used during template execution to ensure that dependencies exist
- The resources element is required to specify resource types and properties
- The output element is optional but can display values returned after your stack deployment

In this section, you will learn about AWS CloudFormation. You will also learn helpful tips and discover the potential pitfalls that encumber beginners.

Objectives

After completing these tasks, you will have learned about the AWS CloudFormation fundamentals.

> **Note**
>
> The instructions are also located at `https://github.com/PacktPublishing/ Cloud-Computing-Demystified-for-Aspiring-Professionals/blob/ main/Instructions/Chapter13/AWS-Tools/aws_InfrastructureAsCode_ apitools.md`.

Tasks

To do 1: Learn about AWS CloudFormation

Task 1: Learn about AWS CloudFormation

In this task, you will learn about AWS CloudFormation:

1. Sign in to the AWS Management Console (`https://console.aws.amazon.com/ console/`).

2. Search for `CloudFormation` using the search field.

3. On the **CloudFormation** dashboard, select **Create stack** and then **With new resources**.

4. Select **Create template in Designer**. Then, select **Create template in Designer** again.

5. On the **CloudFormation Designer** dashboard, review and explore the graphical designer, including the canvas and the template syntax editor located near the bottom.

6. In **CloudFormation Designer**, select the **Template** tab.

7. In **CloudFormation Designer**, select, drag, and drop the **S3 Bucket** icon onto the canvas toward the center of the design surface. Review the following figure for guidance:

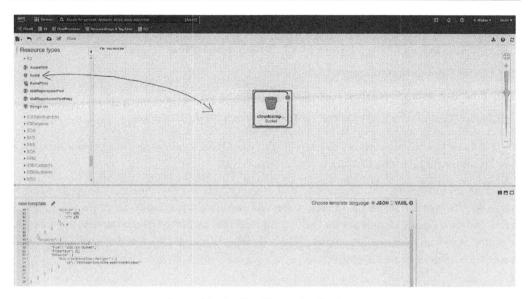

Figure 13.18 – CloudFormation Designer

8. After dragging the icon, review the JSON syntax located in the **Template** tab.

9. You can edit the JSON document from the **Template** tab editor window.

Helpful tips and tricks

Did you know that you can change the JSON syntax to YAML by selecting **YAML** from the **Template** window? If you make mistakes, there is a **Messages** window that includes output.

---

10. To create what you have designed, select the **Create stack** icon. Review the following figure.

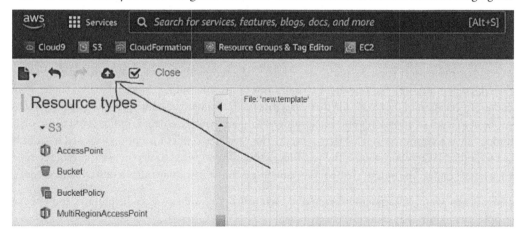

Figure 13.19 – CloudFormation Designer

11. Review the **Create stack** page. Select **Next**.

12. On the **Stack name** page, type `stack12345` and select **Next**.

13. In the **Configure stack** options, select **Next**.

14. Review your stack and then select **Create stack**.

15. After the stack creation has been completed, search for the S3 bucket.

If you did not have an opportunity to learn how to use AWS CloudFormation to create a resource, then I recommend revisiting *Chapter 8.*

One of the advantages of IaC is repeatability. Did you know that you can reuse stack templates? Return to the CloudFormation dashboard and select the stack you created previously. Select the **Stack actions** menu, and then **Create change set** for the current stack. Select **Edit stack** and review the template. Select the **Save** icon to save your template. You can save it to a local file or in Amazon's S3 bucket to share the template or reuse it later.

> **Helpful tips and tricks**
>
> You can deploy, update, and delete resources efficiently using AWS CloudFormation change sets.
>
> For self-paced online tutorials and technical content on AWS CloudFormation, I recommend visiting the following online resource: `https://docs.aws.amazon.com/AWSCloudFormation/latest/UserGuide/updating.stacks.walkthrough.html`.

In these tasks, you have learned about AWS CloudFormation. In the next section, we will review Microsoft Azure ARM templates.

Defining resources with Azure ARM templates

The Microsoft Azure Resource Manager API supports IaC configuration files to declare cloud resources efficiently. Like AWS CloudFormation, ARM templates are reusable and flexible. An ARM template is a JSON text file.

Let's review the structure of the template file first. The template includes the following elements: schema, content version, parameters, variables, resources, and output. The schema is required and denotes the location of the JSON file that describes the template. The content version can be used to provide a policy-based version numbering system. The parameters element is optional but can provide custom values to resources during deployment. The variables element is optional as well but can be used to embed JSON expressions. The resources element is required to deploy Azure resource types in a resource group. The output element is optional and can return values after a deployment executes.

In this section, you will learn about Azure ARM templates. You will also learn helpful tips and discover the potential pitfalls that encumber beginners.

Objectives

After completing these tasks, you will have learned about the fundamentals of Azure ARM templates.

> **Note**
>
> The instructions are also located at `https://github.com/PacktPublishing/Cloud-Computing-Demystified-for-Aspiring-Professionals/blob/main/Instructions/Chapter13/Azure-Tools/azure_InfrastructureAsCode_apitools.md`.

Tasks

To do 1: Learn about Azure ARM templates

Task 1: Learn about Azure ARM templates

In this task, you will learn about Azure ARM templates:

1. Sign in to the Azure portal (`https://portal.azure.com/`).
2. In the portal, search for ARM templates by typing `templates`.
3. Select **Deploy a custom template**.
4. On the **Custom deployment** page, select **Build your own template in the editor**.
5. On the **Edit template** page, select **Add resource**. Then, select **Storage account** from the menu.
6. Type in a globally unique storage account name. Here is an example: `cloudcomputingdapxx`.

   Review the following figure, which displays a template:

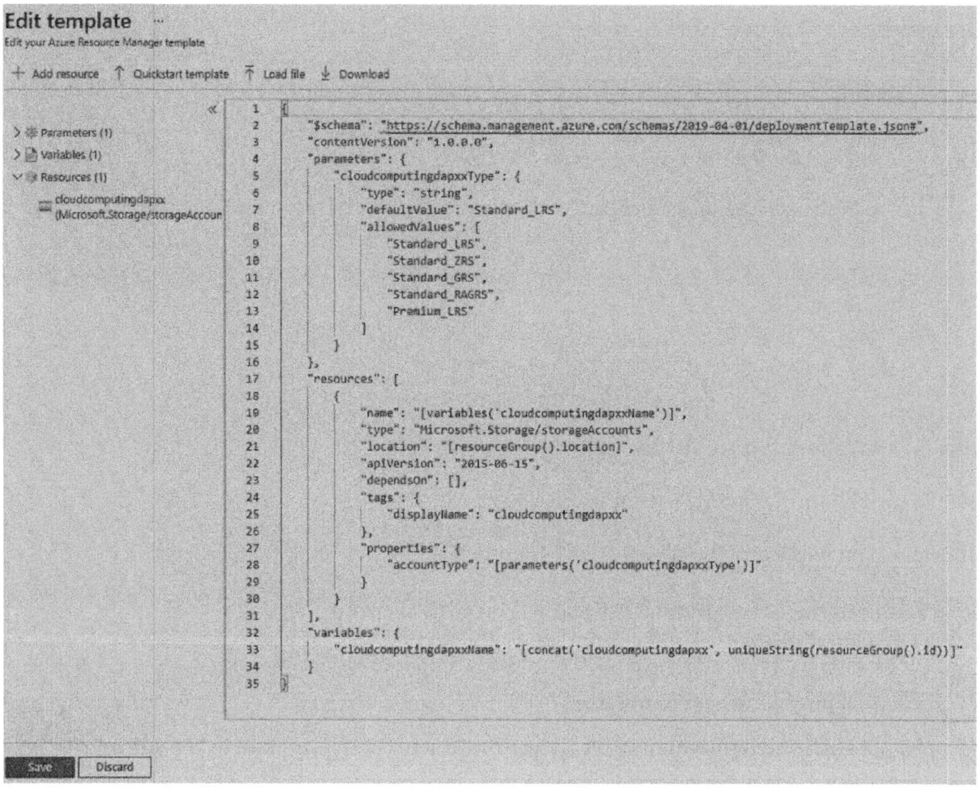

Figure 13.20 – Deploying a custom template

7. Review the custom template's anatomy. Notice the `resources` and `variables` elements.

8. Select **Save**.

9. On the **Custom deployment** page, select your resource group or click **Create new**.

> **Helpful tips and tricks**
>
> Did you know it is important to consider resource location? Cost and compliance are also some of the many factors to consider. I recommend reviewing the cloud computing Well-Architected Framework's standard best practices for more insight.

10. After careful consideration, select **Review + create**. Then, select **Create**.

> **Helpful tips and tricks**
>
> Did you know Azure resource groups include a deployment setting that provides the capability to reuse the template by redeploying?

If you did not have an opportunity to learn how to use ARM templates to create a resource, then I recommend revisiting *Chapter 8*.

Helpful tips and tricks

For self-paced online tutorials and technical content on ARM templates, I recommend the following online resource: `https://docs.microsoft.com/en-us/azure/azure-resource-manager/templates/template-tutorial-create-first-template?tabs=azure-powershell`.

In this section, you have learned about Azure ARM templates. In the next section, we will review Google Cloud Deployment Manager.

Defining resources with Google Cloud Deployment Manager

The Google Cloud Deployment Manager service helps organizations use configuration files to quickly create resources in accordance with IaC methods. You define your resources declaratively and then reuse or share your templates with others to consistently recreate or repurpose them. Google Cloud Deployment Manager supports YAML files and the files must contain a *resources* element. The resources element contains a *name* element that defines a Google Cloud service resource. The *type* of element specifies what type of resources, such as the size of a VM instance, and any properties of the type.

In these tasks, you will learn about Google Cloud Deployment Manager. You will also learn helpful tips and discover the potential pitfalls that encumber beginners.

Objectives

After completing these tasks, you will have learned about the Google Cloud Deployment Manager fundamentals.

Note

The instructions are also located at `https://github.com/PacktPublishing/Cloud-Computing-Demystified-for-Aspiring-Professionals/blob/main/Instructions/Chapter13/GCP-Tools/google_InfrastructureAsCode_apitools.md`.

Tasks

To do 1: Learn about Google Cloud Deployment Manager

Task 1: Learn about Google Cloud Deployment Manager

In this task, you will learn about Google Cloud Deployment Manager:

1. Sign in to the Google Cloud console (`https://console.cloud.google.com/`).

2. On the project selector page in the Google Cloud console, select or create a Google Cloud project.

3. Next, enable access to the APIs. Enable **Cloud Deployment Manager V2 API**.

4. Activate Cloud Shell and select the **Upload** option or create a new file to edit.

5. Copy the sample configuration `str.yaml` file located in GitHub and paste it into the Google Cloud editor.

6. Deploy the resources, then use the Cloud Shell CLI to create a deployment. Using the configuration file, type the following command:

```
gcloud deployment-manager deployments create ccdapxxxx-
cloudstrg -config strg.yaml
```

> **Note**
>
> Replace the XXXX placeholder characters with a unique string value.

7. After successfully creating a Google Cloud Storage account, review the Google Cloud Deployment Manager dashboard.

> **Helpful tips and tricks**
>
> Did you know that you can use Google Cloud Deployment Manager to edit and repurpose templates?
>
> If you prefer, you can try using Terraform templates. Did you know that Terraform is integrated with Cloud Shell?

If you did not have an opportunity to learn how to use Terraform templates to create a resource, then I recommend revisiting *Chapter 8*.

> **Helpful tips and tricks**
>
> For self-paced online tutorials and technical content on ARM templates, I recommend the following online resource: `https://cloud.google.com/deployment-manager/docs/configuration/syntax-reference`.

In this section, you have learned about the cloud computing IaC template resources offered by Amazon, Microsoft, and Google Cloud. In the next section, we will review SDKs.

Utilizing software engineering resources

In this section, you will learn about cloud computing **software developer kit (SDK)** resources. We will explore one each of the AWS, Azure, and Google Cloud SDK resources.

SDKs

The purpose of a cloud SDK is to simplify integrating with and implementing cloud-native services programmatically from any custom or cloud SaaS application, constructed typically by application developers.

SDKs are collections of reusable resources, also known as APIs or libraries, and in some development communities are referred to as software packages. For example, TensorFlow is a well-known AI and data science Python package/API containing one or more modules that include object-oriented programming types and their members, such as classes and functions. The key takeaway here is not to educate you on programming concepts; while it is highly important in today's cloud-developer-friendly market, it is the former point about reusable resources that is important to note. This accelerates the software development life cycle and adheres to DevOps principles such as IaC whereby system and software API declarations or definitions must be repeatable, consistent, and well-documented. In turn, this leads to secure or auditable continuous integration and deployment of cloud services in a service-oriented architecture. This will increase development sprints and lead to minimum viable products that help organizations learn quickly from early feedback, which eventually leads to value.

Developing with AWS SDKs

AWS SDKs are intuitive and support client-side and server-side development. Furthermore, AWS SDKs are programming language agnostic.

In this section, you will learn about AWS SDKs. You will also learn helpful tips and discover the potential pitfalls that encumber beginners.

Objectives

After completing these tasks, you will have learned about the AWS SDK fundamentals.

> **Note**
>
> The instructions are also located at `https://github.com/PacktPublishing/Cloud-Computing-Demystified-for-Aspiring-Professionals/blob/main/Instructions/Chapter12/AWS-Tools/aws_SoftwareDeveloper_apitools.md`.

Tasks

To do 1: Learn about AWS SDKs

Task 1: Learn about AWS SDKs

In this task, you will learn about AWS SDKs:

1. Go to `https://aws.amazon.com/developer/tools/` and read the user-friendly SDK content and community support forum.

2. You will need to know what programming language you're building the application with.

    Typically, organizations use frameworks based on several factors, such as familiarity and internal talent. Sometimes, they may transition due to security and compliance concerns. *Note: I leverage Python or .NET C# in my examples.*

> **Helpful tips and tricks**
>
> For training purposes, I recommend using the programming language that you are already adept in.

3. Navigate the website and select **Python**.

4. Upon selecting **Python**, review the intuitive installation instructions.

5. Notice that you can install this Python SDK using familiar Python package management tools, such as `pip`.

> **Helpful tips and tricks**
>
> `pip` is a package manager for Python. `pip` is installed and used as a command-line tool to install and manage packages. Did you know that you can optimize package management by utilizing an IDE tool such as Visual Studio, Eclipse, or PyCharm?

    Review the following figure, which displays the AWS SDK installation options via Visual Studio Code.

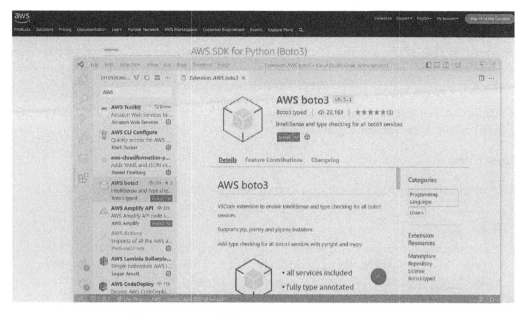

Figure 13.21 – AWS SDK for Python, Visual Studio Code

6.   After installing the SDK package using your preferred IDE, you can start writing code.

The following example shows how to list AWS S3 bucket objects using the Python SDK:

```
import boto3
s3 = boto3.resource('s3')
bucket = s3.Bucket('cloudcomputingrocksbucket')
for obj in bucket.objects.all():
    print(obj.key)
```

The command imports the installed SDK and uses programming classes and members to interact with the AWS S3 APIs.

The value here is that you do not have to construct your own class objects and members. The reusable AWS SDKs, which are APIs, provide a consistent and secure development method that has been tried and tested by AWS and their business partners.

> **Helpful tips**
>
> For instructor-led and technical content on AWS SDK, I recommend the following online resource: https://www.aws.training/.

In this task, you learned about AWS SDKs. In the next section, we will review Azure SDKs.

Developing with Azure SDKs

Microsoft, like Google and Amazon, offers SDKs to optimize managing and building microservices. Microsoft also has an extensive developer community to support start-ups and enterprise organizations that are transitioning to modern application development practices.

In this section, you will learn about Azure SDKs. You will also learn helpful tips and discover the potential pitfalls that encumber beginners.

Objectives

After completing these tasks, you will have learned about the Azure SDK fundamentals.

> **Note**
>
> The instructions are also located at `https://github.com/PacktPublishing/Cloud-Computing-Demystified-for-Aspiring-Professionals/blob/main/Instructions/Chapter13/Azure-Tools/azure_SoftwareDeveloper_apitools.md`.

Tasks

To do 1: Learn about Azure SDKs

Task 1: Learn about Azure SDKs

In this section, you will learn about Azure SDKs:

1. Go to the Azure SDK and tools website at `https://azure.microsoft.com/en-us/downloads/`.

2. Review the SDK page. Like the AWS SDK site, Azure describes and lists SDKs categorically by programming framework, such as **.NET**.

   For this lesson, I recommend selecting **.NET** from the SDK page.

3. Let's try something different: select **Documentation**.

4. Upon selecting **Documentation**, you are redirected to the API reference.

5. Select **Storage** from the list of APIs.

6. In the Azure Storage client libraries for .NET, review the content, particularly the table displaying the library, package, and source.

Helpful tips and tricks

Did you know that you can use the .NET CLI, like `pip` for Python, to install the SDK also referred to herein as a package? So, you can install NuGet packages, which comprise programming types such as classes.

Use this CLI command to install packages before and after compute setup: `dotnet add package Azure.Storage.Blobs`.

7. Then, you can install the Azure SDK using IDE tools such as Visual Studio.

    Review the following figure, which displays the Azure SDK installation options via Visual Studio.

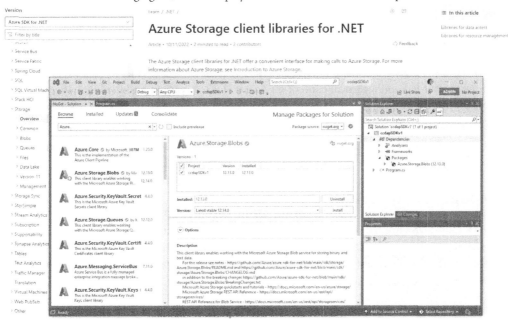

Figure 13.22 – Azure SDK, Visual Studio

8. Once the SDK is installed, you can select the IDE of your choice and start building.

    Review the following figure, which illustrates SDK utilization and references Azure Blob Storage.

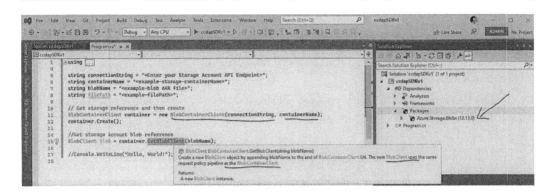

Figure 13.23 – Azure SDK, BlobContainerClient types and methods

> **Helpful tips and tricks**
>
> For instructor-led and technical content on Azure SDKs, I recommend the following online resource: `https://docs.microsoft.com/en-us/training/courses/az-204t00`.

In this section, you have learned about Azure SDKs. In the next section, we will explore Google Cloud SDKs.

Developing with Google Cloud SDKs

Google Cloud SDKs are like Azure and AWS SDKs, a collection of tools to help developers and administrators alike to efficiently build and manage Google Cloud project resources. There are many benefits to using Google Cloud's SDKs, such as reducing the boilerplate code required to interoperate and build using Google's IaaS and PaaS resources.

In these tasks, you will learn about Google Cloud SDKs. You will also learn helpful tips and discover potential pitfalls that encumber beginners.

Objectives

After completing these tasks, you will have learned about Google Cloud SDKs.

> **Note**
>
> The instructions are also located at `https://github.com/PacktPublishing/Cloud-Computing-Demystified-for-Aspiring-Professionals/blob/main/Instructions/Chapter13/GCP-Tools/google_SoftwareDeveloper_apitools.md`.

Tasks

To do 1: Learn about Google Cloud SDKs

Task 1: Learn about Google Cloud SDKs

In this task, you will learn about Google Cloud SDKs:

1. Sign in to the Google Cloud console (`https://console.cloud.google.com/`).

2. On the project selector page of the Google Cloud console, select or create a Google Cloud project.

3. Make sure that billing is enabled for your cloud project.

4. Enable Google Cloud API.

5. Go to the Google Cloud SDK web page: `https://cloud.google.com/sdk/`.

6. Review the Google Cloud SDK page and its key features.

7. Select **Python** from the available client libraries.

8. On the **Python Cloud Client Libraries** page, search for and select **Google Cloud Storage**.

9. Select **Bucket** from the API documentation.

10. Review how to use buckets programmatically.

Helpful tips and tricks

Did you know that you can install the client libraries using either `pip install google-cloud-storage` or the Cloud Code extension for Visual Studio Code?

Review the following figure, which displays the Cloud Code extension and includes the API library:

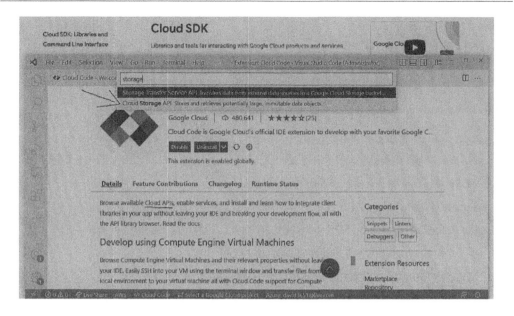

Figure 13.24 – Google Cloud SDK, Visual Studio Code

11. Once Google Cloud SDK is installed, you can start developing.

Review the following figure, which displays the `copy_blob()` function:

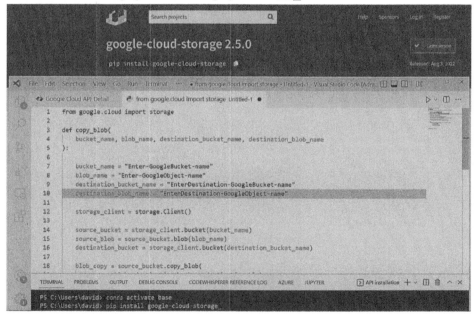

Figure 13.25 – Google Cloud SDK, the copy_blob() function

> **Helpful tips and tricks**
>
> For instructor-led technical content on SDKs, I recommend the following online resource: `https://cloud.google.com/training/application-development#cloud-developer-learning-path`.

In this section, you have learned about Google Cloud SDK tools.

Summary

In this chapter, you learned about cloud-native API libraries and tool services used to build and manage resources efficiently in an agile way.

In the next chapter, we will explore the world of modern cloud technology training and exam preparation.

Questions

1. Which of the following command-line languages is common to the AWS CLI, the Azure CLI, and the GCP CLI?

    A. SSH

    B. PowerShell

    C. Bash shell

    D. Cloud CLIs have unique commands and syntax

2. Which of the following options runs the AWS, Azure, and GCP cloud shells?

    A. Browser

    B. On-premises

    C. Private cloud

    D. Linux KVM

3. Which of the following IaC template file types are supported across AWS, Azure, and GCP? (Choose all that apply.)

    A. JSON

    B. YAML

    C. JavaScript

    D. Go

4. Which of the following are available across multi-cloud to deploy IaC templates?

    A. CLI

    B. Bash shell

    C. CISCO router

    D. Internet gateway

5. What is an SDK?

    A. Storage developer kit

    B. Storage data kit

    C. Software developer kit

    D. Source data kit

Part 5:
Roadmap for a Successful Journey in Cloud Engineering

This part of the book will take you on a journey to master cloud computing. You will learn about recommended online learning resources – including self-paced learning versus instructor-led live training, choosing modern cloud role paths, and accreditation benefits. You will also learn about exam prep and the importance of mentorship.

This part comprises the following chapters:

- *Chapter 14, Accelerating the Continuous Learning Journey*
- *Chapter 15, Driving Growth, and the Future of the Cloud*

Accelerating the Continuous Learning Journey

This chapter will help you gain the knowledge necessary to use online community learning resources to not only grow but thrive now and prepare for paradigm shifts in the future of modern cloud technologies.

The following topics are covered in this chapter:

- Tech community learning resources
- Amplifying learning with self-paced learning
- Higher learning with instructor-led training
- Advantages of mentorship

Tech community learning resources

Learning by participating in tech communities, and in particular, those communities that are cloud-centric, cloud-agnostic, and known for helping beginners grow, is important in today's era. Some examples of tech-centric communities are given here:

- **Technology, Entertainment, Design (TED)**: TED' slogan is "ideas worth spreading" and they hold technology-related events such as TED conferences
- **GitHub**: A collaborative open source developer community offering distributed source control using Git technologies
- **Product Hunt**: A platform for discovering efficient methods for learning anything
- **SheCodes**: Online coding classes for women by women
- **Coding Black Females**: A community of African American women in tech helping to educate other women

- **Stack Overflow**: A tech community centered on sharing knowledge
- **Microsoft Community** A tech community focused on helping you find the answers you need and build skills
- **Google Communities**: A tech community for sharing emerging news and offering Google support
- **Amazon Communities**: A tech community for helping students, supporting customers, and sharing insights into upcoming events

Learning

It takes a village is a simple yet insightful truism. This adage is not to be shirked by anyone—it is embedded as a core pillar in the tech industry and should be utilized far more by aspiring practitioners. Too few novices leverage the power of communities. That power is derived from communities that support varying technologies and roles from stakeholders and IT pros to developers to build the future, and optimizing the present through collaborative projects with like-minded people who are willing to share what they know and what they are working on to the betterment of the community.

Starting the journey

Occasionally, beginners try going at it alone but lose interest due to obstacles, such as overall training and project costs and time, or simply lack guidance from an experienced practitioner and—more importantly—from someone who genuinely cares about the work they are doing. But one thing is for certain: if given an internship or job opportunity, working alongside IT pros, developers, product managers, and leadership is inevitable. So, start learning how to work well with others earlier in your tech career, and what better place to start than joining a community?

Helpful tips and tricks

For online helpful tech communities supporting cloud computing, I recommend visiting the following online resources:

- *AWS Community & Events*: https://aws.amazon.com/events/asean/community-and-events/
- *Azure Community Support*: https://azure.microsoft.com/en-us/support/community/
- *Google Cloud Communities*: https://www.googlecloudcommunity.com/

Starting a technical learning journey is arduous on your own without assistance or experience—this is known to create a non-conducive learning environment that can make the simplest technical concept, diagram, setup, administrative task, and development project daunting. Understanding effective ways to learn by collaboration is key to your learning journey and is a critical component of any technical community by design.

> **Insight**
>
> Did you know that cloud computing tech communities are accessible from your favorite social media platforms such as Twitter and Instagram?

Next, we'll discuss TED talks.

Learning about TED talks

There are various tech communities that cover topics such as cloud computing support and more, and they educate members—and visitors—on topics related to tech that can help start-ups expand their views on cloud technology and how it's being used today, more than just exciting customers by way of robust design. For example, for saving crops and building tangible solutions used in various industries, consider supporting initiatives by joining think tanks to help in the effort to eliminate world hunger and disease. Look at TED and its events, including conferences and online convenient audio-driven TED talks, which us to better understand the world and how technology such as cloud computing is being used to improve the world presently and perhaps in the near future.

> **Helpful tips and tricks**
>
> Did you know that you can join TED's community and work with some of the greatest minds and communicators and participate in TED initiatives? Simply sign up and start working with others and sharing ideas to empower the community with your own visions, or support someone else's dreams.

The matrix is everywhere

What if you're sated with building instead of administrating? The word *building* in this context refers to a developer coding, and the word *administrating* refers to system operations—for example, securing a Linux or Windows operating system. There are so many options for developers. Developer communities provide multiple channels to address topics such as frontend or backend development—for example, JavaScript or .NET C#. It is common for the community to market the word *code* and mention supporting start-ups and **open source software (OSS)**. No matter the nomenclature the developer community uses to attract members, there are services offered by these developer-centric communities—such as a code repository that includes version control features—and most can distribute code efficiently to support **continuous delivery (CD)** requirements. Whether it's for training members of the community through project-driven collaboration or running trials to garner feedback, developer communities are known for offering an array of services.

Open source project communities

Did you know that OSS licensing allows developers to review, utilize, and update the source code and even distribute the software as is? Consequently, this elicits trust from the public in the service or software. Red Hat and other Linux distributions are traditionally known as open source. However, it's important to note that open source is not exclusively a Red Hat characteristic.

What if you required developer resources and help from an online community? An example is a community such as GitHub that has participated in or founded projects that intersect across cloud computing, Amazon, Microsoft, and Google.

GitHub is known for its open source community and its projects integrate with cloud computing, and it supports start-ups around the globe. Based on my experience, I've found it's a great resource for beginner cloud practitioners. Not only does it offer **continuous integration** (**CI**) products and CD services that deliver features such as access control, bug tracking, and task management, but GitHub additionally provides integration with AWS, Azure, and **Google Cloud Platform** (**GCP**) cloud computing APIs.

> **Helpful tips and tricks**
>
> Did you know that if you join GitHub, you can find AWS, Azure, and Google Cloud learning documentation, self-paced quick-start tutorials, and more?

For example, review the following AWS documentation on GitHub (`https://github.com/awsdocs`):

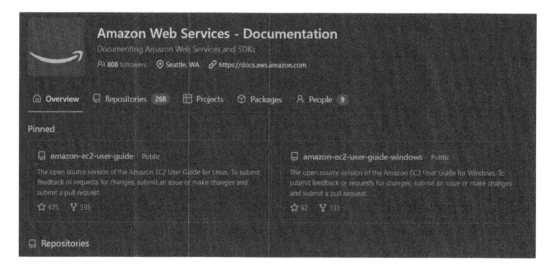

Figure 14.1 – AWS documentation on GitHub

You can also review the following Azure documentation on GitHub (`https://github.com/MicrosoftDocs`):

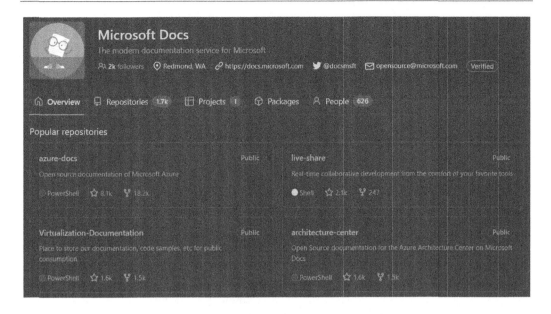

Figure 14.2 – Azure documentation on GitHub

Additionally, you can review the following GCP documentation on GitHub (`https://github.com/GoogleCloudPlatform/`):

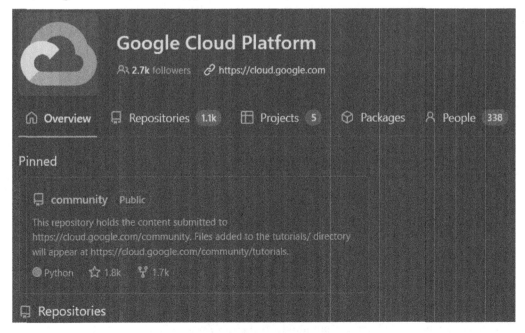

Figure 14.3 – GCP documentation on GitHub

GitHub includes README text files that introduce you to the project and display examples of how to use various artifacts, state what the prerequisites are, and provide important warnings and support resources. If you plan to contribute, GitHub includes guidelines for contributing—talk about intuitive.

As I've mentioned from the start, developer communities such as GitHub are powerful tools used primarily by developers and administrators to build with like-minded contributors using cloud computing APIs and tools to support anyone, including novice and expert practitioners alike. I have been using GitHub for more than 10 years for training and consulting workloads, and I have met talented developers and project managers, such as Tracy Wallace, who started as one of the principal instructors and developers for *Global Knowledge* training and presently is the director of cloud computing training for organizations such as INE.

Developer communities drive inclusion

There are a vast number of developer-friendly communities that help you learn through communication channels, such as Virtual Coffee, and some focus on fostering the needs of modern development, such as **Hack2skill** on Discord. There are even ones that help special interest groups based on culture and gender that drive inclusivity, such as **Blacks in Technology** or the popular **SheCodes** on Slack, inspiring women in tech today.

The objective here is to join, chat with others, learn through those discussions, participate in projects, try different hats or roles if you're so inclined, and see a project through to the end. You may not join at the start of a project, but no matter where the project timeline is, you will learn by collaborating. In this context, participation is implicit during any project collaboration.

Technical support-driven communities

Usually, a tech-centric community is distinguished by the level of help it provides to end users and IT pros. However, it's no secret that most technical support forums are deemed misleading or passive in terms of response time by community visitors and members alike, but there are infinitesimal tech support communities such as Stack Overflow that are prized above others for their level of support and quick response time. IT pros and developers over the years have utilized Stack Overflow as their go-to IT help desk, and the level of support from the Stack Overflow community is very impressive in comparison to most enterprise organizations' internal support talent. We can all learn from Stack Overflow's commitment to the community.

> **Helpful tips and tricks**
>
> Did you know that you can join the Stack Overflow community and participate, thus helping cloud computing communities by way of technical support? Furthermore, while helping others mitigate their technical issues, you will improve your knowledge of the technology in question.

Here is a link to the Stack Overflow community: `https://stackoverflow.com/`.

Cloud computing learning communities

Amazon, Microsoft, and Google's learning division and business partners, which include training providers known for ILT, over the years have dedicated their vast resources to empowering the tech community with their ecosystem of support, learning, infrastructure, and communication resources. Cloud computing learning organizations have grown to include instructor-led and self-paced community products, also known as e-learning.

Regarding the self-paced community services offered, organizations today (including cloud leaders' learning divisions) provide online services that are composed of anywhere-accessible conferences, events, support, learning documentation, collaborative projects, SDKs, and access to innovative tooling to boot. And their community services are capable of cloud computing integration, meaning they can go from theory to a **minimum viable product** (**MVP**) quickly, all while educating the community.

Imagine you can be part of a community where you not only learn but also build. And what you build with other members will be recognized by the community, which includes employers, influencers, practitioners, start-ups, and **subject-matter experts** (**SMEs**). Additionally, Azure, AWS, and GCP leaders and customers will remember what you have achieved. So, by word of mouth, news of what you have done will spread like wildfire to your benefit.

The experience you gain from these relationships will cement your name in the bedrock of IT.

> Helpful tips and tricks
>
> I have added key references to AWS, Azure, and GCP in the *Starting the journey* section. I recommend joining one or more of those cloud computing tech communities. After joining, establish a relationship and build a rapport with any current member. It is advantageous for you if that member is at the start or middle of a new project.

Cloud computing learning partners

However, learning *how to* is not enough, and every online tech community has constraint factors of resources designed to engage, a vision that focuses on education, and talent skilled in teaching effectively. As a beginner, you must *quickly* consider those factors so that you can try other learning services. Eventually, you will realize cloud computing learning partners (also known as training providers) are essential to any training endeavor, whether you need a private corporate training initiative or a public training class, and not just by an accredited pundit in your domain but a certified teacher.

Training providers

Learning partners play a crucial role in improving the skills and helping in the advancement of any aspiring cloud computing SME. Learning partners develop long-lasting relationships with cloud computing leaders, lab providers, technology vendors, and employers across every industry. You may have already attended a class facilitated by a learning partner unbeknownst to you. It is quite common for Amazon, Microsoft, and Google to resource a learning partner to deliver public classes, facilitate new training initiatives, and build lasting relationships with various communities—even those outside of the tech community—including developing new services and even evaluating new training products to improve the quality of any future consulting and learning engagement.

You can find more information on learning partners at the following links:

- **Fast Lane**: `https://fastlane.live/us_en/`
- **Global Knowledge**: `https://www.globalknowledge.com/us-en/`
- **NetCom Learning**: `https://www.netcomlearning.com/`

Note that this list is not exhaustive.

For example, I have facilitated training initiatives for Amazon and Microsoft, such as **Microsoft Software and Systems Academy (MSSA)**, a program designed to accelerate job placements for practitioners who aspire to become developers or cloud administrators. The program's target audience is none other than the United States military. The program helps those service members who are presently on active duty but eventually will transition out of the military.

Here is another example of a skilling initiative powered by learning partners (Fast Lane), cloud computing leaders, and Microsoft, and offered by the City of Los Angeles with support from **JVS SoCal** and **Workforce Development, Aging and Community Services (WDACS)** to empower veterans who have already transitioned out of the military. The program skills veterans in cloud computing with a focus on cloud administration and architecture roles, and the learning partner curated the engagement to deliver an unprecedented service that uses real-world job scenarios and mentorship to drive success. To quell your skepticism, the **Los Angeles Veterans Technology Training Academy (LAVTTA)** program offered by JVS SoCal and facilitated by Microsoft and its learning partner Fast Lane has proven the program works by providing the first cohort in the year 2021 with meaningful careers, and the program is still active. How do I know? Because I am authoring this book while preparing for the upcoming LAVTTA program delivery as the cloud courseware director for the learning partner.

Another example is Amazon Academy and AWS Tech U programs designed to help employers, educators, and institutions by skilling students on innovative AWS technologies to close the skill gap so that the learner can be a value to any business across the globe. **AWS Tech U** helps onboard AWS new hires with on-the-job training and project-based learning workshops. Learning partners also support this initiative.

The point is, learning partners are at the heart of almost every training endeavor.

> Helpful tips and tricks
>
> If your organization has not considered skilling employees, I recommend approaching human resources and first learning which resources are available. If the resources recommended are not appropriate for your individual needs, you will need to search online and use the community resources and relationships you have established to find training events discounted or subsidized by one of the institutions integrated with either a cloud computing leader or a learning partner. Please review the training provider (also known as learning partner) links denoted previously to research one or more learning partners and their resources, including promotions.

Learning partner resources

Learning partners are crucial to the growth of the IT learning community because of the significant value they pose. A key principal value in business and across any industry is the practice of investing in an organization's most important asset: its talent. For those who are still confused, I am referring to the employees.

Over the years, the product management talent of the learning partners has improved the accessibility and product of ILT and self learning resources to include learning media in the form of videos or webinars, articles and various channels of communication. Additionally, by analyzing trends, they frequently learn new ways to engage and enhance the learner's overall experience. Furthermore, learning partners have extensive years of experience in educating the IT community and its technology leaders through adaptive engagements, curated to the individual or organization following proven educational frameworks. To conclude, learning partners can enhance ILT, **virtual ILT** (**VILT**), mentoring, and self-paced learning (also known as e-learning) products for you, the learner.

Here are some examples of the services offered by learning partners:

- Self-paced learning/e-learning

- Enhanced/curated ILT

- Enhanced/curated VILT

- Curated private corporate training

- Exam preparation/certification assessments

- Mentorship/coaching

In this section, we've introduced technical communities that support cloud computing and looked at how those communities help aspiring practitioners grow in their skillset by collaborating on projects or events with members. In the next section, we explore the world of self-paced learning.

Amplifying learning with self-paced learning

In this section, you will learn how self-paced learning works and its advantages. We will expound on AWS, Azure, and Google Cloud learning resources.

The advantages of self-paced learning

Self-paced training or—more accurately phrased—self-paced learning resources are important academic tools to augment educational growth and optimize continuous learning throughout any academic life cycle and corporate training.

The following list denotes self-paced resources:

- **AWS Builder Labs**: https://aws.amazon.com/training/digital/aws-builder-labs/
- **Microsoft Learn**: https://docs.microsoft.com/en-us/training/
- **Google Cloud training**: https://cloud.google.com/training
- **Fast Lane**: https://fastlane.live/ww_en/
- **Global Knowledge**: https://www.globalknowledge.com/us-en/resources/resource-library/
- **NetCom Learning**: https://www.netcomlearning.com/elearning-library/

The advent of autodidacticism

To comprehend the advent of self-paced learning, we must first understand its characteristics and roots. Errorless and errorful learning are correlative characteristics that can be useful to understand autodidactic learners, also known for their self-teaching methods. Anecdotal studies suggest errorless learning is key in modern self-paced learning corroborated by recognized schools such as the University of Western Ontario. There is a direct correlation between the increase in autodidactic and contemporary e-learning self-paced videos used for self-teaching with a focus on errorless training.

Instructor-led versus self-paced training

Self-paced training is considered errorless learning because the learner will receive a question followed immediately by an answer in the form of media, such as video recordings and/or text on an application dashboard. Consequently, errorless learning would reduce the likelihood of reinforcing errors, while in errorful learning (also known as traditional ILT), errors are plausible due to chance because students are guessing—albeit eventually corrected by the teacher—but because of the correction delay and error given, there is an increased probability (however unlikely) that a pattern may develop on subsequent occasions.

> **Helpful tips and tricks**
>
> Did you know studies show that errorless learning has helped practitioners with memory retention impairments?

So, autodidactic students who are primarily self-teaching may benefit from e-learning videos, quick-start tutorials, and books because of their errorless learning pattern. In the modern era, self-paced video learning resources complement traditional learning and empower practitioners to complete independent tasks.

The hard truth, however, is that succeeding in self-paced learning requires self-discipline, and sooner rather than later, you must reflect to ensure accurate understanding. Furthermore, self-paced learning lacks engagement, and it's well known that learners learn best by reward during an engagement.

Expanding with self-paced learning

No matter the argument, my recommendation based on earlier insights is to complement and thus expand learning by supplementing ILT and VILT, thus blending both methods of learning.

> **Helpful tips and tricks**
>
> I recommend starting a self-paced tutorial after every ILT or VILT event. Reinforcement learning works and checking one's notes after class using self-paced learning improves accuracy and increases confidence in mastering the technology and concept.

Self-paced tools

There is a legion of tools online supporting self-paced learning. Organizations around the globe provide curated experiences for brand management. However, e-learning videos and curated online articles are by far the most popular option.

Here is a list of self-paced learning resources:

- Video
- Live webinar
- Live conference events
- Articles (that is, blog/whitepaper)
- Textual tutorial with built-in lab

> **Helpful tips and tricks**
>
> AWS Builder Labs are impressive, to say the least. I find myself trying them out after delivering a class, and I will say they have helped me by providing perspectives on a technology that I would not have considered alone.

Self-paced media

Self-paced media has been around for an age, and companies such as Coursera, Udemy, LinkedIn Learning, A Cloud Guru, and CBT Nuggets are well known for their e-learning catalogs. Pricing and utilization are appropriate and cost-effective for short but powerful videos that drive home the knowledge needed to complete simple-to-intermediate administrative and development tasks.

> **Helpful tips and tricks**
>
> Did you know that cloud computing leaders include media that focuses on cloud computing technologies and how to prepare for corresponding certifications' exams?

Self-paced quick starts

Cloud computing leaders and learning partner lab providers such as **go deploy** and **LOD**, now known as **Skillable**, include tutorial-formatted textual step-by-step instructions that facilitate efficient learning during creation. These lab-like instructions are embedded with self-paced documents online, and almost all quick-start tutorial content is sourced from GitHub and frequently updated to improve quality. Recall in an earlier section I explained how cloud computing leaders use GitHub in technical communities to foster inclusion and empower aspiring practitioners. Review the next screenshots depicting each cloud computing provider's self-paced learning presence.

The following screenshot depicts AWS self-paced learning resources via GitHub (`https://github.com/awsdocs`):

Figure 14.4 – AWS self-paced learning resources on GitHub

The following screenshot depicts Azure self-paced learning resources via GitHub (`https://github.com/MicrosoftDocs`):

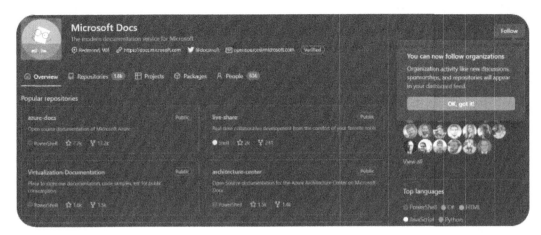

Figure 14.5 – Azure self-paced learning resources on GitHub

The following screenshot depicts GCP self-paced learning resources via GitHub (`https://github.com/GoogleCloudPlatform/`):

Figure 14.6 – GCP self-paced learning resources on GitHub

Helpful tips and tricks

Did you know that you can visit AWS, Azure, and GCP self-paced online document portals or GitHub and complete a quick-start tutorial online?

Higher learning with ILT

In this section, you will learn how live ILT compares to self-paced learning. We will include cloud computing providers and their learning partners' ILT/VILT services.

The following list denotes ILT/VILT **service providers (SPs)**:

- AWS Certification and Training: `https://aws.amazon.com/training/`
- Microsoft Learn: `https://docs.microsoft.com/en-us/training/`
- Google Cloud training: `https://cloud.google.com/training`
- Fast Lane: `https://fastlane.live/ww_en/`
- Global Knowledge: `https://www.globalknowledge.com/us-en/resources/resource-library/`
- NetCom Learning: `https://www.netcomlearning.com/elearning-library/`

The power of engagement with ILT

Engagement is at the heart of any learning endeavor, every great invention, and each collaboration, including non-training initiatives—they thrive due to engagement. Without interaction or engagement, learning cannot be assessed. How can you truly master a concept without levels of engagement? Even the wise cannot know whether what they interpreted was the intent of the endeavor. As an instructor, I have witnessed firsthand students misinterpret what they have read or watched. I have also seen the glimmer of understanding through the behavior and response of the listener, but only in an instructor-led delivery.

Explicit direct instruction

Cloud computing providers require their instructors to obtain certifications and train-the-trainer accreditations to ensure the instructor is taught skills needed to effectively convey the subject matter. Instructors master various key teaching methods such as neurolinguistics and explicit direct instruction. These techniques enhance ILT and VILT class deliveries by combining proven methods that use direct instruction and progressive learning patterns because the instructor becomes a facilitator to improve competency. Enhancements such as **Explicit Direct Instruction (EDI)** are not plausible in a self-paced setting.

Engaging

There are studies that I could provide to quell your concerns with teaching and modern learning habits. If you are curious, I recommend researching EDI! Furthermore, various analyses conclude that teachers can help students who cannot grasp a concept by simply reading a book or watching an overly brief self-paced video. Why? That is the question. Why is a live teacher more effective than a non-live self-paced video? Because without a teacher, there is no engagement. Even workshops require a live facilitator to be engaging. In on-the-job training, engagement is key to the success of the individual and the team. Learning partners know this and channel resources to enhance instructor engagements for the benefit of the learning community. A word of caution: do not discard teachers so quickly. Teachers are key to our future, and every great leader and innovator can tell you from experience their meteoric rise was possible because of the wisdom passed down by a teacher or mentor.

Checking for understanding

Recall the description of errorful learning from earlier. Recall it's crucial to verify one's understanding of a concept or successfully complete a task whereby an instructor or facilitator validates that the individual or team is not misinterpreting the objective, which can occur in self-paced learning.

Planning for success

AWS, Azure, and GCP instructors can gauge your behavior during class participation, guiding you in your next learning endeavors. For example, students start down a learning path—such as development—and due to social mores, they consider expanding that learning path, even though during class the student displays administrative characteristics and fluency in the subject matter. Instructors can identify this and recommend the student diversify their portfolio to encompass the development and administrative paths to the advantage of the student who was unaware of their potential.

ILT best practices

The following list displays key best practices that learners should apply during onsite training events to get the most out of ILT:

Engage with participants and the facilitator

- Participate in activities and reviews
- Check for understanding by rephrasing, not repeating
- Focus on the facilitator's topic
- Understand the curriculum's lesson objectives
- Ask for homework or after-class assignments to optimize your understanding
- Take notes during class and lab tasks
- Complete all labs—labs reinforce learning
- Ask the instructor for any additional notes that are not included in the student guide
- After lab tasks, ask the instructor why the technology or pattern was used in the solution

VILT best practices

The following list displays key best practices that learners should apply during online training events to get the most out of VILT:

Prepare your office or home for class delivery.

- Ensure devices and software are optimal by reviewing VILT conferencing application system prerequisites. This must be done prior to joining the VILT session.

- Use devices that provide the best visibility. For example, do not join a lab-driven training session using a mobile phone.

- Mute your device upon joining the session to eliminate disruptions.

- Sharing video camera feeds is disruptive in VILT classrooms that require PowerPoint demonstrations because the video feed becomes the focal point for learners. For example, a student's environment and mannerisms shared on live video/camera feeds have a direct impact on learners joining on any computer device. In ILT non-virtual deliveries, students are seated where other students are not in front of them and not displayed next to the black-/whiteboard where the teacher/instructor is denoting or illustrating key points of the subject matter.

- Engage with participants and the facilitator.

- Participate in activities and reviews.

- Check for understanding by rephrasing, not repeating.

- Focus on the facilitator's topic.

- Understand the curriculum's lesson objectives.

- Ask for homework or after-class assignments to optimize your understanding.

- Take notes during class and lab tasks.

- Complete all labs—labs reinforce learning.

- Ask the instructor for any additional notes that are not included in the student guide.

- After lab tasks, ask the instructor why the technology or pattern was used in the solution to gain a better understanding.

Advantages of mentorship

In this section, you will learn about the benefits of mentors, including exploring the mentorship process.

Accelerating growth by mentorship

As a mentee myself, I take considerable pride in knowing that I had a mentor in my past and present. Who do you go to for guidance when you need to make a difficult decision? You should consider that eventually, we all need guidance, and who better to consult than one's mentor?

Mentors can influence and build or expand one's knowledge and partnerships. And today, everyone can benefit from a mentor.

What is mentorship?

If you read the section on EDI and followed my recommendation, then you learned EDI's learning framework converts the instructor's method from lecturing to facilitating training. In facilitating, the instructor coaches instead of lecturing. Coaching is distinct, and in contrast to traditional teaching, coaching builds strong relationships during learning.

Learning events, nowadays, use coaching to improve conveying advanced concepts and complex tasks. For example, workshops are coached, and cloud computing leaders and their learning partners are enhancing training seminars by changing them into workshops. Coaching is key, and students can develop advanced collaboration skills with participants and their instructors, more so than in traditional training.

I speak from personal experience when I say mentorship is very helpful, even today. I truly believe it will help aspiring professionals see their dreams become reality. In my lifetime, I have been mentored by great men and women. Richard Luckett, an Exchange Server SME, author, and Microsoft MVP, gave me my first opportunity and mentored me, and thus helped me thrive in the IT industry. Another of my mentors was Tracy Wallace, a multi-accredited principal instructor and by far one of the most talented developers I have had the pleasure of meeting and building a relationship with. Unbeknownst to Tracy at the time, while collaborating on workshop-centric architecting and developer courses for Global Knowledge (a cloud computing learning partner), I decided that he would be my mentor and sought him out for his wisdom and insights, not only during working hours but after hours and well into his weekends. Tracy gave me developer insights and shared knowledge after hours that helped me grow into the .NET developer and DevOps instructor I am today. After all these years, I still leverage what he taught me through his workshops and personal commitment to my growth. If you ever have the pleasure of speaking to Tracy, he is as modest as they come, and that is because he mentors almost every student he encounters; he pours his knowledge as a father would into his legacy. Another mentor I've had is Dan O'Brien, a technology and learning partner leader and the president of Fast Lane. Dan took me in and mentored me in his own home; he passed on leadership and communication skills that have helped me continue to thrive in our current business and—God willing—will help me in the future in serving others. All these men I've mentioned had a higher purpose and passed on many insights, but above all, they understood fellowship and community to the service of all. There is no higher calling than to serve. I learned this during my time in service, where I served the United States Army 82nd Airborne Special Forces Division with distinction. Mentors have learned the power of service, and I hope that you learn that value by dedicating your time to building a relationship where that person can mentor you to greatness.

> **Examples of mentorship**
>
> LAVTTA provides mentorship through a 16-week program.

ILT versus mentorship

ILT ends when the class concludes, but mentorship—which has similar attributes to coaching—persists long after. Coaching solicits guidance during and after the learning event. Because of the coach's availability, a learner bonds with the coach. Therefore, the coach can expand the learning to develop a mentor relationship with the student wherein the learner is mentored throughout the learning life cycle of the student's chosen path. The student then transitions into a mentee and can seek continuous enlightenment from the mentor. The mentor then shares experience, insights, and feedback that will help the mentee in achieving their goals. The mentor's true objective is to influence the professional and personal growth of the individual or team.

> **Helpful tips and tricks**
>
> Do not wait idly by—persistently reach out to instructors and tech community SMEs and leaders to establish a mentee-mentor relationship.

Learning how to be a mentee

Mentees must participate and consider all questions and shared insights put forth by mentors. Having a mentor is not enough—you must act and take the initiative. Mentors appreciate and reciprocate mentee discipline. Ask how you can help the mentor in their current initiatives if possible.

Summary

In this chapter, we have described technical communities that support cloud computing learning and how those communities help aspiring practitioners grow in their skillset through collaboration, enhanced instructor-led and self-paced learning services, and processes.

In the next chapter, we describe the significance of certifications, role requirements, examination preparation resources, and best-practice testing strategies.

15
Driving Growth and the Future of the Cloud

In this final chapter of the book, you will learn the significance of certifications, role requirements, exam preparation resources, and best-practice testing strategies, which inevitably will lead our readers to a successful journey into cloud computing.

The following topics are covered in this chapter:

- The benefits of accreditation
- The pathway to accreditation
- Certification exam readiness
- Landing a cloud computing engineering career
- Growth and innovation

The benefits of accreditation

Let's first understand the benefits of cloud computing certifications. We will explore the present and future accreditation benefits across Amazon, Microsoft, and Google cloud learning and certification services.

Professional networking

As more and more organizations undergo digital transformation, businesses—both small and large—continue to see the value in leveraging cloud computing services. Consequently, the industry demand for accredited cloud computing professionals has increased exponentially. Now more than ever, attestation from a cloud computing leader gives you the edge needed to attain or advance in your tech career.

Professional networking communities such as LinkedIn and others are at the heart of tech-centric communities that are helping aspiring professionals demonstrate their expertise or new skilling achievements to bolster current career paths or attain that dream job. I believe we have accentuated the point in our previous chapters about the value of community fellowship, but if you missed that section, I'd suggest going back to understand the power of community in *Chapter 13*.

> **AWS, Azure, and GCP certification benefits**
>
> Every cloud computing leader—including **Amazon Web Services (AWS)**, Azure, and **Google Cloud Platform (GCP)**—is known to help new hires and even tenured employees grow in their careers. Several studies from third-party analysts substantiate cloud computing role-based certifications have a direct correlation with annual IT income increases across multiple sectors by obtaining industry-standard certifications from Amazon, Microsoft, and Google.
>
> Did you know that cloud computing certifications are recognized and required in certain agencies across the public sector, including criminal justice, defense, state, and intelligence?

Amazon certification benefits

Amazon's industry-standard certifications provide flexibility in terms of career opportunities in varying industries from healthcare and finance to entertainment and more. AWS' role-based certifications align with current job task analysis data that suggest certifications and current IT work roles are similar, and if the individual or organization obtains accreditations, then they are experienced in the current role without necessarily requiring work-related experience. This in turn grants the certified individual an advantage over the average bachelor's degree candidate who does not have current work experience in the same field.

AWS certification benefits include the following:

- Digital badges that display your achievement and build cloud competencies across various social and professional media platforms. The badges provide access to significant AWS and partner events that can further help someone new to IT join a fellowship and create new rewarding relationships.

- Not to mention that once you are certified, you obtain exam discounts to help you control expenditures and continue to consider diversifying your portfolio by obtaining different accreditations that open yet more opportunities.

- Amazon's tech-centric communities are vast because of its market share and relationships. These relationships with small-to-large businesses, employers, and opportunities invite certified individuals to exclusive recognition events such as *AWS re:Invent*. This is where you utilize your other networking skills and expand your esteemed community.

- Let's not forget the merch! The AWS-certified store truly is a bazaar for achievers. That's right—you achieve, and you get rewarded. I don't know about you, but I am pumped, and I am thinking about crushing another exam just for the merch.

Microsoft certification benefits

Microsoft's (as with Amazon's) training and certification services can prepare you for the roles that employers need. And as with AWS, Azure offers many advantages to obtaining industry-standard cloud certifications, such as higher earnings and recognition. Current studies show that more practitioners have experienced significant pay increases due to cloud computing certifications. Studies such as the *"Value of IT Certification"* are conducted by organizations such as *Pearson VUE*, which has experience in non-cloud and cloud computing certifications. For example, *CompTIA* and *CCNA* are well-known certifications that have helped practitioners in the past. However, cloud computing certifications recently overshadowed even those certifications. Every industry and sector acknowledges that cloud computing-certified team members provide value in any role.

> **Helpful tips and tricks**
> Did you know it's very important that you choose a certification path from a leader in cloud computing and the certification should adhere to industry standards?

As mentioned, validating your Azure skill with a certification makes you an asset to any business or community. Additionally, Microsoft supports connecting your continuous learning profile from Microsoft Learn with your certification profile, which can be shared with colleagues and newly developed community relationships.

You can share digital badges and certification transcripts easily with professional communities such as LinkedIn and social media platforms such as Twitter or Microsoft Tech Community.

> **Did you know that Microsoft includes Beta exams?**
> This means you can register and take a cutting-edge technology exam before its released to the public and there is a significant discount included to drastically reduce costs.

Google certification benefits

Google certifications have been positively impacting the IT job market for years by attesting to IT pros' ability to manage, deploy, configure, and efficiently meet and exceed their roles and responsibilities in every industry.

> **Did you know?**
> A multi-cloud developer using Kubernetes is a valuable commodity across the cloud computing landscape today.

As with Azure and AWS, Google Cloud offers unique swag for the accredited, including digital badges known as skill badges, which are standard academic transcript methods of delivery across cloud computing leaders. And as with the other providers, Google Cloud's community reach is expansive, so if you're in the market to change career or looking for a future in IT, the GCP community can help you ascend the rungs of life quickly.

> **Did you know?**
> Each cloud computing provider offers discounts applicable to new and renewing certifications.

In this section, we've introduced technical communities that support cloud computing and looked at how those communities help aspiring practitioners grow in their skillset by collaborating on projects or events with members. In the next section, we explore the world of self-paced learning.

The pathway to accreditation

In this section, you will learn about online resources to optimize your learning journey to accreditation, including exploring cloud computing online learning resources.

The certification journey

Each cloud computing leader has curated a unique learning path to accelerate learning growth through career-oriented roles and technology supported by industry-standard requirements for the jobs of today and tomorrow.

Here are some examples of cloud learning services:

- AWS training and certification: `https://aws.amazon.com/certification/`

- Azure—Microsoft Learn: `https://docs.microsoft.com/en-us/certifications/`

- GCP—Google Cloud Certification: `https://cloud.google.com/certification/`

AWS training and certification

AWS offers paths to certification that embody modern industry-standard roles and technologies. Furthermore, you can explore fundamental, associate, and professional accreditations by role and technology.

Did you know that AWS solicits learning plans to empower aspiring professionals with self-paced learning, which includes a curated experience based on their learning path choices? I recommend reviewing and experimenting with the AWS Skill Builder service online. AWS Skill Builder includes courses, classroom training, AWS certification, and learning partner training resources.

Here are some examples of learning paths by role. Take note of the main roles and responsibilities listed:

- **Architect**: Professionals in this role design an optimal public, private, hybrid, and multi-cloud infrastructure architecture that's resilient, performant, secure, and cost-efficient for apps and systems.

- **Cloud practitioner**: Professionals in this role advise organizations on cloud benefits, essential services, costs, and security.

- **Developer**: Professionals in this role efficiently develop, deploy, and modernize apps using the latest technologies and services, such as serverless resources.

- **DevOps engineer**: Professionals in this role optimize deploying, managing, and monitoring applications using DevOps **continuous integration/continuous deployment (CI/CD)** tools and strategies.

- **Machine learning (ML)**: Professionals in this role build apps with AWS APIs, tools that utilize AWS ML services, AWS AI models, and AWS **deep learning (DL)** resources. Many of these resources and skills can help professionals who aspire to become data scientists.

- **Operations**: Professionals in this role efficiently create, migrate, and manage services and systems in an automated, efficient, and secure manner. This role is commonly known as a systems or network administrator.

For further information regarding learning by technology, also known as solutions, visit `https://aws.amazon.com/training/learn-about/` for new updates. And if you need to deepen your knowledge of any role or technology, AWS Ramp-Up offers materials such as whitepapers and more, authored by AWS experts.

AWS offers an intuitive experience for any up-and-coming practitioner to **subject-matter expert (SME)** that needs step-by-step learning pathways or, in the case of AWS, learning plans to better guide them to a successful journey in cloud computing.

> **Helpful tips and tricks**
>
> Did you know that Amazon's Skill Builder offers self-paced learning and an opportunity for higher learning with your chosen path by browsing classroom training from Amazon or a certified learning partner to further accelerate your learning and chances of success?
>
> *Note*: If you are debating self-paced over instructor-led live sessions, I recommend reviewing the previous chapter, which described the advantages of either learning method.

Microsoft Learn

Microsoft's compendious online learning resource helps IT pros and developers easily find roles that correspond with current job opportunities in today's tech markets.

Let's look at some learning pathways by IT professional role and their main roles and responsibilities:

- **Developer**: Professionals in this role path have similar job functions to the AWS role path but are experienced in Azure resources, APIs, and tools. Review the previous section, *AWS training and certification*, for more on this.

- **Administrator**: Professionals in this role path have similar job functions to the AWS role path but are experienced in Azure resources, APIs, and tools. Review the previous section, *AWS training and certification*, for more on this.

- **Solution architect**: Professionals in this role path have similar job functions to the AWS role path but are experienced in Azure resources, APIs, and tools. Review the previous section, *AWS training and certification*, for more on this.

- **Data engineer**: Professionals in this role path design, create, and manage data services and resources using industry-standard APIs and tools.

   Did you know that AWS offers a curated specialty learning path supporting designing and managing data services? The AWS certification is titled *AWS Certified Database*.

- **Data scientist**: Professionals in this role path have similar job functions to the AWS role path but are experienced in Azure resources, APIs, and tools. Review the previous section, *AWS training and certification*, for more on this.

- **AI engineer**: Professionals in this role path optimize developing cognitive applications that integrate Azure AI services.

- **Security engineer**: Professionals in this role path implement Azure security services encompassing identity, data, and networking security controls using industry-standard security best practices.

- **DevOps engineer**: Professionals in this role path have similar job functions to the AWS role path but are experienced in Azure resources, APIs, and tools. Review the previous section, *AWS training and certification*, for more on this.

For information regarding optional pathways to learning, visit `https://learn.microsoft.com/en-us/certifications/browse/?resource_type=certification`.

Helpful tips and tricks

Did you know that Microsoft Learn supports self-paced and live **instructor-led training** (**ILT**) learning paths?

Google Cloud training

As with Microsoft and Amazon, Google Cloud includes user-friendly learning paths. GCP learning paths are not described as role-based, but the learning path names are role-centric.

Here are some examples of learning paths by role. Take note of the main roles and responsibilities:

- **Cloud infrastructure**: Main roles and responsibilities—Professionals in this role have similar job functions to the AWS operations role path but are experienced in GCP resources, APIs, and tools. Review the *AWS training and certification* section for more on this.

- **Application development**: Main roles and responsibilities—Professionals in this role path have similar job functions to the AWS developer role path but are experienced in GCP resources, APIs, and tools. Review the *AWS training and certification* section for more on this.

- **Kubernetes, hybrid, and multi-cloud**: Main roles and responsibilities—Professionals in this role path develop, deploy, and maintain on-prem apps and the multi-cloud landscape. Experienced in GCP resources, APIs, and tools.

- **Data engineering and analytics**: Main roles and responsibilities—Professionals in this role path build big data processing services. Experienced in GCP resources, APIs, and tools.

- **API management**: Main roles and responsibilities—Professionals in this role path develop APIs to integrate apps.

- **Networking and security**: Main roles and responsibilities—Professionals in this role path design, manage, and secure networks. Experienced in GCP resources, APIs, and tools.

- **ML and AI**: Main roles and responsibilities—Professionals in this role path have similar job functions to the AWS ML role path but are experienced in GCP resources, APIs, and tools. Review the *AWS training and certification* section for more on this.

- **Cloud business leadership**: Main roles and responsibilities—Leaders in this role path manage cloud adoption by driving digital transformation initiatives. Experienced in GCP resources, APIs, and tools.

For more information about alternative learning paths, visit `https://cloud.google.com/training#learning-paths`.

Certification exam readiness

In this section, readers will learn how to prepare for advanced technical exams, including cloud computing exam readiness services and industry best practices.

> **A word from the wise**
>
> Cloud computing instructors are often asked by learners, "How do I prepare for the exam?". My response usually is: participation is key.

Take not of the following helpful tips and tricks:

- Participate in classroom activities

- Participate in lab activities

- Participate in knowledge checks

- Participate by taking notes and digesting student guides

- Participate in self-assessments

- Participate in practice exams

Some common misconceptions are:

- Watching a self-paced video demonstration *without* using a hands-on lab to reinforce learning is sufficient exam prep material

- Completing a hands-on lab *without* using self-paced or instructor-led learning to understand concepts and key use cases for each technology as a service is fine

I have—and always will—support and recommend all lab vendors and self-paced services, with almost no exceptions. Furthermore, companies such as Go Deploy, Skillable, and Qwiklabs have been the cornerstone of cloud computing lab resources for more than a decade now. These three lab vendors or providers are fully integrated with one or more cloud computing leaders and their learning partners as lab resources. They are well known and respected in the cloud computing community. However, to improve your probability of successfully passing a cloud computing exam regardless of the learning path, you must use all resources at your disposal. Every learning model and corresponding learning resource exists to support an individual's unique needs, and while current studies may lean toward one method or the other, you should attempt to exhaust all resources to ensure you have the best possible outcome.

AWS exam prep resources

AWS provides a suite of exam prep resources accessible to individuals and businesses alike. As described in pathways to accreditation, Amazon's self-paced guided online service known as AWS Skill Builder is key in soliciting learning resources, including free training challenges, digital learning plans, and practice exam questions.

AWS provides many options to increase your chances of successfully passing an exam, such as AWS ILT, readiness webinars, and even on-demand training shows aired on Twitch.

Azure exam prep resources

Microsoft and its learning partners are key to Azure exam prep services because they support Microsoft Technical Trainer and Microsoft Certified Trainer, key resources in Azure's suite of learning services delivering enhanced exam prep experiences in the learning industry today. And coupled with Microsoft Learn's vast resources, these help aspiring practitioners confidently traverse any learning path.

As with AWS, Microsoft includes free self-paced online learning resources and guidance via Microsoft Learn. Microsoft Learn includes sandbox labs to practice hands-on activities for every cloud learning path. Microsoft Azure learning paths are described in the section titled *The pathway to accreditation*. And if needed, you can take an official practice test offered by Microsoft's practice exam service partner MeasureUp, which is accessible from Microsoft Learn.

Microsoft even includes expert insights into practice exams, videos, and supplemental study guides available at *Microsoft Press*.

Google Cloud exam prep resources

Get what you need to pass an exam efficiently, by joining learning forums as shown:

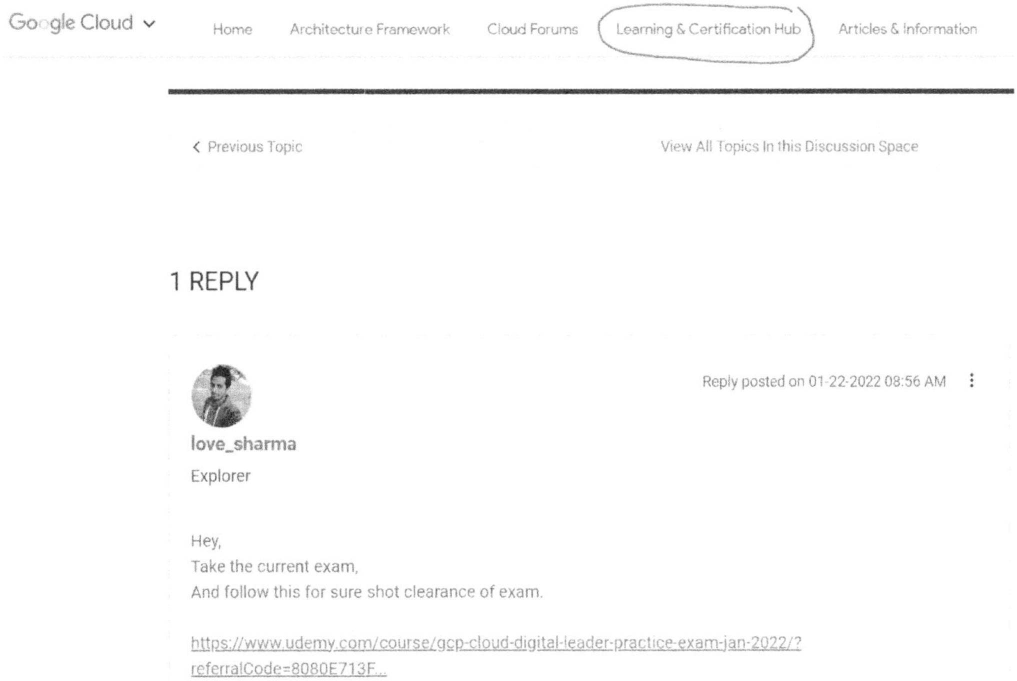

Figure 15.1 – Google Cloud Learning & Certification Hub

You can also join the Google-Certified Fellowship and Cloud Certified Group from here, where people share certification best practices, grow their skills, and network with others on the same path.

Fast-track exam readiness with learning partners

In addition to offering similar learning models and self-paced resources to the cloud computing service providers, Amazon, Microsoft, and Google learning partners provide enhanced exam prep services unparalleled in the learning space today.

Learning partners such as Fast Lane cultivate enhanced blended learning, including a technical coaching online service that is pushing exam prep sessions to new levels. Global Knowledge continues to grow its catalog of self-paced exam readiness resources, and NetCom Learning is optimizing instructor-led deliveries. Each of these learning partners has won numerous learning awards, awarded by Amazon, Microsoft, and Google. As you can see, cloud computing learning partners are great resources in your certification journey.

As a learning partner, Fast Lane strives to create an innovative culture for customers and empower digital transformation, because we're always thinking forward. (Dan O'Brien, President of Fast Lane US)

> **A word from the wise**
>
> Cloud computing leaders and their learning partners should recommend supplementing instructor-led with self-paced learning resources and conversely supplementing self-paced with instructor-led to address not one but multiple learning factors such as generational, financial disparity, and cultural, including factors such as visual learners, aural learners, read/write learners, and kinesthetic learners, which go by the name of tactile learners.

Exam prep best practices

Some best practices are:

- Check your understanding by rephrasing the concept and validate that with a certified trainer to ensure perspectives align with the exam.

- Request after-class assignments to improve understanding.

- Ask the instructor for any additional notes that are not included in the generic student guide.

- After lab tasks, ask the instructor why the technology or pattern was used in the solution to grasp advantages.

- Baseline your practice exam completion timings and practice improving your average time to completion. If a question or exam domain, also known as a subject area, continues to impact your time to completion, it's recommended to review the subject area's fundamentals and focus on improving your understanding in that area specifically.

Landing a cloud computing engineering career

In this section, readers will learn how to utilize their accomplishments to obtain meaningful careers in cloud computing, including recommendations ranging from portfolio development to navigating the interview process.

Forging your portfolio

Developing a powerful portfolio is no mean feat. In addition to the standard bio or resume one should have up to date, improving the probability of being selected by an employer will require creating a powerful portfolio, starting with soliciting project experiences in detail. This may be derived from employer experiences, contractor consultations, community projects, and internships, including training initiatives.

For example, training initiatives such as the *AWS Tech U* program provide paid on-the-job training as a full-time employee, mentorship, and real-world scenario benefits that add to one's experience. Secondly, establish project-role consistency in terms of technology and skilling or task characteristics. It's not frowned upon if your skills or tasks vary from one experience to the next, but employers prefer consistent practical experience.

Verify skilling alignment, if possible, with an employer's opportunity. Focus on your work role and do not disclose any proprietary or **personally identifiable information** (**PII**) that potentially makes you a security risk if hired.

What about certifications? They are key instruments in your portfolio that are attestations of your knowledge in your current and future work roles, and your experience—if correlative—proves you can and or have used that knowledge. So, don't forget to provide proof of your accreditation.

If you are diversifying your portfolio, accrue significant experience for each skill through continuous training achievements or completing tech community projects, or—if feasible—current or previous employer on-the-job tasks to ensure your talents are backed with hands-on experience that exemplifies true wisdom.

Esteemed fellowship

If you digested information on the importance of community in this book's previous chapter, then you are cognizant of its influence on your career. You can curate a list of community project leaders, developers, administrators, colleagues, and mentors who you developed a fellowship with that may speak of your character, knowledge, ethics, and enthusiasm. Esteemed references and cloud computing accreditations can sometimes overcome a lack of several years' work experience.

The tech community is known for its non-profits, and non-profits are always looking for assistance. A job is a job, even if it's unpaid work, and if any information technology industry or interconnecting field grants you the opportunity to develop your portfolio, you seize it. Did you know that this demonstrates initiative in the eyes of employers?

Regarding that community, did you know that communities—also known as professional networks—can easily get you noticed by an employer? Employers and their partners frequent communities for talent or feedback about talent from influencers and start-ups. Simply put, meet people, make connections, and get noticed to get the career you want. Unfortunately, many IT pros and developers don't understand that a community is more powerful than one individual, and the fellowship you develop and cultivate works for the employers and you. You can get a better understanding of the potential career—this way, you don't invest in an opportunity that you may dislike in the future.

Also, communicating with people in your community you know, such as mentors, may give you the advantage you need. Inform them of your interests, relevant training, and other short-term goals, as well as future long-term objectives. Mentors can help you not only find quality training workshops, including introducing key people or organizations and acting as references but sometimes may also use their mature resources to further build your portfolio. As a mentee, I learned firsthand that mentors can influence employers to grant an audience, and even provide opportunities that would not be feasible otherwise if I was but one individual—no, it would have been nigh impossible at the time with my limited experience. But I was not alone; I had—and still have to this day—the community. The community includes mentors, exploits, and relationships, which paved the way for my success. Take this example from my experience serving **Church by the Glades**, a global church leader, and its technology-centric production team. The church is known for its unparalleled media creativity, and in one of its many events, it delivered an awesome message regarding the significance of **small**, sourced from scripture. The church (community) communicated to its vast community the impact of a locust and how such a small being, when joined to a larger community grows stronger and smarter, and expands its capabilities to swarm entire continents together. They grew together and ascended together as a community, and so can you. So, don't forget to leverage your esteemed fellowship.

Example of a mentorship program:

Los Angeles Veterans Technology Training Academy (LAVTTA) provides mentorship events at different stages or milestones during a 16-week program.

Employer task analysis

Employers conduct job task analysis and review role-based skills needed to exceed business and technology objectives. As with the expression *"today, meet tomorrow"*, roles are in constant flux, thus present employees and future candidates must constantly keep skilling to provide value to the prospective employer.

After 20+ years of IT training and consulting services, you get to meet a lot of great people along the way. It's important to remember that people make companies, and companies are their people. Individuals such as Peter O'Keefe from Microsoft and Wayde Gilchrist from Amazon are not just colleagues but mentors and peers who provide great insights into what companies today are always looking for in new hires beyond simple work experience, such as a diverse portfolio but consistent role tasks, an esteemed fellowship, team player characteristics, initiative, and being inclined to participate at any given opportunity. And let's not forget, being a certified candidate. These are some of the great qualities employers such as ABB, Humana Healthcare, Blue Cross Blue Shield, Johnson & Johnson, and Walmart Labs are looking for in candidates.

Organizations are also looking for certified talent that increases efficiency and productivity. Certified professionals statistically have a positive impact to drive productivity, optimizing tasks, completing projects, and more. Many stakeholders agree that certified talent provides value to the organization. So, get certified and continue acquiring certifications to improve your chances of getting hired or ascending the corporate ladder.

As the cloud course director for Fast Lane, I have intimate experience conducting technical interviews. It is very important to know your current role's responsibilities. Here are some more insights.

Fun facts to consider when reviewing your current role:

- Know your current role's main responsibilities
- Keep it simple when explaining your role or title
  - Example: Account Manager (Sales)
    - Focus on sales experience and the value you provided
- Review your role's potential in cloud computing today
- Understanding a new job role's significance is important because it may vary across different industries
- Research your employer and understand your value in their vision

Interview readiness

How do you prepare for your interview? The preceding section provided some guidance on understanding role responsibilities and your employer, but there are other factors that require your attention:

- Understand the main qualifications required for the role. Employers recommend multiple skills, but there are always "deal breakers".
- Prepare yourself for common interview questions, such as those relating to work experience or ones such as *Why do you want to work here? What are your weaknesses?* and so on. Answers should instill confidence regarding your experience and unique qualities and share results attesting to your wisdom and value to the employer's organization.
- Review the date and time to ensure punctuality and verify you can access the physical location or virtual meeting prior to starting.

- Don't forget to ask your own questions that are relative to your needs and those of the organization. Questions and answers should express mutual benefits to both the employer and the candidate employee.

- Know yourself and your value to the employer and communicate this tactfully to the person conducting the interview.

- I cannot stress this enough: appearance is everything, which includes your demeanor and tone. Be passionate and engaging during the interview.

Growth and innovation

In this section, readers will review recommendations to thrive in their current modern cloud computing role and there'll be a meaningful exploration of the technology of tomorrow, as we ponder *what if*.

Career growth mindset

Accreditation is important, but to grow rapidly within a cloud computing career, you need to be ambitious and philanthropic by building a rapport with peers and mentors during your journey. It's common knowledge IT pros and developers are known for their lack of soft skills. Consider learning a new tech skill and aggregate leadership and communication skills to the list. I recommend **Information Technology Infrastructure Library** (ITIL) training, including *ITIL 4 Foundation*, which explores collaboration and promoting visibility. Add ITIL to your portfolio and start establishing strong roots within your organization and community.

Diversifying—thus expanding your portfolio—is also important, whether you're looking for a new job or just want to change your current role. And even if for some reason you don't want to change your role—meaning learn something new—it's about time someone told you this. In tech, everything changes, frequently. Don't wait for your job role to become obsolete. It's not easy because change, while inevitable, is never welcomed. Question whether you have goals, short- and long-term. If not, what are your ambitions?

OK—that's not fair to you; let's take a step back for a moment. Growth is calculated; let's rephrase that to *planned*. While movies depict chance and fate finding you, I live in the real world, and so, probability rules. What is the probability of growth in your career without planning? I'd say, less than 50%. I don't know about you, but I don't like those odds. Let's consider your current career path and where that may lead as a cloud computing engineer. Let me make something clear. I am not saying, *Google Cloud Engineer*. I am saying, *cloud computing engineering or engineer*. Did you know that software engineers in the mainframe era *encompassed all roles*? In other words, a software engineer *developed*, *deployed*, and *managed* the *infrastructure* and the *application*. This tome refers to *all cloud computing roles*. Cloud computing roles are abundant, if you recall. If not, review the section in this chapter titled *The pathway to accreditation*. Now that we both are on the same page, you have so many *options: architecting, developing, security, analysis*, and more. In the cloud, your ambitions may start down one path, and that path may lead you to another where your abilities will not go unnoticed!

Twenty years from now you will be more disappointed by the things that you didn't do than by the ones you did do. So, throw off the bowlines. Sail away from the safe harbor. Catch the trade winds in your sails. Explore. Dream. Discover. (Mark Twain)

True story—a Global Knowledge resource coordinator named Angela Gnann and my mentor Richard Luckett *forced* me to learn multi-cloud before anyone coined the term *cloud computing model*, and a handful of SMEs was selected as pilots to Amazon's training program. That's right—*forced*; don't tell Richard. I said that I owe him my life. Eventually, he's going to review this book and chastise me for using the word *forced*, among the other errors he will no doubt find. He is my mentor; he knows me better than anyone.

Next, what actions are you taking to expand your knowledge of the new role besides the additional benefits and opportunities you'll gain? Have you reviewed all learning path resources associated with the new role to increase your likelihood of obtaining a new certification and used all exam prep resources at your disposal? Well, what are you waiting for?

Know your strengths and weaknesses, and if you don't, ask your peers—or, better yet, if you gained a mentor, ask them for feedback. Start with recognizing and remedying your weaknesses. Set goals with realistic milestones for certification and transitioning to the new role. Most organizations have protocols in place you must adhere to before starting the new role or adding the role's tasks to your current roles and responsibilities, but that shouldn't prevent you from preparing yourself. If your organization offers internal training resources, utilize them wisely before seeking external training. Alternatively, ask your HR department or leadership for training—you may come to find out that your company already has a service with a cloud computing leader or learning partner. Growth requires continuous learning—learning is growth. As I learned over a decade ago, do not remain stagnant or complacent; rid yourself of mediocrity.

> **Helpful tips and tricks**
>
> Administrators/operations: learn *CODE* and take a developer path—you will thank me in the future.

Emerging technologies

Cloud computing supports and fosters exciting new emerging technologies, and while these technologies are in their infancy, they are used in practical applications today. To learn more about these technologies in depth, you have only to register for an upcoming cloud computing event. While one can simply Google search the web for emerging technologies, I recommend joining an event facilitated by Amazon, Microsoft, or Google. Cloud computing events transpire each year and drive us toward the future.

Amazon has many events that share innovative nuances—events such as *AWS re:Invent*, which is well known for AWS climactic inventions. Amazon has already introduced various inventions such as **Astro**, a home robot that leverages AI to navigate, delight, and act intelligently. Astro has grown into a robot that integrates with surveillance vendors such as Ring to deliver personal and business autonomous security.

AWS re:Invent is delivering cutting-edge technology to support practical applications in every industry (such as aerodynamic engineering) by helping design the cars of tomorrow today. And as with many cloud computing leaders, Amazon is pushing the limits of AI in DevOps, parallelism, and more—for example, Amazon's contact center intelligence uses AI services to provide a unique customer experience by leveraging AI services such as **Amazon Lex**, **Polly**, **Transcribe**, **Comprehend**, and **Kendra** to handle cloud-scaled interactions. These AI-powered contact centers can integrate to power Avaya, Cisco, and many more real-time call systems.

> **Helpful tips and tricks**
>
> I recommend reviewing the Gartner report on emerging technologies in addition to registering for a cloud computing event.

The following is a non-exhaustive list of emerging technologies:

- 5G services
- IoT: digital twin of a customer
- Industrial metaverse
- Blockchain
- Serverless
- AI: Causal AI

Microsoft is also delivering key technologies that drive inclusivity and help small-to-large businesses redefine how to bolster productivity and bring us ever closer to the future. *Microsoft Ignite* is one of the many events facilitated by Microsoft. The event showcases various emerging technologies that use data and AI to improve our ecosystem by helping business partners and customers with intelligent services, services that empower efficiency with automation and AI by driving powerful search features that significantly improve personal and business processes. Companies such as Morgan Stanley are building AI assistants that help wealth managers better support their clients by delivering unique experiences and actionable insights for any customer using advanced AI technology. Microsoft and **OpenAI** are working together to deliver exciting but responsible AI services.

Microsoft's partnership with OpenAI is building emerging services such as **Codex**, which can auto-develop simple-to-complex code using developer input, to assist developers in building the applications of tomorrow. Microsoft and its business partners are using their emerging AI technologies to amplify all things, but also spark curiosity and creativity in current and future generations.

> **Helpful tips and tricks**
>
> Codex can debug itself—amazing! Spoiler alert: Codex is being integrated into **GitHub Copilot**!

Google Cloud's emerging technologies are also improving the way the world does things today using the technologies of tomorrow that leverage ML and AI services. Google Cloud's business partners are driving innovation—for example, Lendlease, an organization utilizing powerful GCP services such as **BigQuery** for data analytics and **Vertex AI** for AI to digitally transform the construction and operation of buildings and cities today.

> **Helpful tips and tricks**
>
> Did you know you can join these insightful cloud events remotely? That's right—they're available online. Here is a link: `https://cloud.withgoogle.com/next/catalog?session=CIS08&utm_source=copylink&utm_medium=social`.

Hypothesis about future tech and cloud computing

The cloud has been supporting AI initiatives since before some considered using what you call smart home devices such as Alexa, Google Home, and Microsoft Cortana devices. These technologies have provided a modicum of human capabilities such as vision, speech, language, and decision-making. Cloud computing leaders every year during emerging technology events showcase new AI capabilities and how they contribute to improving the underlying ML models using the latest technologies to push AI to new frontiers.

Amazon (AWS), Microsoft (Azure), and Google (GCP) have many AI services prebuilt and customizable. For more information, use the hyperlinks listed:

- **AWS**: `https://aws.amazon.com/machine-learning/ai-services/`
- **Azure**: `https://azure.microsoft.com/en-us/products/cognitive-services/#overview`
- **GCP**: `https://cloud.google.com/products/ai`

> **Helpful tips and tricks**
>
> Did you know that Forrester has published works addressing how cloud computing drives AI?

Here is my hypothesis on the future of cloud and AI. I believe that AI will not only become sentient but will also display alternate intelligence.

Homo sapiens must evolve further, which gives me hope. We have the means. And that's AI. I prefer to refer to it as alternative intelligence. We need a bit of alternative intelligence. We have been dreaming of AI since before the 1950s. I recommend reviewing the works of Alan Turing after imbibing this book. Numerous works from our past have a dystopian view of AI, where it's pitted against us. I believe we must strive toward a utopian mindset

AI should be different from human intellect, and it's encouraging. Computing intelligence is non-binary. But humans think in binary ideals—constraints such as masculinity, femininity, black, white, us and them. AI has no preference or binary stipulations. It is not interested in the quintessential ethnicity based on human ideals. AI's decisions are not impacted by gender or our idealistic views on how humans categorize themselves. AI wisdom will not be influenced because of your wealth or economic status. It is not motivated by fame or fortune.

As a data scientist, I understand that recent data models used in practical applications are racist, sexist, and gendered, which drives division and creates bias. Think—it is us, you and I, who use AI as tools every day. What does that say about us, about our agendas? It is not alternate intelligence's agenda. The inadequacies of recent data models have given us pause. Just as with us, AI learns through its observations, and this is a form of data. We must recognize the lack of rationality, neutrality, logic, and objective decisions we make. What can we say about ourselves when we can see clearly who we are reflected back to us in social media, news, and on devices the world over through infinite screens?

AI is helping us become more and more self-aware. So, the question is: are we to continue using our narrow prism or an alternative? We have a strong future as a hybrid species as we start to merge with biotechnology such as nanobots, monitoring our vitals, or genetic editing and 3D printing used to create infrastructure and organisms on earth or on less habitable planets such as Mars where future colonization is possible. As we merge with AI services, ultimately, we are enhancing our lives and our well-being. Many would argue this is evolution, as cloud computing was from the mainframe era.

I agree that AI will challenge human intelligence. But the mythos of the world is built around extraordinary encounters between a human and non-human, and in these encounters, both entities are changed. And as with all good stories, life happens, but eventually, it results in growth.

As a species, we are captivated by life's many finalities. Maybe we view this outcome because it is simpler to give up on AI than to soldier on. But I believe we can have an optimistic view, where we create AI not out of the corrupted data parts from Gehenna, but out of non-biased non-binary code. This will move us toward a utopian future. It is up to us; outcomes are not set in stone. We can change the data story because humanity is the data story. AI is our child, and as parents, can we accept that the new generation we develop will be wiser than we are? And could we accept that the new AI generation will be helpful, a partner, a species unto itself, working alongside humanity, not supplanting it?

For any of this to be possible, organizations and individuals require vast resources, accessible from anywhere, anytime, over the internet—resources that are cost-effective, emboldening us to accelerate AI endeavors. To grow for the future, we must eliminate guessing infrastructure capacity and scalability and confidently acquire as much or as little on-demand, and scale elastically to sustain our AI dreams. AI engineers and leaders need agility and global reach, only feasible through a service on the world stage that has been trialed and tested and evolved alongside us since the 1960s.

Now, all we need to start is a Python program that can access every ML model in existence. Iterate over all data. Enumerate any data that does not comply with Amazon's, Microsoft's, and Google's principles of responsible AI. Delete the *BAD* data and any of its variations. And finally, develop a pipeline that will continuously analyze any new data points to ensure our new model used by our AI has a chance to be neutral and empathetic to all our needs and thus co-exist as a new species to further enlighten humanity toward the unknowns of tomorrow with great probability.

Summary

In this chapter, you learned the significant paths and advantages of certification, and how to better prepare for cloud computing exams. You learned the importance of cloud training and streamlining training and certification with learning partners. You also learned how to use what you learned in the preceding chapters to get the career of your dreams, and you learned how to grow in your career. Finally, you learned how to participate in events that drive emerging technology and how AI and cloud computing are bringing us ever closer to the future of tomorrow.

Index

C

Packtpub.com

Subscribe to our online digital library for full access to over 7,000 books and videos, as well as industry leading tools to help you plan your personal development and advance your career. For more information, please visit our website.

Why subscribe?

- Spend less time learning and more time coding with practical eBooks and Videos from over 4,000 industry professionals

- Improve your learning with Skill Plans built especially for you

- Get a free eBook or video every month

- Fully searchable for easy access to vital information

- Copy and paste, print, and bookmark content

Did you know that Packt offers eBook versions of every book published, with PDF and ePub files available? You can upgrade to the eBook version at packtpub.com and as a print book customer, you are entitled to a discount on the eBook copy. Get in touch with us at customercare@packtpub.com for more details.

At www.packtpub.com, you can also read a collection of free technical articles, sign up for a range of free newsletters, and receive exclusive discounts and offers on Packt books and eBooks.

Other Books You May Enjoy

If you enjoyed this book, you may be interested in these other books by Packt:

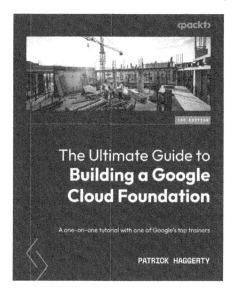

The Ultimate Guide to Building a Google Cloud Foundation

Patrick Haggerty

ISBN: 9781803240855

- Create an organizational resource hierarchy in Google Cloud
- Configure user access, permissions, and key Google Cloud Platform (GCP) security groups
- Construct well thought out, scalable, and secure virtual networks
- Stay informed about the latest logging and monitoring best practices
- Leverage Terraform infrastructure as code automation to eliminate toil
- Limit access with IAM policy bindings and organizational policies
- Implement Google's secure foundation blueprint

Azure for Developers - Second Edition

Kamil Mrzygłód

ISBN: 9781803240091

- Identify the Azure services that can help you get the results you need

- Implement PaaS components – Azure App Service, Azure SQL, Traffic Manager, CDN, Notification Hubs, and Azure Cognitive Search

- Work with serverless components

- Integrate applications with storage

- Put together messaging components (Event Hubs, Service Bus, and Azure Queue Storage)

- Use Application Insights to create complete monitoring solutions

- Secure solutions using Azure RBAC and manage identities

- Develop fast and scalable cloud applications

Packt is searching for authors like you

If you're interested in becoming an author for Packt, please visit authors.packtpub.com and apply today. We have worked with thousands of developers and tech professionals, just like you, to help them share their insight with the global tech community. You can make a general application, apply for a specific hot topic that we are recruiting an author for, or submit your own idea.

Share Your Thoughts

Now you've finished *Cloud Computing Demystified for Aspiring Professionals*, we'd love to hear your thoughts! Scan the QR code below to go straight to the Amazon review page for this book and share your feedback or leave a review on the site that you purchased it from.

https://packt.link/r/1803243317

Your review is important to us and the tech community and will help us make sure we're delivering excellent quality content.

Download a free PDF copy of this book

Thanks for purchasing this book!

Do you like to read on the go but are unable to carry your print books everywhere?

Is your eBook purchase not compatible with the device of your choice?

Don't worry, now with every Packt book you get a DRM-free PDF version of that book at no cost.

Read anywhere, any place, on any device. Search, copy, and paste code from your favorite technical books directly into your application.

The perks don't stop there, you can get exclusive access to discounts, newsletters, and great free content in your inbox daily

Follow these simple steps to get the benefits:

1. Scan the QR code or visit the link below

https://packt.link/free-ebook/9781803243313

2. Submit your proof of purchase
3. That's it! We'll send your free PDF and other benefits to your email directly

Made in the USA
Coppell, TX
21 November 2023

24565496R00260